The Vicissitudes of Nature

*In memory of my friend and colleague Yirmiyahu Yovel,
whose writings on Spinoza and the Marranos inspired this book*

The Vicissitudes of Nature
From Spinoza to Freud

Richard J. Bernstein

polity

Copyright © Richard Bernstein 2023

The right of Richard Bernstein to be identified as Author of this Work has been asserted in accordance with the UK Copyright, Designs and Patents Act 1988.

First published in 2023 by Polity Press

Polity Press
65 Bridge Street
Cambridge CB2 1UR, UK

Polity Press
111 River Street
Hoboken, NJ 07030, USA

All rights reserved. Except for the quotation of short passages for the purpose of criticism and review, no part of this publication may be reproduced, stored in a retrieval system or transmitted, in any form or by any means, electronic, mechanical, photocopying, recording or otherwise, without the prior permission of the publisher.

ISBN-13: 978-1-5095-5519-2
ISBN-13: 978-1-5095-5520-8 (pb)

A catalogue record for this book is available from the British Library.

Library of Congress Control Number: 2022934665

Typeset in 11 on 12.5pt Baskerville MT Pro
by Cheshire Typesetting Ltd, Cuddington, Cheshire
Printed and bound in Great Britain by TJ Books Ltd, Padstow, Cornwall

The publisher has used its best endeavours to ensure that the URLs for external websites referred to in this book are correct and active at the time of going to press. However, the publisher has no responsibility for the websites and can make no guarantee that a site will remain live or that the content is or will remain appropriate.

Every effort has been made to trace all copyright holders, but if any have been overlooked the publisher will be pleased to include any necessary credits in any subsequent reprint or edition.

For further information on Polity, visit our website:
politybooks.com

Contents

Preface	vii
Introduction	1
Part I The Philosophy of Nature	
1 Spinoza: Founder of Modern Naturalism	15
2 Hume: The Experimental Method and the Science of Man	50
3 Kant: Copernican Turn – Nature, Reason, and Freedom	72
4 Hegel: Nature and *Geist*	107
Part II The Hermeneutics of Suspicion	
Prologue	131
5 Marx: The Transaction of Nature and Social Man	133
6 Nietzsche: Nature and the Affirmation of Life	157
7 Freud: Human Nature, Psychic Reality, and Cosmological Speculation	177
Coda	200
Concluding Remarks	204
Notes	209
References	263
Index of Names	275
General Index	279

Preface

When I started this project, I was frequently asked how I became interested in the theme. Why did I decide to write a book about the vicissitudes of nature from Spinoza to Freud? Initially, my answer was vague because it is only in working out my ideas that I discover what I want to say. Actually, there are several strands in the story of writing this book – some dating back to the time when I was a graduate student at Yale. One of the exciting features of graduate school is the discussion groups that arise spontaneously. At Yale, John E. Smith, a philosopher who specialized in American philosophy, organized a small discussion group dealing with John Dewey's *Experience and Nature*. At the time, I shared many of the prevalent prejudices about Dewey's pragmatism – that it was superficial and not really a "serious" candidate for philosophy. (These prejudices were reinforced when I was an undergraduate at the Hutchins College at the University of Chicago, where Dewey's pragmatism was taken as an example of "bad" philosophy.) Reading *Experience and Nature* was a revelation. Dewey's book did not fit the stereotypes of pragmatism that were so prevalent at the time. Dewey's naturalistic vision of the relation of experience and nature – how human beings as natural creatures are related to the rest of nature – spoke deeply to me. Dewey challenged all metaphysical and epistemological dichotomies; he argued for an enriched (naturalistic Hegelian) conception of experience that is continuous with the rest of nature. I decided to write my dissertation on Dewey, "John Dewey's Metaphysics of Experience." Since those early days, I have explored a variety of themes and thinkers, but my early enthusiasm for Dewey's naturalistic vision never left me.[1]

During the first decades of the twentieth century, Dewey was part of a movement of American philosophers who identified themselves as naturalists. They were all deeply influenced by Darwin and the new biology, as well as by the social sciences. With the growing influence of analytic philosophy, the significance of this naturalistic movement was overshadowed – relegated to the "dustbin of history." However, in the mid-twentieth century there was a revival of the new forms of naturalism, stimulated by the work of W. V. O. Quine and Wilfrid Sellars, which had little to do with the American naturalists and more to do with an assessment of the natural sciences and their relation to philosophy.[2] By the later decades of the twentieth century – indeed, right up to the present – most Anglophone philosophers consider themselves naturalists. The contemporary discussion of naturalism has been extremely chaotic, with little agreement about the meaning and scope of the term "naturalism." In my monograph, *Pragmatic Naturalism: John Dewey's Living Legacy*, I work through these debates. Initially, I was struck by the fact that many philosophers were speaking at cross-purposes, but gradually I began to discover a coherent development. A number of analytic philosophers and philosophers of science have been developing a sophisticated version of liberal pragmatic naturalism that is very much in the spirit of Dewey. Consequently, the thesis of my monograph is that the legacy of Dewey's naturalism is very much alive – informed by a new analytic sophistication.

In writing my monograph, I also discovered that many contemporary philosophers are ignorant of the rich debates (pro and con) about the concept of nature and viable forms of naturalism that have been prevalent since the beginning of the modern age.[3] The great discovery for me was Spinoza. Like many contemporary thinkers, I thought of Spinoza as a historical curiosity who proposed a grand metaphysical scheme that is no longer viable in light of criticisms advanced by such thinkers as Hume, Kant, and Hegel. Nevertheless, when I turned to the details of his thinking about nature, I discovered a richness of insight that is relevant to contemporary philosophical debates. In my view, although Descartes was the "father" of modern philosophy, Spinoza was clearly the "father" of modern naturalism. I then followed the twists and turns in the vicissitudes of nature in Hume, Kant, and Hegel. In the nineteenth century, there was something like an intellectual volcanic eruption when the three "masters of the school of suspicion" – Marx, Nietzsche, and Freud – raised critical questions about the viability of a philosophy of nature. Each, in a radically different way, sought to elaborate new ways of thinking about nature that raised provocative critical questions about the relation of human beings and nature.

I fully realize that in carrying out such an ambitious project, questions can always be raised about which thinkers are included or excluded from my primary discussions. For example, one may ask (as a reviewer of my manuscript did ask) why I begin with Spinoza rather than Descartes. After all, Spinoza himself began his philosophizing with reflections on Descartes and debates about Cartesianism. Consequently, a good argument can be made that to achieve a deeper understanding of Spinoza, one should begin with his appropriation and critique of Cartesian themes. I agree with this. Indeed, such a discussion would supplement and enrich my study. But doing this in a historically accurate and thorough manner would have resulted in a very different book.

Another reviewer wondered why I did not spend my time on Schelling's famous philosophy of nature. Schelling is now enjoying a resurgence of contemporary interest. Even in my present narrative, Schelling's insights about nature play a crucial role in challenging mechanistic conceptions of nature and insisting that nature is dynamic and alive. However, following out the rethinking of nature as a vital dynamic force would also require a detailed examination of German idealism. Such an exploration would also enrich my narrative but would require a different book. In focusing on Spinoza, Hume, Kant, Hegel, Marx, Nietzsche, and Freud, I have used my judgment to present a balanced narrative of the vicissitudes of nature during the modern period – well aware that I might have explored other thinkers.

I started this project well before the pandemic. Like many scholars, I encountered a major obstacle in March 2020. I no longer had access to the books in my office. The libraries of The New School and NYU were closed temporarily. Fortunately, I have had a superb research assistant, Olga Knizhnik, who located digital copies of all the primary and secondary sources I needed to continue my research. In addition, Olga carefully edited my manuscript and supervised a team of graduate students who checked the accuracy of all my quotations and references. The team included Agnese Di Riccio, Tatiana Llaguno Nieves, and Veronica Padilla. I would never have been able to complete this manuscript without the help of Olga and the other superb New School graduate students. My acknowledgment of their dedicated assistance is much greater than it would have been if there had not been the pandemic. I am grateful for the meticulous copy editing of Jean van Altena. Finally, I want to acknowledge the dedicated support and encouragement of the editor of Polity Press, John Thompson. He has always been an enthusiastic supporter of my work. He made a number of excellent suggestions for improving the quality of my manuscript. Despite the many problems I had to face writing this book, it has been both an intense and enjoyable experience – intense because of the amount of material I had to master; enjoyable because I learned something new every day.

Introduction

I

In his illuminating essay "The Charm of Naturalism," Barry Stroud perceptively remarks,

> The idea of "nature," or "natural objects or relations, or modes of investigation that are "naturalistic," has been applied more widely, at more different times and places, and for more different purposes than probably any other notion in the whole history of human thought. . . . What is usually at issue is not whether to be "naturalistic" or not, but rather what is and what is not to be included in one's conception of "nature." That is the real question, and that is what leads to deep disagreement. (Stroud 2004: 21–2)

He then notes, "[The] pressure on the one hand [is] to include more and more within your conception of 'nature,' so it loses its distinctiveness and restrictiveness. Or, if the conception is kept fixed and restrictive, there is the pressure on the other hand to distort or even to deny the very phenomena that a naturalistic study – and especially a naturalistic study of human beings – is supposed to explain" (Stroud 2004: 22). Stroud makes a number of important points. The reflection and speculation about the nature of nature has been a primary theme in Western thinking (as well as in other traditions) since its very beginning with the pre-Socratics – and the conception of nature has varied tremendously through the tradition. There are two opposing pressures on thinking about nature: an expansive pressure fraught with the danger that the concept becomes so broad that it loses its distinctiveness, and a narrowing one threatening to distort and deny the phenomena it is supposed to explain. The concept of nature is fundamental for every major philosopher in this tradition. One is almost inclined to say, "Tell me how a thinker conceives of nature, and I can infer the rest of her philosophy." In the seventeenth century, we find the beginnings of revolutionary new ways of conceiving nature. This is the origin of modern natural science – the period of great advances in mathematics, astronomy, and physics – a time associated with Copernicus, Kepler, Descartes, and Galileo, which culminated with the great discoveries of Newton. These new scientific developments presented a great challenge to philosophers – the need to give a philosophical account of the new conception of nature that was emerging in science.

One of the great and most controversial philosophers of the seventeenth century was Spinoza. He was a descendant of the Jewish Marranos who fled Portugal for Amsterdam. Amsterdam, at the time, was one of the most liberal and cosmopolitan cities in Europe – one of the few places where Jews were allowed to practice their religion openly. Spinoza received a rigorous Jewish education, but at the age of twenty-four he was excommunicated – in the harshest and most vicious manner – from the closed Jewish community for his supposedly heretical views. No Jew was allowed to have contact with him or read any of his writings. Spinoza spent the rest of his life earning a living by grinding lenses, working on optics, and dedicating himself to his philosophy. Spinoza was the initiator of the "Radical Enlightenment," to use Jonathan Israel's expression (Israel 2001). He challenged any conception of a transcendent God represented by the Abrahamic religions. He became what Yirmiyahu Yovel calls the "Marrano of Reason" (Yovel 1989). During his lifetime – and long afterward – he was viciously attacked as an unrepentant atheist – although he consistently denied that he was an atheist. His magnum opus, *Ethics*, was published only posthumously. Spinoza was an extremely ambitious thinker with an absolute commitment to philosophy and rationality. He was committed to a version of the principle of sufficient reason according to which everything in the world can be explained rationally. From reading the *Ethics*, it becomes clear that, for Spinoza, God is identified with Nature and Substance. Nature itself can be completely rationally explained by appealing to the universal laws of nature. Spinoza is preeminently a philosopher of immanence – a "this-worldly" philosopher. He rejected the idea of an anthropomorphic transcendent God as superstition, as well as rejecting the appeal to final causes and human free will. He sought to give a completely naturalistic account of human emotions and morality.

With the exception of a few thinkers who engaged with Spinoza's ideas, his influence was marginalized during the century following his death. His ideas were rediscovered only at the end of the eighteenth century during the famous pantheist controversy that played a significant role in the renewal of the interest in Spinoza. What is so impressive about Spinoza is his systematic and rigorous development of a new understanding of nature. In his *Ethics* he adopted a version of Euclid's geometric method consisting of definitions, axioms, propositions, and logical proofs. The geometric method was not limited to mathematics. Rather, it was the method for developing a *grand metaphysical system* that explains nature in a completely determinate manner, offering logically compelling proofs. Although, as has been said, Descartes is frequently called the "father" of modern philosophy, Spinoza is the "father" and founder of modern naturalism, maintaining that everything in nature, including human beings, their emotions, and morality, can be explained by appealing to the universal and necessary natural laws. Initially, Spinoza's grand metaphysical mode of thinking appears completely alien to our contemporary ways of thinking. Virtually every major philosopher has criticized him, including Hume, Kant, and Hegel. Yet, as we will see, the specter of Spinoza hovers over a great deal of modern thought, including that of Marx, Nietzsche, and Freud.

At the same time as Spinoza elaborated his system of nature, another philosophical tradition – empiricism – was emerging in Great Britain, culminating with David Hume. Hume claims that most of what Spinoza wrote in his *Ethics* is metaphysical gibberish and ought to be committed to the flames. He rejects every major concept of Spinoza, including God, Substance, and Nature. Yet, we will see that, despite Hume's repudiation of Spinoza, there are common themes in their conceptions of naturalism and immanence. Hume's beginning point in his *Treatise* is not metaphysics but the epistemological doctrine that all perceptions consist of impressions and ideas. From this starting point, Hume develops an elegant and powerful model of the human mind and nature. Hume rejects the claims of rationalist thinkers like Spinoza that we can justify concepts such as causality by an appeal to reason. It is not reason that lies at the foundation of our empirical knowledge of the world of nature, but rather custom, habit, feeling, and sentiment. Reason *by itself* does not tell us *anything* about the natural world. There is a tension between skepticism and naturalism in Hume's thinking that is evident in his attempt to develop a science of human beings that would complement what Newton had achieved in natural philosophy (what we now call "natural science").

Hume's starting point gets him into trouble. Normally we think of a simple sensory impression such as an impression of a red patch as being *caused* by an actual red patch in the natural world (unless we are hallucinating). Hume, however, claims that *all* our perceptions arise from "unknown causes." Many empiricists before Hume, such as John Locke, presume it to be evident that objects and events in the "real" world cause our perceptions – especially impressions. But if all our perceptions consist exclusively of discrete impressions and ideas, as Hume suggests, then there is no way – it is *impossible* – to get beyond our impressions and ideas to see if they correspond to "real" natural objects and events. Hume's problem, however, is not how we *know* that there are objects and events in the "real" world that are *independent* of our impressions, but rather how and why we come to *believe* that there are such objects and events. This strain in Hume's thinking leads to his skepticism about an objective world independent of our perceptions. At the same time, Hume carries out his naturalistic explanation of human actions and beliefs. Hume is famous for his psychological account of causality and necessary connection. He presents strong arguments to show that we cannot appeal to reason to provide an account of causality. This is Hume's powerful negative conception of causality directed against all rationalist accounts of causality, including Spinoza's.

Immanuel Kant was deeply influenced by Hume's *negative* argument. In Kant's terminology, Hume demonstrated that the causal principle is not an *analytic* principle; it cannot be justified by an appeal to reason alone – by an appeal to the principle of contradiction. There is no logical contradiction in denying that every event must have a cause. According to Kant, Hume's great failure was that he failed to recognize that there are *synthetic a priori principles*. For Kant, the acknowledgment of such principles is *essential* for our understanding of both mathematics and natural science. (Of course, Hume and Humeans would challenge the idea that there are *any* synthetic *a priori* principles.) For all Hume's admiration of Newton, Kant argues, Hume fails to appreciate that the Newtonian conception of nature presupposes universal and necessary deterministic laws of nature.

In order to address the failures of Hume's account of causality, Kant carries out his famous Copernican Revolution. It is not that our ideas and concepts correspond to objects, Kant contends, but rather that our reason (*Verstand*) is the source of concepts (categories) and principles that specify the very conditions for the possibility of our experience of nature. I interpret Kant as confronting an existential crisis in his *Critique of Pure Reason*. Necessary universal laws govern nature. Human beings, insofar as they are natural creatures, are also governed by universal and necessary laws.

If human beings were *exclusively* natural creatures, then there would be no way to account for human freedom, human responsibility, morality, or rational faith. Thus, a large part of Kant's first *Critique* is dedicated to showing that human beings are not *merely* natural creatures; they are also *rational* beings. In his famous Second Analogy, Kant sets out to show that the "causality of nature" is compatible with the nonempirical "causality of freedom." The appeal to nature can never account for human reason and conceptual normativity because it is reason (both *Verstand* and *Vernunft*) that specifies the framework – the very *conditions* for the possibility of *objective nature*. Kant pays a heavy price for his attempt to reconcile freedom and natural necessity. It requires him to say that the *very same event* in the natural world can be explained by both natural causality and the causality of freedom. To see Kant's point, consider the example that I give in my chapter on Kant. Suppose I deliberately raise my hand in a classroom to get a teacher's attention. As an event in the natural world, it can be explained *exclusively* by an appeal to natural causes – that is, I can, in principle, give a *complete* naturalistic explanation of this event. But from a different perspective, we can also say that the very *same event* is the result of the causality of freedom. However, it is unclear precisely how the same event can be explained by *both* natural necessity and the nonempirical causality of freedom. Kant eventually came to realize that his mechanistic account of causality in the first *Critique* is paradoxical. In the *Critique of the Power of Judgment* he attempts to show how freedom and necessity can be reconciled by an appeal to *reflecting* judgment (which is sharply distinguished from *determining* judgment). He also realizes that he needs to enlarge his conception of nature to account for the biological phenomena of organic creatures. In this context, he introduces the concept of purpose (*Zweck*), specifically *Naturzweck*. Once again, we discover unresolved problems in Kant's thinking. *Zweck* is *not* a category of *Verstand* (understanding); it is *not* constitutive of nature. Rather, it is a regulative principle that we human beings employ to understand organic creatures. Yet, although not constitutive, the appeal to purpose is *essential* for describing and understanding biological phenomena. Does it make sense, then, to speak of *Zweck* as only a regulative and not a constitutive principle of nature?

Despite these and other perplexities, Kant's philosophy is a powerful one insofar as it has had a significant influence on twentieth- and twenty-first-century philosophy. Many contemporary thinkers like John McDowell and Robert Brandom are convinced that Kant discovered the independence of conceptual normativity. They agree with Kant that conceptual normativity – the heart of discursive rationality – *cannot* be explained by an appeal to nature. Kant has become a champion of those thinkers who are convinced that an appeal to nature cannot account for human rationality, because this rationality establishes the universal and necessary conditions for an *objective* concept of nature. To the extent that we accept the sharp dichotomy between nature and freedom, or nature and rationality, *all* naturalistic programs (including those of Spinoza and Hume) fail.[1] Kant's critical philosophy is based upon a set of (unstable) distinctions and dichotomies including sensibility and understanding, spontaneity and receptivity, *Verstand* and *Vernunft*, phenomena and noumena, appearance and thing in itself, nature and freedom, nature and rationality. Throughout his three *Critiques* Kant struggles to show how these oppositions (which he sometimes characterizes as heterogeneous) are related to each other.

During Kant's lifetime, many critics attacked these dichotomies – especially the dichotomy between nature and freedom, between appearance and thing in itself, and between nature and rationality. German idealists – Schelling, Fichte, and Hegel – sought to develop alternative accounts of the Kantian dichotomies. Hegel takes Kant's starting point seriously but seeks to show that the Kantian dichotomies are not fixed and rigid. They turn out to be changing moments within a *self-determining* dynamic whole. Developing his speculative identity thesis, Hegel seeks to show both the identity and nonidentity of the Kantian dichotomies. However, Hegel *apparently* leaves us with one great residual dichotomy – the dichotomy between *Geist* and Nature. Many interpreters of Hegel privilege *Geist* over Nature. *Geist* is alive; Nature is dead. As one Hegel commentator, Robert Pippin, claims, *Geist* "leaves nature behind" (Pippin 2002). I argue that this popular interpretation is mistaken. I offer a naturalistic interpretation of Hegel that shows how *Geist* emerges out of Nature. There is no sharp metaphysical or epistemological break between Nature and *Geist*; there is a continuity. When Nature is fully *actualized*, it becomes *Geist*. When *Geist* is fully *actualized*, it is embodied in Nature. Nature and *Geist* are *both* identical and nonidentical. I call those interpreters of Hegel who privilege *Geist* over Nature "Kantian Hegelians." Brandom is the leading Kantian Hegelian; he insists on a sharp distinction between sentience and sapience (Brandom 1994). He argues that discursive rationality *must* be clearly *demarcated* from natural phenomena. From his perspective, it is *conceptually impossible* to give a naturalistic account of human discursive rationality. An opposing tradition, and an opposing reading of Hegel, is the naturalism of John Dewey. Whereas Brandom insists on clear and rigorous *demarcation*, Dewey insists on *continuity*, including the continuity of nature and rationality (what Dewey calls "intelligence"). Many contemporary debates today are the legacy of these different readings of Hegel.

II

Something happened in the mid-nineteenth century that I compare to a volcanic eruption. A volcano erupts when magma builds up to the point that the volcano explodes. Something like this happened with the three "masters of suspicion," as Paul Ricoeur (1970) characterizes Marx, Nietzsche, and Freud. For all the differences between Spinoza, Hume, Kant, and Hegel, they were all committed to a *philosophical* approach to nature. In contrast, Marx, Nietzsche, and Freud are suspicious of philosophical conceptions of nature. In radically different ways, they argue that philosophy mystifies nature. They attack what had been the starting point of so much modern philosophy since Descartes – the appeal to consciousness. They are great destroyers, great demystifiers, and sharp critics of what they take to be false illusions. Their critiques are not merely negative; each of them seeks to elucidate a more adequate conception of nature. Marx, for example, argues that a proper starting point for understanding nature is human activity – human labor. In his writings of the 1840s he critiques alienated labor that is rooted in the historical formation of early capitalism with its institutionalization of wage labor and profit. He develops a new, *transactional* way of understanding the relationship between human beings and nature. Workers are part of nature, and they use nature for production. Capitalists exploit nature for the purpose of profit. Strictly speaking, it is misleading to speak of the human *and* nature; it is more perspicuous to speak of the human-in-nature. Marx is critical of the idea of *nature in itself*. The nature that we encounter is always within a *historical* formation. Some interpreters of Marx, like Louis Althusser (2005), distinguish "two Marxs" – the "early" humanistic Marx and the presumably more "mature" scientific Marx. Some interpreters then defend the humanistic Marx, while others argue that there was an epistemological break that took place in 1845, when Marx presumably abandons his humanism and his early conception of nature. I argue that this demarcation between the "two Marxs" is mistaken. There is certainly development and refinement throughout Marx's career, but by analyzing key passages from the *Grundrisse* and *Das Kapital*, I demonstrate the continuity of Marx's understanding of nature.

Nietzsche is a ruthless critic of Christianity, morality, and the distorting prejudices of philosophy. He disdains straightforward linear arguments. He celebrates contradictory perspectives as the mark of high culture. He experiments with different styles, aphorisms, poems, and imaginative fictions. Recently, there has been a trend among Anglo-American interpreters of Nietzsche to develop a naturalistic interpretation of his thought. I examine what is illuminating and restrictive about these divergent naturalistic readings of Nietzsche. I then turn to what Nietzsche *actually says* about nature – his attempt to demystify and purify nature, to get rid of "God's shadows" that have contaminated nature for the past two thousand years. Nietzsche's nature is chaotic and shaped by instincts and *contradictory* unconscious drives. Nietzsche warns about a type of nihilism that is turning a human into a bland domestic animal – what he calls the "last man." He also warns against turning aggressive instincts against oneself and fostering *ressentiment* and self-hatred. A joyous *life-affirming* way of life is a possibility for a few exceptional and gifted individuals. They are the "Yes-sayers" who affirm the significance of human suffering and tragedy. They are also the ones who purify nature through their way of thinking, feeling, and living.

In many ways, Freud is closer to Nietzsche than to Marx, especially with respect to the role he assigns to the unconscious and the primary drives (sexual and aggressive) that are rooted in the unconscious. In his earliest writings, Freud accepts the positivist credo advocated by his Viennese and German scientific colleagues – the conviction that quantitative natural science *alone* can tell us what nature is. In his 1895 "Project for a Scientific Psychology" he seeks to develop an understanding of human nature based on the constancy principle that he appropriates from physics. Already in the "Project" it becomes increasingly evident that Freud's insights into psychic reality – the key for understanding human nature – exceed his quantitative framework. Primary drives are at once somatic (biological) and psychic. Freud frequently refers to drive as a *borderline* concept. From the time of the "Project" (which he abandoned) to the publication of *The Interpretation of Dreams* in 1900, Freud made a number of discoveries that led to the development of psychoanalysis, which emphasizes the significance of infantile sexuality in shaping who we become. Repressed sexual drives are the source of neurotic symptoms. Patients develop strong *resistance* to acknowledging this repressed material. The task of the psychoanalyst is to help the analysand to come to recognize what she has repressed.

Freud developed the method of "free association" (which is not really "free") in order to get his patients to reveal hidden associations that enable the psychoanalyst to discover what is being repressed and resisted. Transference (as well as counter-transference) between the analysand and the psychoanalyst also turns out to be important in order to discover what the patient is repressing. Freud argues that dreams, as well as slips of the tongue, are *meaningful*. The task of the analyst is to discover the *secret* meaning of dreams and the functioning of dreamwork – the construction, distortion, and condensation of the manifest and latent content of dreams. Freud's great philosophical battle was with those thinkers who maintain that *all* mental activity is *conscious*. In Freud's view, they fail to recognize the powerful role of unconscious psychic activity. Freud's claims about the unconscious are strikingly original. The unconscious is a system – an agency – that is atemporal and knows no negation. Contradictory primal drives are rooted in the unconscious.

Freud developed his views about human nature (not just the nature of "sick souls") from his clinical observations by proposing different models to explain what he was encountering. He developed two different topographical models. The first one distinguishes the conscious, the preconscious, and the unconscious. The major distinction is between the conscious/preconscious and the unconscious that is never *fully* accessible to consciousness. When Freud discovered problems with this model, especially concerning the role of the unconscious, he proposed a second topographical model of the id, ego, and superego. From the 1890s until the 1920s, Freud was primarily concerned with *individual* psychic reality. But beginning in the 1920s, he expanded his speculations to include group behavior, as well as the way in which civilization is a source of frustration, suffering, and unhappiness (despite its technical and cultural achievements). In his notorious and controversial *Beyond the Pleasure Principle* (1920), he proposes an original death principle (*Thanatos*) that is an *internal drive* of organisms to return to what is inorganic. The death drive, when directed *outwards*, is the primary source of human aggressiveness and destruction. Many of Freud's closest associates rejected the hypothesis of an independent death drive. Nevertheless, Freud insisted upon it until the end of his life. *Thanatos* is opposed by *Eros*, which encompasses what Freud had previously characterized as sexuality; it is the drive toward *unification*. In Freud's late speculative theory of instincts, there is a perpetual *battle* between *Thanatos* and *Eros*. In *Civilization and its Discontents* (1930), Freud argues that civilization is the primary source of human suffering and unhappiness. There is no escape from civilization to some idealized innocent state of being. The discontents of civilization are inevitable and intractable. Frequently, Freud's views of human nature are judged pessimistic. Against such views, I argue that Freud develops a *realistic* perspective; he faces up honestly to the limitations of human nature and seeks to ameliorate (not eliminate) human suffering and misery. We need to give up the illusion and fantasy of complete happiness – it is not achievable. Rather, we should live in a manner wherein we seek to negotiate the avoidance of human suffering and misery with the episodic satisfaction of our primary instinctual drives. There is, however, a major difference between Nietzsche and Freud. Freud is skeptical about Nietzsche's joyful affirmation of life – of the human as a "Yes-sayer." From Freud's perspective, this is an unrealistic fantasy. Nietzsche, in turn, might accuse Freud's compromise between living a life that seeks to avoid suffering and misery as a "celebration" of the "last man."

Marx, Nietzsche, and Freud are three destroyers of illusions. Each thinker in a different way seeks to expose how the philosophy of nature distorts nature. Each seeks to develop a *new* way of understanding nature, especially human nature, which emphasizes the *transactional* character of the *human-in-nature*. In different ways, all three belong to the tradition of Spinoza's philosophy of immanence. Each rejects any appeal to what is transcendent. They are "this-worldly" thinkers; they each develop distinctive critiques of religion and the ways in which it distorts the nature of our nature. Each one offers a deep understanding of nature based on a relentless critique – even when it reveals intractable and disturbing facts about human beings.

III

In parts I and II above, I have outlined some of the key points that I develop in this book. In each chapter, I pay close attention to the textual support through which I seek to "flesh out" and texture my key claims. I explicate how each thinker – Spinoza, Hume, Kant, Hegel, Marx, Nietzsche, and Freud – conceives of nature from their own perspective, the reasons that lead them to their distinctive views, and the significance of their contributions to our understanding of nature. There are manifest contradictions and incompatibilities among these thinkers. To take one central example – namely the account of causality, which is crucial for Spinoza's, Hume's, and Kant's analysis of nature – there is no easy way to reconcile Spinoza's *logical* understanding of causality with Hume's *psychological* conception of causality and Kant's *critical* account of causality. But we can engage in a creative dialogue in which we bring out the strengths and weaknesses of their views. Throughout, I indicate unsuspected affinities (as well as differences) among these thinkers.

I have *three* interrelated purposes in writing this book. In the late twentieth and twenty-first centuries, there has been a revival of interest in naturalism and nature. Many contemporary thinkers identify themselves as naturalists. However, when we examine this literature closely, there is simply no consensus about the meaning of nature, natural science, or naturalism. In my previous monograph (Bernstein 2020), I sought to articulate and defend a pragmatic naturalism, which originated with Dewey. I tried to show how some of the best and most sophisticated recent reflections on nature and naturalism enrich and add analytic subtlety to Dewey's legacy. In working on this material, I also discovered that many contemporary thinkers are ignorant of the rich modern tradition of nature, naturalism, and critiques of naturalism. Consequently, I wanted to dig deeper and clarify the variety and vicissitudes of nature in modern thought – from Spinoza to Freud.

A second purpose, closely related with the first one, has been to correct the myths, clichés, and distortions regarding the ways in which past thinkers conceived of nature, and especially the reasons they offered to justify their views. To give one current example, many contemporary thinkers claim that "traditional" philosophers made a sharp distinction between nature and culture – a distinction that is no longer viable. Ironically, *none* of the thinkers I consider introduces or presupposes such a simplistic distinction between nature and culture.

To explain my third, and major, purpose, I need to clarify my own *historical* approach to nature. Some of the thinkers I examine, such as Spinoza and Kant, are committed to the idea that philosophy can offer a conception of nature that stands for all time. I reject such an *ahistorical* view. I accept Hegel's dictum that philosophy is its *own time* comprehended in thoughts. This means that the task of understanding nature must meet new challenges and developments; this is an open task that must be performed over and over again. Many of these new challenges arise from the emergence of new scientific disciplines, such as neuroscience, cognitive science, and ecology, as well as from the changing understanding of the nature of science itself. However, taking on this task also means taking account of the urgent practical challenges that emerge in our time. It is clear that our major practical problems today are climate change, the destruction of the earth by fossil fuels, and the warming of the oceans. Every few months, there are new scientific reports warning about the dire consequences that we will face if we do not *dramatically* try to meet these challenges. In light of recent natural disasters – horrific droughts, hurricanes, tornadoes, intense storms, and widespread wildfires – it is becoming clear that the catastrophe is happening *now*. It is not surprising that today there is so much dystopian literature, film, and media. We still resist the fact that unless human beings *radically* change their behavior and practices *now*, the most likely outcome will be the self-destruction of the human species.

There is *actually* a fourth major purpose of the book that is implicit in the first three purposes. Nature is not a marginal or peripheral concept in the thinkers I consider: it is absolutely *central* for them. I argue that their distinctive concepts of nature shape every aspect of their thinking. It is a key for grasping their overall intellectual orientations toward human beings and the world.

There is also a serious intellectual problem with the way in which we comprehend nature today. While there is a good deal of new and creative thinking about nature, there is also a desperate grouping of new concepts. Coming up with new ways of understanding nature that take account of recent practical and theoretical challenges is our *major* task today. In order to deal with these issues, it is necessary to take into consideration a full account of the insights and challenges of past thinkers. In this sense, my book is a *prolegomenon* – an introduction – to rethinking humanity and nature today. From Kant we learn that a prolegomenon is at once a warning and a guide. It warns us about the limitations of knowledge, illusions, and dead ends, but it also serves as a guide to what we can know and comprehend. As I hope to show, the tradition from Spinoza to Freud offers extremely rich resources for the task of developing an adequate understanding of nature *for our time*, as well as of the challenges that we must confront.

Part I

The Philosophy of Nature

1

Spinoza: Founder of Modern Naturalism

Es Muss Sein

I

There has never been a philosopher like Spinoza – a philosopher so viciously condemned and so ecstatically praised. Spinoza, born in Amsterdam on November 14, 1632, was descended from a Jewish Marrano family that fled Portugal at the end of the sixteenth century. Amsterdam at the time was a wealthy tolerant city where the Jews were allowed to practice their religion. The young Spinoza received a rigorous Jewish education in the relatively closed Jewish community, but on July 27, 1656, when he was not yet twenty-four, he was banned – in the harshest manner – from the Jewish community for his "evil opinions" and his "horrible heresies." The Ruling Council of the Amsterdam Jewish community banished him from "the nation of Israel" and proclaimed the following *herem* (ban) on him:

> "By the degree of the Angels and the word of the Saints we ban, cut off, curse and anathemize Baruch de Espinoza . . . with all the curses written in the Torah [*Ley*]: Cursed be he by day and cursed be he by night, cursed in his lying down and cursed in his waking up, cursed in his going forth and cursed in his coming in; and may the L[ord] not want his pardon, and may the L[ord]'s wrath and zeal burn upon him . . . and ye that did cleave into the L[ord] your G[od] are all alive today."

> We warn that none may contact him orally or in writing, nor do him any favor, nor stay under the same roof with him, nor read any paper he made or wrote.[1]

During his lifetime, especially after he published his *Theological-Political Treatise* in 1670, Spinoza was also severely attacked by Christians – both Protestants (especially Dutch Calvinists) and Catholics – for his heretical views. The *Theological-Political Treatise* was condemned as a book "full of abominations," a book "forged in hell," written by the devil himself.[2]

Spinoza was accused of being an atheist, although he consistently denied this. There is a good reason why some condemned – and others praised – Spinoza for his alleged atheism. If we think of theism as the doctrine asserting the existence of a God that transcends this world, a God who created the world, a God who performs miracles, and a God who possesses such anthropomorphic traits as "wrath" and "jealousy," then there is no ambiguity, for Spinoza rejected such a conception of God. He argued that such a conception is self-contradictory and incoherent. Spinoza was an originator of a higher biblical criticism that interpreted the Bible (both Old and New Testaments) not as the word of God or the source of "sacred truths," but as a human document dealing with moral and political issues. He sought to demystify the Bible.[3]

Spinoza was the key figure in what Jonathan Israel (2001) calls the "Radical Enlightenment." We normally associate the Enlightenment with eighteenth-century French, English, or German thinkers linked and marked by national concerns. But Israel argues that "Spinoza and Spinozism were in fact the intellectual backbone of the European Radical Enlightenment everywhere, not only in the Netherlands, Germany, France, Italy, and Scandinavia but also Britain and Ireland" (Israel 2001: p. vi). This Spinozist "Radical Enlightenment"

> not only attacked and severed the roots of traditional European culture in the sacred, magic, kingship, and hierarchy, secularizing all institutions and ideas, but (intellectually and to a degree in practice) effectively demolished all legitimation of monarchy, aristocracy, woman's subordination to man, ecclesiastical authority, and slavery, replacing these with the principles of universality, equality, and democracy. (Israel 2001: p. vi)

Unlike thinkers of the "moderate Enlightenment," who seek in various ways to reconcile faith in a transcendent God with the demands of reason, Spinoza was uncompromising. He rejected a religious faith in a transcendent God as nothing more than an unwarranted prejudice, a superstition.

We will see that Spinoza's understanding of Nature, which he identifies with God and Substance, is the key to his radical views.[4]

Scholars have frequently asked how such a radical thinker emerged in the seventeenth century – a thinker who challenged the foundations of the Judeo-Christian tradition. Yovel (1989) provides one of the most illuminating analyses of this curious historical phenomenon. He characterizes Spinoza as the "Marrano of Reason." The Marranos were Jews living in Spain and Portugal in the fourteenth and fifteenth centuries who were forced to convert to Christianity. The Jewish Marranos – sometimes called "New Christians" – were publicly compelled to profess Christian beliefs and perform Christian rituals, while secretly and privately keeping their allegiance to the Torah and the laws of Moses. Many of them were persecuted by the Inquisition and burned at the stake in rituals known as "acts of faith" (*autos-de-fé*). Spinoza belonged to those fortunate Marranos who escaped from Portugal and openly practiced their Jewish faith. Yovel describes the main patterns of the Marrano experience that he discerns in Spinoza:

> (1) heterodoxy and the transcendence of revealed religion; (2) a skill for equivocation and dual language; (3) a dual life – inner and external; (4) a dual career with a break between; (5) toleration versus the Inquisition; (6) a zeal for salvation, to be gained by alternative ways to that of tradition; and – coupled with it – this-worldliness, secularism, and the denial of transcendence. All of these Marrano features can be traced in Spinoza, even if in a somewhat different guise. They are reflected not only in his thought but even more in his life or existential case. (Yovel 1989: 28)[5]

Spinoza affirmed that it is reason, and reason *alone*, that is the source of all truth. He had supreme confidence that philosophy as a discipline could discover and logically prove this truth. Extraordinarily ambitious in his claims, Spinoza was confident that he had discovered *the* truth. In one of his letters, he wrote: "I do not presume that I have found the best philosophy, but I know that what I understand is the true one" (Spinoza 1995: 342).[6] For Spinoza, to explain means to show that one true proposition is the logically necessary consequence of another proposition. As Stuart Hampshire notes,

> explanation essentially involves exhibiting necessary connexions, and 'necessary connexion' in this context means a strictly logical connexion to be discovered by logical analysis of the ideas involved. The idea of scientific knowledge is here purely deductive and mathematical; Euclid's geometry

provides the standard example of genuine explanation, in that Euclid is concerned only with the purely logical dependence of the possession of one property or properties on the possession of others. (Hampshire 1951: 29)

Spinoza's rationalism is audacious, because his claims about strictly necessary logical connections are not restricted to the study of mathematics and logic but are applicable to the study and knowledge of *all* of Nature, including the nature of human beings. The spirit of Spinoza's approach to *all* issues is exemplified by what he says in the concluding paragraph to the Preface to Part III of the *Ethics*:

> The Affects, therefore, of hate, anger, envy, etc., considered in themselves follow from the same necessity and force of nature as the other singular things. And therefore they acknowledge certain causes, through which they are understood, and have certain properties, as worthy of our knowledge as the properties of any other thing, by the mere contemplation of which we are pleased. Therefore, I shall treat the nature and powers of the Affects, and the power of the Mind over them, by the same Method by which, in the preceding parts, I treated God and the Mind, and I shall consider human actions and appetites as if it were a Question of lines, planes, and bodies. (III Preface)[7]

One of the reasons why Spinoza's philosophy can seem so remote from us today is because there is no acknowledgment of the fallibility of his philosophical claims and no sense of fallibility in acquiring the *true* knowledge of Nature (and God). He explicitly denies that in Nature there is anything contingent: "In nature there is nothing contingent, but all things have been determined from the necessity of the divine nature to exist and produce an effect in a certain way" (IP29).[8] Like his predecessor Descartes, Spinoza was impressed by the development of the sciences that appeal to the absolute certainty and the logical necessity of mathematics – the type of self-evident certainty and necessity exhibited by Euclid's *Elements*.[9] He was committed to the doctrine that everything in the universe (in Nature) is intelligible – everything can be rationally explained by logical deduction from axioms and adequate definitions. Although he did not use the Leibnizian expression the "principle of sufficient reason," he was committed to this principle in an even more rigorous manner than Leibniz.[10] For Spinoza, to conceive is to make intelligible, and he expresses this conviction in one of his first axioms: "What cannot be conceived through another, must be conceived through itself" (IA2). He affirms: "For each thing there must be assigned a cause, *or* reason, as much for its existence as for its nonexistence" (IP11dem). A philosophical system – or rather *the* philosophical system – can be laid out as a deductive system based on clear and distinct self-evident truths where everything follows by logical necessity. Although Spinoza frequently appeals to experience to *clarify* his meaning, he never does so to *justify* his propositions. In his arguments, he appeals to reason and what is logically necessary. There has never been a philosopher – with the possible exception of Hegel – who has made such ambitious and audacious claims for philosophy and reason. Spinoza has frequently been described as a "naturalist" (an expression he never used), but we will see that his conception of Nature has little to do with the many ways in which the terms "nature" and "naturalism" are used today. Yet, as we will also see, there are some profound affinities between his conception of Nature and the contemporary appeals to nature and naturalism.

As a "Marrano of Reason," Spinoza led a cautious life. *Caute* (cautiously) was his motto. Most of his heretical views were shared only with a close group of friends and correspondents. Spinoza was guarded and frequently used what Yovel calls "double language." Only the sophisticated readers of his anonymously published *Theological-Political Treatise* could discern just how radical a thinker he was. Spinoza, who lived modestly and supported himself by grinding lenses and studying optics, spent most of his later years working on his magnum opus, the *Ethics*.[11] In 1675, two years before his death, Spinoza tentatively explored publishing the *Ethics* in Amsterdam, but because of the increasing attacks upon him by clerics, he decided not to. The *Ethics*, along with the other manuscripts, was published by his friends shortly after his death in 1677.

The *Ethics* employs a geometric method in its style of presentation – one that lists definitions, axioms, postulates, propositions, demonstrations, corollaries, and scholia. Scholars have vigorously debated the significance of Spinoza's use of this method. Opinions about Spinoza's use of a geometric method range from those who take it as absolutely essential for understating his system to those who think it functions more like an external scaffolding.[12] Yovel takes a middle position between these extremes. He claims that the geometrical method is not as sacrosanct to Spinoza as is sometimes supposed, for it neither guarantees nor is indispensable to the attainment of truth.

> The geometrical model is more a matter of philosophical form and mood; it stresses the need for rigor, clarity, and step-by-step consequentiality as necessary conditions of rationality, and it also calls for philosophical detachment in dealing with the most passionate issues. Thus it dramatizes certain major features of Spinoza's philosophical message.... As any readers

> of the work will recognize, the *Ethics* draws heavily from natural language and the traditional vocabulary of philosophy; thus it contains elements of content, allusion, connotation and the like, which an actual formal model will have to reject as opaque; and if the *Ethics* admits them, it is because its language is *not* truly "geometrical" and cannot be so by the nature of its subject matter. Spinoza's actual discourse, even in pure philosophy, is fundamentally non-formal but depends on history, natural language, and the accumulative human experience, although it is organized in weak analogy to a formal system. (Yovel 1989: 139–40)

Nevertheless, one should not underestimate the extent to which Spinoza is committed to the idea that pure philosophy consists in necessary propositions and deductive proofs.[13] Despite Spinoza's use of traditional philosophical expressions, one must be alert to the ways in which he redefines this vocabulary for his systematic purposes.

Although we find anticipations of Spinoza's distinctive concept of Nature in his earlier works, I want to focus on the concept of Nature as it emerges in his mature *Ethics*. The *Ethics* consists of five parts, and the titles that Spinoza gives to each of these parts are important: "I. Of God"; "II. Of the Nature and Origin of the Mind"; "III. Of the Origin and Nature of the Affects"; "IV. Of Human Bondage, *or* of the Powers of the Affects"; "V. Of the Power of the Intellect, *or* of Human Freedom." Spinoza does not begin his *Ethics* with an explicit discussion of Nature but rather with a series of definitions that lay the groundwork for the entire *Ethics*. As the *Ethics* proceeds, we realize that *all* these definitions are definitions of Nature. Nature turns out to be *strictly identical* with God and Substance. In the Preface to Part IV Spinoza introduces his famous (some would say, infamous) expression *Deus sive Natura* (God *or* Nature):

> That eternal and infinite being we call God, *or* Nature, acts from the same necessity from which he exists. For we have shown (IP16) that the necessity of nature from which he acts is the same as that from which he exists. The reason, therefore, *or* cause, why God, *or* Nature, acts, and the reason why he exists, are one and the same. (IV Preface)[14]

Spinoza begins the *Ethics* with eight definitions. These definitions (together with the seven axioms that he lists) are the basis for the thirty-six propositions (and their demonstrations) that constitute our knowledge of God. In the Appendix to Part I, he sums up what he claims to have proved about God:

> With these [demonstrations] I have explained God's nature and properties: that he exists necessarily; that he is unique; that he is and acts from the

necessity alone of his nature; that (and how) he is the free cause of all things; that all things are in God and so depend on him that without him they can neither be nor be conceived; and finally, that all things have been predetermined by God, not from the freedom of the will *or* absolute good pleasure, but from God's absolute nature, *or* infinite power. (I Appendix)[15]

Everything that Spinoza asserts about God in Part I is implicit in his eight definitions – or so he claims. Consequently, it is worthwhile to list his definitions and comment on them to grasp the outlines of Spinoza's metaphysical system.

D1: By cause of itself I understand that whose essence involves existence, *or* that whose nature cannot be conceived except as existing.

D2: That thing is said to be finite in its own kind that can be limited by another of the same nature. . . .

D3: By substance I understand what is in itself and is conceived through itself, i.e., that whose concept does not require the concept of another thing, from which it is formed.

D4: By attribute I understand what the intellect perceives of a substance, as constituting its essence.

D5: By mode I understand the affections of a substance, *or* that which is in another through which it is also conceived.

D6: By God I understand a being absolutely infinite, i.e., a substance consisting of an infinity of attributes, of which each one expresses an eternal and infinite essence. . . .[16]

D7: That thing is called free which exists from the necessity of its nature alone, and is determined to act by itself alone. But a thing is called necessary, or rather compelled, which is determined by another to exist and to produce an effect in a certain determinate manner.

D8: By eternity I understand existence itself, insofar as it is conceived to follow necessarily from the definition alone of the eternal thing. (ID1–D8)[17]

How are we to understand these definitions? Are they merely arbitrary? Is Spinoza simply stipulating the way in which *he* defines these key terms, or is there a sense in which they are "real" definitions – definitions that are true of reality? Are they *necessarily* true? The problem is compounded by the way in which Spinoza introduces several of these definitions with the phrase "I understand" (*intelligo*). Consequently, one may think that these definitions are stipulated and, in that sense, arbitrary, because we are open to stipulating alternative definitions. This is the way that Spinoza's severest critics interpret these initial definitions. As Henry Allison notes, the modern reader is "often left with the impression that Spinoza simply and arbitrarily defines his key terms in such a way as to arrive at his desired conclusions. The argument of the *Ethics* is thus viewed as an impressive and intricate chain of reasoning that nowhere touches reality" (Allison 1987: 40).

Spinoza himself was keenly aware of the problem. He distinguished two kinds of definitions that correspond to the distinction between "nominal" and "real" definitions. "Real" definitions define a thing rather than a name.[18] They can be true or false, and Spinoza claims that his definitions are true – indeed, necessarily true. The question arises, how does Spinoza *know* that his definitions are true, and indeed necessarily true? Here, as Allison observes, we need to see that for Spinoza, the same principles of mathematics apply to his definitions.

> Thus, we have a real definition, an adequate, true, or clear and distinct idea of a thing . . . insofar as we know its "proximate cause" and can see how its properties necessarily follow from this cause. . . . When the mind has a true idea, it immediately knows it to be true, since it grasps the logical necessity with which the properties of the object follow from the idea. The metaphysician, as well as the mathematician, can therefore arrive at genetic definitions of things, and it is through such definitions that one acquires rationally grounded knowledge. (Allison 1987: 41–2)[19]

We fully understand these initial definitions (and axioms) only when we see what propositions can be logically deduced by employing them. We might say that *initially* these definitions are stipulated, but this does not mean that they are arbitrary. On the contrary, when we grasp the full significance of the propositions of Part I, and the demonstrations of these propositions, we come to realize that these definitions are real definitions; we discover that they are true, and indeed necessarily true. Thus, for example, we learn that the proposition that God is an absolutely infinite being – that is, a Substance consisting of an infinity of attributes, of which each one expresses an eternal and infinite existence – is a *necessary truth*.

Spinoza's eight definitions are intimately related to each other. It is significant that Spinoza's first definition is a definition of "cause of itself" (*causa sui*) because it is God – and God alone – that is the cause of itself. Here we see Spinoza's absolute commitment to the principle of sufficient reason: it is impossible to explain God in any other way than to claim that he is the cause of himself. When Spinoza affirms that Substance is conceived through itself, we understand why he identifies God with Substance. Substance is conceived through itself and "does not require the concept of another thing, from which it is formed" (ID3). The term "cause" must be divested of its contemporary empirical associations. Cause is what *logically explains* the existence or qualities of an effect; it is the *logical ground* of what is to be explained. To explain means to show that one true proposition is the logically necessary consequence of another true proposition. We would not be able to explain anything unless we determined that there is a Substance (God) that is the cause of itself. God (or Substance) *necessarily* exists. Furthermore, God is absolutely infinite – a Substance that consists of an infinity of attributes. P18 states that "God is the immanent, not the transitive, cause of all things." God is the immanent and the *eternal* cause of all things. Spinoza categorically rejects any conception of God conceived as being independent of his creation. When we grasp that the terms "God," "Substance," and "Nature" have the same referent, then we realize that natural things cannot be explained by a transcendent cause. Hampshire clarifies this point:

> To say that God is the immanent cause of all things is another way of saying that everything must be explained as belonging to the single and all-inclusive system which is Nature, and no cause (not even a First Cause) can be conceived as somehow outside or independent of the order of Nature. Any doctrine of a transcendent God, since 'transcendent' simply means 'outside the order of Nature', or any doctrine of God as Creator distinguished as transient cause from his creation, involves this impossibility; for it introduces the mystery of an inexplicable act of creation, an act which is somehow outside the order of events in Nature. (Hampshire 1951: 35)

According to D7, God, or Nature, is the eternal cause of all things and of itself and must be *free* in its self-creative activity. "Nothing exists or can be conceived apart from this one, self-contained system, which can be characterized as God, substance, or nature" (Allison 1987: 63). We come to know Nature when we know its eternal and necessary laws – that is, the eternal and necessary laws that define God's nature.

The defining characteristic of Substance is its *existential* and *conceptual* independence. Consequently, Spinoza's concept of Substance is radically different from both Descartes' and Aristotle's conception of substance. Spinoza's conception includes conceptual as well as ontological independence. Conceptual independence means explanatory self-sufficiency:

> Spinoza, in effect, denies that Cartesian substances are really substances. (They are conceived through their attribute, not through themselves). Further, ontological and conceptual independence are not contingently conjoined characteristics of substance for Spinoza. On the contrary, only that which can also be conceived – that is, explained – through itself can also exist in itself, and vice versa. Thus, since Cartesian substances are not conceived through themselves, it follows that they do not exist in themselves either; that is, they do not have the ontological independence claimed for them by the Cartesian theory. (Allison 1987: 47)

Considering that the defining characteristic of Substance is its ontological and conceptual independence, neither the mind nor the body is an independent substance. Descartes, in his *Meditations*, affirms that both the mind and the body are *dependent* on God. He implicitly affirms that there is one and only one substance that is truly *independent* – namely, God. We may say that Spinoza is developing the logical consequences that are already implicit in Descartes' metaphysics.[20]

As the *Ethics* unfolds, we come to understand with increasing clarity that God is strictly identical with Substance, and that Substance is strictly identical with Nature. This progressive development illustrates what Yovel characterizes as Spinoza's use of "double language." In affirming that God is eternal and absolutely infinite, Spinoza adopts a traditional theological way of characterizing God. When we grasp the necessary logical consequences of Spinoza's definitions, axioms, propositions, and demonstrations, we become aware that Spinoza's conception of God is the *antithesis* of the conception of God in the Abrahamic religions. God is *immanent* in, and *identical* with, the universe; God turns out to be *identical* with Nature. We need to read the *Ethics* from a double perspective. On the one hand, there is the "official" perspective of logically rigorous deductions from real and true definitions and axioms. On the other hand, the *Ethics* is a *pedagogical* work, one that is intended to *transform* the reader (a reader capable of using her reason). Starting from a traditional theological conception of God, the reader is led to a radically different conception of God – a God who is thoroughly immanent in the universe and identical with the necessary laws of nature. As the *Ethics* unfolds, we discover not only that the *referents* of "God," "Substance," and "Nature" are identical, but also that, from an *adequate* philosophical perspective, the *senses* of "God," "Substance," and "Nature" are identical.

Spinoza rejects the Aristotelian conception of a plurality of substances, each possessing essential and accidental attributes, just as he rejects the Cartesian claim that there are two substances, defined by the attributes of thought and extension.[21] Unlike Aristotle's and Descartes' conception of substance, Spinoza's view is that finite entities like human beings and trees are *not* substances, but turn out to be *modes* of substance. There are only two attributes of God or Nature that *our human intellect* knows: thought and extension. The attributes of thought and extension are both attributes of the *single* Substance that is God. Spinoza radically departs from Descartes, for whom thought is the essence of one type of substance and extension is the essence of another type of substance. For Spinoza, *all* attributes are conceptually and causally independent of each other; they do not interact with each other. From a traditional religious perspective, Spinoza is making a shocking (and blasphemous) claim – from his definitions it logically follows that the attribute of extension is an attribute of God. There have been interpreters of Spinoza who suggest that, when unmasked, Spinoza is really a materialist because he claims that extension is an attribute that defines the essence of God. There have also been interpreters who think that, when unmasked, Spinoza is an idealist because he affirms that thought is the essential attribute of God. Both interpretations fail to acknowledge what Spinoza clearly affirms: namely, that both attributes are attributes of the *one* and only Substance that is God. These attributes are – to use a Heideggerian turn of phrase – equiprimordial and conceptually independent. Sometimes this view has been characterized as "Spinoza's parallelism," but there is something misleading about this expression. We normally think of parallel lines in geometry as consisting of two or more independent lines that are parallel to each other. But thought and extension are *two* necessary ways of conceiving of the *one* and only Substance. Furthermore, each attribute "expresses an eternal and infinite essence" (ID6). Hampshire nicely brings out what Spinoza is claiming about Substance and the attributes of extension and thought:

> [T]he whole system, which is God or Nature, can be conceived equally, and no less completely, as a system of extended or spatial things or as a system of thinking or animated things; everything extended in space is also truly conceived as animated, and everything animated is also truly conceived as extended in space. In order to appreciate Spinoza's intention, it is essential from the beginning not to attach to the infinite attributes of Thought and Extension only the ordinary associations of the words mind and body; for the attributes of Thought and Extension are not in Spinoza two partly parallel, or somehow co-ordinated, systems of things or events, as mental and physical events are ordinarily imagined to be. They are the same order of causes in the same substance, but conceived under two different attributes

of this substance. Thinking substance and extended substance are one and the same substance, comprehended now under this attribute, now under that ... 'Whether we think of Nature under the attribute of Extension or under the attribute of Thought or under any other attribute whatever, we shall discover one and the same order, or one and the same connexion of causes' (*Ethics Pt.* II. *Prop.* VII. *Note*). The union of individual human minds with individual human bodies is for Spinoza only a special case of the general identity of the order or connexion of causes in Nature. (Hampshire 1951: 49–50)

The precise relation of Substance and its modes has been one of the most intractable and controversial issues among Spinoza's commentators. Recall the definition of a mode: "By mode I understand the affections of a substance, *or* that which is in another through which it is also conceived" (ID5). Spinoza's meaning is certainly not immediately clear. The metaphysical status of familiar objects in the world, such as trees, tables, or even individual bodies or minds, are *modes* of Substance – indeed, all finite objects are modes of Substance (or God). One may ask: are modes only causally dependent on God, or do they somehow inhere in God, and if so, how are we to understand "inhere in God"?[22] But regardless of how we comprehend the relation of Substance and modes, there is no doubt that, first, there is one and only one Substance that is identified with God or Nature; secondly, all attributes are attributes of this single Substance; and thirdly, all modes are modes of these attributes. The claim that the mind and the body (and indeed all finite entities) are modes of God may sound strange to modern ears. I think this is because, despite Spinoza's identification of God with Nature, we still tend to think of God in a traditional way – as the creator of the universe. If we substitute "Nature" for "God" and claim that the mind and the body are modes of Nature, then the strangeness disappears. A naturalistic translation of Spinoza's claim – that finite entities (including the mind and the body) are modes of God – turns out to mean that all finite entities (including the mind and the body) are to be explained by an appeal to the same laws of nature. From ID7 we learn that "[t]hat thing is called free which exists from the necessity of its nature alone." "Free" in this context means truly independent (*causa sui*); everything else is dependent on what is truly – that is, conceptually and causally – independent. Consequently, it is only God who is truly free. This does not mean that God or Nature has free will. There is no such thing as free will. Here, too, we discern Spinoza's anti-Cartesianism: neither God nor man has free will. Spinoza rejects any theological doctrine that ascribes free will to God.

I want to pursue further some of the details of Spinoza's conception of Nature. In IP29, Spinoza asserts: "In nature there is nothing contingent, but all things have been determined from the necessity of the divine nature to exist and produce an effect in a certain way." Spinoza is committed to *both* determinism and necessitarianism. Determinism is the thesis that every event is causally determined from antecedent conditions according to the laws of nature. Determinism does not require the antecedent conditions to be necessary.[23] If the antecedent causes are altered, then the necessary chain of causes and effects will be different. "But, as far as determinism is concerned, there is nothing in principle impossible about the chain of causes having been different all the way back. The laws of nature are necessary, according to determinism, but the particular series of events governed by these laws is not necessary: there could have been a different series of events" (Della Rocca 2008: 75–6). Necessitarianism is a much stronger thesis; it denies that there are other possible worlds. IP16 states: "From the necessity of the divine nature there must follow infinitely many things in infinitely many modes (i.e., everything which can fall under an infinite intellect)." From IP29 we learn that "all things have been determined from the necessity of the divine nature." IP33 explicitly states: "Things could have been produced by God in no other way, and in no other order than they have been produced." Given these claims, it becomes clear that Spinoza is affirming not only determinism but also the much more controversial doctrine of necessitarianism. "The view that there is more than one possible series of events (or, in Spinozistic terms, one possible series of finite modes) is precisely what determinism allows and necessitarianism denies" (Della Rocca 2008: 76).

In the scholium to IP29, where Spinoza affirms that "in nature there is nothing contingent," he elaborates his conception of Nature. Appropriating a distinction from the scholastic philosophers, he distinguishes two ways of thinking about Nature – *Natura naturans* and *Natura naturata*.

> [B]y *Natura naturans* we must understand what is in itself and is conceived through itself, *or* such attributes of substance as express an eternal and infinite essence, i.e. . . . . God, insofar as he is considered as a free cause.
>
> But by *Natura naturata* I understand whatever follows from the necessity of God's nature, *or* from any of God's attributes . . . insofar as they are considered as things which are in God, and can neither be nor be conceived without God. (IP29s)

We can conceive of Nature (or God) as the free, *active*, originating, self-creating cause that expresses itself in its infinite attributes and in the modes of these attributes. We can *also* conceive of Nature (or God) in a *passive* manner, as the created system of Nature. These are two ways of conceiving essentially the *same* Nature. Creator and creation are *identical*. In one of his letters, Spinoza clearly states: "I do not separate God from nature as everyone known to me has done" (Spinoza 1985a: 188). This is the basis for Spinoza's alleged pantheism. We must be extremely careful, however, in using the term "pantheism," which Spinoza himself does not use. If by "pantheism" we mean simply the view that identifies God with Nature (in all its aspects), then Spinoza is a pantheist.[24] However, even this claim is open to various interpretations and misinterpretations. For example, Hegel, who expresses great admiration for Spinoza, charges him with acosmism – the view that finite individuals lack all reality as if everything is "swallowed up" by a God, who is eternal and absolutely infinite. This would be like claiming that Spinoza recognizes only *Natura naturans* and not *Natura naturata*. God and Nature are both *Natura naturans* and *Natura naturata*. Thus, Spinoza subtly takes account of both infinity and finitude (see ID2 and ID6). We must, however, resist the temptation to think that by identifying God with Nature, Spinoza is attributing *independent* divine properties to Nature. All the properties of God are properties of Nature, and all the properties of Nature are properties of God.

Thus far, I have been stressing that the *referents* of "God," "Substance," and "Nature" are strictly identical – although initially, the *senses* of these expressions are strikingly different. The *Ethics* is intended to *transform* how we think, to lead us away from commonsensical and traditional ways of thinking about God, Substance, and Nature to a true and adequate grasp of these concepts. Throughout the *Ethics*, there is a pervasive polemic against any and all anthropomorphic and anthropocentric conceptions of God, as well as a rejection of final causes. In the Appendix to Part I, Spinoza emphatically rejects the prejudices that are the obstacles to a rational understanding of Nature:

> All the prejudices I here undertake to expose depend on this one: that men commonly suppose that all natural things act, as men do, on account of an end; indeed, they maintain as certain that God himself directs all things to some certain end, for they say that God has made all things for man, and man that he might worship God. (I Appendix)[25]

All beliefs based on this prejudice are nothing but superstitions. The sharpness of Spinoza's condemnation is evident when he mocks the idea that "nature does nothing in vain (i.e., nothing which is not of use to men)":

See, I ask you, how the matter has turned out in the end! Among so many conveniences in nature they had to find many inconveniences: storms, earthquakes, diseases, etc. These, they maintain, happen because the Gods . . . are angry on account of wrongs done to them by men, *or* on account of sins committed in their worship. (I Appendix)

Thus, Spinoza's Nature is the eternal system of the laws of nature wherein there are no final causes. The finite human intellect appeals to these necessary laws to explain and make intelligible everything in Nature (all that there is). Our intellect is limited to knowing Nature through the attributes of extension and thought. The Nature that we know is a complete physical system – a system of things extended in space; it is also a complete system of thoughts or ideas. Both conceptions of Nature are complete in themselves and are not reducible to each other. They are conceptually independent, even though they are both conceptions of the one and only Nature. The laws of nature apply to *all* of Nature. The following passage epitomizes Spinoza's understanding of Nature:

[N]ature is always the same, and its virtue and power of acting are everywhere one and the same, i.e., the laws and rules of nature, according to which all things happen, and change from one form to another, are always and everywhere the same. So the way of understanding the nature of anything, of whatever kind, must always be the same, viz. through the universal laws and rules of nature. (III Preface)

Everything in the universe is explained by the same laws. There is absolutely nothing *beyond* or *outside* of Nature.[26]

I have been focusing on Spinoza's general account of Nature as developed in Part I of the *Ethics*. My reason for doing so is to clarify Spinoza's conception of Nature as an all-inclusive system governed by the laws of nature that determine everything in Nature – including human and non-human nature. There are no ontological dualisms within Nature. Before examining the consequences of this conception of Nature, especially as it relates to human beings, I want to stand back and briefly consider how Spinoza's conception of Nature is relevant to contemporary discussions of naturalism. Few philosophers today would accept Spinoza's relentless rationalism, his denial of contingency, his logical and conceptual understanding of causality, his total commitment to a principle of sufficient reason, and his controversial doctrine that "all things have been determined from the necessity of the divine nature to exist and produce an effect in a certain way" (IP29). Most philosophers since Spinoza (including Hume, Kant, and Hegel) have systematically criticized one or more of these claims. But they have also recognized that Spinoza offers a powerful philosophy of immanence and a unified conception of Nature.

Today, the debate between those who seek to defend the viability of a conception of God transcending the natural world and those who reject the belief in a transcendent God is very much alive. Masses of people still believe in some version of a God who has created the natural world and is separate from this world – a God who also exhibits anthropomorphic traits. There are contemporary philosophers and theologians who defend such a conception of God. Spinoza's stand in this debate leaves no doubt. For him, the very idea of an independent transcendent God who creates the universe and everything in it is nothing but a superstition of the human imagination. His categorical rejection of a transcendent God, moreover, has been the basis for the accusation that he is an atheist – an accusation that arose when he was alive and which has persisted until the present.

Suppose we bracket this issue of whether there is a transcendent God and focus on a different issue concerning naturalism. In the passage cited above, Spinoza declares that "the way of understanding the nature of anything, of whatever kind, must also be the same, viz. through the universal laws and rules of nature" (III Preface). Today, there are many varieties of naturalism ranging from reductive forms of naturalism, claiming that everything can ultimately be explained by the physical laws of nature, to more liberal conceptions of naturalism, seeking to account for what is distinctive about human beings – specifically their conceptual capacities and rationality.[27] Some contemporary philosophers reject all versions of naturalism. They argue that a naturalistic scientific account cannot provide an adequate understanding of human intentionality as well as human rational and conceptual abilities. Battles rage between those who seek to defend some version of naturalism (restrictive or liberal) and those who think that naturalistic explanations cannot account for what is distinctive about human beings. Spinoza stands with those who claim that we can give a naturalistic account of *everything*, including human conceptual abilities. Unlike Kant, and those contemporary philosophers influenced by him who draw a sharp distinction between reason and nature or between nature and spirit (*Geist*), Spinoza understands reason as itself an *essential* feature of Nature. Spinoza would be sympathetic to those contemporary philosophers committed to giving a naturalistic account of our conceptual capacities and intentionality.[28] Consequently, the deep issues that stand at the heart of Spinoza's philosophy are still with us. They concern, first, whether or not belief in a transcendent God is to be rejected as unwarranted prejudice, and, secondly, whether there is a single unified system of nature and natural laws that are the basis for explaining everything there is, including human rationality.

To further appreciate Spinoza's distinctive naturalism, I want to consider the consequences of his conception of Nature for understanding *human nature* – especially his understanding of the mind, body, reason, and passions. We have already noted that Spinoza rejects the Cartesian view that the mind and the body are two different substances causally interacting with each other. For him, the mind and the body are finite modes of the attributes of thought and extension – attributes of the one and only nature. "The order and connection of ideas is the same as the order and connection of things" (IIP7). "[W]hether we conceive nature under the attribute of Extension, or under the attribute of Thought, or under any other attribute, we shall find one and the same order, *or* one and the same connection of causes, i.e., that the same things follow one another" (IIP7s). In effect, Spinoza proposes an *identity* theory of the mind and the body. However, this is not an identity theory that claims that everything we take to be distinctive about the mind can be translated into or reduced to a physical system. Nor is it a version of idealism claiming that what appears to be physical or material is completely explicable as mental. In Spinoza, an individual human mind is constituted by a set of causally related *ideas* whose *objects* are states of an individual body.[29] There are two conceptually independent ways of describing and explaining the causal order – the *mental* way of ideas and the *physical* way of material objects. Unlike Descartes (and Malebranche), Spinoza is not claiming that these are ontologically independent orders, somehow "corresponding" to each other. Rather, we are describing and explaining *one and the same order* in two different ways.[30] The relation of the modes of mind and body is a *special case* of the relation of the attributes of thought and extension. "[T]he Mind and the Body . . . are one and the same Individual, which is conceived now under the attribute of Thought, now under the attribute of Extension" (IIP21s).[31] Daisie Radner makes this point clear:

> The human body is a finite mode of the attribute of extension. There is an idea of it in the infinite intellect of God. This idea is the human mind. Since a mode of extension and the idea of that mode are one and the same thing, the human body and the human mind are one and the same thing, viewed on the one hand under the attribute of extension and on the other hand under the attribute of thought. (Radner 1971: 347)

We can also draw another important consequence of Spinoza's naturalism by considering the relation between human beings and nonhuman animals. The modes and the attributes of thought and extension are also applicable to nonhuman animals – just as they are applicable to everything in Nature. The difference between human animals and nonhuman animals is only a difference in the *degree* of complexity in structure and organization. Spinoza would also affirm that the difference between what we now call "organic" and "inorganic" nature is also only a difference of degree of complexity.[32]

Although Spinoza begins the *Ethics* with metaphysical claims about God, Substance, and Nature, his claims depend on a distinctive theory of knowledge. In the *Ethics*, Spinoza distinguishes three levels of knowledge (*cognitio*).[33] The first and lowest level he calls "imagination." It includes sense perception and our common-sense knowledge of the world and ourselves. Imagination is the source of prejudices and superstitions that are obstacles to achieving genuine rational knowledge of the natural causal order. Spinoza frequently condemns this lowest form of knowledge and claims that, for the most part, ordinary people (the "multitude") are limited to this level of knowledge. Sometimes, Spinoza uses "imagination" in a broad sense, to designate common-sense knowledge and sense perception. At other times, he speaks of "imagination" in a more restricted sense. He characterizes bodily affections as "images of things" and their corresponding ideas as "imaginations of the Mind" (IIP17s). He even develops a theory of association of these ideas that anticipates Hume's theory of association. Imagination, however, lacks the rational, logical understanding of causes that characterizes the second and third kinds of knowledge. Imagination is never the source of *adequate* ideas – ideas that are clear and distinct and which provide knowledge of *adequate* causes. Consequently, imagination is the source of error, illusion, and falsity. "Knowledge of the first kind is the only cause of falsity, whereas knowledge of the second and of the third kind is necessarily true" (IIP41). "Knowledge of the second and third kinds, and not of the first kind, teaches us to distinguish the true from the false" (IIP42). Nevertheless, Spinoza does *not* completely reject the knowledge of the first kind. He clearly affirms that it is a form of *knowledge* – although the lowest one. By reflecting on this level of knowledge, by seeing how it leads to contradictions, one is motivated to move to the level of *ratio*, where we achieve the level of scientific knowledge.

To appreciate the contemporary relevance of Spinoza, consider the analogy between Spinoza's first and second kinds of knowledge and Wilfrid Sellars' distinction between the manifest image of man-in-the-world and the scientific image of man-in-the-world. The manifest image is "the framework in terms of which man came to be aware of himself as man-in-the-world. It is the framework in terms of which, to use an existentialist turn of phrase, man first encountered himself – which is, of course, when he came to be man" (Sellars 1963: 6). The manifest image of man-in-the-world corresponds to Spinoza's first kind of knowledge, which has its source in imagination. Like Spinoza, who contrasts the first kind of knowledge with the second, Sellars contrasts the manifest image with the scientific image of man-in-the-world. Sellars is referring to the type of scientific understanding that was emerging during Spinoza's lifetime – especially in the application of mathematics and the postulation of theoretical entities to explain the physical world. There is, however, a clash between these two conceptions of man-in-the-world.[34] Each claims to be the *true* and in principle *complete* account of man-in-the-world. Sellars argues for the ontological primacy of the scientific image. "*[S]peaking as a philosopher*, I am quite prepared to say that the common-sense world of physical objects in Space and Time is unreal – that is, that there are no such things. Or, to put it less paradoxically, that in the dimension of describing and explaining the world, science is the measure of all things, of what is that it is, and of what is not that it is not" (Sellars 1997: 83). This is the analogy between Spinoza and Sellars that I want to emphasize. For although Spinoza and Sellars have very different conceptions of the nature of scientific knowledge, they both maintain that science (what Spinoza calls *ratio*) is the *true* measure of all things and is the basis for determining what is and what is not.[35] Just as Sellars is not suggesting that we abandon the manifest image, Spinoza is not suggesting that we abandon the first kind of knowledge. Rather, we simply need to understand the limitations of this kind of knowledge, its inadequacies, and the role it plays for the "multitude." We are compelled to move beyond the first kind of knowledge when we discern its inadequacies, tensions, and contradictions from a rational (*rationale*) perspective. As Hampshire notes,

> It is therefore, in a sense, misleading to describe our ordinary common-sense statements about the world as simply false: they are not false in any absolute sense, since no idea or judgment is false in any absolute sense. An idea or judgment can only be described as false by comparison with some more logically coherent, and therefore superior, system of ideas of which it is not itself a part. Ideas of the imagination or confused experience, which constitute our common-sense knowledge, are incomplete in the sense that they do not represent the true order of causes in Nature. (Hampshire 1951: 67–8)

The precise character of the third type of knowledge is one of the issues most debated among Spinoza scholars. In part, this is because Spinoza has very little to say about it, and what he does say is not clear. "[T]his kind of knowing proceeds from an adequate idea of the formal essence of certain attributes of God to the adequate knowledge of the [NS: formal] essence of things" (IIIP40s2).[36] The mathematical example that Spinoza provides to explain his meaning only adds to the confusion. Bennett takes an extreme view. He thinks that the latter part of Part V of the *Ethics* where Spinoza deals with intuitive knowledge is "an unmitigated and ... unmotivated disaster" and "rubbish which causes others to write rubbish" (Bennett 1984: 357, 374).[37] At the other extreme, Yovel claims that the third kind of knowledge "gives me a new and deeper perspective on myself and the world" and is a form of secular salvation (Yovel 1989: 166).[38] Fortunately, to understand Spinoza's naturalism, we don't need to resolve the dispute about the third kind of knowledge. We need to acknowledge only that the third kind of knowledge enables one to intuitively grasp the full meaning of *Deus sive Natura* and to grasp how my *individual* nature is related to the whole of Nature.

Thus far, in pursuing the meaning of Spinoza's conception of Nature, I have been concentrating on his basic metaphysical claims and his theory of knowledge. We have learned that human beings are finite modes of God (Nature), that our finite intellects are dependent on the infinite intellect of God, and that by the use of our *ratio* we can gain an understanding of the laws of nature. Spinoza does not limit himself to a metaphysical and epistemological account of Nature. In the third and fourth parts of the *Ethics*, he enriches his conception of Nature by focusing on human nature – especially on how our reason is related to what Spinoza calls "affects" (*affectus*).[39] In his analysis of affects, Spinoza is not exclusively concerned with theoretical issues of understanding their causes. His aim is to give an account of the affects that will show us how to avoid being enslaved by them and how to achieve the highest degree of freedom that is within our human reach. This is the rationale for entitling Part IV "Of Human Bondage, *or* of the Powers of the Affects" and Part V "Of the Power of the Intellect, *or* of Human Freedom." These two parts enable us to grasp why his work is entitled *Ethics*. Spinoza criticizes common conceptions of moral philosophy in order to clear the way for an adequate naturalistic account of ethics. The thesis fundamental for Spinoza's naturalism is that everything in Nature is governed by the same principles, rules, or laws. Consequently, this thesis also applies to his account of human nature. Hampshire beautifully captures the spirit and orientation of Spinoza's naturalistic approach to the study of human nature and human freedom:

> Man is part of Nature, and therefore the moralist must be a naturalist; no moral philosopher has stated this principle of method more clearly, or adhered to it more ruthlessly, than Spinoza. The actual servitude and unhappiness of man, and his ideally possible freedom and happiness, are both to be impartially deduced and explained as the necessary consequences of his status as a finite mode in Nature. Exhortation and appeals to emotion and desire are as useless and as irrelevant in moral, as in natural, philosophy. We must first understand the causes of our passions; our whole duty and wisdom is to understand fully our own position in Nature and the causes of our imperfections, and, by understanding, to free ourselves from them; man's greatest happiness and peace of mind (*acquiescentia animi*) comes only from this full philosophical understanding of himself. (Hampshire 1951: 92)

Thus, the first task is to understand, to gain rational knowledge of the causes of our passions. In the process of achieving rational knowledge of our passions, we are on the way to achieving human freedom.

Spinoza begins his discussion of the affects by taking a swipe at Descartes and the Cartesians:

> Most of those who have written about the Affects, and men's way of living, seem to treat, not of natural things, which follow the common laws of nature, but of things which are outside nature. Indeed they seem to conceive man in nature as a dominion within a dominion. For they believe that man disturbs, rather than follows, the order of nature, that he has absolute power over his actions, and that he is determined only by himself. [*Nam hominem naturae ordinem magis perturbare, quam sequi, ipsumque in suas actiones absolutam habere potentiam, nec aliunde, quam a se ipso determinari, credunt.*] And they attribute the cause of human impotence, not to the common power of nature, but to I know not what vice of human nature, which they therefore bewail, or laugh at, or disdain, or (as usually happens) curse. And he who knows how to censure more eloquently and cunningly the weakness of the human Mind is held to be Godly. (III Preface)[40]

Typically, the definitions that Spinoza gives at the beginning of each part of the *Ethics* provide the key for everything that follows. This is also true for the three definitions that introduce his discussion of affects. Spinoza distinguishes between those affects that are *actions* and those that are *passions*. The distinction between actions and passions is intimately related to the distinction between adequate and inadequate causes – and to our understanding of these causes.

> D1: I call that cause adequate whose effect can be clearly and distinctly perceived through it. But I call it partial, *or* inadequate, if its effect cannot be understood through it alone.

D2: I say that we act when something happens, in us or outside us, of which we are the adequate cause, i.e. (by D1), when something in us or outside us follows from our nature, which can be clearly and distinctively understood through it alone. On the other hand, I say that we are acted on when something happens in us, or something follows from our nature, of which we are only a partial cause.

D3: By affect I understand affections of the Body by which the Body's power of acting is increased or diminished, aided or restrained, and at the same time, the ideas of these affections.

Therefore, if we can be the adequate cause of any of these affections, I understand by the Affect an action; otherwise, a passion. (IIID1–D3)

It is important not to misinterpret IIID3. Affections of the body and the ideas of these affections refer to the same entity – the human individual. We can speak about bodily affections and mental affections, but we are describing the same thing in two different ways. Affections are not exclusively mental or psychological; they are bodily. From Spinoza's previous analysis of the mind and the body, we know that he rejects the very idea of a (Cartesian) interaction of the mind and the body. Spinoza makes this point absolutely clear in IIIP2: "The Body cannot determine the Mind to thinking, and the Mind cannot determine the Body to motion, to rest or to anything else (if there is anything else)." Typically, as I have already suggested, Spinoza adopts the traditional expressions and redefines them for his systematic purposes. Normally, we do not distinguish actions and passions on the basis of whether they do or do not have adequate causes, but for Spinoza this is their distinguishing characteristic. This point turns out to be crucial for him because it links our knowledge (or lack of knowledge) of adequate causes with the distinction between active and passive affects.

One of the impressive features of the *Ethics* is how each part builds on the conclusions of previous parts. The explication of God, Substance, and Nature in Part I and the explication of the mind and body in Part II shape Spinoza's treatment of affects in Part III. This is illustrated in the scholium to IIIP2:

> These things are more clearly understood from what is said in IIP7s, viz. that the Mind and the Body are one and the same thing, which is conceived now under the attribute of Thought, now under the attribute of Extension. The result is that the order, *or* connection, of things is one, whether Nature is conceived under this attribute or that; hence the order of actions and pas-

sions of our Body is, by nature, at one with the order of actions and passions of the Mind. (IIIP2s)

Spinoza, of course, knows that many ordinary people (the "multitude") and philosophers (like Descartes) are "firmly persuaded that the Body now moves, now is at rest, solely from the Mind's command, and that it does a great many things which depend only on the Mind's will and its art of thinking" (IIIP2s).[41] In his response to this common view, Spinoza makes his famous remark that

> no one has yet determined what the Body can do, i.e., *experience* has not yet taught anyone what the Body can do from the laws of nature alone, insofar as nature is only considered to be corporeal, and what the body can do only if it is determined by the Mind. For no one has yet come to know the structure of the Body so accurately that he could explain all its functions – not to mention that many things are observed in the lower Animals that far surpass human ingenuity. (IIIP2s, emphasis added)[42]

This passage is illuminating for another reason: it corrects a common caricature of Spinoza's rationalism. What he says about the body is applicable to everything in the physical world. Spinoza's rationalism is badly misinterpreted when his concept of Nature is taken to mean that he can explain every individual happening in the universe by an appeal to his metaphysical principles. Rather, he claims to provide the necessary *basis* for the explanation of specific events. For Spinoza, it is a *necessary* truth that everything must have a cause and that we can come to know this cause. This does not mean that we can now explain the *specific* external causes of *specific* effects or that we can somehow logically deduce specific external causes of specific effects from logical principles alone. To know specific causes requires detailed scientific inquiry, just as scientific inquiry is required to know what the body (and brain) can do. We might call this the "principle of open inquiry." Consequently, Spinoza's rationalism is not only compatible with, but also demands, open investigation of the specific external causes of phenomena.

Consider the contemporary relevance of his claims about causality. As I have already indicated, every working scientist *presupposes* that we live in a causal universe and that we can eventually discover the specific causes of problematic phenomena. For example, no one doubts that there are specific causes of the different cancers and that researchers are gradually coming to understand these causes. To increase our understanding of cancer, we need to engage in empirical scientific inquiry, just as we need to engage in scientific inquiry to discover what the body and the brain can do. It is true that contemporary conceptions of cause differ from Spinoza's logical conception of cause. The difference between Spinoza and the working scientist is that Spinoza, as a philosopher, claims to *explain* and thereby *justify* what working scientists *presuppose* – namely, that we live in a causal universe determined by natural laws.

Spinoza employs the concept of causality in (at least) two ways. According to IP29, any finite entity is produced (caused) by other finite entities in an endless chain of *external* causation. This is the perspective of explaining the world from the viewpoint of mechanism and finitude. As long as we stick to this perspective, we are restricted to the realm of finite modes and their determinations. When Spinoza says that that "experience has not yet taught anyone what the Body can do," he means that we do not yet have a full understanding of the external causes of the body, just as we do not yet have a complete understanding of other physical entities. In Part I, Propositions 18–25, Spinoza makes it clear that particular things are derived from God or Nature as their immanent cause. This is the sense of cause that goes from Substance through its attributes to a series of modes. This is the logical sense of causality. Yovel refers to the former sense of causality as *horizontal* causality and to the latter as *vertical* causality. He writes:

> Suppose that A is determined by B, C, and D as its mechanistic causes, and that these causes operate in accordance with law L. We may say that L determines A in that it determines how B, C, and D will act upon A. And if we are ready, as Spinoza is, to view as equivalent the following two statements:
>
> 1. A is determined by the logical necessity of the law L
> 2. A is determined by the mechanistic causes B, C, and D whose action obeys and instantiates the law L
>
> then we have acknowledged the equivalence, or complementarity, or the vertical and horizontal views of causation. (Yovel 1989: 158)[43]

We must carefully distinguish the different ways in which Spinoza uses the term "cause." Thus, there is *causa sui* – "cause of itself" – such that the nature of God "cannot be conceived except as existing." This sense of "cause" applies only to God, Substance, or Nature. Then there is the second sense of "cause" – as the logical condition of an effect. This is the primary sense of "cause" that we can explain by logical reason (*ratio*). Third, there is the sense of "cause" whereby we refer to what Spinoza calls "external" causes of finite entities. Hampshire clarifies the difference between the second and third senses of "cause":

> In the widest sense of the word "cause," anything that is an appropriate answer to the question "Why?" gives a cause, irrespective of the category to which the thing to be explained belongs. The question "Why?" may, for example, be asked with reference to a belief, a human action, a human attitude or sentiment, the existence of a physical object, or the properties of numbers and geometrical figures. Anything that counts as an answer to the question "Why?" is an explanation, *whether true or false*, of the belief, action, attitude, sentiment, physical object, or mathematical property (Hampshire 1971: 185–6, emphasis added).

Hampshire goes on to distinguish two fundamental categories or types of cause.

> Let us assume the standpoint of an individual thinker, a finite mode, with his necessarily limited knowledge. Reflecting on the range of knowledge, he will find at least one clear distinction: the distinction between an understanding of causes that is complete and self-justifying, and an understanding of causes that is not complete and self-justifying. There are ideas in reference to which the question "Why is it so?" receives a complete answer, in the sense that, in looking for the explanation, we arrive at self-evident truths, and definitions, in a finite number of steps. There are other ideas in reference to which the question "Why is it so?" leads us back along an infinite series of ideas, with no final and sufficient explanation to be found within the series, however long we continue. . . . For Spinoza the fundamental difference between the two orders of causes is the difference between the series of eternal things and the series of things that come into existence and pass away at a certain time. There is no further difference between the two orders of explanation which is not entailed by this primary difference. . . . The existence of things that are not eternal, and that occupy a determinate position in the time-order, can only be incompletely explained. There must always be an infinite regress of causes required to explain why this particular thing exists at a particular time. (Hampshire 1971: 186–7)

A primary question for Spinoza is whether – and to what extent – the mind can be the adequate cause of its desires. Spinoza thinks this happens when the mind has adequate ideas. He makes this clear in IIIP1: "Our Mind does certain things [acts] and undergoes other things, viz. insofar as it has adequate ideas, it necessarily does certain things, and insofar as it has inadequate ideas, it necessarily undergoes other things." Allison makes Spinoza's point in non-Spinozistic terms:

> [T]he mind acts, as opposed to being merely a passive victim of circumstances, whenever its desires, and hence its decisions, are grounded in

rational considerations – for example, when it desires a particular food because of the knowledge (adequate idea) that it is nutritious. In Spinoza's own terms, "the actions of the Mind arise from adequate ideas alone; the passions depend on inadequate ideas alone" [IIIP3]. (Allison 1987: 130)

When the mind conceives something adequately, it *becomes* the adequate cause of its actions and is not determined by external causes. This does not mean that the mind causes the body to act (as Descartes claims). Rather, because the mind and the body are identical, it means that when the mind acts, the body acts.[44]

In order to justify his alternative view of the mind/body *interaction*, Spinoza introduces the principle of *conatus*. The *conatus* of anything – of any finite mode – is the striving for self-preservation. It is important to emphasize that, given Spinoza's naturalism, *conatus* is a principle that applies to *all* things – not just human beings – but with human beings, "appetite" (*appetitus*) is constitutive of the individual's *conatus*.[45] "When this striving [*conatus*] is related only to the Mind, it is called Will, but when it is related to the Mind and Body together, it is called Appetite. This Appetite, therefore, is nothing but the very essence of man, from whose nature there necessarily follow those things that promote his preservation" (IIIP9s). Appetite in this sense can also be called "desire" (*cupiditas*). The only difference between desire and appetite is that desire implies consciousness of appetite. Desire, then, is defined as appetite together with the consciousness of appetite. Consequently, we can also say that desire is the very essence of man.[46] "The striving [*conatus*] by which each thing strives to persevere in its being is nothing but the actual essence of the thing" (IIIP7). In human beings, this *conatus* is a striving to increase their power – and freedom. This is already implicit in IIID3: "By affect I understand affections of the Body by which the Body's power of acting is increased or diminished, aided or restrained, and at the same time, the ideas of those affections." This can be described as the living organism's level of *vitality*, which can be increased or diminished. From this perspective, Spinoza defines the three *primary* affects:

> We see, then, that the Mind can undergo great changes, and pass now to a greater, now to a lesser perfection. These passions, indeed, explain to us the affects of Joy [*laetitia*] and Sadness [*tristitia*]. By *Joy*, therefore, I shall understand in what follows that *passion by which the Mind passes to a greater perfection*. And by *Sadness*, that *passion by which it passes to a lesser perfection*. The *affect of Joy which is related to the Mind and Body at once* I call *Pleasure* or *Cheerfulness*, and that of *Sadness*, *Pain or Melancholy*. (IIIP11s)

Spinoza adds a third primary affect – desire.[47] These, then, are three primary affects. At the end of Part III Spinoza briefly defines more than forty derivative affects – including love, hate, hope, and fear.

All affects – whether passive or active – can be explained (like the rest of Nature) by the necessary laws of nature. Most of the affects that Spinoza characterizes are *passive*; they are passions in the sense defined by the first three definitions of Part III. But Spinoza also points out that there are *active* affects. Passive affects have *external* causes. Consequently, "we are driven about in many ways by external causes, and . . . like waves on the sea, driven by contrary winds, we toss about, not knowing our outcome and fate" (IIIP59s). In Spinoza's realistic account of human nature, we never *completely* escape being affected by passions. We escape from this condition of being tossed about only *insofar* as we act and thereby have active affects caused internally by ourselves. "Apart from the Joy and Desire that are passions, there are other affects of Joy and Desire that are related to us insofar as we act" (IIIP58). In his demonstration of this proposition Spinoza writes: "When the Mind conceives itself and its power of acting, it rejoices (by P53)" (IIIP58dem). This occurs when the mind has true or adequate ideas. "Therefore, it also rejoices insofar as it conceives adequate ideas, i.e. (by P1), insofar as it acts" (IIIP58dem). This brings us back to the original three definitions of Part III. What we have now learned is that when the mind conceives of itself and its power of *action* – that is, when the mind has adequate knowledge of the causes of its affects – it rejoices. When our mind *acts*, the cause of affects is *within* us; we are *self*-determined. When we are determined by external causes, then we experience passions – in the sense of "passion" defined by the first three definitions of Part III.

We are now in a position to grasp, in a preliminary way, the meaning of human bondage and human freedom in Spinoza. To the extent that we have inadequate (confused) knowledge of our affects, we are constrained by them. To the extent that we have adequate knowledge of our affects, we achieve a degree of power and human freedom. There are *degrees* of bondage and *degrees* of freedom, which depend on the extent to which we have adequate or inadequate ideas of adequate and inadequate causes. Spinoza does not think that human beings can achieve total and perfect freedom, because as finite individuals, we never fully escape from the bondage of the passions. "Man's lack of power to moderate and restrain the affects I call Bondage" (IV Preface). Freedom consists of the active power of the mind or reason to moderate the passions. Those human beings who employ their reason can maximize their freedom and thereby achieve what Spinoza calls "blessedness." This achievement of maximum freedom is a form of naturalistic salvation.[48]

To recap the steps of our transformative journey: at the beginning of the *Ethics* we learn the metaphysical foundations of Spinoza's philosophy of immanence and his naturalism. We then move to the study of the relation of the mind and the body, where we learn that the mind and the body are identical. The mind and the body turn out to be a special case of the general thesis that the attributes of thought and extension are both attributes of the single Substance that is identical with God or Nature. Furthermore, as we move to the study of affects – passions and actions – we gain a richer understanding of human nature. This becomes a necessary condition for the introduction of Spinoza's ethics (his moral theory) – a naturalistic theory that departs radically from the ordinary, traditional philosophical conceptions of morality.[49] In Part IV, we encounter Spinoza's conception of "virtue" and the "good life." We are also provided with the rules for how to live one's life – at least for those guided by reason. Finally, we move to Spinoza's theory of human blessedness. In Part V, we reach the culmination of Spinoza's naturalism, where he develops a naturalist account of human salvation intended to be an alternative to traditional religious conceptions of salvation.

Given Spinoza's conception of Nature, we must keep in mind that when Spinoza turns to probing the meaning of bondage and freedom, the same naturalistic principles of his metaphysics and theory of rational knowledge apply. Spinoza is sharply critical of the common conceptions of morality presupposing that human beings have free will and can freely choose what to do. This is a fiction of the imagination. The ethics that Spinoza proposes is a naturalistic one. The power required to overcome passive affects and thereby minimize our bondage is *not* achieved by an act of free will but rather by achieving adequate ideas – rational (*rationale*) knowledge of the causes of our affects. To the extent that we achieve this knowledge, we increase our power and thereby maximize our human freedom.[50] Much of Part IV is taken up with a sharp critique of the ordinary, as well as the philosophical and theological, conceptions of morality presupposing the faculty of free will in human beings, the existence of final causes, and postulating the transcendent principles determining what is good and evil, and what is right and wrong. In the Preface to Part IV, Spinoza declares:

> As far as good and evil are concerned, they also indicate nothing positive in things, considered in themselves, nor are they anything other than modes of thinking, *or* notions we form because we compare things to one another.

> For one and the same thing can, at the same time, be good, and bad, and also indifferent. For example, Music is good for one who is Melancholy, bad for one who is mourning, and neither good nor bad to one who is deaf. (IV Preface)

Already in IIIP9s Spinoza has declared: "[W]e neither strive for, nor will, neither want nor desire anything because we judge it to be good, on the contrary, we judge something to be good because we strive for it, will it, want it, and desire it." Passages such as this are the basis for the critics' claims that Spinoza is a relativist and a nihilist.[51] Such accusations, however, fail to appreciate Spinoza's claim that desires can be informed by reason – that is, that there are *rational desires*. This claim is basic for understanding what Spinoza means by freedom.

Let me sum up the outlines of Spinoza's naturalistic ethics. First, Spinoza argues that the ordinary conceptions of morality, as well as traditional philosophical and theological conceptions of morality, are totally inadequate. Any conception of morality that presupposes free will or objective transcendent principles is false. These doctrines arise from the limitations of the imagination. Positively, Spinoza argues for an ethics that depends upon having adequate ideas – that is, rational knowledge of adequate causes of our affects. To the extent that we have such knowledge, we are active; we are the immanent cause of our affects – and we escape from the turmoil of conflicting passions that result from external causes. We, in effect, become self-determining. Our desires become rational desires, and we thereby increase our vitality, joy, and freedom. We thereby achieve our true self-interest. Spinoza's ethics is realistic, insofar as he emphasizes that we never completely escape the effects and turmoil of our passions – passions determined by external causes. There are degrees of bondage as well as degrees of freedom, just as there are degrees of ignorance and degrees of rational knowledge.[52] Furthermore, "self-esteem can arise from reason, and only that self-esteem which does arise from reason is the greatest there can be" (IVP52). "Self-esteem is really the highest thing we can hope for" (IVP52s). "A free man thinks of nothing less than of death, and his wisdom is a meditation on life, not on death" (IVP 67). Here, we discover a parallel with Nietzsche in that Spinoza's ethics is life-affirming. This affirmation of life presupposes friendship with others to the extent that they are free: "Only free men are very useful to one another, are joined to one another by the greatest necessity of friendship . . . and strive to benefit one another with equal eagerness for love" (IVP71dem).[53] In Spinoza's ethics, there is no place for a doctrine of original sin. He does not think that ethics depends on the repression of our desires. Nor does he think that there is a conflict between reason and desire. Rather, human freedom demands that reason informs and *transforms* our desires.[54] For Spinoza, all values and norms are immanent in this world; they are immanent in Nature. It is worth repeating what Yovel affirms about the philosophy of immanence: "This world (through the humans in it) is also the sole possible source of valid norms – in morality, law, politics, even religion – and of any justified use of political authority and coercion to support that norm in practice."[55] Spinoza's positive ethics is not based on such traditional concepts as good and evil or natural rights. Rather, it is based on a correct understanding of bondage and freedom.

II

During his lifetime, Spinoza was accused of being an atheist, but when the *Ethics* was published in 1677, the attacks on his philosophy became even more vicious. Leibniz, who shared so much with Spinoza, visited him in The Hague in 1676. He was nevertheless sharply critical of Spinoza's philosophical system. For a century after Spinoza's death, the expression "Spinozist" was primarily a term of abuse and damnation. Pierre Bayle's article on Spinoza in the *Dictionnaire historique et critique* (1697) reinforced the negative attitude toward Spinoza.[56] Although Bayle admired Spinoza as a good person (despite his "atheism"), he abhorred Spinoza's doctrines. He begins his article (the longest in the *Dictionnaire*) in a striking manner: "Spinoza, Benedictus de, a Jew by birth, and afterwards a deserter from Judaism, and lastly an atheist, was from Amsterdam" (Bayle 1965: 288).[57] Bayle canonized the epithet that characterized Spinoza throughout the eighteenth century and long after – *a Jewish atheist*. From the perspective of Christian Europe, Spinoza was a double *pariah* – a Jew and an atheist. Spinoza's philosophy, Bayle claimed, is the most absurd and monstrous hypothesis that can be envisaged. Bayle was particularly offended by Spinoza's monism and his treatment of the problem of evil. Later, Bayle was joined by Voltaire and Diderot in their condemnation of Spinoza. Voltaire claimed that Spinoza's system was based upon a complete ignorance of physics and the most monstrous abuse of metaphysics. Diderot followed Bayle in the chorus of critiques of Spinoza, even though there are Spinozistic elements in his own philosophical outlook. Most contemporary Spinoza scholars agree that the *philosophes*' image of Spinoza is a gross distortion – close to a caricature. Nevertheless, this negative stereotype of Spinoza persisted for more than a century after Spinoza's death. Until recently, Spinoza's theological-political views and his *Ethics* were thought to have had very little influence on European thought and philosophy. Israel (2001) has systematically refuted this widely held belief in his comprehensive study of the "Radical Enlightenment." Omri Boehm (2014) argues that contrary to the conventional belief that Leibniz is the metaphysician whom Kant attacks in his *Critique of Pure Reason*, it is really Spinoza who is the primary object of Kant's critique. Boehm argues that Kant took up the challenge of defeating the alleged "nihilism" implicit in Spinoza's philosophy.

The damning of Spinoza reached its culmination in the famous pantheism controversy (*Pantheismusstreit*). But ironically, this controversy initiated a reevaluation of Spinoza. The controversy began in the most incidental manner in 1783, with a quarrel between Jacobi and Mendelsohn concerning Lessing's Spinozism. According to Jacobi, Lessing had confessed his Spinozism in a private conversation with him in 1780. At the time, Lessing, a good friend of Mendelsohn, enjoyed enormous popularity in Germany. As Frederick Beiser notes in his comprehensive study of the twists and turns of the pantheism controversy, by 1795, "the dispute became public and engaged almost all the best minds of late eighteenth-century Germany. Among the celebrities who took part in it were Kant, Herder, Goethe, and Hamann. Furthermore, each party to the dispute had a large supporting cast, including such later stars as Thomas Wizenmann, who defended Jacobi, and Karl Leonhard Reinhold, who popularized Kant" (Beiser 1987: 44).

> The pantheism controversy completely changed the intellectual map of eighteenth-century Germany; and it continued to preoccupy thinkers well into the nineteenth century. The main problem raised by the controversy – the dilemma of a rational nihilism or an irrational fideism – became a central issue for Fichte, Schelling, Hegel, Kierkegaard, and Nietzsche. It is indeed no exaggeration to say that the pantheism controversy had as great an impact upon nineteenth-century philosophy as Kant's first *Kritik*.
> The first and foremost visible effect of the controversy was the remarkable rise in the fortunes of Spinozism in Germany. Nearly all the major figures of the classical *Goethezeit* – Goethe, Novalis, Hölderlin, Herder, F. Schlegel, Hegel, Schleiermacher, and Schelling – became Spinoza enthusiasts in the wake of the controversy. Apparently overnight, Spinoza's reputation changed from a devil to a saint. The scapegoat of the intellectual establishment in the first three quarters of the eighteenth century became its hero in the last quarter. Thanks to the controversy, pantheism

became, as Heine later put it, "the unofficial religion of Germany." (Beiser 1987: 44–5)

There was, however, little agreement about the meaning of "pantheism" among the disputants and their followers. Sometimes "pantheism" was interpreted as divinizing the world in the sense of ascribing to nature divine characteristics that belong *exclusively* to God. Sometimes it was interpreted as a new form of mysticism. Spinoza, however, categorically rejects the idea that there are special divine characteristics of God that we then ascribe to a natural creation, which is independent of God. God and Nature are identical, and their attributes are identical.

One of the most remarkable features of Spinoza's influence is the appeal he has had for poets and novelists. Not only Goethe and Lessing, but also Heinrich Heine, George Eliot, Jorge Luis Borges, Isaac Bashevis Singer, and Bernard Malamud – among many others – were his admirers. Heine wrote that all of our contemporary philosophers, perhaps without knowing it, are looking through the eyeglasses that Baruch Spinoza polished.[58] In the twentieth century, the character Dr. Nahum Fischelson in Singer's story "The Spinoza of Market Street" illustrates a dilemma that seems to exist at the heart of Spinoza's philosophy.[59] Daniel Garber perceptively describes Dr. Fischelson's problem:

> Dr. Fischelson is striving to be like Spinoza's free man, striving to exemplify the model of a more perfect human nature that Spinoza presents in the *Ethics*. This, he thinks, entails a life alone, a life lived as much as possible without having to depend on the help of others, the imperfectly rational masses that live their lives in the bondage of the passions and in ignorance of the supreme pleasures of the pure intellectual love of God. But in the end, Dr. Fischelson finds this impossible to do; in his family, he needs others, and eventually he marries Black Dobbe, the woman who took care of him when he fell ill. In his marriage bed, Dr. Fischelson sees his strength return, and he finds himself more powerful then when he was alone. Going to the window, he murmurs, "Divine Spinoza, forgive me. I have become a fool." (Garber 2004: 183)

Fischelson's dilemma is that "[o]ur rational need for other people seems to conflict with other demands of complete rationality" (Garber 2004: 184–5). Garber uses this dilemma to explore the relationship between freedom and sociality in Spinoza. He argues (and I agree with his interpretation) that Spinoza is perfectly aware that human beings can never attain a state of complete freedom – only God is completely free. We are finite creatures, and we are always subject to external causes and our passions. At best, we can *maximize* our freedom through rational understanding and thereby limit our bondage. Dr. Fischelson should not regret his need for others; he is not a fool. Instead of asking Spinoza for forgiveness, he should thank Spinoza. He should say, "Divine Spinoza, I thank you for having helped me to see my inevitable finitude, my inevitable need for others of my own kind, my inevitable humanity" (Garber 2004: 204). Spinoza provides us with a *realistic* understanding of human nature. We should work toward achieving freedom – becoming actively self-determined – but we need to recognize that we are flesh-and-blood individuals. We need to recognize the limitations of our humanity; we can never completely escape the effects of external causes that we cannot control. We should never deceive ourselves into thinking that we can become God – the only *completely* free being.

In the twentieth century, Spinoza's philosophical influence was erratic. There was an enormous increase in the sophistication of Spinoza scholarship. We now have a much better understanding of his entire corpus and the many problems and tensions in his work. The French scholarship of Spinoza has been particularly remarkable. A group of French thinkers, including Louis Althusser, Etienne Balibar, Gilles Deleuze, as well as Antonio Negri in Italy, have suggested provocative interpretations of Spinoza showing his contemporary relevance.[60] They argue that Spinoza's philosophy – frequently combined with new interpretations of Marxism – provides us with a more philosophically nuanced understanding of contemporary politics. Spinoza has not, however, been a significant figure for twentieth-century Anglo-American philosophers, despite the flourishing of Anglo-American Spinoza scholarship. His influence has been overshadowed by Hume, Kant, and Hegel. The strong empiricist strain in Anglo-American philosophy has contributed to the neglect of Spinoza. As Della Rocca notes, "Hume's system is the flip-side of Spinoza's" (Della Rocca 2008: 281). Hume argues for the *antithesis* of almost every major claim that Spinoza makes – whether it be about God, reason, causality, knowledge, or necessity. Hume also rejects the principle of sufficient reason that is so central for Spinoza.[61] Contemporary Anglo-American philosophers, influenced by Kant and left Sellarsian Kantianism, categorically reject Spinoza's concept of nature. Although Hegel praises Spinoza's understanding of substance, he (and his contemporary successors), too, find Spinoza's ahistorical philosophy radically deficient. Hegel claims that Spinoza fails to grasp the dialectical development of subjectivity. Our age prides itself on being "post-metaphysical," and Spinoza – the exemplar of a rationalist metaphysical thinker – does not fit it.

Disagreeing with those who think of Spinoza's system as little more than a historical curiosity, I want to claim that the specter of Spinoza – and especially his concept of nature – is perhaps more relevant today than ever. Let me explain. Hilary Putnam was once asked: "What makes a good philosopher?" He answered that there are many kinds of good philosophers. He went on to say that there are two characteristics that he admires in a philosopher: vision and arguments. "[T]here is something disappointing about a philosophical work that contains arguments, however good, which are not inspired by some genuine vision, and something disappointing about philosophical work that contains a vision, however inspiring, which is unsupported by arguments" (Putnam 1999: 44). Many accomplished professional philosophers lack a vision – a sense of how things hang together – despite their argumentative finesse. Having a bold vision of the universe also is never sufficient; it must be textured with powerful arguments. Great philosophers have the rare ability to integrate a bold vision with argumentative sophistication. Spinoza articulates a bold vision of the totality of nature and supports it with detailed arguments. At the beginning of the modern age, Spinoza was the most systematic philosopher of immanence. He denies that there are any ontological dualisms within nature. Unlike philosophers of the "moderate Enlightenment" (such as Kant), who sought to show that a commitment to reason is compatible with faith in a transcendent God, Spinoza will have none of this. He consistently maintains that such a faith is unwarranted – a false projection of the faculty of imagination. Given Spinoza's understanding of reason (*ratio*) – the second form of knowledge – the entire universe can be understood by an appeal to the laws of nature.

Contemporary philosophers reject Spinoza's firm commitment to the unlimited power of pure reason, as well his logical understanding of science, causality, and necessity. Nevertheless, Spinoza's philosophy of immanence – his conviction that there is nothing beyond nature – is strikingly relevant today. Many contemporary Anglophone philosophers consider themselves naturalists, although they sharply disagree about what "naturalism" means.[62] They are opposed by thinkers who claim that there is something distinctive about human rationality – for example, our conceptual capacities and our intentionality – that cannot be accounted for by an appeal to nature and the natural sciences. The battle between naturalists and non-naturalists continues to rage. Some philosophers, like Brandom, claim that humans are *sapient* and nonhuman animals are only *sentient*.[63] For Brandom, human rationality is distinctive and cannot be accounted for by an appeal to nature. This is the view that Spinoza denies.

For Spinoza, reason (*ratio*) is an integral part of the totality of nature, and it can be accounted for by an appeal to nature. Although Spinoza does not use the language of normativity, he would certainly reject the claim that there is something about normativity – whether we take it to be a characteristic of theoretical or practical rationality – that stands outside of nature. In short, I am suggesting that Spinoza is the modern progenitor of a philosophical naturalism maintaining that nature is all-encompassing. Joseph Rouse (2015) argues that philosophical naturalism today is an ongoing *historical* project that must honestly take account of, and meet the objections to, comprehensive naturalism. Spinoza would never put the issue this way, because he thought he had already discovered the "true philosophy." Nevertheless, he stands with those naturalists who argue that as the natural sciences advance and our understanding of what scientific practices involve develops, we discover that nothing *in principle* stands in the way of developing a comprehensive philosophic naturalism – one that is very much in the spirit (if not the letter) of Spinoza. Spinoza also provides strong arguments against a reductive form of naturalism that identifies naturalism with materialism or physicalism. Descartes is frequently labeled the "father of modern philosophy," but Spinoza is the *father of modern naturalism*. At the beginning of the modern age, Spinoza – more *systematically* than any philosopher before him – articulated a bold and powerful vision of naturalism and nature as an all-inclusive philosophic system. There is nothing outside or beyond nature – including reason (*ratio*). Despite the many critiques of Spinoza by subsequent philosophers, who persuasively showed why we must qualify his extreme version of naturalism and his philosophy of immanence, Spinoza nevertheless stands both as an inspiration and a challenge to those who are committed to developing a non-reductive philosophical naturalism. The specter of Spinoza still hovers in the background in the raging disputes about the viability of philosophical naturalism.

2

Hume: The Experimental Method and the Science of Man

Spinoza, a Jewish Marrano, was born in Amsterdam in 1632 and died in 1672. His *Ethics* was published posthumously in the same year that he died. Hume was born in Edinburgh in 1731; his family was Scottish Protestant. His *Treatise on Human Nature* was published in 1739–40 when he was only twenty-eight.[1] Although less than seventy years separated the publication of the *Ethics* and the *Treatise*, an abyss separates these two works. Hume challenges every major thesis advanced by Spinoza. He rejects Spinoza's conception of God, Substance, and Nature. Unlike Spinoza, who demonstrates supreme confidence in the power of reason to understand nature and natural laws, Hume thinks that, strictly speaking, reason alone – what he calls "demonstrative" or "intuitive reason" – does not tell us anything about the world of experience. Spinoza is committed to a rigorous understanding of the principle of sufficient reason: everything can and must be explained rationally. Hume thinks that such a principle is an absurdity. There are brute facts about nature – including human nature – that cannot be explained by an appeal to reason. Hume rejects Spinoza's conception of causality, necessity, and reason; he also claims that Spinoza does *not* understand the relation of reason, human passions, and feelings. Hume's famous claim that "reason is . . . the slave of the passions, and can never pretend to any other office than to serve and obey them" would have scandalized Spinoza (Hume 1978: 415).[2] Hume did not set out explicitly to refute Spinoza, but rather to refute all forms of rationalism that appeal to pure concepts and *a priori* reason. If one tried the thought experiment of imagining a thinker who is the very antithesis of Spinoza, that thinker would surely look like Hume. Yet, as Hegel has taught us, thinkers who initially appear to be antithetical turn out to share more in common than is initially apparent. We will discover that both Spinoza and Hume develop naturalistic orientations – although the distinctive versions of their conception of naturalism and nature are antithetical. Employing the terminology that I used in my discussion of Spinoza, both Spinoza and Hume are *radical* philosophers of immanence; they are "this-worldly" thinkers. They categorically reject any appeal to a transcendent God or transcendent principles to explain phenomena in this world.

To appreciate their differences, let us turn to how they begin their major works. Spinoza, we recall, opens the *Ethics* by laying down eight definitions, including the initial definition of *causa sui*: "By cause of itself I understand that whose essence involves existence, *or* that whose nature cannot be conceived except as existing" (ID1). According to Hume, Spinoza's definitions (including the definition of *causa sui*) are meaningless gibberish – the type of gibberish that is characteristic of metaphysicians who reason in an *a priori* fashion. Hume does not begin his *Treatise* with grand metaphysical claims but rather lays out his *refinements* of the theory of ideas, which he inherits from the tradition of British empiricism. Consider how he opens his discussion in the first section entitled "Of the origin of our ideas":

> All the perceptions of the human mind resolve themselves into two distinct kinds, which I shall call Impressions and Ideas. The difference betwixt these consists in the degrees of force and liveliness, with which they strike upon the mind and make their way into our thought or consciousness. Those perceptions, which enter with the most force and violence, we may name *impressions*; and under this name I comprehend all our sensations, passions and emotions, as they make their first appearance in the soul. By *ideas* I mean the faint images of these in thinking and reasoning; such as, for instance, are all the perceptions excited by the present discourse, excepting only, those which arise from sight and touch, and excepting the immediate pleasure or uneasiness it may occasion. I believe it will not be very necessary to employ many words in explaining the distinction. Every one of himself will readily perceive the difference betwixt feeling and thinking. (Hume 1978: 1–2)

Hume admits that there are some exceptions to this general claim about impressions and ideas. For example, "in sleep, in a fever, in madness, or in any very violent emotions of the soul, our ideas may approach to our impressions," and sometimes our "impressions are so faint and low, that we cannot distinguish them from ideas" (Hume 1978: 2). Despite these exceptions, the general thesis about the relation of impressions and ideas holds. From this simple beginning Hume develops an extremely elegant and powerful structure. We need to distinguish simple impressions and ideas from complex impressions and ideas. A simple sensible impression would be like an image of a red patch, and the corresponding idea would be the faint image or a copy of such a red patch. Consequently, it becomes clear that there is a *dependence* relation between simple impressions and simple ideas. An idea is a *copy* of its impression (although, once again, Hume concedes that on rare occasions, we may have a simple idea without first having a simple impression). Hume claims that "we shall here content ourselves with establishing one general proposition, *That all our simple ideas in their first appearance are deriv'd from simple impressions, which are correspondent to them, and which they exactly represent*" (Hume 1978: 4). In addition to simple impressions and simple ideas, there are also *complex* impressions and ideas made up of simples. For example, I may have a complex impression of a red apple. This is an impression that consists of many distinct and separate elements – an impression of a round, red, hard object with a distinctive taste. A complex idea of a red apple corresponds to this complex impression. Given our memory and imagination, we can be far more creative in mixing and rearranging ideas. We can imaginatively mix our simple ideas, and thereby create ideas that do not *directly* correspond to simple impressions. For example, we can combine the idea of the parts of a horse with a human torso to create the idea of a centaur. In short, we can combine ideas into unique and distinctive patterns. A rough analogy would be a Lego set where we take simple components and combine them in the most ingenious ways.

Thus far, Hume speaks of simple impressions primarily as *sensations*. But the model gets more complicated. Impressions themselves may be divided into two kinds: "those of Sensation and those of Reflexion."

> *The first kind arises in the soul originally, from unknown causes.* The second is derived in a great measure from our ideas, and that in the following order. An impression first strikes upon the senses, and makes us perceive heat or cold, thirst or hunger, pleasure or pain of some kind or other. Of this impression there is a copy taken by the mind, which remains after the impression ceases; and this we call an idea. This idea of pleasure or pain, when it returns upon the soul, produces the new impressions of desire and aversion, hope and fear, which may properly be called impressions of reflexion, because derived from it. These again are copied by the memory and imagination, and become ideas; which perhaps in their turn give rise to other impressions and ideas. So that the impressions of reflexion are only

antecedent to their correspondent ideas; but posterior to those of sensation, and deriv'd from them. (Hume 1978: 7–8, emphasis added)[3]

Impressions of sensations are the basis for corresponding ideas, and these ideas are the basis for new kinds of impressions of reflection such as desire and aversion, hope and fear. For all the complexity of Hume's model, he never departs from the fundamental claim that impressions of sensation are the basis of their corresponding ideas and that these ideas can give rise to a new *type* of impressions – impressions of *reflection*, which in turn are the basis for ideas of reflection. Seeing a scary bear can give rise to a feeling of fear, which is itself an impression of reflection. When I recall my experience of the fear, I recall the idea of fear (which is less forceful and lively than the original impression).

Before proceeding, I want to make a few general remarks about Hume's model: namely, about his refinement of the empiricist theory of ideas. Hume does *not* offer any philosophical justification for his conception of impressions and ideas.[4] He thinks that the distinction between impressions and ideas is evident, and he believes "it will not be very necessary to employ many words in explaining this distinction" (Hume 1978: 1). Hume's model of the relation of impressions and ideas provides a powerful technique for assessing the validity of philosophical claims. When presented with an abstruse philosophical idea, the question to ask is whether we can trace it back to simple ideas and impressions. If not, Hume advises that we commit it to the flames.[5] More importantly, we can begin to see the origins of *one* aspect of Hume's skepticism. If we go back to our examples of a red patch or a red apple, we might be inclined to say that our impressions of these are the result of being confronted with an *actual* red patch or a red ball in the "real" world. These would be the "causes" of the distinctive content of the corresponding impressions. However, Hume says that impressions of sensation arise in the soul from "unknown causes." Simple ideas are *dependent* on first experiencing simple impressions of sensation. Impressions and ideas of reflection are, in turn, *dependent* on experiencing sensible impressions and ideas. Strictly speaking, we *cannot* get behind or beyond our perceptions to a world of objects that is independent of our perceptions. We cannot somehow step outside of impressions of sensation to see how they are related to an independent objective world. We cannot compare our impression or idea of a red patch with an *actual* red patch in the "real" world. Why? Because our epistemological starting point is always perceptions – objects in the mind or soul – *not* objects in an independent empirical world. We cannot know that there are objects in the "real" world that correspond to our perceptions. The *primary* question that Hume addresses is *not* how we come to *know* objects in the "real" world, but rather how we come to *believe* that there is a world of objects that is independent of our perceptions. And his answer is ingenious.[6]

Many commentators have stressed Hume's philosophical skepticism presented in Book I of the *Treatise* and in the corresponding sections of the *Enquiry Concerning Human Understanding*. Hume concludes Book I of the *Treatise* with his own reflections on skepticism with regard to reason and the senses. Yet some interpreters, including Norman Kemp Smith, have been critical of the excessive emphasis on Hume's skepticism. They argue that this emphasis distorts Hume's positive naturalistic project.[7] Barry Stroud presents one of the most persuasive accounts of Hume's naturalistic project.[8] "Hume is a philosopher of human nature. He puts forth a new theory or vision of man, and one that he thinks differs significantly from those of his predecessors. It is a bold and simple theory, and is much more an expression of the unbounded optimism of the enlightenment than of a clever negativism of a man at the end of his intellectual rope" (Stroud 1977: 1). The *Treatise* carries the subtitle: "An Attempt to Introduce the Experimental Method of Reasoning into Moral Subjects." Hume was a great admirer of Newton, and he sought to achieve for moral (that is, distinctively human) subjects the type of comprehensive explanations that Newton had achieved for the natural world. Of course, humans are part of the natural world, and the laws described by what was then called "natural philosophy" are applicable to human beings. (A human being falling off a high building conforms to the same natural laws as a brick falling off the building.) Stroud notes:

> Moral philosophy differs from natural philosophy only in the *way* it deals with human beings – it considers only those respects in which they differ from other 'objects of nature'. Men think, act, feel, perceive and speak, so 'moral subjects' deal with human thought, actions, feelings, perception, passions and language. Hume is concerned with what it is like to be human, with what is special or different about being human – with human nature. The non-human parts of animate nature come under his scrutiny only briefly, but the question of how humans differ from animals is in fact extremely important for Hume. He sees men as much more like the animals than most earlier theories had done. (Stroud 1977: 2)[9]

The principles and explanations of "natural philosophy" (what today we call "natural science") apply to *all* natural beings – inanimate and animate. Moral philosophy – Hume's primary topic – is concerned with what is distinctive about *human* nature. Hume's proposed "science of man" requires more than general or even universal principles. The principles must be arrived at by "the experimental method of reasoning."[10] This means drawing conclusions that are supported by experience. Great progress had been made in natural philosophy by Newton, who rejected *a priori* theorizing. Hume expects that employing the experimental mode of theorizing will lead to similar progress in the science of human nature or moral subjects: "We must . . . glean up our experiments in this science from a cautious observation of human life, and take them as they appear in the common course of the world, by men's behaviour in company, in affairs, and in their pleasures" (Hume 1978: p. xix). Comparing Hume to Newton, Stroud observes:

> Newtonian theory provides a completely general explanation of why the things in the world of nature happen as they do. It explains various and complicated physical happenings in terms of a relatively few extremely, perhaps universal principles. Similarly, Hume wants a completely general theory of human nature to explain why human beings act, think, perceive and feel in all the ways that they do. (Stroud 1977: 3)[11]

Discovering the various principles of association is the key to Hume's natural "science of man."

> [S]o far as regards the mind, these are the only links that bind the parts of the universe together, or connect us with any person or object exterior to ourselves. For as it is by means of thought only that anything operates upon our passions, and as these are the only ties of our thoughts, they are really *to us* the cement of the universe, and all the operations of the mind must, in a great measure, depend on them. (Hume 1993: 138)

Hume believes that the "use he makes of the principle[s] of the association of ideas" is his most original contribution to philosophy (Hume 1993: 138). Strongly influenced by Francis Hutcheson, Hume denigrates the role of *a priori* reason and elevates *feeling* and *sentiment* into a total natural theory of man. In opposition to Spinoza and Leibniz, Hume argues that not everything can be explained. Human beings can be studied scientifically, but when we empirically discover the principles of association, we can offer no further explanation of *why* these principles are the principles that determine what we think and feel. Unlike Descartes, who maintains that the human mind cannot be explained naturalistically, Hume insists that *every* aspect of human life can be explained naturalistically.

> Hume's theory sees every aspect of human life as naturalistically explicable. It places man squarely within the scientifically intelligible world of nature. . . .

> Some of his most original contributions to philosophy are made in his attempt actually to discredit the traditional 'rationalistic' conception on its own terms. He does not just advance a positive theory that plays down the role of reason; he tries to show independently that reason does not, and in fact cannot, have the kind of role in human life that had traditionally been supposed. (Stroud 1977: 13–14)

What, then, are the principles of association? Hume specifies three: *resemblance, contiguity in time and space,* and *cause and effect.* (The principle of cause and effect presupposes the principles of resemblance and contiguity.)

I want to focus on the principle of cause and effect for several reasons. This is a key principle for all thinking – the principle of *inference* whereby we can infer from something that is observed to something that is not observed. Hume's analysis of causation presents one of the clearest examples of why he rejects any appeal to a rational justification for knowledge of matters of fact.[12] In this respect, Hume challenges the entire tradition that takes causation to be a fundamental rational principle. Hume's *negative* critique of the appeal to reason to justify causation and his *positive* nonrational account of causation are among the most original and revolutionary features of his philosophy. They are fundamental for comprehending his distinctive version of naturalism – a naturalism that takes feeling, sentiment, and custom to be more central for the understanding of human nature than the appeal to reason. Hume presents his analysis of causation in his three primary texts: *Treatise of Human Nature, Enquiry Concerning Human Understanding,* and the anonymous *Abstract* of the *Treatise* that he published in order to encourage a more favorable reading of his early work.[13] There are variations in each of these presentations. I want to focus on his discussion in the *Abstract* because this was Hume's attempt to restate what he took to be one of the most important topics of his *Treatise*. Throughout our discussion, it is important to distinguish Hume's negative critique and his positive statement. The main point of the *negative* critique is to challenge the claim that the causal principle can be justified by an appeal to reason. The main point of the *positive* statement is to offer a naturalistic explanation of causation.

Hume begins his discussion in the *Abstract* by reiterating his distinction between two types of perceptions: impressions and ideas that are copies of these impressions. He indicates why this distinction is so important for settling philosophical controversies:

> Our author thinks "that no discovery could have been made more happily for deciding all controversies concerning ideas than this, that impressions

always take the precedence of them, and that every idea with which the imagination is furnished, first makes its appearance in a correspondent impression. These latter perceptions are all so clear and evident, that they admit of no controversy; though many of our ideas are so obscure, that it is almost impossible even for the mind, which forms them, to tell exactly their nature and composition." Accordingly, wherever any idea is ambiguous, he has always recourse to the impression, which must render it clear and precise. And when he suspects that any philosophical term has no idea annexed to it (as is too common) he always asks *from what impression that pretended idea is derived?* And if no impression can be produced, he concludes that the term is altogether insignificant. It is after this manner he examines our idea of *substance* and *essence*; and it were to be wished, that this rigorous method were more practised in all philosophical debates. (Hume 1993: 128–9)[14]

Hume does not explicitly state here his thesis that each simple impression and idea is *distinct* and *separable* – like independent atoms. From a simple idea by *itself* we cannot infer any other idea. Then he introduces his famous billiard-ball example:

Here is a billiard-ball lying on the table, and another ball moving towards it with rapidity. They strike; and the ball, which was formerly at rest, now acquires a motion. This is as perfect an instance of the relation of cause and effect as any which we know, either by sensation or reflection. Let us therefore examine it. (Hume 1993: 129)

The two balls touched each other before the motion was communicated. Consequently, there is *contiguity* in time and place. Furthermore, there is *priority* in time. Hume generalizes from this example and claims that contiguity and priority are the requisite circumstances in every cause. If we try any similar balls in the same kind of situation, we shall always find that the impulse of one produces motion in the other. In addition to contiguity and priority, there is "a *third* circumstance, *viz*. that of a *constant conjunction* between the cause and effect. Every object like the cause, produces always some object like the effect. Beyond these three circumstances of contiguity, priority, and constant conjunction, I can discover nothing in this cause" (Hume 1993: 129).

Hume then turns to the question that primarily concerns him. If he sees a ball moving in a straight line toward another ball, he immediately infers that the second ball will be set in motion. Hume generalizes the point:

Suppose I see a ball moving in a straight line towards another, I immediately conclude, that they will shock, and that the second will be in motion. This is the inference from cause to effect; and of this nature are all our reasonings

> in the conduct of life: on this is founded all our belief in history: and from hence is derived all philosophy, excepting only geometry and arithmetic. If we can explain the inference from the shock of two balls, we shall be able to account for this operation of the mind in all instances.
>
> Were a man, such as *Adam*, created in the full vigour of understanding, without experience, he would never be able to infer motion in the second ball from the motion and impulse of the first. It is not any thing that reason sees in the cause, which makes us *infer* the effect. Such an inference, were it possible, would amount to a demonstration, as being founded merely on the comparison of ideas. But no inference from cause to effect amounts to a demonstration. Of which there is this evident proof. The mind can always *conceive* any effect to follow from any cause. (Hume 1993: 129–30)

We can easily *conceive* that, instead of the second billiard-ball moving when there is the shock of impact, it flies off the table. There is no *contradiction* in conceiving of this or any other event as following from the impact. This is the heart of Hume's *negative* thesis: demonstrative or intuitive reason cannot account for the inference from cause to effect. An individual must have *experienced* the constant conjunction of one ball striking another and a second moving when impacted to warrant the inference from cause to effect.

It follows, then, that all our reasonings concerning cause and effect, are founded on experience, and that all reasonings from experience are founded on the supposition, that the course of nature will continue uniformly the same. We conclude, that like causes, in like circumstances, will always produce like effects. It may now be worth while to consider, what determines us to form a conclusion of such infinite consequence. (Hume 1993: 130)

Hume claims that the "uniformity of nature" *cannot* be justified by demonstrative reason. We can easily *conceive* that the course of nature will change. If we can conceive of this change without any formal contradiction, this shows that we cannot rationally demonstrate that the future must be like the past. Indeed, neither demonstrative nor probable arguments can justify the thesis that the future must be conformable to the past. There is no argument that can *rationally* justify the uniformity of nature; there is no rational *proof* that the future will be like the past. This is simply a matter of fact. So why do we believe that the future will conform to the past?

> We are determined by CUSTOM alone to suppose the future conformity to the past. When I see a billiard-ball moving towards another, my mind is immediately carried by habit to the usual effect, and anticipates my sight by conceiving the second ball in motion. There is nothing in these objects,

abstractly considered, and independent of experience, which leads me to form any such conclusion: and even after I have had experience of many repeated effects of this kind, there is no argument, which determines me to suppose, that the effect will be conformable to past experience. *The powers, by which bodies operate, are entirely unknown. We perceive only their sensible qualities: and what reason have we to think that the same powers will always be conjoined with the same sensible qualities?*

It is not, therefore, reason, which is the guide to life, but *custom*. That alone determines the mind, in all instances, to suppose the future conformable to the past. However easy this step may seem, reason would never, to all eternity, be able to make it. (Hume 1993: 131, emphasis added)

I want to stress two aspects of this passage. First, Hume's appeal to custom is an appeal to a nonrational feature of human nature. It is a *matter of fact* that custom and habit operate in this manner. No further explanation can be given of *why* custom operates the way it does.[15] Second, the passage that I have italicized is ambiguous. In a straightforward reading, Hume appears to be asserting that there *are* powers by which bodies operate, but these are unknown to us. A more skeptical reading indicates that if they are really *unknown* to us, then we cannot even know that there are powers by which objects (not perceptions) operate. If the thesis that "[a]ll the perceptions of the human mind resolve themselves into two distinct kinds, which I shall call Impressions and Ideas" is true, then to speak about the "powers of objects" that are *not* perceptions turns out to be (on Hume's own principle) one of those obscure philosophical ideas that ought to be rejected.

Hume now has to confront a further problem. He says he has made a "curious discovery": "*When I see a billiard-ball moving towards another, my mind is immediately carried by habit to the usual effect, and anticipates my sight by conceiving the second ball in motion. But is this all? Do I nothing but* CONCEIVE *the motion of the second ball? No surely. I also* BELIEVE *that it will move. What then is this belief?*" (Hume 1993: 131). Stroud nicely underscores the problem that Hume must confront:

> So far only one such principle has been invoked. It explains why the idea of a B appears in the mind whenever the idea of an A appears there in terms of a 'union in the imagination' between As and Bs. But there is more to explain. When we get an *impression* of an A we do not just get an *idea* of a B – we actually come to *believe* that a B will occur. That is just the inference Hume wants to explain. All that has been explained so far is why the idea of a B comes into the mind. Hume's further explanation of how an actual belief arises is primarily an explanation of how believing something differs from merely having an idea of it. Believing involves having an idea, but it is also something more. (Stroud 1977: 69)

What is the *more* involved in *believing* something? Stroud clarifies Hume's understanding of belief.

> He concludes that what distinguishes an idea or simple conception from a belief is therefore whatever it is that distinguishes an impression from an idea. And an impression differs from an idea only in its degree of 'force and vivacity'. So Hume feels he has no alternative but to say that a belief is 'a more vivid and intense conception of an idea, proceeding from its relation to a present impression'. . . , or, in his more common formulation, 'a lively idea related to or associated with a present impression'. (Stroud 1977: 70)

This account of belief is strained and awkward. It illustrates how Hume's insistence on the doctrine of impressions and ideas constrains his explanations.

> Since therefore belief implies a conception, and yet is something more; and since it adds no new idea to the conception; it follows, that it is a different MANNER of conceiving an object; *something* that is distinguishable to the feeling, and depends not upon our will, as all our ideas do. My mind runs by habit from the visible object of one ball moving towards another, to the usual effect of motion in the second ball. It not only conceives that motion, but *feels* something different in the conception of it from a mere reverie of the imagination. The presence of this visible object, and the constant conjunction of that particular effect, render the idea different to the *feeling* from those loose ideas, which come into the mind without any introduction. (Hume 1993: 132)[16]

Hume seems to be aware of the constrained quality of this explanation since he adds: "This conclusion seems a little surprising; but we are led into it by a chain of propositions, which admit of no doubt" (Hume 1993: 132).[17]

There remains something more that needs to be explained to provide a full account of cause and effect – an issue with which Hume struggles in the *Treatise* but barely mentions in the *Abstract*. He is fully aware that previous philosophers have claimed that the necessary connection of cause and effect is the heart of any understanding of causation. We think that cause and effect are *necessarily* connected – they are not just two events constantly following each other like day and night. Hume, moreover, has argued that there is no *simple* sensible impression of necessary connection or power. Necessary connection, as it pertains to matters of fact, is an idea that *cannot* be justified by appeal to reason alone; it is not a rational principle. Considering Hume's fundamental principle that all ideas must be traced back to impressions, this might seem to be the end of the matter.

We might conclude that necessary connection is a pseudo-idea that must be rejected. But this is *not* the conclusion that Hume draws. On the contrary, Hume raises the question:

> *What is our idea of necessity, when we say that two objects are necessarily connected together.* Upon this head I repeat what I have often had occasion to observe, that as we have no idea, that is not deriv'd from an impression, we must find some impression, that gives rise to this idea of necessity, if we assert we have really such an idea. (Hume 1978: 155)

After repeated instances (constant conjunction) of objects, a *new impression* is produced.

> For after a frequent repetition, I find, that upon the appearance of one of the objects, the mind is *determin'd* by custom to consider its usual attendant, and to consider it in a stronger light upon account of its relation to the first object. 'Tis this impression, then, or *determination*, which affords me the idea of necessity. (Hume 1978: 156)[18]

Consequently, there is a "legitimate" idea of necessary connection, but the impression that is the source of the idea of necessary connection is not a simple sensible impression. The impression of necessary connection arises only from the frequent repetition of objects that are conjoined together. This repetition gives rise to a *new* impression of reflection – *the determination of the mind* presented with an object to consider its usual attendant. This particular impression of reflection arises only after a very complicated process. First, there must be sensible impressions that give rise to their corresponding ideas. Second, there must be a frequent repetition of the conjoining of ideas retained in the memory. Once both conditions are satisfied, a new *internal* impression in the imagination arises: namely, the *determination of the mind* presented with an object to conceive its "usual attendant" in a stronger light.

> The idea of necessity arises from some impression. There is no impression convey'd by our senses, which can give rise to that idea. It must, therefore, be deriv'd from some internal impression, or impression of reflextion. There is no internal impression, which has any relation to the present business, *but that propensity, which custom produces*, to pass from an object to the idea of its usual attendant. This therefore is the essence of necessity. Upon the whole, *necessity is something, that exists in the mind, not in objects*; nor is it possible for us ever to form the most distant idea of it, consider'd as a quality in bodies. Either we have no idea of necessity, or *necessity is nothing but that determination of the thought to pass from causes to effects and from effects*

to causes, according to their experienc'd union. (Hume 1978: 165–6, emphasis added)[19]

Hume's analysis of the idea of necessary connection is quite subtle. When he affirms that "upon the whole, necessity is something, that exists in the mind," he is not affirming that necessity is *merely* a subjective idea locked up in our minds.

> As to what may be said, that the operations of nature are independent of our thought and reasoning, I allow it; and accordingly have observ'd, that objects bear to each other the relations of contiguity and succession; that like objects may be observ'd in several instances to have like relations; and that all this is independent of, and antecedent to the operations of the understanding. But if we go any farther, and ascribe a power or necessary connexion to these objects; this is what we can never observe in them, but must draw the idea of it from what we *feel* internally in contemplating them. And this I carry so far, that I am ready to convert my present reasoning into an instance of it, by a subtility, which it will not be difficult to comprehend. (Hume 1978: 168–9, emphasis added)

Contrary to what some interpreters claim, Hume affirms that there is an idea of necessary connection. Furthermore, this idea is based on an internal impression – the determination of the mind to pass from the presence of an object to its usual attendant – something we learn from past constant conjunctions. This is not a *rational* inference, but rather a *feeling* we have, which results from *custom*. Hume, however, rejects the traditional accounts of necessary connection – namely, that necessary connection is a principle known by reason alone. His positive account shows how we can explain the idea of necessary connection by an appeal to custom and the *feeling* of determination of the mind that it generates.[20] Hume has *shifted* the entire question of necessary connection "out there" – as something independent, objective, and distinct from the mind – to the issue of how the mind comes up with the idea of necessary connection. Thus, although there is an idea of necessary connection in Hume, it is not the idea that philosophers traditionally have taken it to be – not a rational or objective principle that is independent of how the mind works. Rather, Hume's idea of necessity is based upon a *feeling* – an internal impression of reflection.

Annette Baier's book, *A Progress of Sentiments* (1991), captures something essential about the movement of the *Treatise*. As we progress through it, we observe Hume showing us that the natural "science of man" and moral philosophy depend upon an appeal to custom, habit, feelings, and sentiments. Hume's distinction between merely *conceiving* of an idea and *believ-*

ing it appeals to the lively *feeling* we have when we believe something – a manner of feeling that is difficult (Hume says "impossible") to put into words.

> Our author proceeds to explain the manner of feeling, which renders belief different from a loose conception. He seems sensible, that it is impossible by words to describe this feeling, which every one must be conscious of in his own breast. He calls it sometimes a *stronger* conception, sometimes a more *lively*, a more *vivid*, a *firmer*, or more *intense* conception. And indeed, whatever name we may give to this feeling, which constitutes belief, our author thinks it evident, that it has a more forcible effect on the mind than fiction and mere conception. (Hume 1993: 132)

The appeal to feeling and sentiment is also important for Hume's positive account of causality and necessary connection; it is an extension of his strategy for distinguishing mere or "loose conception" from belief. The idea of necessary connection is dependent on a particular impression of reflection – namely, the *feeling* that arises after experiencing constant conjunction – "the propensity, which custom produces, to pass from an object to the idea of its usual attendant" (Hume 1978: 165). This is the necessity that pertains to *matters fact*, and as such it must be distinguished from the necessity of *relations of ideas* exhibited in such disciplines as geometry and arithmetic. Hume is fully aware of how "paradoxical" his explanation of necessity appears. He anticipates the resistance and prejudice against his doctrine. Nevertheless, he claims that his reasoning appears to him as "the shortest and most decisive imaginable" (Hume 1978: 167).

> Before we are reconcil'd to this doctrine, how often must we repeat to ourselves, *that* the simple view of any two objects or actions, however related, can never give us any idea of power, or of a connexion betwixt them; *that* this idea arises from the repetition of their union: *that* the repetition neither discovers nor causes anything in the objects, but has an influence only on the mind, by that customary transition it produces: *that* this customary transition is, therefore, the same with the power and necessity; which are consequently qualities of perception, not of objects, and are internally felt by the soul, and not perceiv'd externally in bodies? (Hume 1978: 166)

There is thus a progress of sentiments in the *Treatise* in the sense that we become increasingly aware that instead of appealing to reason to explain and justify his most important theses about human nature, Hume is appealing to sentiment, feeling, custom, and habit.

The realization of the importance of these impressions of reflection in accounting for belief and necessary connection leads us to a broader discussion of the passions, which are also impressions of reflection.[21] The upshot of Book I of the *Treatise* leads smoothly to Book II, "Of the Passions," which sets the stage for Book III, "Of Morals." We can discern Hume's thematic consistency in the *Treatise*: at the beginning of Book II, Hume repeats his thesis that all perceptions consist of impressions and ideas. He opens Book II by declaring:

> As all perceptions of the mind may be divided into *impressions* and *ideas*, so the impressions admit of another division into *original* and *secondary*. This division of the impressions is the same with that which I formerly made use of when I distinguish'd them into impressions of *sensation* and *reflexion*. (Hume 1978: 275)

At the beginning of Book III, he also reiterates the doctrine of impressions and ideas. In the *Advertisement* that opens Book III, he states:

> It must only be oberv'd, that I continue to make use of the terms, *impressions* and ideas, in the same sense as formerly; and that by impressions I mean our stronger perceptions, such as our sensations, affections and sentiments; and by ideas the fainter perceptions, or the copies of these in the memory and imagination.

Just as we cannot account for causality by an appeal to reason, we cannot give an account of morality by an appeal to reason by itself. "Reason of itself is utterly impotent in this particular. The rules of morality, therefore, are not conclusions of our reason" (Hume 1978: 457). The *causes* for actions are "propensities" and "aversions." Hume calls them "emotions" and "passions," and contrasts them with anything that can be derived by reason. Reason and sentiment belong to different faculties of the mind for Hume. Many philosophers before Hume have maintained that when there is a conflict between reason and a temptation of passion to do otherwise, we ought to follow the dictates of reason. Hume maintains that the very idea of a conflict between reason and the passions is *mistaken*. Strictly speaking, reason and passion *cannot conflict* with each other.

> Reason is the discovery of truth or falshood. Truth or falshood consist in an agreement or disagreement either to the *real* relations of ideas, or to *real* existence and matter of fact. Whatever, therefore, is not susceptible of this agreement or disagreement, is incapable of being true or false, and can never be an object of our reason. Now 'tis evident our passions, volitions, and actions, are not susceptible of any such agreement or disagreement; being original facts and realities, complete in themselves, and implying no

reference to other passions, volitions, and actions. 'Tis impossible, therefore, they can be pronounced either true or false, and be either contrary or conformable to reason. (Hume 1978: 458).

The only items that can be true or false are the propositions of reason. If something is to conflict with reason, it must also be something that is true or false.[22] Passions, emotions, and sentiments belong to a *different* faculty. They are not the type of mental states that can be *either* true or false. Consequently, they cannot, strictly speaking, be in conflict with reason.[23] If a given passion or desire is to be altered, this can only occur by an opposing passion or desire. This account of passions adds force to Hume's claim that reason is impotent.[24]

Hume's thematic consistency is evident when he takes up the issue of morality. For he argues that necessary connection is just as relevant for understanding morality. Hume defends the thesis that all our actions are naturally caused. Many philosophers claim that if all our actions are causally determined, then this amounts to the denial of human liberty and human *responsibility*. Hume argues that this is to misunderstand what liberty means.

> For what is meant by liberty, when applied to voluntary actions? We cannot surely mean that actions have so little connexion with motives, inclinations, and circumstances, that one does not follow with a certain degree of uniformity from the other, and that one affords no inference by which we can conclude the existence of the other. For these are plain and acknowledged matters of matters of fact. By liberty, then, we can only mean *a power of acting or not acting, according to the determinations of the will*; that is, if we choose to remain at rest, we may; if we choose to move, we also may. Now this hypothetical liberty is universally allowed to belong to every one who is not a prisoner and in chains. Here, then, is no subject of dispute. (Hume 1975: 95)[25]

Given this definition of liberty, there is *no* incompatibility between liberty and causal necessity in Hume. Necessary connection is just as relevant to explaining human actions as it is to explaining causality in the rest of the natural world. Contrary to those who think that causal necessity undermines human responsibility, Hume argues that causal necessity is the *only* way to make sense of responsibility. Hume makes an even *stronger* claim: "It is not merely that liberty and the ascription of responsibility are compatible with necessity – they actually require it; they would make no sense without it" (Stroud 1977: 149). In the development of a "science of man," it is essential to show that the *same* principle of causal necessity is applicable to both human and nonhuman nature. Finally, Hume's thematic consistency is also evident in his discussion of miracles, for he argues that events called "miracles" turn out to be events that, when properly understood, are also subject to causal necessity. Hume's deconstruction of the idea of a miracle is one of the primary reasons why he was condemned as an atheist.[26]

Discussing Spinoza, I cited Joseph Rouse, who specifies *three* core commitments of philosophical naturalism. Let us see how these commitments apply to Hume. "First, ... [naturalists] refuse any appeal to or acceptance of what is supernatural or otherwise transcendent to the natural world" (Rouse 2015: 3). Second, "naturalists regard scientific understanding as relevant to all significant aspects of human life and only countenance ways of thinking and forms of life that are *consistent* with that understanding" (Rouse 2015: 3). Third, "naturalists repudiate any conception of 'first philosophy' [what Hume calls "metaphysics" – RJB] as prior to or authoritative over scientific understanding" (Rouse 2015: 3). Hume is a philosophical naturalist who satisfies all three commitments, although he never uses the expression "naturalist" or "naturalism" to define his philosophical vision. His primary aim is to develop a natural "science of man" based on matters of fact – a science that complements Newton's science of nature. Newton rejects any appeal to *a priori* principles in explaining our knowledge of the external natural world; Hume rejects any appeal to *a priori* principles in explaining human nature. Reason alone does not tell us anything about the world of experience and matters of fact. This is the negative aspect of Hume's thinking. Positively, he seeks to show that custom, habit, feeling, and sentiment are foundational for a proper "science of man." Note how antithetical Hume's naturalism is to Spinoza's. Whereas Spinoza thinks that his philosophy is solely dependent on the proper exercise of reason, Hume argues that reason alone – the type of reason exhibited by Spinoza's geometric method – does not tell us anything about matters of fact. For Hume, Spinoza's *Ethics* exemplifies the type of metaphysics that needs to be totally abandoned.

Hume's naturalism is in the tradition of British empiricism, but it has a *unique* character that is also one of the sources of Hume's skepticism. As we have seen, the thesis that perceptions consist of impressions and ideas is fundamental for Hume. This doctrine also turns out to be the *Achilles' heel* of Hume's philosophy and naturalism. We can think of perceptions (either impressions or ideas) in two ways: on the one hand, we can think of them as discrete and separable items or events that are "before the mind" or soul, arising from *unknown causes*.[27] On the other hand, we can focus on what perceptions are *about* – what contemporary philosophers call "intentional content" of perceptions. For example, if we have an impression of a red patch, this sensible impression is an item present to the mind like all other sensible impressions. When we think of perceptions in this way, they are all on the "same footing." "[E]very impression, external and internal, passions, affections, sensations, pains and pleasures, are originally on the same footing; and that whatever other differences we may observe among them, they appear, all of them, in their true colours, as impressions or perceptions" (Hume 1978: 190). What distinguishes one perception from another is its *intentional content* – what it purports to be *about*. One sensible impression is *about* a red patch, and it is distinguished from another impression that is *about* a blue patch.

Hume never *systematically* distinguishes these two ways of understanding perceptions and ideas: namely, the items or events that occur before the mind and the intentional content of impressions and ideas (what they are *about*). This distinction is important, because once we grasp what an impression or idea is *about*, we can raise the question as to the relation between the intentional content of an impression or idea and the objective empirical world of matters of fact. Normally, we think that if we have an *impression* of a red patch, it is caused by us being in the presence of an actual red patch in the empirical world (unless we are dreaming or hallucinating). This seems to be a matter of common sense. Throughout the *Treatise*, Hume does speak of objects, events, and causality as features of matters of fact. However, from his own *philosophical* perspective, it is misleading to use this "common" way of thinking about the presence of an *actual* empirical red patch as giving rise to the appearance of a sensible impression. It is misleading because for Hume the mind has *no* access to anything but its own perceptions. We have no independent access to an external world of objects and events that are independent of our perceptions.

We confront here a problem: a paradox that is at the heart of Hume's philosophy. *We cannot compare our impressions or ideas to what they purport to be about*. It is, of course, quite natural to think that what gives rise to this particular impression is an actual red patch in the world. But Hume's doctrine of impressions and ideas exposes the fallaciousness of this natural or common-sense way of thinking. The problem for Hume is *not* whether we can *know* that there are objects and events in the world that are independent of perceptions – objects and events that give rise to our impressions and ideas. *His* problem is how we come to *believe* that there are objects, events, causal relations, and powers in the external world – matters of fact to which we have no *direct* access. As long as we take this doctrine of perceptions as fundamental (as Hume does), Hume's naturalistic project – his attempt to develop a natural "science of man" – leads to "mitigated" (not total) skepticism about the very existence of the world of matters of fact.[28] While Hume seeks to explain why we *believe* that there is such a world, he cannot explain why we can *know* that such a world "really exists."

Whether we are dealing with inanimate objects or personal selves, we need to explain why we *believe* they have continued existence when we are not perceiving them. But how are we to account for this belief when in fact all our perceptions are about discrete, separable, non-continuous items?[29] We cannot explain this by an appeal to reason. We must appeal to another faculty of the mind – the imagination. Hume does confront the paradox that his philosophical reflections lead him to: the conclusion that we cannot *know* that there is an independent natural world of matters of fact of our perceptions.[30] He nevertheless struggles with the tension between what his philosophical reflections lead him to believe and what we naturally believe: namely, that there really is a natural world "out there" that *directly* influences us – a world that is independent of what we perceive.

> There is a great difference betwixt such opinions as we form after a calm and profound reflection, and such as we embrace by a kind of instinct or natural impulse, on account of their suitableness and conformity to the mind. If these opinions become contrary, 'tis not difficult to foresee which of them will have the advantage. As long as our attention is bent upon the subject, the philosophical and study'd principle may prevail; but the moment we relax our thoughts, nature will display herself, and draw us back to our former opinion, Nay she has sometimes such an influence, that she can stop our progress, even in the midst of our most profound reflections, and keep us from running on with all the consequences of any philosophical opinion. Thus tho' we clearly perceive the dependence and interruption of our perceptions, we stop short in our career, and never upon that account reject the notion of an independent and continu'd existence. That opinion has taken such deep root in the imagination, that 'tis impossible ever to eradicate it, nor will any strain'd metaphysical conviction of the dependence of our perceptions be sufficient for that purpose. (Hume 1978: 214)

Even this statement about how "nature will display herself" and how nature can sometimes interrupt our philosophical reflections is *paradoxical*. How are we to understand what he means by "nature" in this passage? Clearly, Hume intends to speak about a nature that is really "out there" and independent of what we think or believe – a nature that can influence us. He speaks about nature as "obstinate" and forcing itself upon us. But given his doctrine that perceptions "before the mind" are our *only* access to knowledge about matters of fact and that the impressions (the basis for ideas) have "unknown causes," we have no direct access to nature. We have an *idea* of nature, but we do not know whether the *intentional content* of this idea corresponds to or is caused by a nature that is truly independent of our perceptions. We can explain why we *believe* that the natural world exists, but not how we *know* that such a natural world exists.

What is the source of these paradoxes and tensions? Why does Hume struggle so valiantly to explain why we *believe* in a world of physical objects and selves that have continued existence – a world that is independent of the mind? The source of these difficulties is Hume's *starting point* – his doctrine of the origin of ideas – or, more specifically, his claim that simple impressions arise from "unknown causes." With a beginning point like this, Hume cannot escape from the skeptical doubts about the existence of an objective independent world of matters of fact.[31] I agree with Stroud when he affirms that Hume's *dominant* interest was in human nature, not in the origin of human ideas:

> [A]nd his interest took the form of seeking extremely general truths about how and why human beings think, feel and act in the ways they do. . . . He thought we could understand what human beings do, and why and how, only by studying them as a part of nature, by trying to determine the origins of various thoughts, feelings, reactions and other human 'products' within the familiar world" (Stroud 1977: 222).

I want to return now to what I said at the beginning of this chapter, where I mentioned that, although Spinoza and Hume radically disagree on many key points, they are both advocates of a thoroughgoing naturalism. Hume makes many nasty and insulting comments about Spinoza in his *Treatise*. Nevertheless, when we probe what he is saying, it turns out that he shares a great deal with Spinoza.[32] Their respective understandings of nature are totally different. Hume, for example, would never use an expression such as "God or Nature." For Hume, such an expression is pure nonsense. Although Hume is not directly concerned to refute Spinoza, his multifaceted attack on the appeal to reason to explain matters of fact is intended to refute the type of rationalism that is fundamental for Spinoza. Hume would never accept Spinoza's commitment to a principle of sufficient reason. For him our knowledge is far more limited. For example, when Hume gives his positive account of causality and necessary connection by an appeal to custom and sentiment, we reach the limits of our knowledge. For Hume, it would be absurd to try to explain why we are creatures of custom and feeling. That is just what human beings *are* (full stop). For Spinoza, there is a hierarchy of types of knowledge. Intuitive knowledge is the highest form of knowledge, and then comes rational knowledge, and, finally, imagination – the lowest form of knowledge and the source of human error. What Spinoza takes to be the lowest faculty of the mind – imagination – for Hume turns out to be the key faculty for understanding the natural world. Spinoza seeks to avoid any appeal to experience in *justifying* his propositions in the *Ethics*. His use of the geometric method, modeled on Euclid's method, is intended to show that we can develop a complete philosophical system based on demonstrative reason – one in which logical necessity prevails in the proofs. Hume's naturalistic project – both his negative and positive theses – categorically rejects the very idea of the possibility of a demonstrative science of nature based on rigorous proofs. Demonstrative reason is restricted to dealing with relations of ideas; it is appropriate for such disciplines as geometry and arithmetic, but it does not tell us *anything* about matters of fact in the natural world. Although Hume believes that every event has a cause, he maintains that it is at least *conceivable* that an event or object does not have a cause. Spinoza would never agree to this. For Hume, all distinct ideas are *separable* from each other. Spinoza rejects such a claim. Hume mocks Spinoza's monism. And so on. One can continue the list of the striking differences between Spinoza and Hume, showing that their naturalistic projects are antithetical. But let me turn to what they share in common.

Both Spinoza and Hume are philosophers of immanence. They reject any appeal to what is divine or supernatural to account for the phenomena of this world. Although they have radically different conceptions of necessity, both held that everything that happens in this world is determined by causal necessity. There is no incompatibility in reconciling freedom (liberty) and necessity. Both Spinoza and Hume maintain even stronger positions: a proper understanding of freedom (liberty) *requires* the appeal to causal necessity. Although their conceptions of the nature of reason and passions differ, they both maintain that reason *alone* is not *sufficient* to oppose or counter a given passion. Only another passion can oppose a given passion – for example, joy opposing sadness. But perhaps the most significant similarity that justifies characterizing them as philosophical naturalists is that they are both committed to the doctrine that the same natural laws apply to all of nature – including human nature. Neither of them is a philosophical reductionist. Neither maintains that all natural phenomena can be explained by a single natural science such as physics. For Spinoza, this would violate his principle that God or Nature has an infinite number of attributes, even though we humans have knowledge of only two of these attributes – thought and extension. Hume is not a reductionist, because he maintains that there are distinctive principles for explaining how humans think and feel, but these principles are natural. Both Spinoza and Hume maintain that there are *no metaphysical* gaps in nature and no *epistemological* gaps in our knowledge of the natural world.

If we had to point to a single principle that accounts for their radical differences, it would be their antithetical conceptions of causality and necessary connection. Spinoza's rational conception of causal necessity as a form of *logical necessity* seems excessive. The notion of *causa sui*, which is the beginning point of Spinoza's *Ethics*, is open to skeptical doubts. Hume certainly thought it was absurd – nothing more than a metaphysical gibberish. However, Hume's own *psychological* account of causality and necessary connection, based upon custom and sentiment, is equally inadequate to account for causality as an objective principle governing nature.

The philosopher who had the deepest understanding of the strengths and weaknesses of both Spinoza's and Hume's conception of causality was Kant. Kant saw that the problem of necessary connection was not an isolated problem but a systemic one. In his critical philosophy – especially in the *Critique of Pure Reason* – Kant sought to develop a transcendental philosophy that would at once transform our understanding of metaphysics (by exposing its limitations) and explain the possibility of experience and a science of nature. Kant's critical philosophy poses a deep challenge to *all* varieties of naturalism – including Spinozistic and Humean. Kant argues that both Spinoza and Hume fail to develop adequate conceptions of nature and natural laws; their naturalisms also cannot adequately account for human reason. The insight and power of Kant's philosophy have had a remarkable endurance. Many contemporary philosophers are deeply sympathetic to his critique of naturalism – a naturalism that claims that everything, including *human reason* and our discursive conceptual capacities, may be explained by an appeal to nature and the natural sciences.[33] Yet, as we will also see, despite the power and brilliance of Kant's critical philosophy, he leaves us with a series of his own perplexities and paradoxes concerning nature and its relation to human reason.

3
Kant: Copernican Turn – Nature, Reason, and Freedom

In my discussion of Spinoza and Hume, I argued that they are both "this-worldly" thinkers and philosophers of immanence. Although they have radically different conceptions of nature and the proper method for coming to know nature, they are both committed philosophical naturalists. The world of nature is all that there is and all that we can know. Both Spinoza and Hume hold that the explanation of nature (including human nature) is by appeal to the laws of nature. They reject any appeal to transcendent principles. They both acknowledge that there are differences within nature, but these are differences of *degree*, not *kind*; there are no metaphysical or epistemological gaps or dualisms within nature. Both Spinoza and Hume reject Cartesian dualism, but for different reasons. For Spinoza, the final court of appeal is reason; for Hume, it is experience. Both seek to explain causality and necessary connection. Spinoza claims that causal necessity is a form of *logical* necessity; Hume, on the contrary, claims that our idea of necessary connection is *psychological*: it is based on custom and feeling. Both accounts of causal necessity are problematic and have been severely criticized by subsequent philosophers.

Kant presents the greatest challenge to naturalism – whether it be the metaphysical naturalism of Spinoza or the empirical naturalism of Hume. Champions of Kant claim that he has definitively shown the failure of *any* form of naturalism. He seeks to demonstrate the *impossibility* of naturalism as a doctrine that can account for human rationality (both theoretical and practical). Furthermore, naturalism fails to account for human freedom and morality. Kant's influence has been so pervasive and deep that even today, in the twenty-first century, philosophical battles continue to rage between those who advocate some version of naturalism and those who, like Kant, argue that all naturalist accounts of human rationality are doomed to failure. Because Kantian arguments (or arguments in a Kantian spirit) against naturalism have been so dominant, it is important to get clear about Kant's understanding of nature. In his Copernican Revolution, he seeks to demonstrate that the very possibility of experience and an objective science of nature *presupposes* that reason dictates the form of the universal and necessary laws of nature.[1]

Before turning to the details of Kant's conception of nature and natural science, I want to present informally the existential crisis that Kant was facing when writing the *Critique of Pure Reason*. Despite its dry, almost scholastic, style, there is a high drama lurking in the background. Like so many eighteenth-century thinkers, Kant was impressed by the scientific achievements of his time, especially those of Newton. As Kant understands Newtonian science – and, more generally, the science of nature – it is committed to a *strong* conception of causality whereby every event is determined by a cause according to the universal laws of nature. To use Kant's own words in the Second Analogy, "[e]verything that happens (begins to be) presupposes something which it follows in accordance with a rule" (*CPR* A 189/B 232).[2] In the second edition of the *Critique of Pure Reason*, Kant reformulates his claim: "All alterations occur in accordance with the law of the connection of cause and effect" (*CPR* A 189/B 232). In the realm of nature, there are no exceptions to strict objective necessary causation. The laws of nature are universal and necessary. This applies to *everything* in nature, including physical nature and animate nature. *Insofar* as humans are natural creatures, the rigorous universal causal principle applies to them. If we were to affirm that human beings are *exclusively* natural beings, then there would be *no* possibility of human freedom. We would be committed to fatalism; morality would turn out to be a sham and an illusion. This is the high drama of the *Critique*. Unless Kant can show – *demonstrate* – that human beings are not *exclusively* natural creatures, there is no basis for claiming that they can freely choose what they ought to do. A primary objective of the *Critique of Pure Reason* is thus a negative one: to refute the claim that human beings are *totally* subject to the laws of nature. To state the point more positively, Kant's aim is to make room for the *possibility* of human freedom, morality, and faith. To the extent that his arguments in the first *Critique* are successful, we can affirm that human beings are *natural* creatures and *rational* beings capable of free action. Kant seeks to show that natural causality and the "causality through freedom"

(*CPR* A 538/B 566) do not conflict with each other – they are *compatible*. At the conclusion of his discussion of the third antinomy, Kant states: "[To show] that this antinomy rests on a mere illusion, and that nature at least **does not conflict** with causality through freedom – that was the one single thing we could accomplish, and it alone was our sole concern" (*CPR* A 558/B 586).[3]

I want to turn to an explication of Kant's conception of nature, natural science, and the laws of nature by commenting on the significance of his Copernican Revolution. In the Preface to the second edition of the *Critique of Pure Reason*, Kant first describes the revolutions that took place in mathematics and natural science. In the field of mathematics,

> [a] new light broke upon the first person who demonstrated the isosceles triangle (whether he was called "Thales" or had some other name). For he found that what he had to do was not to trace what he saw in this figure, or even trace its mere concept, and read off, as it were, from the properties of the figure; but rather that he had to produce the latter from what he himself thought into the object and presented (through construction) according to *a priori* concepts, and that in order to know something securely *a priori* he had to ascribe to the thing nothing except what followed necessarily from what he himself had put into it in accordance with its concept. (*CPR* B xi–ii)[4]

Kant then tells us that in the natural sciences it took much longer to turn away from idle groping and to find the highway to science.

> When Galileo rolled balls of a weight chosen by himself down an inclined plane, or when Torricelli made the air bear a weight that he has previously thought to be equal to that of a known column of water, or when in a later time Stahl changed metals into calx and then changed the latter back into metal by first removing something and then putting it back again, a light dawned on all those who study nature. They comprehended that reason has insight only into what it itself produces according to its own design; that it must take the lead with principles for its judgments according to constant laws and compel nature to answer its questions, rather than letting nature guide its movements by keeping reason, as it were, in leading-strings; for otherwise accidental observations, made according to no previously designed plan, can never connect up into a necessary law, which is yet what reason seeks and requires. (*CPR* B xii–iii)

Both of these revolutions provide the background for Kant's own Copernican Revolution in metaphysics. Kant sought to escape the battlefield of the endless disputes in metaphysics and to establish metaphysics on a firm foundation.

> I should think that the examples of mathematics and natural science, which have become what they now are through a revolution brought about all at once, were remarkable enough that we might reflect on the essential element in the change in the ways of thinking that has been so advantageous to them, and, at least as an experiment, imitate it insofar as their analogy with metaphysics, as rational cognition, might permit. (*CPR* B xv–vi)

The *Critique of Pure Reason* initiates the type of revolution for metaphysics that historically took place in mathematics and natural science.

> Up to now it has been assumed that all our cognition must conform to the objects; but all attempts to find out something about them *a priori* through concepts that would extend our cognition have, on this presupposition, come to nothing. Hence let us once try whether we do not get farther with the problems of metaphysics by assuming that the objects must conform to our cognition, which would agree better with the requested possibility of an *a priori* cognition of them, which is to establish something about objects before they are given to us. This would be just like the first thoughts of Copernicus, who, when he did not make good progress in the explanation of celestial motions if he assumed that the entire celestial host revolves around the observer, tried to see if he might not have greater success if he made the observer revolve and left the stars at rest. (*CPR* B xvi)

This is the revolutionary hypothesis that Kant set out to demonstrate in sophisticated detail in the first *Critique*. In the final analysis, the hypothesis that "objects must conform to our cognition" turns out to be an apodictic truth. Yovel succinctly states the significance of this Copernican Revolution for comprehending nature and natural science.

> For, according to the "Copernican" principle set by the Critique, the conditions for *thinking* objects in nature are equally the conditions for these *to be* objects in nature. Therefore, in knowing the grounds of thinking natural objects we at once know the first grounds of nature itself, that is, we possess what Kant calls "a pure science of nature" (and also "nature in a formal sense"). Based on these foundations and on sensible materials, we also need an *empirical* science of nature (such as physics and its derivatives in astronomy, organic chemistry, biology), since it is only by empirical science that we come to know particular objects and specific natural laws, and even to know there is a world. And since empirical science is based on the a priori science, we are able to know in advance, as a conditional proposition, that *if* there is a natural world and there are natural objects in it, they all necessarily obey certain primary conditions, which the Critique determines and formulates a priori. In this respect, the Critique that exhibits the science of consciousness generates, by the same move, an a priori science of the foundations of nature. (Yovel 2018: 6)

Yovel makes several important points that we need to keep in mind. For contemporary readers it may sound strange and confusing to distinguish between an *empirical* science of nature and a pure *a priori* science of nature. Most scientists and philosophers today think that there are *only* the empirical natural sciences; there is no such thing as an *a priori* science of nature. But for Kant, the distinction between *a priori* natural science and empirical natural science is absolutely key. By a pure *a priori* science of nature Kant means a science that lays out the foundational conditions for the possibility of empirical natural science. We can illustrate this with a reference to the causal principle (although it is only one of the principles of the pure science of nature). For example, in medical research, we seek to discover the empirical causes of diseases like cancer. No one doubts that there are natural causes of cancer; the empirical scientific problem is to discover them. But empirical experience by itself cannot *justify* the causal principle that is presupposed in our search for empirical causes of cancer. Empirical research cannot justify the principle that every event *must* have a cause – a cause determined by the universal laws of nature. This is a *synthetic a priori* claim. By the pure science of nature Kant means the *complete* system of *a priori* principles that constitute the foundation of the empirical natural sciences. The very possibility of empirical natural science presupposes the pure *a priori* science of nature. Consequently, we do not *derive* the concept of cause by generalizing from empirical experience. Our understanding (*Verstand*) is so constituted that we *a priori* impose the requirement of causal necessity. In a famous passage that shows how strongly Kant departs from Hume, he writes:

> If one were to think of escaping from the toils of these investigations by saying that experience constantly offers examples of a regularity of appearances that give sufficient occasion for abstracting the concept of cause from them, and thereby at the same time thought to confirm the objective **validity** of such a concept, then one has not noticed that the concept of cause cannot arise in this way at all, but must either be grounded in the understanding completely *a priori* or else be entirely surrendered as a mere fantasy of the brain. For this concept always requires that something *A* be of such a kind that something else *B* follows from it **necessarily** and **in accordance with an absolutely universal rule**. Appearances may well offer cases from which a rule is possible in accordance with which something usually happens, but never a rule in accordance with which the succession is **necessary**; thus to the synthesis of cause and effect there attaches a dignity that can never be expressed empirically, namely, that the effect does not merely come along with the cause, but is posited **through** it and follows **from** it. The strict universality of the rule is therefore not any property of empirical

rules, which cannot acquire anything more through induction than comparative universality, i.e., widespread usefulness. But now the use of the pure concepts of the understanding would be entirely altered if one were to treat them only as empirical products. (*CPR* A 91–2/B 123–4)

The relationship between the pure *a priori* science of nature and empirical science is more complicated than I have suggested. Kant actually introduces a *threefold* distinction: (1) There are the pure *a priori* principles that are established in the Transcendental Analytic. The systematic set of these principles constitutes transcendental philosophy – and the formal science of nature. (2) There are empirical regularities that we discover by observation and induction. (3) There are also specific *causal laws* that constitute the natural sciences, which cannot be identified either with the pure *a priori* formal principles or with the empirical regularities that we discover based on induction. And these causal laws are themselves *necessary* and *universal*. In his *Metaphysical Foundations of Natural Science*, Kant clearly distinguishes *two* aspects of the metaphysics of nature:

> *Properly* so-called natural science presupposes, in the first place, metaphysics of nature. For laws, that is, principles of the necessity of that which belongs to the *existence* of a thing, are concerned with a concept that cannot be constructed, since existence cannot be presented *a priori* in any intuition. Thus proper natural science presupposes metaphysics of nature. Now this latter must always contain solely principles that are not empirical (for precisely this reason it bears the name of a metaphysics), but it can still either: *first*, treat the laws that make possible the concept of nature in general, even without relation to any determinate object of experience, and thus undetermined with respect to the nature of this or that thing in the sensible world, in which case it is the *transcendental* part of the metaphysics of nature; or *second*, concern itself with a particular nature of this or that kind of things, for which an empirical concept is given, but still in such a manner that, outside of what lies in this concept, no other empirical principle is used for its cognition (for example, it takes the empirical concept of matter or of a thinking being as its basis, and it seeks that sphere of cognition of which reason is capable *a priori* concerning these objects), and here such a science must still always be called a metaphysics of nature, namely, of corporeal or of thinking nature. However [in this second case] it is then not a general, but a *special* metaphysical natural science (physics or psychology), in which the above transcendental principles are applied to the two species of objects of our senses. (*MFN* 4:469–70)

Although this passage is extremely turgid, the point Kant is making is important for his understanding of a *critical metaphysics* (a metaphysics that results from the critique of reason). A critical metaphysics consists of two parts. The first part consists of the complete system of *a priori* principles articulated and defended in the Transcendental Logic. These principles apply to all natural science. They are the principles of nature in *general*. Kant, however, claims that there is a second aspect of a metaphysics of nature. It consists of the principles (laws of nature) that are relevant to the *specific* domain of nature.[5]

Both in the first *Critique* and in the *Prolegomena to Any Future Metaphysics*, Kant insists on a clear distinction between the pure *a priori* principles and the particular empirical laws of nature (which are not to be confused with the discovery of empirical regularities).

> The pure faculty of understanding does not suffice, however, to prescribe to the appearances through mere categories *a priori* laws beyond those on which rests a **nature in general**, as lawfulness of appearances in space and time. Particular laws, because they concern empirically determined appearances, **cannot** be **completely derived** from the categories, although they all stand under them. Experience must be added in order to come to know particular laws **at all**; but about experience in general, and about what can be cognized as an object of experience, only those *a priori* laws offer instruction. (*CPR* B 165)[6]

The particular laws that constitute an empirical science such as physics require the contribution of experience, but these empirical laws are *universal* and *necessary*. The universality and necessity of empirical laws are *grounded* in the transcendental principles that constitute the pure *a priori* science of nature. Michael Friedman emphasizes that "Kant recognizes two types of necessity (and thus apriority)":

> The transcendental principles of the understanding are absolutely necessary and *a priori*: they are established entirely independent of all perception and experience. Empirical laws that somehow fall under these transcendental principles are then necessary and *a priori* in a derivative sense. They, unlike the transcendental principles themselves, indeed depend partially on inductively obtained regularities (and thus on perception), yet they are also in some sense grounded in or determined by the transcendental principles, and thereby acquire a necessary and more than merely inductive status. (Friedman 1992a: 174)[7]

In the *Prolegomena*, published shortly after the first edition of the *Critique of Pure Reason*, Kant declares: "I freely admit the remembrance of *David Hume* was the very thing that many years ago first interrupted my dogmatic slumber and gave a completely different direction to my researches in the field of speculative philosophy" (*P* 4:260).[8] This barely indicates why Kant thought Hume was so important for philosophy and for understanding the proper scope and limits of metaphysics.

> *Hume* started mainly from a single but important concept of metaphysics, namely that of the *connection of cause and effect* (and of course also its derivative concepts, of force and action, etc.), and called upon reason, which pretends to have generated this concept in her womb, to give him an account of by what right she thinks: that something could be constituted that, if it is posited, something else necessarily must thereby be posited as well; for that is what the concept of cause says. He undisputably proved that it is wholly impossible for reason to think such a connection *a priori* and from concepts, because this connection contains necessity; and it is simply not to be seen how it could be, that because something is, something else necessarily must also be, and therefore how the concept of such a connection could be introduced *a priori*. From this he concluded that reason completely and fully deceives herself with this concept, falsely taking it for her own child, when it is really nothing but a bastard of the imagination, which, impregnated by experience, and having brought certain representations under the law of association, passes off the resulting subjective necessity (i.e. habit) for an objective necessity (from insight). From which he concluded that reason has no power at all to think such connections, not even merely in general, because its concepts would then be bare fictions, and all of its cognitions allegedly established *a priori* would be nothing but falsely marked ordinary experiences, which is as much as to say there is no metaphysics at all, and cannot be any. (*P* 4:257–8)

Hume's great achievement is a negative one. He showed definitively that reason alone, by *conceptual analysis*, cannot generate the causal principle – a principle that establishes an objectively necessary connection between cause and its effect. In Kantian terminology, the causal principle is not an *analytic* truth – that is, not one whose truth can be established solely by an appeal to the principle of contradiction. Consequently, Hume refutes all dogmatic rationalist conceptions of causality (whether offered by Leibniz, Wolff, or Spinoza) presupposing that the causal principle is an *a priori* analytic truth.[9] The causal principle (like the other key principles of the pure science of nature) is *synthetic*, but it is not a synthetic *a posteriori* principle. It is not a principle that can be justified by an appeal to empirical experience. Despite Hume's challenge to rationalist conceptions of causality, his great failure, Kant claims, was not to realize that the causal principle is a *synthetic a priori* principle. Of course, there is no place in Hume's epistemology for synthetic *a priori* principles or judgments. The empiricists, right up to the twentieth-century logical empiricists, have denied that there are any synthetic *a priori* judgments. For Kant, however, it is clear that both mathematics and natural science require synthetic *a priori* judgments and principles. The key philosophical question for Kant is not whether there are synthetic *a priori* judgments but rather, "How are synthetic *a priori* judgements possible?" This is *the* question that structures the *Prolegomena*. Kant proceeds by raising the question first for mathematics, then for the pure science of nature, and finally for metaphysics.

In the *Prolegomena*, Kant distinguishes two different philosophical methods: the synthetic (progressive) and the analytic (regressive).[10] The synthetic method is the one adopted in the first *Critique*, and the analytic method structures the *Prolegomena*. Gary Hatfield provides a succinct account of the difference between these methods.

> In the *Prolegomena*, Kant attributed two features of the synthetic method to the *Critique*. First, as regards method of exposition, the big book [the *Critique of Pure Reason*] "had to be composed according to the *synthetic method*, so that the science [viz., transcendental philosophy] might present all of its articulations, as the structural organization of a quite peculiar faculty of cognition, in their natural connection" (*P* 4:263). It examined first the "elements" of pure reason and then the "laws of its pure use" (*P* 4:274), moving from parts to whole and from ground to consequent. Second, as regards the source of conviction, he could accept nothing as given "except reason itself" and so had to "develop cognition out of its original seeds without relying on any fact whatever" (*P* 4:274). He had to argue directly for his account of the elements and the laws of pure reason. The analytic method of the *Prolegomena* proceeded differently on both counts, starting from something known and familiar and proceeding to discover its elements or grounds. The method was nonetheless intended to justify the discovered elements or grounds, in this case by showing that Kant's theory of synthetic *a priori* cognition is the only possible account of the knowledge we actually possess. (Hatfield 2002: 36)

Strictly speaking, the analytic method of the *Prolegomena* presupposes the success of the synthetic method of the first *Critique*. In the *Prolegomena* Kant presupposes that mathematics and natural science are based upon synthetic *a priori* judgments. The analytic method proceeds by asking *how* synthetic *a priori* judgments are possible in mathematics and how synthetic *a priori* judgments are possible in natural science: that is, *how* pure mathematics is possible and *how* pure natural science is possible. This provides the basis for raising the question: "How is metaphysics in general possible?" But a good empiricist (like Hume) would never grant that there are any synthetic *a priori* judgments. Consequently, the question of *how* such judgments are possible is moot. That is why the analytic method in the *Prolegomena* is dependent on the synthetic method in the first *Critique*, where

Kant seeks to prove that pure mathematics and a pure science of nature consist of synthetic *a priori* judgments.

To appreciate fully Kant's conception of nature, we must keep in mind his larger philosophical project in the first *Critique*. Kant begins the *Critique* in a most arresting manner. Reason is burdened by questions that it cannot dismiss yet cannot answer. It is at war with itself and falls into obscurity, contradictions, and endless controversies. "The battlefield of these endless controversies is called metaphysics" (*CPR* A viii). Kant seeks to determine the proper domain and scope of metaphysics. In order to carry out this task, he must determine what human beings can know and what is beyond human knowledge. The *Critique* synthetically (progressively) begins with the Transcendental Doctrine of Elements. In the Transcendental Aesthetic, Kant argues that our sensibility is structured by the pure *a priori* intuitions of space and time. We then move to the Transcendental Logic, in which Kant first explains what he means by transcendental logic (as distinguished from general logic). He proceeds to the analysis of the pure *a priori* concepts of the understanding – the categories. From there, he moves to what many take to be the culmination of his achievement, namely, the Transcendental Deduction of the Pure Concepts of the Understanding from the "I think" – the transcendental unity of apperception.[11] In the *Prolegomena*, Kant states: "Nothing can be more desirable to a philosopher than to be able to derive, *a priori* from one principle, the multiplicity of concepts or basic principles that previously had exhibited themselves to him piecemeal in the use he had made of them *in concreto*, and in this way to be able to unite them all in one cognition" (*P* 4:322). Kant claims that this is precisely what the Transcendental Deduction accomplishes; that is why it is the coping stone of the first *Critique*. After ascending to his Deduction from the transcendental unity of apperception, Kant turns to the Analytic of Principles – "a canon for the power of judgment that teaches it to apply to appearances the concepts of the understanding, which contain the condition for rules *a priori*" (*CPR* A 132/B 171). We can roughly describe the structure of the Transcendental Doctrine of Elements as an *ascent* that begins with the analysis of the *a priori* conditions of sensibility – the pure intuitions of space and time – and then moves to the analysis of the twelve categories of the understanding, and culminates in the Transcendental Deduction of the Pure Concepts of the Understanding. This movement then provides the basis for a *descent*, in which we learn how the pure concepts of the understanding (the categories) apply to appearances.[12] Kant claims to present a systematic representation of *all* the principles of pure understanding.

What, then, can humans know? The opening sentence of the Transcendental Aesthetic provides the essential clue for grasping what we human beings can know. "In whatever way and through whatever means a cognition may relate to objects, that through which it relates immediately to them, and at which all thought as a means is directed as an end, is intuition (*CPR* A 19/B 33). Human beings are capable *only* of having *empirical* intuitions, not *intellectual* intuitions. Kant categorically rejects the rationalist claim that humans can have intellectual (nonsensible) intuitions. The faculty by which we receive empirical intuitions is sensibility. Sensibility (which is the faculty of receptivity) is structured by the pure intuitions of space and time. These pure intuitions provide the universal framework for receiving all empirical intuitions; they provide the *formal* structure for empirical intuitions.

> The effect of an object on the capacity for representation, insofar as we are affected by it, is **sensation**. That intuition which is related to the object through sensation is called **empirical**. The undetermined object of an empirical intuition is called appearance.
>
> I call that in the appearance which corresponds to sensation its **matter**, but that which allows the manifold of appearance to be intuited as ordered in certain relations I call **the form** of appearance. (*CPR* B 34/A 20)

We can restate Kant's claims more directly. There is the faculty of sensibility – the faculty of receptivity possessed by all human beings. This faculty is structured by the pure formal *a priori* intuitions of space and time. These pure intuitions provide the formal framework for all the empirical intuitions that we receive. There is an element of sensation in every empirical intuition – that is, the affect of the object upon our faculty of representation. The undetermined object of an empirical intuition is appearance, and appearance itself has form and content. (I will say more about the significance of appearance later.) In the Transcendental Aesthetic, Kant introduces one of the clearest early statements of transcendental idealism:

> We have therefore wanted to say that all our intuition is nothing but the representation of appearance; that the things that we intuit are not in themselves what we intuit them to be, nor are their relations so constituted in themselves as they appear to us; and that if we remove our own subject or even only the subjective constitution of the senses in general, then all constitution, all relations of objects in space and time, indeed space and time themselves would disappear, and as appearances they cannot exist in themselves, but only in us. What may be the case with objects in themselves and abstracted from all this receptivity of our sensibility remains entirely unknown to us. We are acquainted with nothing except our way of perceiv-

ing them, which is peculiar to us, and which therefore does not necessarily pertain to every being, though to be sure it pertains to every human being. We are concerned solely with this. Space and time are its pure forms, sensation in general its matter. We can cognize only the former *a priori*, i.e., prior to all actual perception, and they are therefore called pure intuition; the latter, however, is that in our cognition that is responsible for it being called *a posteriori* cognition, i.e., empirical intuition. The former adheres to our sensibility absolutely necessarily, whatever sort of sensations we may have; the latter can be very different. (*CPR* A 42–3/B 59–60)

According to the Copernican hypothesis, *everything* that we can know is *conditioned* by us. As the *Critique* synthetically progresses, it becomes clear that an account of human knowledge requires that we also grasp the contribution of the discursive faculty of understanding – the faculty of spontaneity that is the source of the *concepts* required to yield knowledge. Human knowledge requires both *intuitions* and *concepts* – both the contributions of sensibility and of understanding. The table of judgments of the Transcendental Logic provides the basis for the *complete* list of the pure concepts – that is, the categories that are essential for achieving objective knowledge.[13] To gain empirical knowledge of the world of appearance, we require the *cooperation* of concepts and empirical intuitions. In a famous passage, Kant summarizes his stance:

> If we will call the **receptivity** of our mind to receive representations insofar as it is affected in some way **sensibility**, then on the contrary the faculty for bringing forth representations itself, or the **spontaneity** of cognition, is the **understanding**. It comes along with our nature that **intuition** can never be other than **sensible**, i.e., that it contains only the way in which we are affected by objects. The faculty for **thinking** of objects of sensible intuitions, on the contrary, is the **understanding**. Neither of these properties is to be preferred to the other. Without sensibility no object would be given to us, and without understanding none would be thought. Thoughts without content are empty, intuitions without concepts are blind. (*CPR* A 51/B 75)[14]

The empirical intuitions of the receptive faculty of sensibility are the *necessary* conditions for the possibility of knowledge. Without sensibility, no objects would be given to us. Nevertheless, the intuitions of sensibility are not *sufficient* to yield knowledge. These intuitions must be organized by the concepts of understanding. Sensibility and understanding must function *together* to yield knowledge. Sensible empirical intuitions are required for us to gain concrete knowledge of the natural world.

Transcendental philosophy specifies the *a priori* principles that provide the necessary form for the knowledge of mathematics and natural science.

Pure mathematics presupposes the pure intuitions of space and time. Nevertheless, the pure intuitions of space and time are not *sufficient* to yield mathematical knowledge. All knowledge requires concepts that have their source in the faculty of understanding. Pure mathematics itself requires the cooperation of *pure* intuitions of the faculty of sensibility and the *pure* concepts of the faculty of understanding. When it comes to natural science, the issue is more complicated. Like mathematics, natural science presupposes the pure intuitions of space and time as well as the pure concepts (the categories) of the understanding. In order to achieve concrete empirical knowledge of the world, however, we must receive empirical intuitions. Kant makes his position absolutely clear in the *Prolegomena*.

> We must, however, distinguish empirical laws of nature, which always presuppose particular perceptions, from the pure or universal laws of nature, which, without having particular perceptions underlying them, contain merely the conditions for the necessary unification of such perceptions in one experience; with respect to the latter laws, nature and *possible* experience are one and the same, and since in possible experience the lawfulness rests on the necessary connection of appearances in one experience (without which we would not be able to cognize any object of the sensible world at all), and so on the original laws of the understanding, then, even though it sounds strange at first, it is nonetheless certain, if I say with respect to the universal laws of nature: *the understanding does not draw its* (a priori) *laws from nature, but prescribes them to it.* (*P* 4:320)

We can now see how Kant proposes to answer Hume.[15] From Kant's perspective, Hume cannot account for the *universality* and *necessity* of the laws of nature because he fails to realize that the faculty of understanding *prescribes* these laws. "There are many laws of nature that we can know only through experience, but lawfulness in the connection of appearances, i.e., nature in general, we cannot come to know through any experience, because experience itself has need of such laws, which lie *a priori* at the basis of its possibility" (*P* 4:318–19). The world we come to know is the world of appearance, but appearance is *not* illusion; it is *the empirically real world – the natural world*. This empirically real world is not to be identified with the "thing in itself" (*Ding-an-Sich*). Kant's notion of the "thing in itself" has been problematic for many of his interpreters; it has been criticized and even ridiculed. *Initially*, all that Kant meant by this expression was to name what is *impossible* for us to know – a world that is *unconditioned* by us, by our sensibility and understanding. For some critics, Kant is the "all destroyer" skeptic who claims that we can never know "true reality." This criticism misses Kant's primary point. If we want to comprehend the *objectivity* of the natural world, then this can be accomplished by appealing to a *universal subjectivity* – the *a priori* structure of sensibility and understanding. The world of things in themselves is *not* another independent world that lies behind the world of appearance. It *is* the world of appearance, but understood *counterfactually* – what appearance would be if it were not conditioned by us. Sometimes Kant uses "noumena" as a synonym for "thing in itself." In their introduction to the Cambridge edition of the *Critique of Pure Reason*, Paul Guyer and Allen Wood emphasize the negative sense of "noumena":

> Kant says it is legitimate for us to speak of noumena only "in a negative sense," meaning things as they may be in themselves independently of our representation of them, but not noumena "in a positive sense," which would be things known through pure reason alone. A fundamental point of the *Critique* is to deny that we ever have knowledge of things through pure reason alone, but only by applying the categories to pure or empirical data structured by the forms of intuition. (Kant 1998: 13)[16]

When the first *Critique* was published in 1781, several reviewers claimed that Kant's transcendental idealism was little more than a version of Berkeleyan subjective idealism. Kant was stung by this criticism. He felt that it completely distorted what he attempted to demonstrate: namely, that transcendental idealism was the *only* way to guarantee the universality, necessity, and objectivity of our knowledge of the natural world – the empirically real world. When he wrote the *Prolegomena*, and when he revised the *Critique* for a second edition, he emphatically sought to refute the charge of *subjective* idealism.[17]

> Idealism consists in the claim that there are none other than thinking beings; the other things that we believe we perceive in intuition are only representations in thinking beings, to which in fact no object existing outside these beings corresponds. I say in opposition: There are things given to us as objects of our senses existing outside us, yet we know nothing of them as they may be in themselves, but are acquainted only with their appearances, i.e., with the representations that they produce in us because they affect our senses. Accordingly, I by all means avow that there are bodies outside us, i.e., things which, though completely unknown to us as to what they may be in themselves, we know through the representations which their influence on our sensibility provides for us, and to which we give the name of a body – which word therefore merely signifies the appearance of this object that is unknown to us but is nonetheless real. *Can this be called idealism? It is the very opposite of it.* (*P* 4:289, emphasis added)[18]

We can now understand the type of metaphysics that Kant defends and the pretensions of a metaphysics that he categorically rejects. Let us recall that in the first edition of the *Critique of Pure Reason* Kant tells us that human reason is burdened by questions it cannot dismiss but which it cannot answer because "they transcend every capacity of human reason" (*CPR* A vii). Kant indicates that the principles employed by reason are *unavoidable* in the never-ending quest to know what is unconditioned. Reason sees itself as "necessitated to take refuge in principles that overstep all possible use in experience" (*CPR* A viii). Consequently, it falls into obscurity and contradictions. The entire first part of the *Critique*, from the Transcendental Aesthetic through the Analytic of Principles, has taught us what is the proper domain of human knowledge of nature. We have learned that the pure concepts of understanding (the categories) yield knowledge *only* when applied to the empirical intuitions yielded by sensibility. The contribution of what we receive via sensibility is absolutely essential for achieving knowledge of the natural world. Kant claims to have set forth the *complete* system of synthetic *a priori* principles that are required for human knowledge of the natural world. The synthetic *a priori* principles that define nature in *general*, together with the *specific* metaphysical principles applicable to the different domains of nature, constitute the *only legitimate* metaphysics for Kant.[19]

We have also learned that the pure concepts of reason do not have any built-in *intrinsic* restrictions. When we are tempted to use these concepts to transcend all possible experience, we fall into the error of thinking that we can know what is beyond experience. This is the empty domain of *transcendent* dogmatic metaphysics, which must be distinguished from the legitimate critical *transcendental* metaphysics. In the Transcendental Dialectic, Kant shows that the attempt to employ reason to gain *theoretical* knowledge of objects beyond possible experience results in illusion, but that this illusion is *unavoidable*. Nevertheless, he shows that there is an important positive function performed by the *Ideas* of pure reason (*Vernunft*). These Ideas are *not* constitutive; they are *regulative*. They drive us on to achieve completeness and systematic unity of our knowledge of the natural world.

> To take the regulative principle of the systematic unity of nature for a constitutive one, and to presuppose hypostatically, as a cause, what is only in the idea as a ground for the harmonious use of reason, is only to confuse reason. The investigation of nature takes its own course, following only the chain of natural causes according to their universal laws in conformity to the idea of an author, to be sure, yet not to derive from that idea the purposiveness it is seeking everywhere, but rather in order to cognize its

existence from this purposiveness which it seeks in the essence of natural things, where possible in the essence of all things in general as well, and hence to cognize it as absolutely necessary. Whether or not this latter may succeed, the idea always remains correct, and so does its use, if it has been restricted to the conditions of a merely regulative principle. (*CPR* A 693–4/B 721–2)[20]

The *Ideas* of reason (*Vernunft*) are regulative; the *categories* of understanding (*Verstand*) are constitutive. The Ideas of reason play a vital role in the project of its *critique*, but we are deceived if we think that they lead us to the *knowledge* of what transcends the possibility of experience and the natural world.

I want to return to what I earlier called the existential reading of the first *Critique*. As rational beings, we are never satisfied with limiting ourselves to possible experience and the domain of nature. We seek to gain knowledge of what is unconditioned. We seek to gain speculative (theoretical) knowledge about God, freedom, and immortality (traditional topics of transcendent metaphysics). We cannot give up asking such questions, because we employ principles that are unavoidable in the course of experience. Yet, when we employ these principles in our attempt to gain knowledge of what is *beyond* possible experience, we inevitably fall into illusion, error, and obscurity. Reason's perplexity is not an *abstract* perplexity. Kant *personalizes* reason when he claims that it is *burdened* by questions which it cannot dismiss but which it cannot answer either. This is *our* fundamental human condition because we are rational creatures. The temptation to strive to gain knowledge of objects that are beyond possible experience is *unavoidable*. Even when we come to know that knowledge of a transcendent "realm" is *impossible*, we are still *tempted* to acquire such knowledge. This is why the Transcendental Dialectic can be understood as an ongoing *task* (*Aufgabe*) that needs to be performed over and over again whenever human beings are tempted by the illusion of gaining theoretical knowledge of objects beyond the world of nature.[21] "[This is] an **illusion** that cannot be avoided at all, just as little as we can avoid it that the sea appears higher in the middle than at the shores, since we see the former through higher rays of light than the latter, or even better, just as little as the astronomer can prevent the rising moon from appearing larger to him, even when he is not deceived by this illusion" (*CPR* A 297/B 354).

The result of the Transcendental Dialectic is not merely negative. On the contrary, it is crucial for Kant's overall project. We can now comprehend the full significance of the claim that Kant "had to deny **knowledge** in order to make room for **faith**" (*CPR* B xxx). The knowledge that Kant is *denying* is the knowledge of objects that are beyond possible experience – the "realm" of transcendent metaphysics. This means that those dogmatic philosophers (like Spinoza) and the theologians who claim to have speculative knowledge of God are making empty claims. They *falsely* claim to know what we cannot know. But the atheists who claim to *know* that there is *no* God are in the same position. They are also claiming to know what they cannot possibly know. We can neither *theoretically* prove nor disprove that there is a transcendent God.[22] This limitation leaves room for "rational faith," where we provide *practical* (not theoretical) arguments to justify faith. This reasoning also applies to freedom, as well as immortality. We cannot gain theoretical (speculative) knowledge of freedom; nor can we disprove that there is freedom. What the *Critique* demonstrates is the *possibility* of freedom and that "causality through freedom" is compatible with "the universal law of natural necessity" (*CPR* A 538/B 566). Once we have established the possibility of freedom, then the space is open to provide *practical* arguments to justify why we must *presuppose* freedom – a project that Kant fully undertakes in the *Critique of Practical Reason*.

Let me summarize what we have learned about Kant's conception of nature, natural science, and the universal and necessary laws of nature. Kant frequently speaks of "nature in general." "Nature is the existence of things, insofar as that existence is determined according to universal laws" (*P* 4:294). The Copernican Revolution has taught us that nature is not to be identified with things in themselves – things that are unconditioned by the faculties of sensibility and understanding. We do, however, actually possess "a pure natural science, which, *a priori* and with all of the necessity required for apodictic propositions, propounds laws to which nature is subject" (*P* 4:295). The transcendental philosophy lays out in systematic detail the complete pure science of nature. The principles articulated constitute the *formal* science of nature. Our knowledge of the *particular* material laws of nature not only must conform to these formal principles; it is *grounded* in these pure principles. This pure science of nature is not sufficient to provide substantive knowledge of the empirical world. Without the contribution of empirical intuitions, there is *no* concrete knowledge of nature. Consider how Kant defines nature in the *empirical* sense:

> By nature (in the empirical sense) we understand the combination of appearances as regards their existence, in accordance with necessary rules, i.e., in accordance with laws. There are therefore certain laws, and indeed *a priori*, which first make a nature possible; the empirical laws can only obtain and be found by means of experience, and indeed in accord with its origi-

nal laws, in accordance with which experience itself first becomes possible. (*CPR* A 216/B 263)

We have also indicated that Kant makes a threefold distinction concerning our knowledge of the natural world. There are the synthetic *a priori* principles of the *pure* science of nature; there are empirical regularities discovered by observation and induction; and there are universal and necessary laws of nature (e.g., physics) that are at once grounded in empirical intuitions and in the pure science of nature. In the *Metaphysical Foundations of Natural Science*, Kant states:

> A rational doctrine of nature thus deserves the name of a natural science, only in case the fundamental natural laws therein are cognized *a priori*, and are not mere laws of experience. One calls a cognition of the first kind *pure*, but that of a second kind is called *applied* rational cognition. Since the word nature already carries with it the concept of laws, and the latter carries with it the concept of the *necessity* of all determinations of a thing belonging to its existence, one easily sees why natural science must derive the legitimacy of this title only from its pure part – namely, that which contains the *a priori* principles of all other natural explanations – and why only in virtue of this pure part is natural science to be proper science. Likewise, [one sees] that, in accordance with demands of reason, every doctrine of nature must finally lead to natural science and conclude there, because this necessity of laws is inseparably attached to the concept of nature, and therefore makes claim to be thoroughly comprehended. (*MFN* 4:468–9)

Although Kant claims to specify the complete transcendental analytic of principles, I have been stressing, as Kant himself frequently does, the causal principle: that is, the principle of temporal succession according to the law of causality. According to this law, we know *a priori* that "everything that happens (begins to be) presupposes something which it follows in accordance with a rule" (*CPR* A 189/B 232). This means that there is an *objectively* necessary connection between cause and effect. Nature consists of an empirical world in which there is strict determinism – a determinism that excludes freedom. The antithesis of the third antinomy states: "There is no freedom, but everything in the world happens solely in accordance with laws of nature" (*CPR* A 445/ B 473). This antithesis is *true* of the natural world (the world of appearance). Kant's understanding of nature, as it emerges from the first *Critique*, is a grand deterministic system grounded on a pure science of nature articulated by synthetic *a priori* principles. Kant is not claiming that we will ever achieve complete *empirical* knowledge of the natural world – this depends on the ongoing empirical research – but we know *a priori* that nature consists of universal and necessary laws. In the first edition of the *Critique* – in one of the few poetic passages, which comes after his transcendental analysis of the principles of the understanding – Kant declares:

> We have now not only traveled through the land of pure understanding, and carefully inspected each part of it, but we have also surveyed it, and determined the place for each thing in it. This land, however, is an island, and enclosed in unalterable boundaries by nature itself. It is the land of truth (a charming name), surrounded by a broad and stormy ocean, the true seat of illusion, where many a fog bank and rapidly melting iceberg pretend to be new lands and, ceaselessly deceiving with empty hopes the voyager looking around for new discoveries, entwine him in adventures from which he can never escape and yet also never bring to an end. (*CPR* A 235–6/B 294–5)

Even though Kant stresses that we are tempted to think that we can achieve objective *theoretical* knowledge of noumena, the concept of noumena plays an absolutely fundamental role. To "make room" not only for faith but also for the *possibility* of freedom, Kant had to determine what we can know and what we cannot know. By delineating the boundaries of human knowledge, Kant has also provided for the *possibility* of freedom. He has opened the space for *practical* arguments to show why we must *presuppose* freedom – and specifically why we human beings are capable of exercising this freedom. The price that Kant pays for his elegant solution to reconciling natural causality with the causality of freedom is a heavy one – one that leaves us with some extraordinary paradoxes and perplexities.

I want to take a closer look at how Kant seeks to reconcile freedom and natural necessity in the first *Critique* and in the *Prolegomena*.[23] We have already learned that Kant claims that the "causality of nature" does not conflict with "causality through freedom." But we also want to know *precisely* how freedom and nature are related. "In respect of what happens, one can think of causality in only two ways: either according to **nature** or from **freedom**" (*CPR* A 532/B 560). There is something strikingly odd about this claim. Kant speaks about "what happens," but strictly speaking, what happens involves *temporality*. If what happens involves temporality, it is subject to natural causality and the laws of nature. Kant is explicit about this feature of natural causality.

> Within appearance, every effect is an event, or something that happens in time; the effect must, in accordance with the universal law of nature, be preceded by a determination of the causality of its cause (a state of the

cause), from which the effect follows in accordance with a constant law. But this determination of the cause to causality must also be something *that* occurs or *takes place*; the cause must have *begun* to *act*, for otherwise no sequence in time could be thought between it and the effect. (*P* 4:343–4)

The question arises: How can we speak of "what happens" issuing from the *causality of freedom* – a causality that does not involve temporality? Kant understands freedom as "the faculty of beginning a state **from itself,** the causality of which does not in turn stand under another cause determining it in time in accordance with the law of nature" (*CPR* A 533/B 561). He adds that "[f]reedom in this signification is a *pure transcendental idea*, which . . . contains nothing borrowed from experience" (*CPR* A 533/B 561, emphasis added). This means that freedom is a causality that is *independent* of time and experience. "[R]eason creates the idea of a spontaneity, which could start to act from itself, without needing to be preceded by any other cause that in turn determines it to action according to the law of causal connection" (*CPR* A 533/B 561). This is the "**transcendental idea of freedom**" (*CPR* A 533/B 561).[24] Even when Kant speaks of the causality through freedom, his language is *saturated* with temporal expressions. There is also a *practical* concept of freedom, which is "the independence of the power of choice from **necessitation** by impulses of sensibility" (*CPR* A 533/B 561). This practical concept of freedom is fundamental to Kant's moral philosophy. However, in the *Critique of Pure Reason*, Kant stresses that practical freedom – the power of choice – is *grounded* in the transcendental idea of freedom. Without the transcendental idea of freedom, it would make no sense to speak about freedom in a practical sense. Kant is emphatic in stressing the dependence of the practical sense of freedom on the transcendental idea of freedom:

> It is easy to see that if all causality in the world of sense were mere nature, then every occurrence would be determined in time by another in accord with necessary laws, and hence – since appearances, insofar as they determine the power of choice, would have to render every action necessary as their natural consequence – *the abolition of transcendental freedom would also simultaneously eliminate all practical freedom*. For the latter presupposes that although something has not happened, it nevertheless ought to have happened, and its cause in appearance was thus *not so determining* that there is not a causality in our power of choice such that, independently of those natural causes and even opposed to their power and influence, it might produce something determined in the temporal order in accord with empirical laws, and hence begin a series of occurrences **entirely from itself**. (*CPR* A 534/B 562, emphasis added)

It is not clear what Kant means when he says that "its cause in appearance [is] . . . not so determining that there is not a causality in our power of choice." Up until now, everything that Kant has claimed would lead us to think that every event and every action in the world of appearance is causally determined by *strict* universal laws of nature. This excludes any freedom or "power of choice." Consequently, it is not so easy to understand the *intelligibility* of the idea of transcendental freedom – a freedom that spontaneously "initiates" and "starts" what happens in the world but that is *not* itself conditioned by temporality and natural necessity. Kant tells us that the third antinomy would be a genuine contradiction *only* if we assumed that appearances are things in themselves. "For if appearances are things in themselves, then freedom cannot be saved" (*CPR* A 536/B 564). In the *Prolegomena*, Kant stresses this point:

> If the objects of the sensible world were taken for things in themselves, and the previously stated natural laws for laws of things in themselves, contradiction would be unavoidable. In the same way, if the subject of freedom were represented, like the other objects, as a mere appearance, contradiction could again not be avoided, for the same thing would be simultaneously affirmed and denied of the same object in the same sense. But if natural necessity is referred only to appearances and *freedom only to things in themselves*, then no contradiction arises if both kinds of causality are assumed or conceded equally, however difficult or impossible it may be to make causality of the latter kind conceivable. (*P* 4:343, emphasis added)

During Kant's lifetime, many of his critics questioned his distinction between appearance and thing in itself, as well as his claim that freedom refers *only* to things in themselves. This became one of the key issues in the pantheism controversy.[25] We can now understand why Kant was so adamant in insisting on this distinction. The distinction between appearance and thing in itself is *essential* for resolving the third antinomy and for showing that it is not a blatant contradiction. If we identify the world of appearance with the thing in itself, we would not be able to make sense of transcendental freedom, and this would undermine the very possibility of practical and moral freedom. Kant's transcendental idealism speaks of causality in *two aspects*: "as **intelligible** in its **action** as a thing in itself, and as **sensible** in the **effects** of that action as an appearance in the world of sense" (*CPR* A 538/B 566). Nevertheless, it is perplexing to claim that *one and the same event* in the world of appearance can be strictly determined by natural causality and at the same time be the result of a free act of choice. Kant has affirmed over and over again that everything in the world of appearance (the realm of nature) is strictly determined. Every event (including action) has a natural cause determined by the laws of nature. But if this is so, how can there be another type of causality – causality through freedom – that presumably has *effects in the natural world* but is not part of the natural world?

Kant's restatement of this critical point about how freedom and nature are reconciled in the *Prolegomena* does not alleviate this perplexity, but rather increases the paradoxical character of his "solution." "I can now say without contradiction: all actions of rational beings, insofar as they are appearances (are encountered in some experience or other), are subject to natural necessity; but *the very same actions*, with respect only to the rational subject and its faculty of acting in accordance with bare reason, are free" (*P* 4:345, emphasis added). What are the *criteria* for speaking about "the very same actions"? Kant appears to mean this as a strict identity: the very same *temporal* action that is part of a chain of necessary causes can *also* be conceived of as free – as the effect of the *non-temporal* rational faculty of choice. However, Kant's attempt to elucidate what he means does not really help, because it simply affirms that one and the same action can be explained as an effect of natural causes and as the effect of the rational capacity for free choice.

> In this way practical freedom – namely, that freedom in which reason has causality in accordance with the objective determining grounds – is rescued, without natural necessity suffering the least harm with respect to the very same effects, as appearances. This can also help elucidate what we have had to say about transcendental freedom and its unification with natural necessity (in the same subject, but not taken in one and the same respect). For, as regards transcendental freedom, any beginning of an action of a being out of objective causes is always, with respect to these determining grounds, a *first beginning*, although the same action is, in the series of appearances, only a *subalternate beginning*, which has to be preceded by a state of the cause which determines that cause, and which is itself determined in the same way by an immediately preceding cause: so that in rational beings (or in general in any beings, provided that their causality is determined in them as things in themselves) one can conceive of a faculty for beginning a series of states spontaneously, without falling into contradiction with the laws of nature. For the relation of an action to the objective grounds of reason is not a temporal relation; here, that which determines the causality does not precede the action as regards time, because such determining grounds do not represent the relation of objects to the senses (and so to causes within appearances), but rather they represent determining causes as things in themselves, which are not subject to temporal conditions. Hence the action can be regarded as a first beginning with respect to the causality

of reason, but can nonetheless at the same time be seen as a mere subordinated beginning with respect to the series of appearances, and can without contradiction be considered in the former respect as free, in the latter (since the action is mere appearance) as subject to natural necessity. (*P* 4:346–7)

To see just how paradoxical Kant's "solution" is, consider a concrete example: raising my hand in a classroom in order to be recognized by a teacher. Raising my hand is an event that takes place in the world of appearance. We know *a priori* (according to the Second Analogy) that it is necessarily determined by preceding natural causes. Kant even affirms that "if we could investigate all the appearances of [a human being's] power of choice down to their basis, then there would be no human action that we could not predict with certainty, and recognize as necessary given its preceding conditions" (*CPR* A 550/B 578). Consequently, we could (in principle) predict the raising of my hand with certainty and recognize that it is the result of preceding natural causes – and yet say that from an "intelligible" point of view, it is the result of a free choice.[26]

There is another way of seeing the paradoxical character of Kant's attempt to reconcile strict determinism in the natural world and freedom. Freedom is "the faculty of beginning a state **from itself**" (*CPR* A 533/B 561). How are we to make sense of a *non-temporal beginning* – a non-temporal beginning that has effects in the temporal world of appearance? Insofar as actions and events are part of the natural world, we have criteria for individuating and identifying them. I can distinguish my actions from other people's actions. But how do we individuate acts of non-temporal and non-spatial freedom? What are the criteria for specifying what is *my* freedom and *my* power of choice as distinguished from *your* freedom? The criteria for distinguishing different acts of freedom (the non-temporal beginnings) clearly cannot be empirical. Freedom and nature are so heterogeneous that it is difficult to grasp that they can even relate. But according to Kant, if we do not accept the concept of the thing in itself, then we cannot give an account of transcendental freedom – the ground of practical freedom.[27]

The heterogeneity between freedom and natural necessity was a troubling issue for many of Kant's contemporary critics. It became a major – perhaps *the* major – problem for German idealism. Fichte, Schelling, and Hegel are critical of the way in which Kant distinguished between appearance and thing in itself in order to show how freedom and natural necessity can be reconciled. Each sought to rethink the relation of nature and freedom without endorsing the Kantian distinction between appearance and thing in itself. Kant himself came to realize that he needed to tackle the issue of how to *mediate* between freedom and natural necessity. He addresses this issue in the *Critique of the Power of Judgment*, where he claims that the power of judgment

> provides the mediating concept between the concepts of nature and the concept of freedom, which makes possible the transition from the purely theoretical to the purely practical, from lawfulness in accordance with the former to the final end in accordance with the latter, in the concept of a **purposiveness** of nature; for thereby is the possibility of the final end, which can become actual only in nature and in accord with its laws, cognized. (*CJ* 5:196)

This passage from the published introduction to the third *Critique* indicates that Kant was keenly aware of the *need* for "a mediating concept between the concepts of nature and the concept of freedom."

In the first (unpublished) introduction to the third *Critique*, Kant speaks of philosophy as the system of rational cognition and tells us that "this real system of philosophy itself . . . cannot be divided except into **theoretical** and **practical** philosophy; thus, the one part must be the philosophy of nature, the other that of morals, the first of which is also empirical, the second of which, however (since freedom absolutely cannot be an object of experience), can never contain anything other than the pure principles *a priori*" (*CJ* 20:195). Theoretical and practical philosophy are *unified* in a *single* system of philosophy. How does Kant understand the systematic unity of philosophy – specifically the unity of reason? Near the end of the first *Critique*, in the section entitled "The architectonic of pure reason," Kant writes: "By an **architectonic** I understand the art of systems. . . . Under the government of reason our cognitions cannot at all constitute a rhapsody but must constitute a system, in which alone they can support and advance its essential ends. I understand by a system, however, the unity of the manifold cognitions under one idea" (*CPR* A 832/B 860). Kant draws the analogy between the unity of a system and the unity of an *organism* – that is, an animal body. "The whole is therefore articulated (*articulatio*) and not heaped together (*coacervatio*); it can, to be sure, grow internally (*per intus susceptionem*) but not externally (*per appositionem*), like an animal body, whose growth does not add a limb but rather makes each limb stronger and fitter for its end without any alteration of proportion" (*CPR* A 833/B 861). This analogy between the unity of the system of reason and the growth of an organism turns out to be fundamental for the third *Critique*. It is one of several reasons why Kant focuses on the significance of purpose (*Zweck*) and purposiveness (*Zweckmässigkeit*) in organisms. Judgment – specifically *reflecting judgment*, which Kant distinguishes from understanding and reason – enables us to understand this systematic unity.[28]

> Now although there is an incalculable gulf fixed between the domain of the concept of nature, as the sensible, and the domain of the concept of freedom, as the supersensible, so that from the former to the latter (thus by means of the theoretical use of reason) no transition is possible, just as if there were so many different worlds, the first of which can have no influence on the second: yet the latter **should** have an influence on the former, namely the concept of freedom should make the end that is imposed by its laws real in the sensible world; and nature must consequently also be able to be conceived in such a way that the lawfulness of its form is at least in agreement with the possibility of the ends that are to be realized in it in accordance with the laws of freedom. – Thus there must still be a ground of the **unity** of the supersensible that grounds nature with that which the concept of freedom contains practically, the concept of which, even if it does not suffice for cognition of it either theoretically or practically, and thus has no proper domain of its own, nevertheless makes possible the transition from the manner of thinking in accordance with the principles of the one to that in accordance with the principles of the other. (*CJ* 5:176)[29]

Reflecting judgment – which has no proper domain of its own – presumably makes the transition between the theoretical and practical domains and unifies them.

If, however, one expects that a major theme of the third *Critique* will be an explication of how the concepts of nature and freedom are reconciled in a unified system of philosophy, one will be disappointed. The Critique of the Aesthetic Power of Judgment and the Critique of the Teleological Power of Judgment (the two parts of the *Critique of the Power of Judgment*) are tangentially related to the problem of mediating between nature and freedom. Kant has very little to say explicitly about the relation of nature and freedom, and what he does say hardly advances our understanding beyond what he has claimed in the first two *Critiques*. Reflecting judgment is supposed to unite nature and freedom, but Kant does not explain how reflecting judgment accomplishes this. Most of what Kant says about freedom in the third *Critique* concerns *practical freedom* (and specifically moral freedom): that is, the freedom that is grounded in *transcendental freedom*. Kant repeats what he said in the first *Critique*: namely, that the power of choice of practical freedom – and specifically moral freedom – is based on the idea of transcendental freedom (*CJ* 5:343). But the really hard task is to make sense of *how* the non-temporal causality of transcendental freedom determines what happens in the temporal natural world. Unless we can make this intelligible, the very foundation of practical freedom is called into question. Kant repeatedly insists that practical freedom is grounded in transcendental freedom, and the *only* way to make room for freedom is to accept transcendental idealism. This entails affirming the fundamental distinction between appearance and thing in itself. Even if one claims that all Kant means by "transcendental freedom" is the *possibility* of freedom and that it is only with the *Foundations of the Metaphysics of Morals* and the *Critique of Practical Reason* that we find a full explication of practical freedom, this does not advance our understanding of how one and the same action can be explained by a necessary chain of natural causes and yet also be the effect of transcendental freedom.[30] It does not help to say that we have two different *methods* or *perspectives* for dealing with one and the same event or action, because this does not *explain how* the event or action, can be one and the same. Kant never qualifies his claim that nature (whether understood from a transcendental or an empirical perspective) excludes freedom. *Pure theoretical and practical reason can never be accounted for by the appeal to nature.* If we understand naturalism (whether in its metaphysical or empirical variety) to be the view that we can explain everything that *is* — including human reason and freedom — by an appeal to nature, then Kant stands as one of the greatest opponents of naturalism.[31]

There is, however, another key problem concerning the concept of nature that Kant does address in the third *Critique*.[32] This concerns the role of purpose (*Zweck*) and purposiveness (*Zweckmässigkeit*) in nature. Kant had already raised the issue of purposiveness in the first *Critique*. Purposiveness is the key idea of the physico-theological proof of the existence of God. Kant rejects this proof, as well as the ontological and cosmological proofs, because they all seek to transcend the limits of possible experience. But he acknowledges the power and allure of the argument that claims that there is an intelligent designer of the world.

> This proof always deserves to be named with respect. It is the oldest, clearest and the most appropriate to common human reason. It enlivens the study of nature, just as it gets its existence from this study and through it receives ever renewed force. It brings in ends and aims where they would not have been discovered by our observation itself, and extends our information about nature through the guiding thread of a particular unity whose principle is outside nature. (*CPR* A 623/B 651)

The concept of purposiveness does *not* warrant the proof of the existence of a supreme intelligent designer and creator – God. Nevertheless, the concept of purposiveness, interpreted as a *regulative idea*, turns out to be absolutely essential for understanding organisms as natural beings.[33] Initially, this might seem perplexing. On the basis of the Second Analogy and the third antinomy in the first *Critique*, we might be left with the impression that natural causality consists of a *mechanical* system that is *sufficient* to explain everything that comprises the domain of nature. How can we reconcile the mechanism of nature with the claim that some natural beings (organisms) can only be understood as purposes?[34] This is a primary subject of the second part of the third *Critique* – the Critique of the Teleological Power of Judgment.[35]

Before turning to the details of Kant's view, I want to present informally the basic problem that Kant is confronting. Kant increasingly came to realize that the depiction of nature in the first *Critique* was incomplete.[36] Many issues were left open that needed to be addressed – especially the questions concerning those natural objects that we call "organisms." When dealing with the transcendental and empirical science of nature in the first *Critique*, Kant primarily had Newtonian physics in mind as the paradigm of an empirical natural science with its universal and necessary natural laws. In the *Metaphysical Foundations of Natural Science*, he focuses on the foundations of Newtonian science. But Kant, who had a deep interest in the biological sciences of his time, came to realize that the first *Critique* did not provide a sufficient basis for understanding the foundations of biology. "Organisms" ("organized beings") are part of nature, but "mechanism" cannot account for organisms. To account for organisms, we need to appeal to the concept of purpose.[37] The Second Analogy does not *logically entail* a mechanistic account of causality, but it certainly suggests that this is the only way to understand nature's causality. In the third *Critique*, Kant is keenly aware that normally, when we speak about a purpose or end (*Zweck*), we are referring to artificial objects that we deliberately intend or design. He emphasizes, however, that there is a difference between artificial objects and natural organic beings. Hannah Ginsborg succinctly states Kant's essential claim about organic creatures.

> It is a central and often repeated claim in Kant's Critique of Teleological Judgment that we must regard organisms as purposes. We cannot understand their possibility, Kant says, unless we invoke the notion of design. At the same time, however, he insists that we cannot assert that organisms are in fact the product of design. On the contrary, we both do, and must, regard them as natural products rather than as artefacts. Thus while the concept of purpose plays an indispensable role in our understanding of the organic world, its use is, in Kant's terminology, regulative rather than constitutive: it

belongs to reflective judgment, rather than to determining judgment. The concept of purpose plays a merely heuristic role, serving as a guiding-thread in our observation and investigation of organisms without being invoked to explain directly how they come to be. (Ginsborg 2015: 255)[38]

When we speak of an organism as a purpose, we mean a *natural* purpose (*Naturzweck*).[39] Purposiveness is *not* a category of the understanding (*Verstand*), and there is no mention of purposiveness in the Analytic of Principles in the first *Critique*. So the challenge that Kant faces is how to reconcile the *necessity* of appealing to purpose and purposiveness when dealing with organisms (or parts of organisms) without violating the fundamental claims of his transcendental idealism.[40] Unlike the natural objects of physics, which can be explained by mechanistic causal principles, we cannot understand organisms *unless* we appeal to the concept of purposiveness. The following example illustrates why Kant thinks organisms cannot be understood solely by an appeal to mechanistic principles:

> For if one adduces, e.g., the structure of a bird, the hollowness of its bones, the placement of its wings for movement and its tail for steering, etc., one says that mere *nexus effectivus* in nature, without the help of a special kind of causality, namely that of ends (*nexus finalis*), this is all in the highest degree contingent: i.e., that nature, considered as a mere mechanism, could have formed itself in a thousand different ways without hitting precisely upon the unity in accordance with such a rule, and that it is therefore only outside the concept of nature, not within it, that one could have even the least ground *a priori* for hoping to find such a principle. (*CJ* 5:360)

Quarfood elucidates this distinction between *nexus effectivus* and *nexus finalis*:

> The organism with its typical features (reproduction, growth, regeneration) exhibits a kind of causal structure where effective causes seem to be reciprocally conditioned by their own effects. The organism is thus in a way both cause and effect of itself. In order to handle this situation we resort to the *nexus finalis* known to us from the production of a work of art. So it might appear that Kant just presupposes that organisms are artefacts. But in presenting the criteria for calling a thing a "natural purpose" (*Naturzweck*, Kant's term for a teleologically conceived organism) he explicitly adds the requirement that the thing produces itself. The notion of an external agency forming the thing according to a plan (which is how the production of artefacts is conceived) is replaced by an internal teleology in which each part "must be thought of as an organ that *produces* the other parts (consequently each produces the others reciprocally)" (*CJ* 5:374). For something to be a natural purpose, it must be "an *organized* and *self-organizing*

being" (*CJ* 5:374), and this self-organization is not a matter of replacing the external agent with an internal, conscious agency. Even though we describe the organism with locutions borrowed from the sphere of intentional production, "one says far too little about nature and its capacity in organized products if one calls this *an analogue of art*" (*CJ* 5:374), "strictly speaking, the organization of nature is therefore not analogous with any causality that we know" (*CJ* 5:375). (Quarfood 2004: 147)

When we claim that an organic creature is a natural purpose (*Naturzweck*), we are judging from the perspective of *reflective judgment* and not from that of the understanding (*Verstand*) or reason (*Vernunft*). Kant characterizes a natural purpose as follows: "I would say provisionally that a thing exists as a natural end (*Naturzweck*) **if it is cause and effect of itself** (although in a twofold sense), for in this there lies a causality the likes of which cannot be connected with the mere concept of nature without ascribing an end to it, but which in that case also can be conceived without contradiction but cannot be comprehended" (*CJ* 5:370–1).[41] In the introduction to the *Critique of the Power of Judgment,* in a section entitled "On the power of judgment as an *a priori* legislative faculty," Kant defines the power of judgment (*Urteilskraft*) in general as "the faculty for thinking the particular as contained under the universal" (*CJ* 5:179). He then distinguishes two ways in which this faculty can be *exercised*: determining and reflecting. The two ways are defined as follows:

> If the universal (the rule, the principle, the law) is given, then the power of judgment, which subsumes the particular under it (even when, as a transcendental power of judgment, it provides the conditions *a priori* in accordance with which alone anything can be subsumed under that universal), is **determining**. If, however, only the particular is given, for which the universal is to be found, then the power of judgment is merely **reflecting**. (*CJ* 5:179)

The power of judgment is a *single* faculty that can be *exercised* in two different ways. In the first *Critique*, Kant was primarily concerned with determining judgments, especially the determining judgments of the understanding (*Verstand*). In the third *Critique*, the reflecting exercise of judgment is his primary concern.[42] Kant follows his architectonic design, dividing the third *Critique* into three sections: Analytic, Dialectic, and Methodology. He presents the antinomies of teleological judgment in the Dialectic, but these are antinomies of reflecting judgment.

The **first maxim** of the power of judgment is the **thesis**: All generation of material things and their forms must be judged as possible in accordance with merely mechanical laws. The **second maxim** is the **antithesis**. Some products of material nature cannot be judged as possible according to merely mechanical laws (judging them requires an entirely different law of causality, namely that of final causes. (*CJ* 5:387)

Both of these maxims are regulative principles of the power of reflecting judgment. They do not make claims about the *constitutive* principles of the possibility of the objects themselves. Kant argues that "if one were to transform these regulative principles for research into constitutive principles of the possibility of the objects themselves" (*CJ* 5:387), they would read:

> **Thesis**: All generation of material things is possible in accordance with mere mechanical laws.
> **Antithesis**: Some generation of such things is not possible in accordance with merely mechanical **laws**. (*CJ* 5:387)

The first formulation of the antinomy refers to *judging* in both the thesis and the antithesis, but the second formulation does *not* refer to judging. Let's label the first formulation T and A and the second formulation as T' and A'. Commenting on Kant's formulation of the antinomy, Quarfood writes:

> As soon as we clearly understand that we have nothing but maxims for judging (*Beurteilung*) here, not principles determining objects *a priori*, the antinomy is dissolved, because the maxims T and A do not have to be taken as contradictory. The thesis just says that all "products" of nature must be judged according to mechanism, which should be applied "so far as I can," and that is not, according to how Kant presents the matter here, incompatible with the other maxim, which says that we occasionally should reflect on some "products" using a different principle, that of final causes (*CJ* 5:387–8).
>
> At this point, it seems that this is all there is to the solution. The antinomy of teleological judgment is a conflict between two putative constitutive principles of reason. The solution consists in pointing out that the principles have the more modest status of being regulative maxims for reflective judgment. (Quarfood 2004: 164)[43]

The more closely one examines what Kant says about purpose and purposiveness as relating to organisms, the more perplexing it becomes. Purpose is not a category of the understanding (*Verstand*), and it is *not* an empirical concept. Yet, in the third *Critique*, Kant claims that purpose is absolutely essential for understanding organisms. He *appears* to resolve the antinomy of teleological judgment by claiming that T and A are maxims of *reflective* judgment. These maxims are heuristic principles that guide research. In Kant's example of the bird, the appeal to the *nexus finalis* does not make an ontological claim about the nature of birds. Consider a more contemporary example. Before the discovery of the structure of DNA, a teleological characterization of the heredity of genes guided research. But once the discovery was made, the way was open for an explanation of inherited characteristics by an appeal to a mechanistic causal account of how genes are transmitted through generations. *But this way of showing the compatibility of the appeal to purposes and functions with mechanical natural causality is not Kant's position.* He is *not* saying that speaking of organisms as purposes or speaking of the functions of an organism is *merely* an aid for discovering the mechanical causes of organisms. He makes a different and much *stronger* claim – that it is *impossible* for human beings to give an account of the genesis and structure of organisms by appealing *exclusively* to mechanistic principles.

> For it is quite certain that we can never adequately come to know the organized beings and their internal possibility in accordance with merely mechanical principles of nature, let alone explain them; and indeed this is so certain that we can boldly say that it would be absurd for humans even to make such an attempt or to hope that there may yet arise a Newton who could make comprehensible even the generation of a blade of grass according to natural laws that no intention has ordered; rather, we must absolutely deny this insight to human beings. (*CJ* 5: 400)

Although Kant was a fierce opponent of dogmatism throughout his career, this passage sounds like sheer dogmatism. He constantly reaffirms the claim that organisms are mechanically inexplicable, but he never provides adequate reasons to justify this claim.[44] If we consider the achievements of contemporary biological science – especially since the advent of molecular biology and its remarkable developments – we have the beginnings of a *non-teleological* account of the origins and structure of organisms. We need to be extremely wary of *a priori* claims about what is inexplicable in the progressive development of the natural sciences (including biology).

There is a deep tension in the Critique of the Power of Teleological Judgment. On the one hand, Kant frequently speaks of the appeal to purposiveness as "merely" a maxim of reflecting judgment that guides our recognition and understanding of organisms. From this perspective, purposiveness is "a subjective fundamental principle merely for the reflecting power of judgment, hence a maxim that reason prescribes to it" (*CJ* 5:398).

Purposiveness is not an *objective* feature of nature in the way in which the categories of the understanding provide us with formal objective features of empirical reality. Purposiveness, as a regulative principle, carries no ontological commitment about what organisms are as natural products.[45] It tells us only that, from a *human* point of view, we must understand organisms in this way. As Ginsborg emphasizes, "We invoke a teleological mode of judging "to bring nature under principles of observation and investigation, without presuming to *explain* it accordingly (*CJ*, §61, 360)" (Ginsborg 2015: 259).

Terry Pinkard provides a summary of this strain in Kant's thinking. He writes:

> On the one hand, the world as we must experience it requires a mechanical explanation. On the other hand, we cannot make sense of organic life without bringing in the conception of teleology (of what an organ is for). As with several of Kant's other antinomies, his solution was to say that although we find it unavoidable to ascribe purposes to organisms, we nonetheless cannot make sense of that within the way we must think of the world as a causal system. Our ascription of purposes has only subjective validity, something "we" must do in studying things – which we find unavoidable – and is not a feature of the things being studied. (Pinkard 2012: 23)

In paragraph 79, entitled "Whether teleology must be treated as part of the doctrine of nature," Kant raises the question: "Does [teleology] belong to natural science (properly so called)?" And he answers that it does *not* "seem to belong in natural science, which requires determining and not merely reflecting principles in order to provide objective grounds for natural effects" (*CJ* 5:417). He goes on to clarify what he means as follows:

> In fact, nothing is gained for the theory of nature or the mechanical explanation of its phenomena by its efficient causes when they are considered in light of the relations of ends to one another. Strictly speaking, positing ends of nature in its products, insofar as it constitutes a system in accordance with teleological concepts, belongs only to the *description of nature*, which is composed in accordance with a particular guideline, in which reason certainly plays a role that is magnificently instructive and purposive in many respects, but in which it *provides no information at all* about the origination and the inner possibility of these forms, although it is that with which theoretical natural science is properly concerned. (*CJ* 5:417, emphasis added)[46]

On the other hand, Kant claims that it is absolutely necessary to think of organisms as *Naturzwecke* (natural purposes). For example, Kant writes:

It might always be possible that in, e.g., an animal body, many parts could be conceived as consequences of merely mechanical laws (such as skin, hair, and bones). Yet the cause that provides the appropriate material, modifies it, forms it, and deposits it in its appropriate place must always be judged teleologically, so that *everything in it must be considered as organized*, and everything is also, in a certain relation to the thing itself, an organ in turn. (*CJ* 5:377, emphasis added)

If it is true that both an animal body and its organs *must* be judged as self-organized (as *Naturzweck*), then it looks like this principle does not "merely" heuristically guide research but tells us something *substantive* about the distinctive nature of organisms. Furthermore, Kant insists that what distinguishes organisms from objects that are intentionally designed is that they exhibit *internal purposiveness*, which he sharply distinguishes from external purposiveness. As Quarfood notes, "If a teleological point of view is a condition for biology, teleology should rather be seen as a constitutive principle for this science" (Quarfood 2004: 119).[47] It is almost as if Kant wants to have his cake and eat it too. He wants to insist that teleological judgments are reflecting and not determining judgments; yet he claims that these teleological judgments tell us something that is *necessarily true* about organisms. What is even more perplexing is that Kant seems to allow for the possibility that organisms are mechanically produced, while also maintaining that they are mechanically inexplicable.

Kant's understanding of nature leaves us with a number of tensions and unresolved problems. Whether we conceive of nature from a transcendental or an empirical perspective, it is clear that nature consists of universal and necessary deterministic laws. There is no place in nature for freedom. This is why the resolution of the third antinomy is so important for Kant's entire critical project. Unless we can establish that there is transcendental freedom, we cannot account for practical freedom. Without establishing that there is practical freedom, we cannot account for morality and human responsibility. If human beings were *exclusively* natural beings, this would entail that freedom is an illusion, and we would be committed to fatalism. Allowing for the *possibility* of freedom is one of the major aims of the *Critique of Pure Reason*, and this requires establishing the boundaries of human knowledge and showing the impossibility of any theoretical knowledge of a transcendent reality. The Copernican Revolution requires that the natural world *must* conform to the *a priori* conditions that we, as rational beings, impose on the world.

Articulating and justifying this thesis is the task of the first division of the first *Critique* – the Transcendental Doctrine of Elements. Kant consistently argues that transcendental idealism is the *only* way to establish the *a priori* conditions for our knowledge of the natural world and allow for the possibility of freedom at the same time. Transcendental idealism requires the acceptance of the distinction between appearance (the world that we can know) and the thing in itself (which it is impossible to know). This sharp distinction between the phenomenal natural world of appearance and an unknowable noumenal world of the thing in itself troubled many of Kant's contemporary critics and was a source of provocation for the entire tradition of German idealism. Fichte, Schelling, and Hegel all rejected the way in which Kant draws the distinctions between phenomena and noumena, as well as appearance and thing in itself. Kant is adamant when he insists that the very possibility of transcendental freedom is dependent on acknowledging the thing in itself. Throughout his critical philosophy, Kant had to confront the problem of how to mediate between what he takes to be heterogeneous: sensibility and understanding, intuitions and concepts, phenomena and noumena, theoretical and practical reason – and especially freedom and nature. I have argued that Kant never succeeds in showing us how the causality of nature and the causality of freedom are compatible. At best, he provides an *abstract* solution in the third antinomy. But when we ask how one and the same event or action can be the result of a necessary series of temporal natural causes and the result of a non-natural non-temporal transcendental freedom, we are left with a mystery.

Furthermore, although Kant, in the *Critique of the Power of Judgment*, tells us that the reflecting judgment, which he distinguishes from understanding (*Verstand*) and reason (*Vernunft*), *mediates* between nature and freedom, he does not adequately explain how such a mediation is accomplished. He is acutely aware that the causality of nature that he describes and justifies in the first *Critique* is inadequate for accounting for biological organisms. Organisms (self-organized beings) are mechanically inexplicable, yet they are products of nature. This is why we need to introduce the concept of purpose in order to understand organisms. Yet the problem Kant faces is that purpose is neither a category of the understanding nor an empirical concept. In this respect, there is an analogy with the concept of freedom, which is neither a category of the understanding nor an empirical concept. It is only by appealing to what is "beyond" natural causality that we claim that organisms are purposes. Once again, we discover a deep tension. On the one hand, Kant claims that the appeal to final causes is a heuristic regulative principle guiding our discovery about what is distinctive in organisms. On the other, he claims that the concept of purpose is "absolutely necessary" to describe organisms. It is almost as if Kant is suggesting that purpose functions *as if* it were a constitutive feature of organisms, but that it is not *really* a constitutive principle.

The source of Kant's problems is the way he characterizes nature in the first *Critique* – consisting of universal and necessary laws that exclude the possibility of freedom or purpose. For all his revisions of how we are to understand nature in the third *Critique*, Kant never revises his account of natural necessity in the first *Critique*. It is this hard deterministic way of thinking of the laws of nature that is the source of so many unresolved problems. Kant sets out to show that we can correct the deficiencies of Spinoza's and Hume's conception of nature. He rejects Spinoza's rationalistic metaphysics – a metaphysics that seeks to attain knowledge of what is *beyond* experience. At the same time, Kant seeks to correct what he takes to be the inadequacies of Hume's psychological conception of experience – Hume's doctrine that all perceptions consist of impressions and ideas. The key to overcoming the deficiencies of Spinoza's and Hume's conception of nature is the Copernican Revolution, which enables us to develop a complete system of the pure *a priori* principles of transcendental philosophy. Nevertheless, Kant leaves us with a series of deep perplexities and unresolved tensions. These concern the precise relation between natural necessity and freedom. Does it really make sense to claim that one and the same event can be explained by natural necessity and yet can also be seen as a result of the "causality of freedom"? Furthermore, although he claims that the concept of purpose (*Zweck*) is "absolutely essential" for describing organisms, he conceives of purpose *only* as a regulative principle, not a constitutive one. Purposiveness is *only* how we human beings understand biological organisms. He never gives a satisfactory account of how purpose is *absolutely essential* for understanding organisms but is *not* a constitutive principle of biological nature. In the next chapter, we will see how Hegel seeks to resolve these Kantian perplexities in order to develop a more adequate understanding of nature.

4

Hegel: Nature and *Geist*

Kant's critical philosophy is based upon a whole series of dichotomies – sensibility and understanding, receptivity and spontaneity, intuitions and concepts, understanding (*Verstand*) and reason (*Vernunft*), appearance and thing in itself, phenomena and noumena, the conditioned and the unconditioned, necessity and freedom, finite and infinite, theoretical philosophy and practical philosophy, determining judgment and reflecting judgment – and especially, nature and freedom. At times, Kant describes the opposing elements of these dichotomies as heterogeneous. How are these elements related to each other? In all three *Critiques* Kant struggles to show how the oppositions can be related to each other. Nevertheless, during his lifetime, critics began to question what they took to be untenable dualisms in Kant's philosophy. Furthermore, Kant scholars – right up to the present – fiercely debate how these dichotomies are to be interpreted and how their opposing terms are related to each other.

These debates are not mere scholarly quibbles. They indicate how one understands and evaluates the success of Kant's critical project. For example, can we really *separate* the contributions of receptivity and spontaneity in our knowledge of the world? Is it correct to say – as McDowell claims – that we cannot even make a notational distinction between the contributions of receptivity and spontaneity?[1] Do phenomena and noumena designate two different ontological realms, or do they refer to the *same* thing understood in *different* ways? Is there a unity of reason that encompasses both theoretical and practical philosophy? The problematic aspect of Kant's dichotomies is most evident when he contrasts nature and *reason*, and nature and *freedom*. From Kant's Copernican Revolution, we learn that understanding (*Verstand*) provides the *a priori* categories and principles that constitute the possibility of experience and the conditions for knowledge of nature. Kant defines the pure *a priori* science of nature in such a manner that nature consists of universal and necessary deterministic causal laws. There is no place for freedom, and consequently no place for morality, in this natural realm. In the third *Critique*, we learn that the concept of internal purpose (*Zweck*) is absolutely essential for identifying and describing living organisms. But this concept is only regulative, *not* constitutive of nature. There is no place for purpose or final causes in Kant's depiction of nature and natural laws in the first *Critique*. In the third *Critique*, we learn that the appeal to purpose is the way that we (human beings) must *judge* natural organisms. However, this judging is a reflecting judging, not a determining one.

Kant's contemporaries argued that his dichotomies lead to inescapable *aporias*. Not even Kant's most fervent admirers were satisfied with the distinction between appearance and thing in itself. Nevertheless, Kant claims that this distinction is fundamental for the articulation and defense of his transcendental idealism. Philosophers of German idealism – especially Fichte, Schelling, and Hegel – attempted to *rethink* the problematic and unsatisfactory Kantian dichotomies. Hegel's attempt was more systematic and rigorous than either Fichte's or Schelling's, although he appropriated a great deal from their critiques of the Kantian dichotomies.[2]

Before turning to the details of Hegel's concept of nature, I want to outline four different interrelated goals for orienting my discussion: (1) to present a sketch of Hegel's master strategy in dealing with dichotomies; (2) to indicate what Hegel appropriates from Schelling's early *Naturphilosophie*; (3) to show what Hegel took to be Kant's *positive* contribution in the third *Critique* – the philosophical significance of "internal purposiveness"; (4) to explore how Hegel conceives of the relation of the nature of human beings and the nature of nonhuman animals. All four goals will help to orient our understanding of the role of nature in Hegel's systematic philosophy.

Hegel employs a master strategy in dealing with philosophical oppositions and dichotomies. He takes these oppositions seriously, including the Kantian dichotomies; but, unlike Kant, he does not take them to be fixed and permanent. Hegel seeks to show that when we think through these dichotomies, we come to grasp that they are *moments* within a *single dynamic whole* – the whole that *encompasses* these opposing elements. Consider the famous opening dichotomy that initiates the *Science of Logic* (1812–16). We start with the apparent opposition between being and nothing. If we focus on the meaning of pure being – being without any determination – and hold fast to the purity of being, we discover that it is pure indeterminateness and emptiness. In short, pure being, "the indeterminate immediate, is in fact *nothing*, and neither more nor less than *nothing*" (Hegel 1969: 82). Now suppose that we focus our attention on nothing, pure nothing, a "complete emptiness, absence of all determination and content" (Hegel 1969: 82). Pure nothing turns out to be identical with pure being. The realization that pure being and pure nothing are the same, or identical, is not the end of the matter. We grasp that being and nothing are also *different* from each other; they are identical and nonidentical.

> *Pure being* and *pure nothing* are, therefore, the same. What is the truth is neither being nor nothing, but that being – does not pass over but has passed over – into nothing, and nothing into being. But it is equally true that they are not undistinguished from each other, that, on the contrary, they are not the same, that they are absolutely distinct, and yet that they are unseparated and inseparable and that each immediately *vanishes in its opposite*. Their truth is, therefore, this movement of the immediate vanishing of the one in the other: *becoming*, a movement in which both are distinguished, but by a difference which has equally immediately resolved itself. (Hegel 1969: 82–3)[3]

When Hegel speaks of movement and becoming, he is not referring to any temporal or empirical movement. It is a *logical* movement that asserts the identity and nonidentity of being and nothing. If we simply focus on being and nothing without grasping the logical movement between them, we are dealing with reified abstractions.

This opening movement of the *Science of Logic* is intimately related to Hegel's speculative identity thesis: a thesis already present in one of Hegel's earliest publications, the *Difference Between Fichte's and Schelling's System of Philosophy* (1801), often referred to as *Differenzschrift*, and is developed and refined in the *Phenomenology of Spirit* (1807) and the *Science of Logic*.[4] Karen Ng notes that "speculative identity refers to the relation between subjective and objective elements that is at stake in any attempt to understand the nature of knowledge" (Ng 2020: 69). *Speculative* identity is contrasted with *reflection* and with "common sense" (*der gesunde Menschenverstand*). Hegel characterizes modern philosophers, including Locke, Hume, Descartes, Leibniz, and especially Kant, as committed to a philosophy of reflection that is at once *formal* and *dualistic*.

> In one form or another, all of these thinkers construct their philosophies based on an assumed dualism and opposition between, roughly, mind and

world (subject and object), and the distinct causal orders that each represents. This fixed opposition is never given independent justification and, moreover, results in a situation where these dualisms lead to skeptical or dogmatic conclusions concerning the possibility of their nonetheless necessary reconciliation, where the impossibility of reconciliation would amount to the impossibility of knowledge. (Ng 2020: 69)

If we return to the Kantian dichotomies, we can see Hegel's master strategy at work. In Hegel's view, Kant is *right* in drawing these dichotomies and insisting that the elements comprising them are distinct. However, because Kant is entrapped in the philosophy of reflection, he fails to realize how the opposing elements are also identical with each other; that is, he fails to recognize a dialectical movement between these opposing elements that overcomes these dualisms. For example, although we initially *distinguish* between phenomena and noumena, we discover that they are also *identical*. To use a Hegelian turn of phrase, we are confronted with a distinction that is no distinction. Or, to use a Heideggerian turn of phrase, the distinctness and opposition of these dichotomies is equiprimordial with their identity and unity. Of course, it is never sufficient simply to state that there is both identity and nonidentity. Such a statement is, in Hegel's view, merely abstract and consequently false. The philosophical task is to show *concretely*, to demonstrate systematically, this identity and nonidentity.

How do these brief remarks about the thesis of speculative identity relate to Hegel's concept of Nature?[5] Let us return to the Kantian dichotomies – nature and *reason*, nature and *freedom*, and nature and *purpose*. Each of the terms opposed to nature – *reason*, *freedom*, and *purpose* – are manifestations of what Hegel calls *Geist* (Spirit).[6] We can therefore speak of the opposition and dichotomy between Nature and *Geist*.[7] However, taking account of Hegel's master strategy, we come to realize that Nature is not only *distinct* from, and stands *opposed* to, *Geist*; it is also *identical* with *Geist*. Appreciating the sense in which Nature is both distinguished from and identical with *Geist* has the utmost significance for Hegel's understanding of Nature. There are interpreters of Hegel who stress the distinctness and opposition between Nature and *Geist*; they privilege *Geist*, and thus characterize Hegel as an anti-naturalist.[8] These Kantian Hegelians insist upon a radical distinction between Nature and the normativity of reason. Their interpretation is *not wrong*, but it is one-sided insofar as it neglects Hegel's own insistence on the identity of Nature and *Geist*. The Kantian Hegelian commentators fail to do justice to *both* the nonidentity and identity of Nature and *Geist*. They also tend to downplay the way in which Hegel's philosophy "combines a distinctive strand of Aristotelian naturalism with core insights from Kant's transcendental idealism, incorporating concepts of teleology and function alongside conceptions of self-consciousness and freedom" (Ng 2020: 4).[9] Terry Pinkard summarizes the sense in which we as human beings are *natural creatures* for Hegel: "We are self-conscious, self-interpreting animals, natural creatures whose 'nonnaturalness' is not a metaphysical difference (as that between spiritual and physical 'stuff') or the exercise of a special form of causality. Rather, our status as *geistig*, as 'minded' creatures is a status we 'give' to ourselves in the sense that it is a practical achievement" (Pinkard 2012: 18). Hegel, like Aristotle, stresses our continuity with the rest of the natural world. Below, I will be exploring the sense in which Nature and *Geist* are identical and at the same time stand in opposition to each other. If Nature and *Geist* are identical, then Hegel – who starts with the Kantian dichotomies – ends up with a radically anti-Kantian position. Kant's transcendental idealism is based upon the sharp dichotomies between nature and reason, nature and freedom, nature and final causes. Hegel argues that these are not fixed dichotomies but *moments* in a dynamic unified whole.[10]

The second perspective for understanding Hegel's concept of Nature is to see how much his conception shares with Schelling's early *Naturphilosophie*. To set the context for the influence of Schelling on Hegel, one needs to dig deeper into other philosophical currents that were shaping German philosophy in the late eighteenth century. With the growth of philosophical Romanticism, there was a reaction against the type of Enlightenment thinking represented by Kant. Specifically, there was a strong reaction to the mechanistic and lifeless conception of nature that emerges from the *Critique of Pure Reason*. In opposition to a conception of nature that consists of fixed universal and necessary deterministic laws, the Romantic critics of Kant stressed the dynamic and organic character of nature based on the concept of life. The Romantic opposition to Kant is exemplified by the heated debates between Herder (Kant's former student) and Kant. Herder was one of the thinkers inspired by Spinoza in the Pantheist controversy initiated by Jacobi. Against Kant, Herder advocated a Spinozistic naturalism, although he interpreted Spinoza in a novel way. Beth Lord describes Herder's conception of Spinoza's substance as "the *dynamic* immanent unity of an *active* being." She writes:

> Herder ... presents Spinoza as a vitalist concerned to promote a single dynamic system of God and nature, the force of which powers the progressive development of an ever-changing universe. Herder made it more difficult for Kant and others to refute Spinoza, but also more important that they do so; Spinoza could no longer be dismissed as an atheist, but had

to be considered as a serious contributor to debates on the organization of nature and God's place in it. This way of reading Spinoza was to supersede Jacobi's, setting the terms for German Romantic and Idealist uses of Spinoza. (Lord 2011: 57)[11]

This conception of a dynamic living nature – of nature as *both objective and subjective* – is also integral to Schelling's early philosophy of nature – his *Naturphilosophie*. In the *First Outline of a System of the Philosophy of Nature* (1799), Schelling presents the following conception of nature:

> *Nature* as a mere *product* (*natura naturata*) we call Nature as *object* (with this alone all empiricism deals). *Nature as productivity (natura naturans)* we call *Nature as subject* (with this alone all theory deals). (Schelling 2004: 202)[12]
> We can say of Nature as object that it *is*, not of Nature as subject; for this is being or productivity itself. (Schelling 2004: 203)
> Nature must originally be an object to itself; this change of the *pure subject* into an *object to itself* is unthinkable without an original diremption [*urspüngliche Entzweyung*] in Nature itself. (Schelling 2004: 205)
> [A]ll *persistence* also only exists in Nature as *object*; in Nature as *subject* there is only infinite *activity* [*unendliche Tätigkeit*]. (Schelling 2004: 205)
> [Nature] must therefore be at once infinite and finite; it must be only seemingly finite, but in infinite *development*. (Schelling 2004: 206)[13]

Schelling's conception of nature departs radically from the formal conception of nature in the *Critique of Pure Reason*. For Kant, the *transcendental subject*, the source of spontaneity, brings thought and the categories to bear on empirical intuitions. The only kind of subjectivity that we find *within* nature is empirical subjectivity, which can be studied and known like any other *object* characterized by universal and necessary deterministic laws. For Kant, the productive spontaneous subject is "outside" of nature – it is the transcendental subject. Schelling seeks to develop a conception of nature in which *productive subjectivity* is *not* "outside" nature but is *integral* to it.

Despite Hegel's many criticisms of Schelling, Hegel accepts (and builds upon) Schelling's understanding of nature as *at once* active subject and object. In the *Differenzschrift*, Hegel shares Schelling's criticism of Fichte, claiming that Fichte's conception of nature is dead and lifeless. This is also Hegel's and Schelling's criticism of the conception of nature that Kant elaborates in the Transcendental Analytic of the first *Critique*. In his criticism of Fichte, Hegel declares: "From this highest standpoint [of reflection] nature has the character of absolute objectivity, that is, of death" (Hegel 1977: 140). In Fichte, "[t]he standpoint which posited nature as living, disappears. . . . Reason is nothing but the dead and death-dealing rule of formal unity" (Hegel 1977: 142). The theme that Nature, Self-Consciousness, Reason, Freedom, the Concept (*Begriff*), and *Geist* are *active* and *alive* persists throughout Hegel's works, culminating in the Absolute Idea in the final section of the *Science of Logic*.

For a third perspective on Hegel's conception of Nature – closely related to the speculative identity thesis – I want to consider Hegel's interpretation of the purposive theme elaborated in Kant's third *Critique*. In my earlier discussion of the concept of purpose (*Zweck*) in Kant's third *Critique*, I noted some deep unresolved tensions and perplexities. Kant claims that the concept of purpose is essential for identifying and describing organisms and is integral to reflecting judgment. Yet he steadfastly denies that it is a *constitutive* principle of nature; for Kant, it is only a regulative principle. Purpose tells us how we (humans) *judge* nature (natural organisms), but it does not tell us what nature really *is*. Against Kant, Hegel maintains that internal purpose is a *constitutive principle* of Nature and *Geist*, but he also has a more favorable and hermeneutically generous interpretation of Kant's achievement. In the section dealing with teleology in the *Science of Logic*, Hegel states:

> One of Kant's great services to philosophy consists in the distinction he has made between relative or *external*, and *internal* purposiveness; in the latter he has opened up the Notion of life, the Idea, and by so doing has done *positively* for philosophy what the *Critique of Reason* did but imperfectly, equivocally, and only *negatively*, namely, raised it above the determinations of reflection and the relative world of metaphysics. It has been remarked that the opposition of teleology and mechanism is in the first instance the more general opposition of *freedom* and *necessity*. (Hegel 1969: 737)

Hegel is referring to the distinction that Kant draws at the beginning of the third *Critique*. External or relative purposiveness is based on the model of artifacts, intentional design, and means–end thinking. For example, when I am building a house, my purpose is to build a house, and my actions are *intentionally* organized to fulfill this purpose. *Internal purposiveness*, on the contrary, is the purposiveness that is manifested by *self-organized* organisms and their reproduction.[14] Internal purposiveness does not involve *external* human intentions. The distinction between external and internal purposiveness closely parallels Aristotle's distinction between artifacts and natural organisms. In the above quotation, Hegel claims that the concept of internal purposiveness "opens up" "the Notion of *life*, the *Idea*."[15] Despite Kant's resistance to ascribing a constitutive role to the concept of internal purposiveness, Hegel argues that there are already the seeds for a *positive* substantive role (and not merely a regulative function) of purpose in Kant's first and third *Critiques*. Hegel reads these *Critiques* as offering a unified account of purpose and its internal relation to judging. In this respect, Hegel thinks of himself as making *explicit* what is already *implicit* in Kant. As Ng notes, "Hegel's reading of Kant suggests that he views the first and the third *Critiques* as offering one, unified account of judging activity, an account that is indispensable for understanding the orientation of Hegel's idealism as grounded in the relation and opposition between self-consciousness and life" (Ng 2020: 25). Internal purposiveness is *constitutive* of Nature and *Geist*. Once again, we see how Hegel, starting with, and building upon, themes already present in Kant, develops them in a way that culminates in a thoroughly anti-Kantian conception of both Nature and *Geist*.

A fourth perspective for orienting our comprehension of Hegel's conception of Nature is to focus on Hegel's understanding of the relation between the naturalness of human beings and the naturalness of nonhuman animals. Kant thinks there are distinctions within nature: distinctions between what we today would call the inorganic, organic, and human nature. Internal purposiveness only occurs with biological organisms, although this internal purposiveness is not a *constitutive* feature of biological organisms.[16] Just as there is a sharp break between inorganic and the organic nature, there is also a sharp break between nonhuman and human animals. Human beings are animals that share many characteristics with nonhuman animals, but they are *rational* animals capable of theoretical and practical reasoning. In Kant's view, human rationality *cannot* be explained by an appeal to nature because, according to Kant's transcendental idealism, it is the understanding (*Verstand*) that sets the formal conditions for what constitutes nature. Hegel, on the contrary, argues for *continuity* between inorganic, organic, and human nature. Continuity does not mean homogeneity. The distinctions between humans and nonhumans are just as important for Hegel as they are for Kant. But there are no fixed and permanent distinctions between humans and nonhumans. As Pinkard notes,

> our continuity with the natural world (specifically, with animals) is at the center of Hegel's Aristotelian conception of mindful agency. . . . In Hegel's terms, animals also have the capacity to be "at one with themselves" and even to have both "selves" and . . . "subjectivity." However, Hegel holds that human agents, by virtue of thinking of themselves as animals, thereby become special animals, namely, self-interpreting ones. (Pinkard 2012: 18)[17]

Thus, the four perspectives that I have suggested for approaching Hegel's concept of Nature are: (1) the identity and nonidentity of Nature and *Geist*; (2) the appropriation and development of Schelling's conception of nature as living and both productive and product; (3) the thesis that internal purposiveness is a constitutive feature of both Nature and *Geist*; and (4) the continuity of human animals with the rest of nature. All four perspectives are intertwined and intimately related.

I now want to explore in detail Hegel's concept of Nature, specifically its relation to *Geist*. Earlier I mentioned that there is a divide among contemporary interpreters of Hegel: those who stress the continuity between Nature and *Geist* and those who think there is something so distinctive about *Geist* that it cannot be explained by an appeal to Nature. I have labeled the latter group "Kantian Hegelians" because they stress the *break* between Nature and *Geist*.[18] In opposition to the Kantian Hegelians, Willem deVries, Italo Testa, Terry Pinkard, and Steven Levine all stress Hegel's naturalism.[19] DeVries boldly states:

> Thus I read Hegel as a great naturalist, as one who saw man as arising out of and continuous with nature and capable of being understood only in this natural context. He was certainly not a total naturalist, but no ultimate break is to be found between nature and spirit in Hegel's system. In his dislike of absolute dichotomies Hegel shares an important trait with his (to me most congenial) successors, the pragmatists. (deVries 1988: p. xii)[20]

Here is how Testa characterizes Hegel's naturalism:

> [O]ne must combat any conception that sees Spirit in its various degrees – Subjective, Objective, Absolute – as a type of being other than the natural, which subsists prior to and independently of the natural or which is added to it from outside. By contrast, Spirit for Hegel is "return out of Nature" (Zurückkommen aus der Natur), which is to say, Nature that returns to itself and awakens from its sleep. Spirit, accordingly, far from constituting another type of thing, is for Hegel nothing other than a determinate constellation of relations of Nature itself as the one single reality. This thesis could be called *Hegel's naturalism*: the idea that there is one single reality – living reality – and different levels of description of it. . . . On one hand, spiritual activities must be conceived in such a way that they do not prove to be something other than and independent of human natural being. On the other hand, there is a need for a conception of Nature that is not restricted, a conception that accounts for the fact that the space of Reason does not necessarily have to be conceived on the basis of a sort of dualism between itself and the space of nature. (Testa 2013: 23–4)

The Philosophy of Nature

Pinkard characterizes this naturalistic approach by stressing Hegel's conception of human agency.

> For Hegel, to be an agent is to not to be made of any particular stuff (say, "mental" as distinct from "physical" stuff), since agents are, after all, natural creatures. To be an agent is to be able to assume a position in a kind of normative space, which, so it will turn out, is a kind of social and historical space. To be able to do this, the natural creatures who are human beings are brought up within a form of life, and in doing so, they acquire an array of social skills, dispositions, and habits that function for them as a "second nature." In becoming "second nature" and not simply a nonnatural capacity to respond to norms, a form of life remains a form of "life," that is, part of the natural world but different from the forms of life of other natural creatures. (Pinkard 2012: 7)[21]

Levine argues that Pinkard's view of Hegel is not sufficiently naturalistic. In Levine's view, Pinkard is still committed to a separation of *Geist* and Nature because he endorses a dichotomy between the "space of reasons" and the "space of nature." Levine claims that Pinkard does not recognize that "natural conditions maintain some *authority* with respect to our thinking and doing even after Spirit's emergence" (Levine 2015: 640). A thoroughly naturalistic interpretation of Hegel rejects the fixed dichotomy between the "space of nature" and the "space of reasons."[22] The naturalist interpretation of Hegel emphasizes the *historicity* of Spirit and its *natural embodiment*. Just as Nature requires full *actualization* in Spirit, Spirit requires *actualization* in Nature. This is the way that Levine describes the relation of Nature and Spirit:

> As Hegel demonstrates in the *Encyclopedia* Subjective Spirit, when nature becomes Spirit – or when Soul, the organized form of our natural bodies, becomes Mind – spirit does not leave the natural conditions of its emergence behind, rather sensibility, self-feeling and habit *continue to condition* Spirit's activity. So Spirit is not a product of itself on this interpretation but a return to itself out of the Otherness of nature, or Spirit is nature awakening from its 'sleep'. (Levine 2015: 640)

Pinkard also emphasizes that normativity is not exclusively a feature of human conceptual activity. *Normatively is already at work in nonhuman animals.*

> On Hegel's account, the difference between animal and human mentality does not rest on the idea that the former is nonnormative (or that it is merely sentient, in Robert Brandom's phrase) whereas human mentality is also normative (or what Brandom calls sapient). In the Hegelian view, there is a

normativity already at work in nature in the sense that for organic life, there can be goods and evils for plants and animals – and thus reasons for plants and animals to respond in one way or another. In animals, the concept of an action takes shape in that the animal (depending on the complexity of, for example, its nervous system) can form plans, take steps to satisfy those plans, in some cases reevaluate the plan in light of new information, and so forth. Hegel notes (with an explicit reference that he is following Aristotle on this point) that the difference between human mindful agency and animal action is that the animal nonetheless does not "know his purposes as purposes." (Pinkard 2012: 26)[23]

Implicit in these several descriptions of Hegel's naturalism is the theme of "internal purposiveness." We can now fully appreciate why Hegel claimed that one of the great services to philosophy of Kant was to stress this theme and that it "opened up the Notion of *life*, the Idea." Internal purposiveness is not only a *constitutive* feature of living organisms; it is an intrinsic and essential characteristic of Nature. The internal purposiveness of Nature – when fully realized or *actualized* – becomes the internal purposiveness of *Geist* itself.[24] Later I will explain how *Geist* is nonidentical with Nature and even opposes Nature.

The above statements, characterizing the intimate relation between Nature and *Geist*, provide a segue to Hegel's *Philosophy of Spirit*, where we find one of the clearest accounts of the relation between sentient nature and *Geist*.[25] The *Philosophy of Spirit* consists of three parts: Anthropology – the Soul; The Phenomenology of Spirit – Consciousness; and Psychology – Spirit.[26] Hegel uses the term "soul" (*Seele*) in a technical way that departs from the way in which previous modern philosophers referred to the soul. The word "soul" (*Seele*) is reserved by Hegel for the lowest level of Spirit. Testa comments, "The different images Hegel uses to speak of the soul – natural Spirit, the sleep of Spirit, Spirit immersed in Nature – fundamentally express the idea that we are dealing here with a '*natural determinateness*' (*Naturbestimmtheit*)" (Testa 2013: 25). Yet Hegel also says that soul is not *yet* Spirit – not fully actualized Spirit. The first part of the *Philosophy of Subjective Spirit* is a genealogy of Spirit based on natural conditions. Hegel begins with sensation and feeling of the natural soul, passes on to consciousness, and culminates with an explicit analysis of Spirit (theoretical, practical, and free Spirit).[27]

I want to focus on the stage of *habit*, where Hegel makes the transition from what he calls the "feeling soul" to the "actual soul." By focusing on this transition, we can see how intimately Spirit in the form of soul is related to the *corporeality* of sentient nature. This is where Hegel (appropriating the

Aristotelian term) introduces the concept of *second nature*. In §410 Hegel writes, "Habit has rightly been called a second nature: *nature*, because it is an immediate being of the soul; a *second* nature, because it is an immediacy *posited* by the soul, incorporating and moulding the bodiliness that pertains to the determinations of feeling as such and to the determinacies of representation and of the will in so far as they are embodied" (Hegel 2007a: 131). Hegel is sensitive to the difference between habits as mere repetition and habits that become flexible, plastic, and *critical*. Habits themselves can be "dead" or "alive."[28] "[B]y habit a man becomes free, yet, on the other hand, habit makes him its *slave*" (Hegel 2007a: 134).[29] Testa notes that

> a dialectics of relative freedom and relative un-freedom is also understood by Hegel as a process of "Liberation (*Brefreiung*)" which involves a distinction between "bad habits (*üblen Gewohnheiten*)" (inertial, enslaving) and good ones (expansive, expressive of life's freedom) meaning that habit is not in itself identical neither with enslaving repetition nor with freedom, but can be expressive of both in different contexts or under different aspects. (Testa 2017: 4)

Testa also points out that

> [t]he mechanism of habit – the fact that habit has to function as something automatic, embodied in preintentional physiological mechanisms, and operates at a prereflexive, unconscious level – is thus a sliding door, since it can be the natural basis of the expression of spiritual freedom – a necessary, even if not sufficient condition of it, expressed by the idea that habit "has the content of freedom" – but can also implement an enslaving pattern and thus take the form of un-freedom. Which means that neither freedom nor un-freedom are identical with habitual mechanism. (Testa 2017: 4–5)

When Hegel introduces the concept of habit as second nature, we are still at a relatively early stage of the development and the actuality of Subjective Spirit. The soul, at this simple (immediate) stage of Spirit, involves corporeality. We still have to rise to the level of Consciousness, Self-Consciousness, and Spirit (in its higher and more restrictive sense). Prior to the stage of habit, the animal soul is absorbed in sensations, feelings, and desires. With habituation, we are no longer "sunk" into them. Human beings gain liberation from this absorption in feeling and begin to make the distinction between their own inwardness and what is *other* than their inwardness. This becomes the *transition* to Consciousness, where there is the distinction between what is inward (subjective) and what is other (objective). This is a crucial stage because it is here that the distinction between subject and object arises. Eventually, Spirit will sublate this dichotomy. The dialectical sublation (*Aufhebung*) of the subject–object dichotomy is what distinguishes speculative identity from the reification of this dichotomy by philosophies of reflection.[30]

Although Hegel vehemently rejects reductive forms of sensationalism and materialism, he does maintain that Spirit has its origin in sentient nature. Even more important, at the higher levels of the development of Spirit, sentient nature continues to *condition* Spirit. *Spirit presupposes its natural embodiment*.[31] We can also say that when we grasp the internal purposiveness of Nature (*Naturzweck*), we realize that its full *actuality* is achieved by Spirit. Hegel makes it perfectly clear that thinking (a higher level of Spirit), which is free and active, presupposes and *requires* habit. Hegel introduces a bit of humor into his analysis when he declares:

> Thinking too, however free and active in its own pure element it becomes, no less requires habit and familiarity ... by which it is the property of my single self where I can freely and in all directions range. It is through this habit that I come to realize my *existence* as a thinking being. Even here, in this spontaneity of self-centered thought, there is corporeity (hence, want of habit and too-long continued thinking cause headache); habit diminishes this feeling, by making the natural function an immediacy of the soul.[32]

John Dewey was deeply influenced by Hegel's understanding of the role of habit in human development. In 1897, Dewey gave a lecture course dealing with Hegel's *Philosophy of Spirit*, focusing on the early stages of Subjective Spirit, where Hegel introduces the concept of second nature and habit. Consider how Dewey describes this stage in the development of Subjective Spirit:

> Feeling, by which Hegel means sensation, appetites, impulses and passions, so far as it loses its independence and becomes reduced to a capacity of the soul itself, – is habit. The soul in this way comes to possess its experiences instead of being absorbed in them. It has them in itself, without being obliged to feel them, and it thus moves freely in them. It is free from them so far as it not interested in them, as it is not constantly taken up with them, and thus is not only left open to other occupations but also has an additional power to bring to bear on this other occupation. Habit, then, is the freedom which the soul obtains over its particular experiences by reducing them into powers of its own. It is the mechanism of feeling by which the particular feelings are reduced to organs of the soul itself. (Dewey 2010: 130)[33]

Dewey then describes three stages in the development of habit, noting that it is in the third stage that

> habit takes the form of skill, active habit, and from the soul makes itself felt through the body and subjects the latter to its own use. Habit is thus the process by which the soul comes to possess itself, to know its experiences instead of being lost in them. That unity of the body and the soul which merely *existed* in feeling is transformed in habit into a *made* unity, a unity which is the outcome of the soul's own activity. (Dewey 2010: 131)[34]

Thus far, I have been exploring how nature is continuous with, and is presupposed by, Spirit, and how the internal purposiveness of Nature, when fully actualized, becomes identical with Spirit. We need to explore the way in which Spirit is *not* identical to Nature – and indeed, how it is opposed to Nature. Although soul is the lowest level of Spirit, Spirit – when actualized – is pure self-generating and self-determining activity. Spirit manifests internal purposiveness; or more accurately, Spirit *is* internal purposiveness.

> Hegel's shift from "soul" to "spirit" emphasizes the nonthingishness, the active nature of the human essence as well as its communal or social nature. Hegel thereby emphasizes that he is investigating what is universal to us all, one and the same in us all, something in which we each participate rather than an entity we each individually possess (or are) independently of all others. As comprehension of the nature of spirit, which informs not only the intellectual and practical life of the individual but of the whole of humanity as well, the philosophy of spirit must be seen as a much broader discipline than the philosophy of soul. (deVries 1988: 25–6)

Spirit does not develop in a smooth continuous manner; it develops by a process of *self-diremption* and *self-division* wherein there is opposition, rupture, and contradiction.[35] We witness this already in the division of subject and object that characterizes Consciousness. This is especially relevant for grasping the opposition of Nature and Spirit. Despite Hegel's praise and acknowledgment of the influence of Aristotle, it is important to see how he departs from Aristotle. This becomes evident in the way in which he describes how Spirit emerges out of Nature. This emergence

> must not be so conceived as though nature were the absolute immediate, the first, the original positing, and spirit only something posited by nature. Rather nature is posited by spirit, and spirit is the absolute first. Spirit existing in and for itself is not the mere result of nature, but in truth, spirit is its own result. It brings itself forth from presuppositions that it constructs for itself, from the logical idea and from external nature: spirit is the truth of both ... The appearance that spirit is mediated through an other [nature] is thus suspended by spirit itself, because spirit has, so to speak, the sovereign

ingratitude to suspend that through which it appears to be mediated, to mediate its mediator, to reduce its mediator to something that exists and endures only through spirit. In this way spirit makes itself completely independent. This implies that the transition from nature to spirit is not a transition to something utterly other, but only a process wherein spirit comes to itself out of its self-externality in nature. Just as little is the specific distinction between nature and spirit suspended because *spirit does not proceed out of nature in a natural way.*[36]

Roughly speaking, we can say that there are three major stages in the development of Nature and Spirit. There is the initial stage in which (to use Hegel's metaphor) Spirit is "slumbering" in the natural soul – it is implicit in the natural soul. Then there is a second major stage where there is a tense *opposition* between Spirit and Nature. Nature becomes the *other* of Spirit. Finally, we come to realize that the full actualization and truth of Nature coincides with Spirit. Spirit returns to itself in and through the process of a dialectical overcoming of its opposition with Nature. The actualization of Spirit is achieved in and through the overcoming of its opposition to Nature.

How are we to understand the stage of the opposition of Spirit and Nature – the stage when Nature is taken to be the other of Spirit? To answer this question, we must turn to the second major section of the *Encyclopaedia*, the *Philosophy of Nature*. This is the most maligned and neglected of all of Hegel's writings. It is the book that is frequently held up to ridicule, showing what is worst about Hegel – his presumed ignorance of science and his fallacious attempt to impose *a priori* categories on natural science. Many philosophers of science view Hegel's *Philosophy of Nature* as an example of the type of pretentious philosophizing about nature and natural science that ought to be completely condemned and rejected.[37] It is true that the natural sciences of his time and much of Hegel's understanding of these sciences are outdated and antiquated. Nevertheless, there are several misleading myths about the *Philosophy of Nature*.

Myth 1: Hegel was totally ignorant of the sciences of his time; he was simply imposing his own arbitrary speculative system on the natural sciences. Dispelling this myth, Houlgate writes, "It is, however, now being recognized by a small but growing number of Hegel scholars and philosophers of science that Hegel was neither ignorant of, nor indifferent to, natural science, as is often claimed, but was in fact deeply knowledgeable about the science of his day" (Houlgate 1998: p. xii). Michael Petry in the introduction to his three-volume edition of Hegel's *Philosophy of Nature* points out that "the 'Philosophy of Nature' far from being an arbitrary and irresponsible exposition of partially understood subject matter, is a sensitively structuralized, deeply informed and infinitely rewarding assessment of the whole range of early nineteenth century science" (Petry 1970: 60).

Myth 2: Hegel's conception of a philosophy of nature (*Naturphilosophie*) is an *a priori* science that falsely imposes its categories on the actual practice of the natural sciences. Two aspects of this myth are misleading. The first one is the misleading claim that Hegel accepts the Kantian distinction between the *a priori* and the *a posteriori*. Ironically, Hegel was one of the sharpest critics of this Kantian distinction wherein the *a priori* science of nature is the basis for laying out the *formal* conditions for the possibility of experience and the objectivity of nature. Hegel certainly does speak of his *Logic* as a science of pure thinking. But as deVries notes, "Hegel does not believe that there is a clear distinction between the a priori and the a posteriori – not because the distinction itself is unclear, but because it is really a matter of degree. In order to do Hegel full justice, we need to abandon the a priori–a posteriori dichotomy and employ instead the notion of degrees of empirical sensitivity" (deVries 1998: 14, n. 5).[38] What is even more misleading about this myth is that it distorts Hegel's conception of the relation between a philosophy of nature and natural science (what Hegel calls "physics"). At the very beginning of the *Philosophy of Nature*, Hegel states: "Not only must philosophy be in agreement with our empirical knowledge of Nature, but the *origin* and *formation* of the Philosophy of Nature presupposes and is conditioned by empirical physics" (Hegel 1970: 6). Hegel is not questioning the achievements of the natural sciences but is raising the philosophical question of whether the natural sciences by themselves provide an adequate philosophical conception of Nature. To maintain, as some philosophers do, that the natural sciences *alone* tell us what Nature is, is *not* a scientific but a philosophical claim – one that needs to be justified. Pinkard tells us that

> what thus distinguishes Hegel's *Naturphilosophie*, his "philosophy of nature," from physics itself is that the philosophy of nature aims at producing a metaphysics or, as Hegel calls it, "the diamond net" into which we make the world intelligible – a comprehension, in Wilfrid Sellars's famous phrase, of how things (in the broadest sense of the term) hang together (in the broadest sense of the term). (Pinkard 2012: 19)[39]

We must distinguish our direct *encounters* (what Peirce calls "Secondness") with nature as it *exists* – that is, with singular natural entities, whether they be inorganic or organic – from the task of making nature *intelligible* (what Peirce calls "Thirdness").[40] A philosophy of nature must do justice to both aspects of how we are related to nature. Hegel has a robust sense of our encounters with natural objects. "Nature, for Hegel," as Collingwood tells us, "is real, it is in no sense an illusion, or something which we think to exist when what really exists is something else, nor is it in any sense a mere appearance, something which only exists because we think it. It really exists, and exists independently of any mind whatever" (Collingwood 1945: 124). Hegel mocks the position that is frequently falsely attributed to him: that we *never* encounter physical nature, but only our own mental ideas.[41] Hegel would agree with Dewey when Dewey reminds us that "it is not experience [or mere mental ideas – RJB] that is experienced, but nature – stones, plants, animals, diseases, health, temperature, electricity, and so on" (Dewey 1981: 12). At the beginning of the *Philosophy of Nature*, Hegel affirms:

> In thinking things, we transform them into something universal; but things are singular and the Lion as Such does not exist. We give them the form of something subjective, of something produced by us and belonging to us, and belonging to us in our specifically human character: for *natural objects do not think, and are not presentations or thoughts*. (Hegel 1970: 7, emphasis added)

Hegel celebrates the contingency, singularity, immediacy, and infinite variety of Nature: "The more thought enters into our representation of things, the less do they retain their naturalness, their singularity and immediacy. The wealth of natural forms, in all their infinitely manifold configuration, is impoverished by the all-pervading power of thought, their vernal life and glowing colours die and fade away" (Hegel 1970: 7). Hegel sounds almost like a Romantic poet mocking his own project of seeking intelligibility when he adds: "The rustle of Nature's life is silenced in the stillness of thought; her abundant life, wearing a thousand wonderful and delightful shapes, shrivels into arid forms and shapeless generalities resembling a murky northern fog" (Hegel 1970: 7). This passage reminds us of Hegel's characterization of logic in his *Science of Logic* as "the realm of shadows, the world of simple essentialities freed from all sensuous concreteness" (Hegel 1969: 58).[42] It also calls to mind the famous passage from the *Elements of the Philosophy of Right* (1820): "When philosophy paints its grey in grey, a shape of life has grown old, and it cannot be rejuvenated, but only recognized, by the grey in grey of philosophy; the owl of Minerva begins its flight only with the onset of dusk" (Hegel 1991: 23).

Despite the radical otherness and nonidentity between Nature and Spirit, we seek to comprehend the Nature that we encounter – to make it *intelligible* not only for us but as it exists in itself. Stated in a different way, we do not stand dumb before the Nature that we encounter, but we seek to understand its *actuality* (*Wirklichkeit*), its *energeia* – the inner purposiveness of organic objects and, ultimately, of Nature itself. This culminates in the recognition of the inner purposiveness, *self-activity*, and *self-determination* of *Geist*. We must take seriously the otherness of Nature – the way in which Nature is other than Spirit and is opposed to it (and the way in which Spirit is other than and opposed to Nature). In achieving this task, we do *not* leave Nature behind; rather, we integrate the radical difference of Nature into a more comprehensive intelligibility. This is a long, difficult journey involving many stages and culminating in grasping the internal purposiveness of Nature. We move from mechanics to physics and to organics (the three main divisions of the *Philosophy of Nature*). Despite the many deficiencies of the *Philosophy of Nature*, an overall narrative shapes its structure. It is the story of how Nature initially appears to be absolutely external to Spirit; but, as we gradually come to realize, it is not a fixed and permanent other of Spirit. The full actualization of Nature culminates in the transition to, and reconciliation with, Spirit. We are led away from the way in which Nature first appears to us from the perspective of *Verstand*, where there is a sharp opposition between consciousness and its object. Kant leaves us with this dualistic perspective when he emphasizes the dichotomies of nature and freedom, nature and rationality, nature and purpose. Hegel argues that when we pursue the dialectic of *Vernunft*, we discover the speculative identity of Nature and Spirit – when both are fully *actualized*. Pinkard describes how Hegel seeks to show that Nature becomes less and less external and how the otherness of Nature is *aufgehoben*.

> Hegel tries to make a case for the irreducibility of other spheres of nature to the sphere of mechanics. The sphere of "physics" (heat, light, magnetism, electricity, sound, meteorology, and chemical processes) does not account for nature in terms of the pure externality of matter in motion; instead matter is said within those accounts to exhibit an affinity for other determinate matters (as in chemical processes), and, of course, he distinguishes organic life and (quasi-organic processes) from both of them. *In each case, nature is said to become less and less "external," and in the case of organic animal life, as self-organizing, begins to prefigure the shape of subjectivity and self-direction themselves.* (Pinkard 2005: 28, emphasis added)

In terms of Hegel's *Encyclopaedia Logic*, we move from mechanism to chemism and to teleology. Different versions of mechanism had been dominant from the time of Galileo, and a mechanistic conception of nature was reinforced by Newton (and especially by the philosophical interpretations of Newton). This is also a mechanistic conception of nature that emerges from Kant's *Critique of Pure Reason*. In Hegel's *Encyclopaedia Logic*, the triad of mechanism, chemism, and teleology appears in the third (and final) subdivision, The Doctrine of the Concept. Hegel opens his analysis of the Concept by declaring that "the Concept is the principle of all life, and hence, at the same time, it is what is utterly concrete" (Hegel 1991a: 236). In order to understand what this means, we have to pass through several stages in the development of the Concept. We pass from the subjective concept, to the object, and finally to the *Idea* – the culmination of the *Logic*. The triad of mechanism, chemism, and teleology occurs in the analysis of the object. Hegel begins his discussion of mechanism as follows:

> In its immediacy, the object is only the Concept *in-itself*; initially it has the Concept *outside it*, and every determinacy is [present] as one that is posited externally. Hence, as a unity of distinct [terms], it is *something-composite*; it is an aggregate, and its operation upon another remains an external relation. This is *formal mechanism*. – In this relation and dependence the objects remain equally independent; they offer resistance, and are *external* to each other. (Hegel 1991a: 274)

Although the idiom is distinctively Hegelian, the point is clear. Note the emphasis on "externality," "aggregate," and "independence" of objects. We find an anticipation of this type of mechanism in Hume when he emphasizes that every simple impression and idea is independent, discrete, and separable. Consequently, when he analyzes causality, we come up with *external* constant conjunction of independent units. Even when Kant challenges Hume's account of causality, he claims that causes and effects are *independent* events that are *externally* related and governed by universal and necessary laws. Hegel characteristically does *not* deny the importance of mechanical explanation. He defends it as a universal logical category. He acknowledges that it even has a role to play in explaining spiritual phenomena.

> Even in the domain of the spiritual world, mechanism has its place, though again it is only a subordinate one. It is quite right to speak of "mechanical" memory, and of all manner of "mechanical" activities, such as reading, writing, and playing music, for example. As for memory specifically, we may note, in this connection, that a mechanical mode of behaviour belongs even to its essence; this is a circumstance that is not infrequently overlooked by modern pedagogy in a mistaken zeal for the freedom of intelligence – something that has caused great harm to the education of youth. (Hegel 1991a: 275)

The key point here is that mechanical explanations are perfectly appropriate and even *essential* for a wide variety of physical and spiritual phenomena. Hegel, however, criticizes the claim that mechanical explanations are *sufficient* to account for the distinctive character of *both* natural and spiritual phenomena. In this respect, Hegel is in agreement with Kant that one needs to introduce the non-mechanical concept of purpose to account for organic life. For Hegel, we pass from mechanism to chemism and finally to teleology.[43] The move to teleology is a move to the greater *concreteness* of the Concept. Against many of those who take mechanism to be the *primary* mode of explanation of nature and claim that the appeal to purposes is either unnecessary or derivative, Hegel argues for the opposite thesis. Purposiveness is *primary* and more *concrete*; mechanism is an *abstraction* from teleology. Hegel acknowledges the contributions of Kant and Aristotle for understanding the internal purposiveness of Nature and the Concept.

> In dealing with the purpose, we must not think at once (or merely) of the form in which it occurs in consciousness as a determination that is present in representation. With his concept of *internal* purposiveness, *Kant* has resuscitated the Idea in general and especially the Idea of life. The determination of life by *Aristotle* already contains this internal purposiveness; hence, it stands infinitely far above the concept of modern teleology which had only *finite*, or *external*, purposiveness in view. (Hegel 1991a: 280)

Unlike Kant, however, and more in the spirit of Aristotle, Hegel argues that internal purposiveness is constitutive of Nature and Spirit. He sets out to show the *logical primacy* of teleology and internal purposiveness. For Kant, mechanism, as understood in the first *Critique*, is the *primary* category for understanding nature. With Hegel, there is a dialectical reversal: teleology understood as internal purposiveness is logically primary. Mechanism turns out to be an *abstraction* from teleology and is consequently a *subservient* category for making nature intelligible. Hegel goes beyond Kant and Aristotle in claiming that internal purposiveness is the essential feature of the Concept. It is internal purposiveness that provides the transition to the culmination of Hegel's *Logic* – the analysis of the logical concept of life and the full actualization of the Concept into the *Idea*.[44] Returning to the *Philosophy of Nature*, Hegel concludes this work by showing the transition from Nature to Spirit.

> This is the transition from Nature to spirit; in the living being, Nature finds its consummation and has made its peace, in that it is transformed into a higher existence. Spirit has thus proceeded from Nature. The goal of Nature is to destroy itself and to break through its husk of immediate, sensuous existence, to consume itself like the phoenix in order to come forth

from this externality rejuvenated as spirit. Nature has become an other to itself in order to recognize itself again as Idea and to reconcile itself with itself. But it is one-sided to regard spirit in this way as having only *become* an actual existence after being merely a potentiality. True, Nature is the immediate – but even so, as the other of spirit, its existence is a relativity: and so, as the negative, its being is only posited, derivative. It is the power of free spirit which sublates this negativity; spirit is no less *before* than *after* Nature, it is not merely the metaphysical Idea of it. Spirit, just because it is the goal of Nature, is *prior* to it, Nature has proceeded from spirit: not empirically, however, but in such a manner that spirit is already from the very first implicitly present in Nature which is spirit's own presupposition. (Hegel 1970: 444)

This passage must be read carefully. When Hegel says the goal of "Nature is to destroy itself," he does not mean the complete and *total* annihilation of Nature, for he qualifies it to mean that it "breaks through its husk of immediate, sensuous existence." Furthermore, he is quite explicit in asserting that Spirit from the very beginning is implicit in Nature.

We can now understand the dialectical relation between Nature and Spirit. From one perspective, we begin with Nature and see its culmination – its full actualization – in Spirit. We witness this in the progression from the natural soul – the lowest form of Spirit – to the full development of the Subjective, Objective, and Absolute Spirit. Nature becomes transformed. But from another perspective, Spirit is logically prior to Nature. Spirit dirempts itself – divides itself into a Nature that *opposes* Spirit. It is only when this opposition is overcome that Nature is sublated (*aufgehoben*). But this does not mean that Nature is annihilated. If we simply focus on those passages in Hegel where he stresses the contrast between "dead" Nature and the Spirit that is *alive*, we can come away with the conclusion that, for all Hegel's concern to overcome dichotomies, to see oppositions as moments within a single dynamic whole, there is one *fundamental* dichotomy that Hegel never really overcomes – the dichotomy between Nature and Spirit. I have been arguing that such an interpretation is mistaken. It is like taking an isolated snapshot of what is a dynamic process. Hegel follows the same speculative logic in dealing with Nature and Spirit as he does in dealing with being and nothing. We must grasp how Nature and Spirit are both nonidentical and identical. In the *Philosophy of Subjective Spirit*, he shows in concrete detail how Spirit emerges out of Nature, how Spirit is *implicit* in Nature, and how Spirit actualizes Nature. Employing Hegel's metaphor, Spirit is "slumbering" in Nature, and as Nature is actualized, Spirit awakens from its sleep. Spirit is always *conditioned* by Nature. There is no such thing as "pure Spirit" that is completely removed and separate from Nature.[45] "Pure Spirit" devoid of Nature is a false abstraction, just as the idea of "pure Nature" devoid of Spirit is an equally false abstraction. Without Nature there is no Spirit. We can also make the *opposite* claim. Without Spirit, there is no Nature. There is no permanent ontological or epistemological gap between Nature and Spirit.

We can now also appreciate the conflicting contemporary legacies between the Kantian Hegelians and the pragmatic naturalistic Hegelians. Philosophers in the Kantian tradition insist on the dichotomy of the logical "space of reasons" and the "space of nature." They insist that conceptual normativity cannot be accounted for by an appeal to nature; they are heirs to the dichotomy that Kant draws in the *Critique of Pure Reason* between nature and reason, and between nature and freedom. The twentieth-century patron saint of these Kantian Hegelians is Wilfrid Sellars – especially the Sellars of *Empiricism and the Philosophy of Mind*.[46] Perhaps the most dedicated follower of Sellars in this respect is Brandom, but there are many others who share this Kantian approach to Hegel.[47] Their Hegel is one who is "anti-naturalist." *Geist* prevails over Nature. These Kantian Hegelians are opposed by the pragmatic naturalistic Hegelians who stress the continuity and the unity of Nature and Spirit. In the twentieth century, the most famous philosopher who followed this line of thinking was Dewey. Like Hegel, Dewey stresses the continuity between Nature and Spirit (what Dewey calls "culture").[48] Dewey rejects a sharp dichotomy between the "space of nature" and the "space of reasons." All too frequently, when the Kantian Hegelians stress the contrast between Spirit and Nature, they take as paradigmatic what we learn from existing (or past) natural sciences. The pragmatic naturalists emphasize science as a set of *future-oriented changing dynamic historical* practices. They are critical of appeals to "conceptual analysis" or "transcendental arguments," claiming that there is a fixed boundary between science and philosophy. They insist that philosophy must always be open to what we learn from sciences – including sciences like climatology and ecology. Our understanding of nature and natural sciences changes in the course of history. The pragmatic naturalists are inspired by the Hegelian thesis that there is a genuine continuity between Nature and *Geist* and seek to show how new developments in the sciences and philosophy support this continuity thesis.[49]

Part II

The Hermeneutics of Suspicion

Prologue

When the red-hot magma below the earth's surface builds up, it can violently explode through a volcanic vent and spew destructive lava. Volcanic eruption is an apt metaphor for what happened in the nineteenth century concerning new ways of thinking about nature. For all the consequential differences among Spinoza, Hume, Kant, and Hegel in their conceptions of philosophy, they all held that a philosophical understanding of nature was a viable and important contribution to knowledge. There were, however, subterranean destructive forces at work that exploded with Marx, Nietzsche, and Freud, who sought to demystify the very idea of a philosophy of nature. Indeed, their critiques cut deeper because (in radically different ways) they sought to expose how philosophy distorted and obscured a deeper layer of reality and nature. Ricoeur distinguishes two opposing "interpretations of interpretation": "the one as recollection of meaning, the other as reduction of the illusions and lies of consciousness" (Ricoeur 1970: 32). The latter, which he calls the "school of suspicion," is dominated by three masters – seemingly mutually exclusive – Marx, Nietzsche, and Freud. For all their differences, they shared a suspicion of the appeal to consciousness, which had been so fundamental in philosophy since the time of Descartes. They looked upon "the whole of consciousness primarily as 'false' consciousness" (Ricoeur 1970: 33).

> They thereby take up again, each in a different manner, the problem of the Cartesian doubt, to carry it to the very heart of the Cartesian stronghold. The philosopher trained in the school of Descartes knows that things are

> doubtful, that they are not such as they appear; but he does not doubt that consciousness is such as it appears to itself; in consciousness, meaning and consciousness of meaning coincide. Since Marx, Nietzsche, and Freud, this too has become doubtful. After the doubt about things, we have started to doubt consciousness. (Ricoeur 1970: 33)

Marx, Nietzsche, and Freud argue that consciousness is determined by what is not *immediately* available to consciousness: by unconscious dynamics. These three "masters of suspicion" are not three masters of skepticism. Skepticism is a philosophical position that has an ancient lineage and frequently reappears in modern versions – for example, in Hume. The "masters of suspicion" are "great destroyers," but they destroy in order to build afresh and to reveal new ways of understanding nature, especially the *relation* and *transaction* that takes place between human and nonhuman nature. All three approach the critique of false consciousness with a certain amount of ironic guile.

> All three begin with suspicion concerning the illusions of consciousness, and then proceed to employ the stratagem of deciphering; all three, however, far from being detractors of "consciousness," aim at extending it. What Marx wants is to liberate *praxis* by the understanding of necessity; but this liberation is inseparable from a "conscious insight" which victoriously counterattacks the mystification of false consciousness. What Nietzsche wants is the increase of man's power, the restoration of his force; but the meaning of the will to power must be recaptured by meditating on the ciphers "superman," "eternal return," and "Dionysus," without which the power in question would be but worldly violence. What Freud desires is that the one who is analyzed, by making his own the meaning that was foreign to him, enlarge his field of consciousness, live better, and finally be a little freer and, if possible, a little happier. (Ricoeur 1970: 34–5)

We will now probe the thinking of these three "masters of suspicion" – these great demystifiers – who lead us into new ways of coming to grips with nature, including the nature of human beings.

5
Marx: The Transaction of Nature and Social Man

On November 10, 1837, Marx, who was nineteen years old, wrote a remarkable letter to his beloved father. His letter takes on a richer meaning in light of Marx's life story. At the time, Marx was in his second year of university studies of jurisprudence at the University of Berlin, having spent his first year at the provincial University of Bonn. Berlin was the cosmopolitan capital of Prussia where radical free thinkers gathered. Marx opens his letter declaring: "There are moments in life which mark the close of a period like boundary posts and at the same time definitely point in a new direction" (Marx 1997: 40). This statement is prophetic, in that Marx's life and intellectual development can be told as a narrative of boundary posts that definitely point in new directions. Some of these resulted from being exiled from Germany to Paris, then to Brussels, and finally to London. He arrived in London in 1849, and (except for a few brief excursions) lived in London until his death in 1883. Even more important were significant changes in his revolutionary thinking.

At the beginning of his letter, Marx first speaks of his longing and love for Jenny von Westphalen. Jenny was the daughter of Ludwig von Westphalen, the top Prussian officer in Trier, who was a mentor to the young Marx and a good friend of Marx's father. Marx was secretly engaged to Jenny before he left for Bonn, and they were finally married in 1843 with the blessing of both fathers. Marx confesses that despite his legal studies, lyrical poetry became his first concern – and Marx sent many of his poems to Jenny. Throughout his life, Marx had a deep love of poetry and literature, especially Goethe and Shakespeare. Jenny and Karl had an extraordinarily close marriage, even though at times they suffered from extreme poverty. Jenny came to share Karl's revolutionary opinions and provided emotional and intellectual support for him throughout her life.

In his letter, Marx next turns to a review of his studies of jurisprudence and describes the schema for a work of "nearly three hundred pages" that he had written. (Remember, Marx was nineteen.) He declares that he "was greatly disturbed by the conflict of what is and what ought to be, a conflict peculiar to idealism" (Marx 1997: 42). This incidental remark looms large over the rest of Marx's intellectual career. He is referring to the sharp distinction between the "is" and the "ought" that had been canonized by Kant and his followers. Throughout his life, Marx was ruthlessly critical of thinkers (including utopian socialists) who based their thinking on this dichotomy. Overcoming the is/ought dichotomy was one of the primary reasons for his initial attraction to Hegel. After outlining what he plans to write about, the philosophy of law, he exclaims, "But why should I continue filling pages with things I have discarded?" (Marx 1997: 45). He confesses: "I could not make my way without philosophy. Hence, I was again able, with good conscience, to throw myself into the arms of philosophy, and I wrote a new basic metaphysical system. Upon its completion I was again constrained to recognize its futility and that of all my previous endeavors" (Marx 1997: 45).

This passage reveals a trait that Marx displayed throughout his life – his enormous capacity for *self-criticism*, his ability to revise and even abandon claims when he recognized them as inadequate or wrong. The reason *why* he abandoned these projects is revealing. He abandoned or modified them when he realized that he was forcing artificial abstract categories upon actual concrete historical living reality. The letter demonstrates Marx's constant drive to do justice to the concrete details of actually existing historical reality and not to get caught up in mystifying abstractions. His letter also displays the extraordinary range of his intellectual interests and describes a procedure he was to follow all his life: he would make excerpts of passages he was reading and then "scribble down some reflections."[1] This became his favored way to criticize claims that he judged to be false or misleading. A classic early example of this type of critique is his manuscript *Critique of Hegel's Philosophy of the State* (1843) in which he comments on paragraphs 261–308 of Hegel's *Outlines of the Philosophy of Right*.[2] Marx then describes his move from the narrow confines of jurisprudence to philosophy. "Setting out from idealism – which, let me say in passing, I had compared to and nourished with that of Kant and Fichte – I hit upon seeking the Idea in the real itself. If formerly the gods had dwelt above the world, they had now become its center" (Marx 1997: 46). When Marx speaks of the Idea, he is referring to Hegel's Concept (*Begriff*) of the Absolute Idea. Hegel claimed at the end of his *Science of Logic* that the Idea has to be sought in the real itself. Ironically, we will see that in Marx's critique of Hegel, he accuses Hegel of a *failure* to seek the Idea in the real itself – in the real sensuous lives of suffering human beings. When Marx first read fragments of Hegel's philosophy, he found "its grotesque craggy melody unpleasing." Nevertheless, he decided "to dive into the ocean once again" and to read Hegel from beginning to end (Marx 1997: 46). Isaiah Berlin eloquently describes this period in Marx's life:

> Hegelianism at first repelled his naturally positivist intelligence. In a long and intimate letter to his father he described his efforts to construct a rival system; after sleepless nights and disordered days spent wrestling with the adversary, he fell ill and left Berlin to recuperate. He returned with a sense of failure and frustration, equally unable to work or to rest. His father wrote him a long paternal letter, begging him not to waste his time on barren metaphysical speculation when he had his career to think of. His words fell on deaf ears. Marx resolutely plunged into an exhaustive study of Hegel's work, read night and day, and after three weeks announced his complete conversion. He sealed it by becoming a member of the *Doktorklub* (Graduates' Club), an association of free-thinking university intellectuals, who met in beer cellars, wrote mildly seditious verse, professed violent hatred of the King, the church, the bourgeoisie, and above all argued endlessly on points of Hegelian theology. (Berlin 1948: 67–8)

To speak of Marx's "conversion" is an overstatement, since Marx was never a slavish disciple of Hegel. From his first encounter with Hegel, he felt that there was something essentially right and something desperately wrong with Hegelianism. In the course of the next few years, he tried over and over again to articulate what was of lasting value in Hegel and what had to be rejected as mystification. In rapid succession, he absorbed, utilized, and rejected tools of critique that he picked up from the other left Young Hegelians. At the same time, preparing for an academic career that never materialized, Marx began to work in 1839 on his dissertation, "The Difference between Democritean and Epicurean Philosophy of Nature." This was Marx's earliest attempt to come to grips with ancient concepts of nature. Because of his radical activities, it soon became clear that he would never gain an academic appointment. Already in his dissertation, he engaged in a critique of religion, arguing that philosophy after Hegel (like after Aristotle) became practical, turning to the real problems confronting human beings. The 1840s were an extremely fertile period in

Marx's intellectual and practical life. Much of what he wrote during the mid-1840s, including the *Paris Manuscripts* (1844), the *Theses on Feuerbach* (1845), and *The German Ideology* (1845), was not published at the time. Yet, we find in these manuscripts his earliest reflections on the relation of nature, society, humanism, and communism. Marx became increasingly dissatisfied with the Young Hegelians. He felt that their criticisms never really got further than the critique of religion. They talked and acted as if their criticism of religion would bring about radical changes in the world, but they had no real understanding of genuine practical activity (*praxis*).

Marx moved rapidly from the critique of religion to the critique of philosophy, the critique of the state, and the critique of political economy (even though in the 1840s, he had only just begun to study political economy seriously). Marx was true to the meaning of "radical," trying to get at roots (*radix*). Critique, for Marx, was not simply negative criticism. Critique meant cutting through mystification and ideology in order to understand what is happening. In an exchange of letters with Arnold Ruge, his fellow radical thinker, Marx writes, "[W]e . . . wish to find the new world through criticism of the old" (Marx 1997: 212). He then goes on to say, "Even though the construction of the future and its completion for all times is not our task, what we have to accomplish at this time is all the more clear: *relentless criticism of all existing conditions*, relentless in the sense that the criticism is not afraid of its findings and just as little afraid of the conflict with the powers that be" (Marx 1997: 212). Marx held to this conviction throughout his life. How is this criticism to become efficacious, to become practical, to make a difference in the real world? Marx turned against his fellow Young Hegelians, who frequently wrote and acted as if their intellectual posturing would shake worlds.

> The weapon of criticism obviously cannot replace the criticism of weapons. Material force must be overthrown by material force. But theory also becomes a material force once it has gripped the masses. Theory is capable of gripping the masses when it demonstrates *ad hominem*, and it demonstrates *ad hominem* when it becomes radical. To be radical is to grasp things by the root. . . . The criticism of religion ends with the doctrine that *man is the highest being for man*, hence with the *categorical imperative to overthrow all conditions* in which man is a degraded, enslaved, neglected, contemptible being. (Marx 1997: 257–8)[3]

Marx's rapid development during the 1840s is a movement from relentless criticism to revolutionary practice. At the same time as Marx was writing articles about current affairs in Prussia, he continued his philosophical struggle with Hegel. Feuerbach's critique of Hegel provided a breakthrough by exposing Hegel's mystification. "*Feuerbach* is the only one who has a *serious, critical* relation to Hegel's dialectic, who has made genuine discoveries in this field, and who above all is the true conqueror of the old philosophy. The magnitude of Feuerbach's achievement and the unpretentious simplicity with which he presents it to the world stand in a strikingly opposite inverse ratio" (Marx 1997: 316). Feuerbach's demystification of Hegel provided a fresh perspective for interpreting Hegel's *Phenomenology of Spirit*. Marx notes:

> The great thing in Hegel's *Phenomenology* and its final result – the dialectic of negativity as the moving and productive principle – is simply that Hegel grasps the self-development of man as a process, objectification as loss of the object, as alienation and transcendence of this alienation; that he thus grasps the nature of *work* and comprehends objective man, authentic because actual, as the result of his *own work*. (Marx 1997: 321)

Soon after his high praise, however, he engages in a sharp critique of Feuerbach, who he sees as too much concerned with nature rather than radical politics. In the first of his famous *Theses on Feuerbach*, Marx tells us:

> The chief defect of all previous materialism (including Feuerbach's) is that the object, actuality, sensuousness is conceived only in the form of *object or perception* [*Anschauung*], but not as *sensuous human activity, practice* [*Praxis*], not subjectively. Hence in opposition to materialism the *active* side was developed by idealism – but only abstractly since idealism naturally does not know actual, sensuous activity as such. Feuerbach wants sensuous objects actually different from thought objects: but he does not comprehend human activity itself as *objective*. (Marx 1997: 400)

Marx departs from *all* forms of mechanical materialism and reinforces his claim that Hegel grasped (though mystified) the self-development of man as a *process*. Hegel grasped the nature of human activity – work. Although Marx speaks of human activity, his focus is on activity as *laboring* in the current historical situation that he was confronting. He consistently opposes "sensuous human activity, practice [*Praxis*]" to the mere "thought-determinations" of philosophy. It is in practice that "man must prove the truth, that is, actuality and power, this-sidedness of his thinking" (Marx 1997: 401). For Marx, "[a]ll social life is essentially *practical*. All mysteries which lead theory to mysticism find their rational solution in human practice and the comprehension of this practice" (Marx 1997: 401–2). In his sixth thesis, Marx declares: "Feuerbach resolves the religious essence into the *human* essence. But the essence of man is no abstraction inhering in each single individual. In its actuality it is the ensemble of social relationships" (Marx 1997: 402).[4]

Marx's *Theses on Feuerbach* conclude with the famous eleventh thesis: "The philosophers have only *interpreted* the world in various ways; the point is, to *change* it" (Marx 1997: 402) – a thesis that is frequently misinterpreted. Marx is not condemning the project of interpretation. Rather, he is condemning the varieties of interpretation that mystify concrete historical reality. A true interpretation of this historical reality expresses the need for radical change; it is a theory that can become a material force. Throughout his life, Marx was deeply skeptical of calls for action that are not informed by a correct interpretation of historical reality – one that confronts the contradictions and seeks to resolve them by revolutionary practice.

Marx develops his early reflections on nature from this radical orientation. Unlike Spinoza, Hume, Kant, and Hegel, who are committed to a *philosophical* understanding of nature, Marx approaches the meaning of nature from his conception of man as a laboring animal. I want to reconstruct Marx's early reflections on nature. Although the *language* here in his early writings such as the *Paris Manuscripts* – especially the reference to "species-being" and his understanding of what is "authentically human" – is indebted to Feuerbach, the *substance* of his claims is distinctively Marxian. I hope to show that even though Marx abandons this Feuerbachian idiom, major themes in these early reflections on nature persist throughout his later writings – including *Das Kapital*.

The *Paris Manuscripts* are most famous for Marx's analysis of alienated labor. Frequently, the very meaning of alienation and the specific rationale for Marx's discussion of alienation are ignored. If we want to understand the meaning of alienation, we need to go back to Hegel. From a traditional philosophical perspective (and even from a common-sense perspective), we normally make a sharp distinction between persons and objects. A craftsman makes a chair, or a factory worker makes an automobile, but we normally consider the chair or automobile to be a distinct object that is completely independent of the person producing it. Neither Hegel nor Marx thinks of the relation of producer to product in this way. Rather, for them, the object produced is the *congealed* or *embodied form* of the *activity* that produces it. We come closest to this understanding of the relation of human actors to the objects they produce when we *identify* Rembrandt or Rothko with the works of art they create. This is the *objectification* of the activity of the producer. The first stage in understanding alienation is grasping that the *object* the laborer makes is his *activity* congealed.[5] This is not simply a metaphor but rather a statement of the relation of the maker to the object made. However, under specific historical circumstances (wage labor and capitalism), the object produced also stands opposed to and becomes hostile to the producer. "[T]he object which labor produces, its product, stands opposed to it as an *alien thing*, as a *power independent* of the producer. The product of labor is labor embodied and made objective in a thing. It is the *objectification* of labor" (Marx 1997: 289). The object produced by wage labor both *is* and *is not* the laborer. It *is* the laborer insofar as his activity is congealed in a product, but it *is not* the laborer insofar as it degrades and dehumanizes him. Marx analyzes alienation from the perspective of political economy. By political economy he means the actual *historical* situation of private property and wage labor and the way it has been conceptualized by political economists such as Adam Smith and David Ricardo. He makes his perspective clear:

> We have proceeded from the presuppositions of political economy. We have accepted its language and its laws. We presupposed private property, the separation of labor, capital and land, hence of wages, profit of capital and rent, likewise the division of labor, competition, the concept of exchange value, etc. From political economy itself, in its own words, we have shown that the worker sinks to *the level of a commodity, the most miserable commodity*. (Marx 1997: 287, emphasis added)

Thus, traditional political economy proceeds by taking private property as a given; it doesn't *explain* private property. The rationale for analyzing alienation is to explain private property and all that it entails. "In the viewpoint of political economy this realization of labor appears as the *diminution* of the worker, the objectification as the *loss of and subservience to the object*, and the appropriation as *alienation* [*Entfremdung*], as externalization [*Entäusserung*]" (Marx 1997: 289). Marx goes on to say, "The more the worker exerts himself, the more powerful becomes the alien objective world which he fashions against himself, the poorer he and his inner world become, the less there is that belongs to him" (Marx 1997: 289–90). Alienation is a denial of the capacities of human beings to realize themselves fully and freely. Instead, the worker becomes a slave to the objects that he produces. This is the context in which Marx introduces the concept of nature. "The worker can make nothing without *nature*, without the *sensuous external world*. It is the material wherein his labor realizes itself, wherein it is active, out of which and by means of which it produces" (Marx 1997: 290). Initially, Marx conceives of nature as the sensuous external world that the worker uses in his production. Soon we will see how this understanding of nature becomes more complex.

Marx summarizes this form of alienation – alienation from the product that the worker produces when he makes use of nature as the sensuous external world:

> The alienation of the worker in his object is expressed according to the laws of political economy as follows: the more the worker produces, the less he has to consume; the more values he creates, the more worthless and unworthy he becomes; the better shaped his product, the more misshapen is he; the more civilized his product, the more barbaric is the worker; the more powerful the work, the more powerless becomes the worker; the more intelligence the work has, the more witless is the worker and the more he becomes a slave of nature. (Marx 1997: 291)

Political economy *conceals* this alienation because it ignores the direct relationship between the worker (laborer) and the products that he makes. Marx proceeds to consider two other aspects of alienation. The worker is not only alienated from the *product* of his labor, but the very *activity* of his laboring is alienating. "[A]lienation is shown not only in the result but also in the *process of production*, in the *producing activity* itself" (Marx 1997: 291). Laboring as producing activity is *external* to the worker, "it is not part of his nature" (Marx 1997: 292). The worker does not *affirm* himself in his work but denies himself. His labor is not voluntary and free; it is coerced. "The result, therefore, is that man (the worker) feels that he is acting freely only in his animal functions – eating, drinking, and procreating, or at most in his shelter and finery – while in his human functions he feels only like an animal. The animalistic becomes the human and the human the animalistic" (Marx 1997: 292). Note the strong contrast that Marx draws between man's *animal* functions (functions man shares with nonhuman animals) and his *human* functions. Marx summarizes these two aspects of alienation thus:

> We have considered labor, the act of alienation of practical human activity, in two aspects: (1) the relationship of the worker to the *product of labor* as an alien object dominating him. This relationship is at the same time the relationship to the sensuous external world, to natural objects as an alien world hostile to him; (2) the relationship of labor to the *act of production* in *labor*. This relationship is that of the worker to his own activity as alien and not belonging to him, activity as passivity, power as weakness, procreation as emasculation, the worker's *own* physical and spiritual energy, his personal life – for what else is life but activity – as an activity turned against him, independent of him, and not belonging to him. *Self-alienation*, as against the alienation of the *object*, stated above. (Marx 1997: 292–3)

Marx proceeds to derive a third aspect of alienated labor based on the first two aspects. He introduces the controversial idea of "species-being" (*Gattungswesen*). This is a further refinement of Marx's concept of nature. Man is a species-being as "he considers himself to be a *universal* and consequently free being" (Marx 1997: 293). Man, as well as animal, lives physically by inorganic nature, but the universality of man "appears in practice in the universality which makes the whole of nature his *inorganic* body: (1) as a direct means of life, and (2) as the matter, object, and instrument of his life activity" (Marx 1997: 293).

> Nature is the *inorganic body* of man, that is, nature insofar as it is not the human body. Man *lives* by nature. This means that nature is his *body* with which he must remain in perpetual process in order not to die. That the physical and spiritual life of man is tied up with nature is another way of saying that *nature is linked to itself, for man is a part of nature*. (Marx 1997: 293, emphasis added)

When Marx initially introduced the concept of nature, he distinguished man (the worker) from nature. Nature is the material – the sensuous external world – that the worker *uses* to make products, like the wood one uses to make a chair. Now we see that man himself not only lives by nature: he is *a part of nature*. Man is a natural creature who uses nature to produce objects. Nonhuman animals are identical with their life activity, but "[m]an makes his life activity itself into an object of will and consciousness. He has conscious life activity" (Marx 1997: 294). In asserting that man is a species-being, Marx is asserting that human beings have a distinctive character, but this is not to be interpreted as a *fixed permanent essence*.[6] Man as a species-being is changeable and malleable. (Recall that in his sixth thesis on Feuerbach, Marx asserts that the essence of man is in its actuality *"the ensemble of social relationships,"* and this ensemble changes in the course of history.) In alienated labor, man's species-being is degraded; it becomes merely a means for physical existence. But man as a species-being has the *capacity* for "free spontaneous activity" – a capacity (or rather a set of capacities) that can be *actualized* only with the transformation of the system of alienated labor. Marx does not think of alienation as primarily a psychological condition, although it has psychological consequences for alienated workers who experience misery. Nor is alienation a *permanent* existential condition of human beings. Alienation is an *objective* historical condition that results from the whole system of private property and wage labor; it is built into the structure of capitalism.[7]

A direct consequence of man's alienation from the product of his work, from his life activity, and from his species-existence, is the *alienation of man from man*. When man confronts himself, he confronts *other* men. What holds true of man's relationship to his work, to the product of his work, and to himself, also holds true of man's relationship to other men, to their labor, and the object of their labor. (Marx 1997: 295)

This is the third aspect of alienation. Man is alienated not only from the product of his labor and his life activity, he is also alienated from other men. Only with the overthrow of the whole system of alienated labor can the free spontaneous activity of human beings flourish. The rationale for Marx's analysis of these aspects of alienation is that he seeks to explain what is at the *root* of private property and the political-economic system of capitalism. The emergence of capitalism is fundamentally a *historical* phenomenon. The system of wage labor has not always existed; one needs to understand how it arose in the course of history. In *The German Ideology*, Marx begins to provide a sketch of the emergence of capitalism from earlier forms of the material activity of human life – the "different forms of ownership" – beginning with tribal ownership and culminating with the emergence of modern private property (Marx 1997: 410–11). "We know only one science, the science of history. History can be viewed from two sides; it can be divided into the history of nature and that of man. The two sides, however, are not to be seen as independent entities. *As long as man has existed, nature and man have affected each other*" (Marx 1997: 408, emphasis added).

Marx makes a crucial move here that refines his understanding of nature and the *transaction* that takes place between human beings as natural creatures and the rest of nature.[8] Originally, when Marx spoke of the laborer working upon and using nature as a resource, it appeared that there was a clear distinction between the actor – the laborer – and the natural material that he uses. But what becomes increasingly clear is that there is no duality here. We overcome the suggested duality by reminding ourselves that "as long as man has existed, nature and man have affected each other" (Marx 1997: 408). Marx is developing a *new* and different way of thinking about the relationship of man and nature in which – to use a Hegelian turn of phrase – they are *moments* within a *single relational transactional process*. Marx illustrates this when he describes how human beings produce food as a means of subsistence:

> The way in which man produces his food depends first of all on the nature of the means of subsistence that he finds and has to reproduce. This mode

of production must not be viewed simply as reproduction of the physical existence of individuals. Rather it is a definite form of their activity, a definite way of expressing their life, a definite *mode of life*. As individuals express their life, so they are. What they are, therefore, coincides with what they produce, with *what* they produce and *how* they produce. The nature of individuals thus depends on the material conditions which determine their production. (Marx 1997: 409)

This analysis of food production supports a more general conclusion: that "[h]istory itself is an *actual* part of *natural history*, of nature's development into man. Natural science will in time include the essence of man as the science of man will include natural science: There will be *one* science" (Marx 1997: 312).

Earlier, in discussing Marx's letter to his father, I noted that Marx was greatly disturbed by the conflict of the "is" and the "ought"; this was one of the reasons for his attraction to Hegel. Marx sought to bring forth what he took to be the *material* truth in Hegel. We can now see how this is manifest in his analysis of alienation. Hegel makes a sharp distinction between what *exists* and what is fully *actualized*. What exists is what is *presently* before us. For Marx, what presently exists is the system of private property and alienated labor. For Hegel, what exists needs to be *negated* and transformed, in order to be fully *actualized* – to fully realize its potential. Actualization is the *process of development* by which an entity actualizes the potential implicit in its Concept (in the Hegelian sense of *Begriff*). Thus, for Hegel, the alienated form of man's species-being must be *negated* and *transformed* in order for man's species-being to be *actualized* as "free spontaneous activity." For Marx, this actualization takes place not within consciousness and self-consciousness but in the *material* life of sensuous human beings.[9] Man's species-being as "free spontaneous activity" can only be *actualized* by revolutionary *praxis*. "In taking from man the object of his production, alienated labor takes from his *species-life*, his actual and objective existence as a species. It changes his superiority to the animal to inferiority since he is deprived of nature, his inorganic body" (Marx 1997: 295). Nature then is not simply the "sensuous external world" – the nature that man uses in his labor. In the actualization of man's species-being, both nature and human beings are *transformed*. Marx does not deny that there are laws of the natural world discovered by the progress of the natural sciences. Throughout his life, Marx kept himself informed of developments in the natural sciences, including Darwin's theory of evolution. Knowledge of the laws of nature is essential for grasping the *constraints* on human activity. Marx's central concern, however, was to understand the *relation* and *transaction* of man (who is a natural creature) with nonhuman nature.

> Immediately, *man* is a *natural being*. As a living natural being he is, in one aspect, endowed with the *natural capacities* and *vital powers* of an *active* natural being. These capacities exist in him as tendencies and capabilities, as *drives*. In another aspect as a natural, living, sentient and objective being man is a *suffering*, conditioned, and limited creature like an animal or plant. The *objects* of his drives, that is to say, exist outside him as independent, yet they are *objects* of his *need*, essential and indispensable to the exercise and confirmation of his *essential capacities*. The fact that man is a *corporeal*, actual, sentient, objective being with natural capacities means that he has *actual, sensuous objects* for his nature as objects of his life-expression, or that he can only *express* his life in actual sensuous objects. (Marx 1997: 325)

In alienated labor, nature is taken to be something other and alien to man. This *relation* is transformed when man's species-being is fully actualized by the negation of alienated labor. Nature becomes humanized.

> The *human* essence of nature primarily exists only for *social* man, because only here is nature a *link* with *man*, as his existence for others and their existence for him, as the life-element of human actuality – only here is nature the *foundation* of man's own *human* existence. Only here has the *natural* existence of man become his *human* existence and nature become human. Thus *society* is the completed, essential unity of man with nature, the true resurrection of nature, the fulfilled naturalism of man and humanism of nature. (Marx 1997: 305–6)[10]

Marx is euphoric in his description of what the overcoming of private property and alienated labor means – what the humanization of nature means.

> For not only the five senses but also the so-called spiritual and moral senses (will, love, etc.), in a word, *human* sense and the humanity of the senses come into being only through the existence of *their* object, through nature *humanized*. The development of the five senses is a labor of the whole previous history of the world. *Sense* subordinated to crude, practical need has only a *narrow* meaning. . . . For the starving man food does not exist in its human form but only in its abstract character as food. It could be available in its crudest form and one could not say wherein the starving man's eating differs from that of *animals*. The care-laden, needy man has no mind for the most beautiful play. The dealer in minerals sees only their market value but not their beauty and special nature; he has no mineralogical sensitivity. Hence the objectification of the human essence, both theoretically and

practically, is necessary to *humanize* man's *senses* and also create a *human sense* corresponding to the entire wealth of humanity and nature. (Marx 1997: 309–10)

Although Marx's language is florid and even romantic, the point he is making is extremely important. Nature is not taken to be something that exists completely independent of man's (the worker's) laboring activity. Rather, it is shaped and reshaped by human activity. In changing the sensuous external world by their practical activity, *human beings change themselves*. Marx is deeply skeptical of an innocent conception of nature untouched by human activity and history. Nature is always related to the historical societal activity. And societal activity is always related to historical nature. There is an interdependence between nature and history. What we take to be nature changes in the course of changing historical social formations. Neil Smith and Phil O'Keefe succinctly state Marx's understanding of the relation of society and nature.

> Nature separate from society had no meaning for Marx; nature is always related to societal activity.... Writing as long ago as the 1840s, when Africa was still known as the Dark Continent, Marx and Engels could conclude that a "nature [which] preceded human history ... no longer exists anywhere (except perhaps on a few Australian coral-islands of recent origin)". ... Historically and practically, the relation with nature is at the centre of human activity since people rely on nature for the fulfillments of fundamental needs. (Smith and O'Keefe 1980: 32)

Marx wrote long before the contemporary concern with climate change and the human destruction of the earth by the excessive use of fossil fuels, but his insights are directly relevant to what is happening today. The nature that we confront today is a nature that is determined by capitalist imperatives. Under the present capitalist system, nature is primarily a resource to be exploited for profit. Marx would be skeptical about the attempts of various environmental movements to change fundamentally this exploitive relation to nature unless one seeks to transform capitalism.[11] If one is serious about establishing a greater ecological harmony between human beings and nonhuman nature, then the system of capitalism needs to be transformed.

In his early writings, Marx claims that man's senses are directly related to his *practical activity* and consequently change in the course of history. But this is also true of Marx's distinctive understanding of our higher cognitive capacities. Leszek Kolakowski explains this in the following terms:

> Human consciousness, the practical mind, although it does not produce existence, produces existence as composed of individuals divided into species and genera. From the moment man in his onto- and phylogenesis begins to dominate the world of things [and nature – RJB] intellectually – from the moment he invents instruments that can organize it and then expresses this organization in words – he finds that world already constructed and differentiated, not according to some alleged natural classification but according to a classification imposed by practical need for orientation in one's environment. (Kolakowski 1968: 46)

Man does not confront a nature that exists in itself completely independently of his *relation* to it. There is always a nonhuman "natural substratum," or "stuff," that man works upon and shapes. I agree with Kolakowski when he says that Marx's basic idea is

> that man as a cognitive being is only part of man as a whole; that that part is constantly involved in a process of progressive autonomization, nevertheless it cannot be understood otherwise than as a function of a continuing dialogue between human needs and their objects. This dialogue, called work, is created by both the human species and the external world, which thus becomes accessible to man only in its humanized form. (Kolakowski 1968: 66)[12]

Let me summarize Marx's view of nature and man's *transactional* relationship to nature as it emerges from his writings in the mid-1840s. Using Shlomo Avineri's helpful description, to Marx, man is essentially "the creative being who has a unique dialectical relationship to nature and to the objective world, which both sustains him and is also formed by his labor and his activity. This human activity constantly changes both nature and man himself" (Avineri 2019: 65).[13] Avineri states what Marx takes to be the essential difference between humans and other animals:

> To Marx, the major difference between humans and other animals is that animals are sustained by the means that nature puts at their disposal and are therefore constrained and limited by what nature offers them as food or shelter: their relationship to nature is basically passive, constant, and limited to their biological determination. Humans, on the other hand, shape nature, change it, and mold it to their need; in doing this, they also create new needs, whereas the needs of other animals are unchanged and strictly determined biologically. By creating new needs, humans also create history – as history is the developmental way by which they supply their needs through labor. Labor obviously needs a material, natural foundation, but it is changing nature, whereas animals just take from nature what it offers

and leaves it as it is. Without naming it "historical materialism," this is the crux of Marx's philosophical anthropology: labor is thus the foundation of human active consciousness: before being *Homo sapiens*, man is *Homo faber*. (Avineri 2019: 65–6)

Marx focuses on the activity of alienated labor – whereby man is alienated from his product, his productive activity, his fellow human beings, and from nature. Nature designates "the sensuous external world" that man *uses* in his labor (although he also uses tools and artificial objects), but man is *also* "a part of nature." There is a mutual interdependence between man (as a natural producer) and the nonhuman nature that man uses. Georg Lukács summarizes how nature is socially conditioned: "Nature is a societal category. That is to say, whatever is held to be natural at any given stage of social development, however this nature is related to man and in whatever form his involvement with it takes, i.e. nature's form, its content, its range and its objectivity are all socially conditioned" (Lukács 1971: 234). However, as Alfred Schmidt notes, responding to Lukács, "If nature is a social category, the inverted statement that society is a category of nature is equally valid. Although nature and its laws subsist independently of all human consciousness and will for the materialist Marx, it is only possible to formulate and apply statements about nature with the help of social categories" (Schmidt 1971: 70). Because the relation between man and nature is *transactional*, we can say that man as a social being *acts* in shaping nature. But we can also say that the *historical* shape of nonhuman nature is not merely passive but *active* in shaping the determinate character of human beings. Marx is not interested in "nature in itself" (nature that is completely independent of its relation to man); nor does he think that this is even *intelligible*. He does not question that the natural sciences can inform us about the character of nature, but even the categories of science are historically and socially determined. Marx focuses on how the historical "practical mind" organizes and shapes nature. The interdependent transactional relation between man and nature means that *as man changes, so does nature*. Just as there is a history of man, so too there is a history of nature. Both these histories are part of a *single* history of changing social and economic structures. The social structure of alienated labor is an *objective* historical social structure – *not* a permanent human condition. We need to understand the *historical genesis* and *consequences* of alienated labor in order to grasp how it can be changed and transformed. This is not something that happens in the realm of consciousness and self-consciousness; it happens only in the active, sensuous, material natural world. The detailed analysis of the present structure and development of alienated labor, private property, and capitalism reveals deep contradictions – contradictions that provide the *conditions* for the revolutionary transformation of capitalism. Such overcoming and transformation do *not* happen automatically without the intervention of human activity. Consequently, the type of transformation that is required for the flourishing of human freedom is *contingent* – it is not a matter of rigid historical necessity. The aim of this activity is to overcome the deformation of man's species-being as an ensemble of social relations that is inherent in alienated labor and private property.

Marx's early discussion of the concept of nature, his analysis of alienated labor, the critical demand to overcome alienated labor in order to *actualize* the positive flourishing of capacities of free human beings in society, the analysis of what it means for nature to be humanized and for human beings to be fully naturalized – all these discourses are based primarily upon Marx's unpublished writings of the mid-1840s. The *Paris Manuscripts* became available only in the 1920s. They were barely known until a critical edition was prepared after World War II. The availability of these manuscripts provided the basis for a new interpretation of Marx that emphasized his humanism. These manuscripts provided the basis – especially in Eastern Europe – for a sharp critique of the Stalinist deformation of Marxism. For the *Praxis* group in the former Yugoslavia, these early manuscripts became the basis for advocating a Marxist humanism. It became fashionable to speak of "two Marxs" – the early *humanistic* Marx and the more mature *scientific* Marx of *Das Kapital*. However, the growth and spread of "Marxist humanism" coincided with a strong counter-movement led by the French philosopher Louis Althusser, who argued that there was good reason that Marx never published the 1844 *Paris Manuscripts*. Althusser (2005) claimed that there was an epistemological rupture in Marx's thinking – one that presumably took place in 1845 when Marx abandoned his humanism as an ideology (indebted to Feuerbach) and began his project of *scientific* Marxism that culminated in *Das Kapital*. The debate between Althusser and his humanistic opponents was not only a theoretical matter; it had practical consequences concerning the status of the "really existing" Communist parties throughout Western and Eastern Europe. Many humanistic Marxists broke with the "official" Communist parties and became dissidents at a time when Althusser and his followers still supported them. The more extreme claims of Althusser about the rupture in Marx's development have since been refuted or significantly modified on the basis of both textual and theoretical grounds.[14] Nevertheless, one cannot ignore the fact that terminology so characteristic of the *Paris Manuscripts* disappears (or recedes into the background) from Marx's thinking. No longer is there a significant reference to "species-being" or "human essence"; nor does Marx make grand claims about a naturalism that becomes humanism or a humanism that becomes naturalism. This has led many to claim that Marx completely abandons his understanding of nature elaborated during the 1840s.

I want to challenge this thesis. I do not deny that significant changes took place in Marx's development. Nor do I want to deny that Marx abandons or modifies many of the key concepts that he employs in his 1840s writings, such as "species-being" and "humanization of nature." Nevertheless, the key points that Marx makes about nature in his "early" writings persist in a modified form in his "later" writings. These points include: (1) approaching questions of nature from the perspective of how they are related to human beings; (2) arguing that human beings transform nature in their laboring activity; (3) arguing that in changing nature, human beings change themselves; (4) recognizing that in a capitalist society there is a deformation of both human beings and nature; (5) arguing that a capitalist system of exploitation is a form of alienated labor whereby human beings are alienated from their products, from their laboring activity, from other human beings, and from nature; (6) claiming that there are tensions and contradictions in capitalism that will eventually lead to its destruction and provide the *conditions* for revolutionary *praxis* that will enable free self-determination. To support these claims fully would require a detailed examination of Marx's unpublished and published works. But I can still justify them with the key discussions in his later works, including the *Grundrisse* and *Das Kapital*.

After the defeat of the 1848 revolutions, Marx, who remained engaged in his political activities and the analysis of contemporary affairs, turned to a more thorough and detailed analysis of the political economy of capitalism. One of his most important and ambitious works is the *Grundrisse*, a series of seven roughly drafted notebooks that he wrote during the winter of 1857–58.[15] These notebooks were not published during his lifetime and only became available in a very limited edition when they were published in Moscow in 1939 and 1941. They became more generally available when a photo-offset reprint was made available in Berlin in 1953. Despite the rough character of these notebooks, they provide a gold mine of information for understanding Marx's intellectual development. They connect with 1840s writings, especially the *Paris Manuscripts*, and provide the background for the composition of *Das Kapital*. In these notebooks Marx outlines an ambitious six-part project of a work on economics. *Das*

Kapital was originally supposed to be only *one* part of this six-part volume. David McLellan notes:

> The *Grundrisse* remains in many ways the most central of Marx's works. It is of wider scope than any later writings and takes up themes from the earlier works, in particular the *1844 Manuscripts*. The ideas of alienation, man as a social being, the dialectical categories of Hegel, and 'communist man' as the aim of history reappear here, though mediated through a profounder study of history and economics than was available to Marx in 1844. (Marx 2000: 379)[16]

There is also a continuity of this work with Marx's reflections on nature in his writings from the 1840s. In his introduction to the *Grundrisse*, Marx reaffirms a point that he made in the *Paris Manuscripts*: "All production is appropriation of *nature* by the individual within and through a definite form of society" (Marx 2000: 383). This reiterates the point made in the *Paris Manuscripts* when Marx first introduces the concept of nature, informing us that that the worker can make nothing without nature – "without the sensuous external world" (Marx 1997: 290). To speak of production in general is to speak about an abstraction. Production always takes place in a specific socio-economic structure. Marx's primary focus is the socio-economic structure and dynamics of capitalism. By the time of the *Grundrisse*, Marx had introduced several refinements. He distinguishes between "use value" and "exchange value"; he refines his thinking about labor by speaking of the "labour power" of the worker and the "surplus value" that the worker creates in a capitalist system. Consider Marx's description of how capitalism shapes nature:

> Thus capital first creates bourgeois society and the universal appropriation of nature and of social relationships themselves by the members of society. Hence the great civilizing influence of capital, its production of a stage of society compared with which all early stages appear to be merely local progress and idolatry of nature. Nature becomes for the first time simply an object for mankind, purely a matter of utility; it ceases to be recognized as a power in its own right; and the theoretical knowledge of its own independent laws appears only as a stratagem designed to subdue it to human requirements, whether as the object of consumption or as the means of production. Pursuing this tendency, capital has pushed beyond national boundaries and prejudices, beyond the deification of nature and the inherited, self-sufficient satisfaction of existing needs confined within well-defined bounds, and the reproduction of the traditional way of life. It is destructive of all this, and permanently revolutionary, tearing down all obstacles that impede the development of productive forces, the expansion of needs, the

diversity of production and the exploitation and exchange of natural and intellectual forces. (Marx 2000: 398)

If we analyze this passage carefully, we see how Marx is describing the transformation of both nature and human beings under the dynamic power of capitalism. This transformation of nature also changes the way in which both workers and capitalists approach nature. Wage laborers need to *use* nature in order to survive in a capitalist system, and capitalists need to exploit nature in order to secure economic profits.

We can also see Marx's analysis of alienated labor reappearing in the *Grundrisse*. The exploitation of workers under a capitalist system results in the alienation of laborers. Marx distinguishes the *objectified labor* that is appropriated by the capitalist and the *living labor* of the wage laborer who needs to labor in order to survive. The objectified labor that the wage laborer creates becomes an *alien power* over the worker. Marx speaks of

> the alien nature of objective conditions of labour as against living labour power, reaching the point that –
>
> (1) these conditions face the worker, as a person, in the person of the capitalist (as personifications with their own will and interest), this absolute separation and divorce of ownership (i.e. of the material conditions of labour from living labour power); these conditions are opposed to the worker as alien property, as the reality of another legal person and the absolute domain of their will –
>
> and that
>
> (2) labour hence appears as alien labour as opposed to the value personified in the capitalist or to the conditions of labour. (Marx 2000: 401)

Marx reaffirms the analysis of alienated labor that he elaborated in the *Paris Manuscripts*, emphasizing that the *objectification* of labor ("labour power") in a capitalist system is *alienated labor*. The products that the worker produces become an alien and hostile power over him. Although the worker uses nature in his productive activity, he also becomes alienated from nature when nature is taken by the capitalist to be a primary resource for exploitation and profit.

Even though the concept "species-being" does not appear in the *Grundrisse*, we can discern its *functional equivalent*. "Species-being," as characterized in the *Theses on Feuerbach*, designates the distinctive flexible, plastic character of human beings – the ensemble of social relationships. These relationships take on different forms in different historical socio-economic systems. In the capitalist system, this ensemble of social relationships is degraded in the form of alienated labor. Nevertheless, because alienation is the *historical* result of the capitalist system (not the ontological or existential condition of human beings), the revolutionary transformation of capitalism enables the potential for human self-determination – the flourishing of positive human capacities. This is not a potential that is actualized *ceteris paribus*. It is not like the potential of a seed to become a tree if the environmental conditions are right. Rather, it is a potential that can be realized *only* if we change the world by *praxis* – a *praxis* that transforms capitalism into a genuinely communist society. Consequently, there is a radical *contingency* about whether the various forms of alienation can be overcome, because this depends on collective social action (*praxis*). Throughout the *Grundrisse* Marx makes references to the flourishing of these human capacities and to creative self-determination. Consider, for example, his criticism of Adam Smith's conception of labor as repulsive and a curse:

> It seems to be far from A. Smith's thoughts that the individual, 'in his normal state of health, strength, activity, skill, and efficiency', might also require a normal portion of work, and of cessation from rest. It is true that the quantity of labour to be provided seems to be conditioned by external circumstances, by the purpose to be achieved, and the obstacles to its achievement that have to be overcome by labour. But neither does it occur to A. Smith that the overcoming of such obstacles may itself constitute an exercise in liberty, and that these external purposes lose their character of mere external necessities and are established as purposes which the individual himself fixes. *The result is the self-realization and objectification of the subject, therefore real freedom, whose activity is precisely labour.* Of course he is correct in saying that labour has always seemed to be repulsive, and forced upon the worker from outside, in its historical forms of slave-labour, bond-labour and wage-labour, and that in this sense non-labour could be opposed to it as 'liberty and happiness'. This is doubly true of this contradictory labour which has not yet created the subjective and objective conditions . . . which make it into attractive labour and individual self-realization. . . . Really free labour, the composing of music for example, is at the same time damned serious and demands the greatest effort. The labour concerned with material production can only have this character if (1) it is of a social nature, (2) it has a scientific character and at the same time is general work, i.e. if it ceases to be human effort as a definite, trained natural force, gives up its purely natural, primitive aspect and becomes the activity of a subject controlling all the forces of nature in the production process. (Marx 2000: 402–3, emphasis added)

In a society in which unalienated labor eventually prevails, *subjective* and *objective* conditions have been created such that human beings control "all the forces of nature in the production process." In such a society, *objectification* is no longer *alienation* but the full positive expression of human *self-realization*.[17] Marx was always resistant to spelling out the details of a future communist society. They have to be worked out by the participants in such a society. (Remember his early declaration that "even though the construction of the future and its completion for all times is not our task, what we have to accomplish at this time is all the more clear: *relentless criticism of all existing conditions*" [Marx 1997: 212].) But he is perfectly clear that in such a society, nature would no longer be encountered as a hostile force or a resource to be exploited solely for profit. Without sentimentalizing man's relation to nature, Marx claims that human beings would be able to relate to nature in a more rational and harmonious manner.

We can also discern the thematic consistency of the transactional relationship between social man and nature in *Das Kapital*.[18] This is evident in his discussion of the fetishism of commodities. Initially, a commodity appears to be a trivial thing, but it turns out to be "a very queer thing" (Marx 2000: 472). Marx repeats a point he made in the *Paris Manuscripts* when he says: "It is as clear as noonday, that man, by his industry, changes the forms of the materials furnished by Nature, in such a way as to make them useful to him. The form of wood, for instance, is altered, by making a table out of it. Yet, for all that, the table continues to be that common, everyday thing, wood" (Marx 2000: 472). Nevertheless, when the table becomes a commodity, "it is changed into something transcendent." The "mystical character" of commodities does not arise from their use value but from their exchange value.

> A commodity is therefore a mysterious thing, simply because in it the social character of men's labour appears to them as an objective character stamped upon the product of that labour; because the relation of the producers to the sum total of their own labour is presented to them as a social relation, existing not between themselves, but between the products of their labour. This is the reason why the products of labour become commodities, social things whose qualities are at the same time perceptible and imperceptible by the senses. . . . [T]he existence of the things *qua* commodities, and the value relation between the products of labour which stamps them as commodities, have absolutely no connection with their physical properties and with the material relations arising therefrom. There it is a definite social relation between men, that assumes, in their eyes, the fantastic form of a relation between things. (Marx 2000: 473)

The analysis of the fetishism of commodities follows the same logic that Marx pursued in his earlier analysis of alienation, albeit at a more advanced level. Initially, a commodity appears as something produced from nature for its use value (like the table built from wood), but in a capitalist society, commodities take on a life of their own that stands in *opposition* to the laborers that produced them. At the same time, the laborer becomes a commodity. In the *Paris Manuscripts*, Marx already states:

> [T]hat the worker sinks to the level of a commodity, the most miserable commodity; that the misery of the worker is inversely proportional to the power and volume of his production; that the necessary result of competition is the accumulation of capital in a few hands and thus the revival of monopoly in a more frightful form; and finally that the distinction between capitalist and landowner, between agricultural laborer and industrial worker, disappears and the whole society must divide into the two classes of *proprietors* and propertyless *workers*. (Marx 1997: 287)

Commodities are the expression of human labor, but they degrade the ensemble of social relations that constitute human beings. *Das Kapital* is not primarily a revolutionary tract but a detailed analysis of the internal dynamics and contradictions of capitalism. Nevertheless, all three volumes are informed by the fundamental conviction that the alienating character of capitalism can be overcome in a manner whereby freedom is achieved when the transaction between men and nature is transformed. The following passage is typical of Marx's affirmation of the *possibility* of human self-determination and genuine freedom.

> In fact, the realm of freedom actually begins only where labour which is determined by necessity and mundane considerations ceases; thus in the very nature of things it lies beyond the sphere of actual material production. Just as the savage must wrestle with Nature to satisfy his wants, to maintain and reproduce life, so must civilized man, and he must do so in all social formations and under all possible modes of production. With his development this realm of physical necessity expands as a result of his wants; but, at the same time, the forces of production which satisfy these wants also increase. *Freedom in this field can only consist in socialized man, the associated producers, rationally regulating their interchange with Nature, bringing it under their common control, instead of being ruled by it as by the blind forces of Nature; and achieving this with the least expenditure of energy and under conditions most favourable to, and worthy of, their human nature.* (Marx 2000: 534–5, emphasis added)

Consequently, there is a thematic consistency in Marx's transactional (dialectical) account of socialized man and nature that was first articulated in the *Paris Manuscripts*, the *Theses on Feuerbach*, and *The German Ideology*, and continued in the *Grundrisse* and *Das Kapital*. There is no epistemological break or rupture, although there is considerable refinement based on Marx's more sophisticated understanding of the political economy and the dynamics of capitalism.

Let me return to Ricoeur's characterization of Marx as a master of the "school of suspicion." What precisely is Marx suspicious of, and why? He is suspicious of what has been so fundamental for modern philosophy since the time of Descartes: the appeal to consciousness as foundational. He doubts the autonomy of consciousness. More specifically, he is suspicious of Hegel's appeal to consciousness and self-consciousness in his *Phenomenology*. He seeks to demystify Hegel's appeal to speculation and to show that, in an obscure manner, Hegel grasps "the self-development of man as a process," that "he grasps the nature of labour and understands objective man, true, because real, man as the result of his own labour" (Marx 2000: 109). The trouble with Hegel, so Marx claims, is that Hegel doesn't understand his own discovery. He doesn't get at the roots; he (along with Feuerbach) is not sufficiently *radical*. He does not grasp the dynamics of concrete sensuous reality – the sensuous suffering and the laboring activity of human beings. To get at the roots that lie buried in Hegel's speculative project, we must appeal to the transaction between human beings (who are part of nature) and nonhuman nature. Although Marx frequently speaks of humans *and* nature, it is more accurate and perspicuous to speak of *humans-in-nature*. Once we fully realize that alienation is an objective *historical* reality determined by capitalism (and not a permanent ontological condition), then the *possibility* is open to transcending capitalism. When (and if) transformation is *actualized* by collective radical *praxis*, then the realm of freedom emerges. Human beings are no longer determined by the blind forces of nature, and only then can socialized human beings regulate their transaction with nature in a more rational and harmonious manner. Only then can the potentialities implicit in the ensemble of social relations that constitute human beings be fully actualized and flourish.

Finally, I want to return to my prologue – the volcanic eruption that took place in grasping the dialectical historical transaction of man and nature. Initially, Marx's project was to demystify what he took to be the pretensions of philosophy. But Marx is not engaged exclusively in a negative critique of a philosophy of nature. His systematic drive is to understand human *praxis* as a manifestation of labor and the way in which *praxis* could be transformed into revolutionary *praxis* – a *praxis* that would finally overcome the alienation of man. Alienation, including the alienation from nature, is an *objective* historical phenomenon that is the result of the present system of wage labor and private property. In his *Paris Manuscripts*,

Marx uses the Feuerbachian language of "species-being" and "dehumanizing nature" to clarify what he means by alienation – alienation from the objects that workers produce, from the laboring activity itself, and from other human beings. I have argued that in his later works, especially in the *Grundrisse* and *Das Kapital*, we find a genuine continuity with his 1840s writings, although there is a considerable development and sophistication in his analysis of the political economy and in his understanding of the structure and dynamics of capitalism. Marx shares a traditional aim of modern philosophy, which sees human *telos* in the achievement of freedom as self-determination. He felt, however, that so much of modern thinking failed to come to grips with how genuine freedom as self-determination is to be concretely achieved. Hegel had already interpreted the world in such a manner that the *telos* of history is freedom, but he failed to realize that freedom can be actualized – concretely realized – by changing the world. Achieving this goal requires a new understanding of nature. Nature is not exclusively a resource used and exploited by human beings, although this is what it has become in a capitalist society. We must grasp that human beings are also natural beings and that their essence includes malleable social relations. We must grasp the transactional character of the *human-in-nature*. Marx in not an idealistic utopian. On the contrary, he holds out the *real possibility* that we can achieve a more rational, humane, and sustainable transactional relation with nature.

6

Nietzsche: Nature and the Affirmation of Life

On July 30, 1881, Nietzsche sent a postcard to his friend Franz Overbeck, on which he excitedly declared:

> I am utterly amazed, utterly enchanted. I have a *precursor*, and what a precursor! I hardly knew Spinoza: that I should have turned to him just *now*, was inspired by "instinct." Not only is his over-all tendency like mine – making knowledge the *most powerful* affect – but in five main points of his doctrine I recognize myself; this most unusual and loneliest thinker is closest to me precisely in these matters: he denies the freedom of the will, teleology, the moral world order, the unegoistic, and evil. Even though the divergences are admittedly tremendous, they are due more to the difference in time, culture, and science. *In summa*: my lonesomeness, which, as on very high mountains, often made it hard for me to breathe and made my blood rush out, is at least a twosomeness [*Zweisamkeit*]. Strange. (Nietzsche 1976: 92)[1]

What underlies this striking sense of affinity is that both thinkers are radical thinkers of immanence – the commitment that the only world is this earthly world and that there is no God, Platonic Forms, or Kantian Ideas that transcend this world. Both are thoroughly committed to rooting out all temptations that appeal to a realm that transcends *this* world and everything in it. We must resist all forms of explanation of this immanent world that – to use Nietzsche's phrase – are "shadows" of a transcendent realm (*GS* 109).[2] This immanent world coincides with nature, and there is nothing behind or beyond it. This is not the first (or the last) time that Nietzsche mentions Spinoza. References to Spinoza appear throughout his works. Nietzsche not only praises Spinoza but also attacks him in the most ruthless manner. In *Beyond Good and Evil* (1886), where Nietzsche mocks the "prejudices of philosophers," he writes:

> Or consider the hocus-pocus of mathematical form with which Spinoza clad his philosophy – really "the love of *his* wisdom," to render that word fairly and squarely – in mail and mask, to strike terror at the very outset into the heart of any assailant who should dare to glance at that invincible maiden and Pallas Athena: how much personal timidity and vulnerability this masquerade of a sick hermit betrays! (*BGE* 5)[3]

Nietzsche mocks the very idea of *causa sui* – the first and most important concept in Spinoza's *Ethics* and the *foundation* of his entire system. "The *causa sui* is the best self-contradiction that has been conceived so far, it is a sort of rape and perversion of logic; but the extravagant pride of man has managed to entangle itself profoundly and frightfully with just this nonsense" (*BGE* 21). There is a deep affinity between Nietzsche and Spinoza, but Spinoza is also Nietzsche's "mortal enemy." Nietzsche frequently praises the need for worthy enemies. Yovel eloquently epitomizes the basic affinity between Spinoza and Nietzsche, as well as the extreme differences between them:

> In Spinoza the immanent world inherits the divine status and many of the properties of the defunct transcendent God. Self-caused and self-justified, it is eternal and infinite (both in quantity and in perfection). Its existence follows necessarily from its essence, is governed by fixed and eternal laws, and is rationally intelligible throughout. As for man, he exists "in God" and shares in the same universal rationality by which eventually he can rise above his finitude and realize eternity within his temporal existence. By contrast, Nietzsche's experience of immanence leaves no room for order, permanence, fixed laws, inherent rationality, or truth; it presupposes a mode of existence from which not only God, but, as Nietzsche says, "God's shadows" have also been removed. Man exists here in an ever-transient flux of (cosmic) "will to power," without redemption, without fixed truth, with nothing to explain his life or justify his death. As for the concept of *necessity* – the object of love – it signifies in Spinoza that existence flows from the essence of God and is rational and divine throughout, whereas in Nietzsche necessity is opaque, an unintelligible *fatum*, devoid of essence or rational ground and pressing upon all creatures as an inescapable burden. (Yovel 1986: 186)[4]

One of the sharpest statements of Nietzsche's commitment to this immanent world appears in the section "Let us beware" of *The Gay Science* (1882): "The total character of the world . . . is for all eternity chaos, not in the sense of a lack of necessity but of a lack of order, organization, form, beauty, wisdom, and whatever else our aesthetic anthropomorphisms are called" (*GS* 109).

There are serious obstacles that stand in the way of any interpretation of Nietzsche. No thinker (philosopher or non-philosopher) ever wrote like Nietzsche, employing aphorisms, fragments, poems, songs, metaphors, and polemics in quite the way he does. He celebrates experimental writing; his books frequently read more like creative works of fiction than sustained arguments. He praises contradictions – the mark of a free thinker – and disdains boring linear arguments.

> *Being able to contradict.* – Everybody knows now that being able to stand contradiction is a high sign of culture. Some even know that the higher human being desires and invites contradiction in order to receive a hint about his own injustice of which he is as yet unaware. But the *ability to* contradict, the acquired *good* conscience accompanying hostility towards what is familiar, traditional, hallowed – that is better yet than both those abilities, and constitutes what is really great, new, and amazing in our culture; it is the step of all steps of the liberated spirit: who knows that? (*GS* 297)

Given almost any interpretation of Nietzsche, one can find passages that appear to contradict it. Clearly, some interpretations are off the wall – like reading Nietzsche as a proto-Nazi or a vicious anti-Semite, interpretations that were prevalent during Hitler's time.[5] This still leaves room for extremely divergent readings of Nietzsche.[6] It is almost as if Nietzsche delights in provoking divergent readings or emphases because of his celebration of pluralism and his perspectivism. As Lanier Anderson notes:

> For Nietzsche, a person's ability to deploy and be responsive to a multiplicity of values, virtues, of outlooks and "perspectives", is a positive good in its own right. Nietzsche's defense of this idea is perhaps clearest in the epistemic case, where he insists on the value of bringing multiple perspectives to bear on any question: the thinker must "know how to make precisely the *difference* in perspectives and affective interpretations useful for knowledge", because
>
>> There is *only* a perspectival seeing, *only* a perspectival "knowing"; and *the more* affects we allow to speak about a matter, *the more* eyes, different eyes, we know how to bring to bear on one and the same matter, that much more complete will our "concept" of this matter, our "objectivity", be. (*GM* III:12) (Anderson 2017: 3.2.6.)[7]

We should not think that the multiplicity of perspectives can or should be reconciled with each other in a *harmonious* whole. Different perspectives may clash and even contradict each other. This is not a defect. It is essential for seeking *genuine* knowledge.

> But precisely because we seek knowledge, let us not be ungrateful to such resolute reversals of accustomed perspectives and valuations with which the spirit has, with apparent mischievousness and futility, raged against itself for so long: to see differently in this way for once, to *want* to see differently, is no small discipline and preparation of the intellect for its future "objectivity" – the latter understood not as "contemplation without interest" (which is a nonsensical absurdity), but as the ability *to control* one's Pro and Con and to dispose of them, so that one knows how to employ a *variety* of perspectives and affective interpretations in the service of knowledge. (*GM* III:12)

To appreciate the radicalness of the above claims, note how Nietzsche speaks of "knowledge" and "objectivity."[8] Virtually every philosopher prior to Nietzsche (and also after Nietzsche) claims that the minimal necessary condition for knowledge is a consistency of epistemic claims. If these claims really contradict each other, then something is wrong – this is a sure sign that we have not achieved "genuine" knowledge. Nietzsche, however, claims that knowledge requires the ability to employ a variety of perspectives and affective interpretations – even those that contradict each other. Furthermore, here, and in many other places, he mocks the idea of a disinterested knowledge to achieve objectivity. He insists that this conventional understanding of objectivity is an absurdity. There is no disinterested knowledge; there is no such thing as the "view from nowhere."

We might mention another source of perplexity, which could be labeled as "double reading." For any fundamental philosophical concept – knowledge, objectivity, truth, necessity, rationality, virtue, value, etc. – Nietzsche seeks to expose *both* its negative and its positive features, or, to use his terminology, its dark, sick aspects and its bright, illuminating, healthy features. He condemns and ridicules typical philosophical conceptions of knowledge, objectivity, truth, and so on. If we focus exclusively on those passages, we will come to the misleading conclusion that Nietzsche does not think that there is *any* genuine knowledge or truth. We may conclude that Nietzsche is a radical nihilist.[9] In the above passage from the *Genealogy of Morals* (1887), Nietzsche defends the need for "resolute reversals of accustomed perspectives and valuations" in order to seek knowledge and the objectivity of the future. A vivid example of holding together conflicting perspectives is the "good/bad" distinction and "good/evil" distinction in the *Genealogy*. A straightforward reading of the *Genealogy* might lead to the conclusion that Nietzsche favors, and even has nostalgia for, the ancient aristocratic class – the class that thought of themselves as noble, excellent, and good, and of those who are not like them as bad. Nietzsche also seeks to expose and discredit the good/evil distinction that lies at the heart of Christianity and arises out of *ressentiment*. Nevertheless, this is how he concludes his discussion of these two distinctions.

> The two *opposing* values "good and bad," "good and evil" have been engaged in a fearful struggle on earth for thousands of years; and though the latter value has certainly been on top for a long time, there are still places where the struggle is as yet undecided. One might even say that it has risen ever higher and thus become more and more profound and spiritual: so that today there is perhaps no more decisive mark of a *"higher nature,"* a more spiritual nature, than that of being divided in this sense and a genuine battleground of these opposed values. (*GM* I:16)[10]

Nietzsche celebrates the *struggle*, the *battleground* of opposing powerful drives; this is the decisive mark of a healthy "higher nature." The desire for a harmonious reconciliation is the mark of weaker, sick creatures.

Nietzsche's radical claims about knowledge and objectivity serve as a warning to anyone who seeks to interpret his philosophy. Many commentators and interpreters of Nietzsche have a tendency to emphasize *one* idea or theme that presumably unlocks the *key* to his thinking – for example, appealing to the will to power, eternal recurrence, nihilism, or the claim that God is dead. None of these really works as a basis for a *single* unified interpretation. Approaching Nietzsche from his conception of nature is only *one* perspective – one that *should be supplemented* by other perspectives. There are always "many eyes." This, of course, does not mean that all perspectives are equally valid. One must support an interpretation with the strongest possible textual evidence – evidence that acknowledges different, even opposing, perspectives and interpretations.

Unlike Spinoza, Hume, Kant, and Hegel, Nietzsche is skeptical – or, more accurately, suspicious – of the very idea of a "philosophy of nature" – just as Marx and Freud are. Nietzsche, along with these two other masters of the "school of suspicion" – are suspicious of what they take to be the misleading pretenses and prejudices of philosophy. All too frequently, what philosophers call "rational" turns out to be nothing but a "rationalization" of conflicting instincts, drives, and affects that are hidden from consciousness. What is worse is that when philosophy is taken to be an autonomous discipline, it obscures and distorts the underlying dynamics of nature. The three "masters of suspicion" also question the basis of modern philosophy – the appeal of consciousness itself.[11] Marx, Nietzsche, and Freud are three great "destroyers." They "destroy" in order to clear the way for a deeper and more *honest* understanding of human beings as natural creatures – natural creatures who are not always consciously aware of the instincts, drives, and forces that shape them.

Recently, Anglo-American commentators and interpreters of Nietzsche have developed a naturalistic reading of Nietzsche. "Naturalism" is a label that covers a wide diversity of meanings, some of which are even contradictory. There is *no* philosophical consensus about what naturalism means or *ought* to mean.[12] Nietzsche would resist being labeled by any "ism," including "naturalism." He would take this as an example of the misguided philosophical attempt to classify, police, and find order where there is plurality, conflict, struggle, and tensions that resist classification.

Richard Schacht – one of the contemporary Anglo-American Nietzsche scholars who interprets him as a naturalistic thinker – notes that there are clearly versions of naturalism that Nietzsche disdains and scathingly attacks.[13]

> For example, there is the "mechanistic" kind he calls one of "the *stupidest*" ("der dümmsten") ways of assessing and construing music (and not only music) in the second edition of *The Gay Science* (*GS* 373), and the kind he attributes (in *Beyond Good and Evil*) to "Naturalisten," whose "clumsiness" ("Ungeschick") is such that "they no sooner touch 'the soul' than they lose it." (*GS* 373, *BGE* 12, cited in Schacht 2012: 185)

Let us begin exploring the issue of Nietzsche's "naturalism." Previously, in the chapter on Hume, I cited the three core commitments that Joseph Rouse lists to describe philosophical naturalism. First, naturalists "refuse any appeal to or acceptance of what is supernatural or otherwise transcendent to the natural world." (Rouse 2015: 3). Nietzsche shares this commitment. Throughout his career, he approaches the issue of religion and God from a variety of perspectives; he debunks anything that "smells" of the transcendent and the supernatural; he roots out the debilitating consequences of religions – especially Christianity. He seeks to unmask the *shadows* of the divine as it appears in philosophy and metaphysics.

The second core commitment is to a "scientific understanding of nature." "At a minimum, naturalists regard scientific understanding as relevant to all significant aspects of human life" (Rouse 2015: 3). When Nietzsche speaks of the sciences, he is following the nineteenth-century conception of sciences as *Wissenschaften*. The concept includes much more than our contemporary understanding of the natural sciences; it includes such disciplines as history, philology, and linguistics. Schacht suggests that when Nietzsche refers to *Wissenschaften*, "they . . . are better construed . . . to mean something like 'cognitive inquiry' and 'cognitive disciplines' of various sorts, devoted to the attainment of a variety of forms of knowledge" (Schacht 2012: 186).[14] Nevertheless, there is plenty of historical evidence that Nietzsche had a good understanding of the natural sciences of his time – and frequently drew on these to support his claims.[15] Throughout his works, Nietzsche appeals to *his* understanding of physics, biology, physiology, and psychology.

The third core commitment is a repudiation of any conception "of 'first philosophy' as prior to or authoritative over scientific understanding" (Rouse 2015: 3). Rouse is thinking primarily of W. V. O. Quine, although Nietzsche is perhaps the most thoroughgoing critic of the very idea of a "first philosophy" or metaphysics that is prior to and authoritative over scientific thinking.

Even if one agrees that Nietzsche shares these core commitments, they are so abstract and general that they do not illuminate what is distinctive about Nietzsche's understanding of nature. To explore these details, especially as they pertain to human beings, I want to consider the Anglo-American naturalistic reading of Nietzsche. Schacht was among the first contemporary philosophers to advance a naturalistic reading of Nietzsche in his 1983 book *Nietzsche*. But the heated controversy about Nietzsche's naturalism really took off with Brian Leiter's book *Nietzsche on Morality* (2015 [2002]), in which he sets out to give a systematic reading of Nietzsche as a philosophical naturalist. Leiter claims that Nietzsche's naturalism "is fundamentally a *methodological* view, which holds that philosophical inquiry should be both *modelled on* the methods of the successful sciences, and, at a minimum, *consistent with* the results of those sciences" (Leiter 2004: 77)[16] Leiter distinguishes between "Methodological Naturalism" and "Substantive Naturalism." While Nietzsche is committed to "the (ontological) view that the only things that exist are *natural*" (Leiter 2015 [2002]: 5) – the view that Leiter labels "Substantive Naturalism" – Nietzsche also shares the principles of "*Methodological* Naturalism (M-Naturalism)," according to which "philosophical inquiry . . . should be continuous with empirical inquiry in the sciences" (Leiter 2015 [2002]: 3). Furthermore, according to Leiter, Nietzsche's version of M-Naturalism is distinguished by two commitments. Building on his earlier claims, in his 2013 essay, "Nietzsche's Naturalism Reconsidered," Leiter argues that Nietzsche is a "Speculative M-Naturalist, that is, a philosopher, like Hume, who wants to 'construct theories that are "modeled" on the sciences . . . in that they take over from science the idea that natural phenomena have deterministic causes' (Leiter 2002: 5)" (Leiter 2013: 577). Speculative M-Naturalists do not appeal to *actual* causal mechanisms, but their theories of human nature are informed by the sciences and a scientific picture of how things work.[17] Nietzsche "appears to be a skeptic about determinism based on his professed (if not entirely cogent) skepticism about laws of nature" (Leiter 2013: 577–8). Nevertheless, Nietzsche "has a sustained interest in explaining why 'human beings act, think, perceive and feel' as they do, especially in the broadly ethical domain" (Leiter 2013: 578). There is also a second aspect of Nietzsche's Speculative M-Naturalism. "[S]*ome* M-Naturalists demand a kind of 'results continuity' with existing science" (Leiter 2013: 578); for them, "philosophical theories should . . . 'be supported or justified by the results of the sciences' (Leiter 2002: 4)" (Leiter 2013: 578). But Leiter claims that "the only one kind of 'results continuity' at work in Nietzsche" is "'that man is not of a "higher . . . [or] different origin" than the rest of nature' (Leiter 2002: 7)" (Leiter 2013: 578).

Leiter introduces a further distinction between a "Humean Nietzsche" and a "Therapeutic Nietzsche" (Leiter 2013: 582–4).[18] The "Humean Nietzsche" aims to *explain* morality naturalistically; the "Therapeutic Nietzsche" wants "to get select readers to throw off the shackles of morality" (Leiter 2013: 582). The "Therapeutic Nietzsche" enlists the explanations of the "Humean Nietzsche" for therapeutic purposes, relying on many rhetorical devices to achieve his ends of persuasion. "Nietzsche's naturalism, and the prominent role it assigns to non-conscious drives and type-facts, leads him to be skeptical about the efficacy of reasons and arguments. But a skeptic about the efficacy of rational persuasion might very well opt for persuasion through other rhetorical devices" (Leiter 2002: 155, cited in Leiter 2013: 582). Leiter makes an even stronger claim. The "Humean Nietzsche" not only offers theories to explain human phenomena that draw upon (or are at least constrained by) actual scientific results; he puts forth theories that "are mainly *modeled* on science in the sense that they seek to reveal the *causal determinants* of these phenomena, typically in various physiological and psychological facts about persons" (Leiter 2013: 585–6, emphasis added). Causation plays a prominent role in Leiter's characterization of Nietzsche's Speculative M-Naturalism. "On my reading of M-Naturalism, the Humean Nietzsche emulates the methods of science by trying to construct causal explanations of the moral beliefs and practices of human beings" (Leiter 2013: 587). In short, the "Humean Nietzsche" "emulates the methods of science," albeit in a speculative manner.

Before considering some of the criticisms of Leiter's claims regarding Nietzsche's Speculative M-Naturalism, I want to highlight a key feature of

Leiter's methodological approach. Leiter states that his interest in Nietzsche "is not simply antiquarian" but is a "function of the extent to which he [Nietzsche] gets nature and the facts right" (Leiter 2013: 594). When Leiter encounters passages in Nietzsche that conflict with *his* understanding of philosophical naturalism – such as Nietzsche's striking claims about the will to power – Leiter tends to dismiss them and say, "so much the worse for Nietzsche" (Leiter 2013: 594). "We may do Nietzsche *the philosopher* a favor, however, if we reconstruct his Humean project in terms that are both recognizably his in significant part, and yet at the same time far more plausible once the crackpot metaphysics of the will to power (that all organic matter 'is will to power') is expunged" (Leiter 2013: 594). Rather than doing justice to what Nietzsche *actually* says, Leiter is prepared to dismiss or explain away a great deal that does not fit his Speculative M-Naturalist interpretation.

Leiter's interpretation has been sharply criticized by a number of scholars, many of whom accept a naturalistic reading of Nietzsche but argue that Leiter's "scientistic" claims about Nietzsche's Speculative M-Naturalism are not only far too restrictive but also distort what Nietzsche is doing. Maudemarie Clark and David Dudrick argue against Leiter's version of Nietzsche's naturalism. They contend that the mature Nietzsche rejects the view that "everything can be explained scientifically." They write, "[A]lthough human beings are part of nature, Nietzsche's version of naturalism insists that science does not tell us all there is to know about their doings . . . ; rather, it says that fully natural beings have developed in such a way as to admit of true descriptions that cannot be had from and empirical perspective" (Clark and Dudrick 2006: 164–5). Several critics object to Leiter's emphasis on the centrality of "causal determinism" and what Leiter labels "causal essentialism" in his depiction of Nietzsche's Speculative M-Naturalism.[19] Christa Davis Acampora argues that Leiter fails to consider Nietzsche's skepticism about science. "The problem with science, for Nietzsche, is that it quite often sneaks in principles or articles of faith that smack of the very metaphysical and theological conceptions that it seeks to overcome. Two such ideas that were crucial to the science of his day, and one of which remains the bedrock of scientific inquiry, are the teleological conception of nature and the concept of causation" (Acampora 2006: 316–17).

Two other notable critics of Leiter are Christopher Janaway and Schacht. Both claim that Nietzsche is a naturalistic thinker, but they reject what they take to be Leiter's narrow reading of Nietzsche's naturalism. In contrast to Leiter, Janaway gives a broad characterization of Nietzsche's naturalism:

> [Nietzsche] opposes transcendent metaphysics, whether that of Plato or of Christianity or of Schopenhauer. He rejects notions of the immaterial soul, the absolutely free controlling will, or the self-transparent pure intellect, instead emphasizing the body, talking of the animal nature of human beings, and attempting to explain numerous phenomena by invoking drives, instincts, and affects which he locates in our physical, bodily existence. Human beings are to be 'translated back into nature', since otherwise we falsify their history, their psychology, and the nature of their values. (Janaway 2007: 34)[20]

Schacht agrees with Janaway, but distances himself further from Leiter's claim that Nietzsche primarily seeks "causal-deterministic" explanations of human phenomena.

> I would thus amend and expand Janaway's statement as follows: "Nietzsche can be read as a naturalist in that he seeks explanations and interpretations of all things human that do not conflict with science, that are scientifically informed where appropriate, and that make reference to nothing beyond entirely mundane developments and transformations of our original and fundamental human animality" (By "mundane" I mean simply to pick up on the spirit of Nietzsche's themes of "this-worldliness" and of the humble origins of everything human). (Schacht 2012: 192)

Schacht brings us back to the dominant theme of immanence and "this-worldliness" that so deeply marks Nietzsche's thinking. Janaway and Schacht do not read Nietzsche's project as *primarily* a version of Speculative M-Naturalism. They both emphasize Nietzsche's "this-worldliness" but also seek to take full account of his stylistic experiments.

> Philosophy for Nietzsche involves attempting and proposing accounts of various sorts – some "genealogical" or otherwise developmental, others interpretative or otherwise sense making. They are sometimes modeled on natural-scientific modes of explanation, but this is by no means always or even for the most part the case; and they are rarely (if ever) based explicitly on appeals to results of research of the sorts based in natural-scientific disciplines. These accounts are often developed imaginatively and proposed merely hypothetically; and I take their basic function to be to show the plausibility of the guiding idea that all things human can be made sense of in this-worldly developmental terms, even though they may well be problematic as they stand. (Schacht 2012: 194)

The naturalistic interpretations of Nietzsche – especially in their more liberal varieties – have been a healthy corrective to those readings that neglect these aspects of Nietzsche's thinking. They teach us that despite

Nietzsche's criticisms of the philosophical prejudices that distort the sciences, Nietzsche had a healthy respect for the sciences. In opposition to interpretations of Nietzsche that find *no* place for knowledge or truth, naturalistic interpretations emphasize the extent to which Nietzsche is firmly committed to a healthy revision of both notions. I think, however, there is something *askew* in these depictions of Nietzsche's naturalism. Much of the discussion is focused on Nietzsche's understanding and attitude toward the sciences. This is especially the case with Leiter, who claims that Nietzsche is a methodological naturalist seeking causal explanations of phenomena – especially morality and values – that are modeled on the empirical sciences. Leiter downplays the way in which Nietzsche *actually* speaks of nature. He believes that it is the well-established sciences – and the sciences *alone* – that provide us with our *knowledge of nature*. To quote once again a famous phrase of Sellars, "in the dimension of describing and explaining the world, science is the measure of all things, of what is that it is, and of what is not that it is not" (Sellars 1997: 83). Given the remarkable progress of the sciences since the seventeenth century, there are powerful reasons for turning to them for knowledge of nature. However, it does not follow that this is the *best* way or *only* way to develop an understanding of nature.[21] Leiter presupposes that when Nietzsche appeals to psychology to explain religious and moral phenomena, he refers to what we currently identify as the empirical science of psychology. This ignores the highly distinctive, multifaceted manner in which Nietzsche conceives of psychology and employs psychological explanations.[22]

I want to turn to passages where Nietzsche *actually* speaks of "nature" and "naturalizing humanity." In *The Gay Science*, he asks: "When will all these shadows of god no longer darken us? When will we have a completely de-deified nature? When may we begin to *naturalize* humanity with a pure, newly discovered, newly redeemed nature? [*Wann werden uns alle diese Schatten Gottes nicht mehr verdunkeln? Wann werden wir die Natur ganz entgöttlicht haben! Wann werden wir anfangen dürfen, uns Menschen mit der reinen, neu gefundenen, neu erlösten Natur zu vernatürlichen*]" (*GS* 109).[23] Nietzsche also declares, "Let us beware of saying that there are laws in nature." This certainly does not sound like a thinker advancing a naturalism modeled on the natural sciences. Before turning to the questions raised in this passage, I want to cite the passage where Nietzsche speaks "against the slanderers of nature."

> I find those people unpleasant in whom every natural inclination immediately becomes a sickness, something disfiguring or even contemptible – *they*

have seduced us into the belief than man's natural inclinations are evil; *they* are the cause of our great injustice towards our nature, towards *all* nature! There are enough people who could well entrust themselves to their inclinations with grace and without care, but who do not fear the imagined 'evil essence' of nature! *That* is why there is so little nobility among human beings; its distinguishing feature has always been to have no fear of oneself, to expect nothing contemptible from oneself, to fly without misgivings wherever we're inclined – we free-born birds! And wherever we arrive, there will always be freedom and sunlight around us. (*GS* 294)

What does Nietzsche mean when he speaks of "de-deifying nature"? We can sharpen Nietzsche's meaning by returning to the contrast with Spinoza. Although they are both radical philosophers of immanence, they stand at opposite extremes when it comes to nature. Spinoza identifies Nature with God. Nature is eternal and infinite; it is a necessarily existing Substance and is self-caused. Nature consists of permanent universal natural laws that govern *all* of Nature, including human nature. From Nietzsche's perspective, Spinoza's Nature is a *deified* nature in a blatant form. The deification of nature stubbornly persists in conceptions of nature in which "God's shadows" are still present. Kant, for example, rejects the rationalism of Spinoza and Leibniz; he also rejects the possibility of theoretical knowledge of God. Nevertheless, he seeks to develop a metaphysics of nature (as well as a metaphysics of morals) that is grounded on universal and necessary principles. From Nietzsche's perspective, these claims about metaphysics are only "God's shadows." To the extent that we still accept metaphysical or epistemological foundations of nature, we have *not* de-deified nature. At the same time, Nietzsche fully recognizes the appeal and *power* of faith in a transcendent God for the "multitude" – the "herd" (just as Spinoza did). It is a deep need for the weak herd. "Christianity, it seems to me, is still needed by most people in old Europe even today; hence it still finds believers. For that is how man is: an article of faith could be refuted to him a thousand times; as long as he needed it, he would consider it 'true' again and again, in accordance with that famous 'proof of strength' of which the Bible speaks" (*GS* 347). There is an analogy with Marx's description of religion as the "opium of the masses"; religion serves as a palliative for real human suffering. When Nietzsche criticizes Christianity and morality, he is not merely claiming that they are *false* doctrines. He digs deeper. He shocks because he claims that Christian morality is not based on love but on self-hate and *ressentiment*. He shows remarkable psychological insight when (in a manner that anticipates Freud) he writes:

> All instincts that do not discharge themselves outwardly *turn inward* – this is what I call the *internalization* of man: thus it was that man first developed what was later called his "soul." The entire inner world, originally as thin as if it were stretched between two membranes, expanded and extended itself, acquired depth, breadth, and height, in the same measure as outward discharge was *inhibited*. Those fearful bulwarks with which the political organization protected itself against the old instincts of freedom – punishments belong among those bulwarks – brought about that all those instincts of wild, free, prowling man turned backward *against man himself*. Hostility, cruelty, joy in persecuting, in attacking, in change, in destruction – all this turned against the possessors of such instincts. *That* is the origin of "bad conscience." (*GM* II:16)

The dialectical character of Nietzsche's thinking is vividly illustrated in the way in which he analyzes "bad conscience." He is scathing in his characterization of bad conscience, but at the same time indicates the *positive* role it plays in the development of the human being.

> The man who, from lack of external enemies and resistances and forcibly confined to the oppressive narrowness and punctiliousness of custom, impatiently lacerated, persecuted, gnawed at, assaulted, and maltreated himself; this animal that rubbed itself raw against the bars of its cage as one tried to "tame" it; this deprived creature, racked with homesickness for the wild, who had to turn himself into an adventure, a torture chamber, an uncertain and dangerous wildness – this fool, this yearning and desperate prisoner became the inventor of the "bad conscience." But thus began the gravest and uncanniest illness, from which humanity has not yet recovered, man's suffering *of man, of himself* – the result of a forcible sundering from his animal past, as it were a leap and plunge into new surroundings and conditions of existence, a declaration of war against the old instincts upon which his strength, joy, and terribleness had rested hereto. (*GM* II:16)

It certainly looks as if Nietzsche is portraying human beings who invent "bad conscience" as if they are terminally ill, caught up in a never-ending spiral of self-hate, self-laceration, and self-torture. However, Nietzsche's use of such active verbal forms ("lacerated," "persecuted," "forcible sundering") should warn us that there is something more going on than unconditional condemnation. In the very next paragraph, Nietzsche makes this explicit.

> Let us add at once that, on the other hand, the existence on earth of an animal soul turned against itself, taking sides against itself, was something so new, profound, unheard of, enigmatic, contradictory, *and pregnant with a future* that the aspect of the earth was essentially altered. Indeed, divine spectators

were needed to do justice to the spectacle that thus began and the end of
which is not yet in sight – a spectacle too subtle, too marvelous, too paradoxical to be played senselessly unobserved on some ludicrous planet! From
now on, man is *included* among the most unexpected and exciting lucky
throws in the dice game of Heraclitus's "great child," be he called Zeus or
chance; he gives rise to an interest, a tension, a hope, almost a certainty, as
if with him something were announcing and preparing itself, as if man were
not a goal but only a way, an episode, a bridge, a great promise. (*GM* II:16)

If we are caught in the metaphysician's trap of faith in opposite values, then the above claims may seem thoroughly baffling. But Nietzsche's dialectical thinking makes it clear that *ressentiment* and "bad conscience" are double-edged. If *ressentiment* is left to fester, it becomes a dangerous poison. But the illness that Nietzsche describes is *"pregnant with a future."* Internal to this illness is a great promise, "as if . . . something were announcing and preparing itself." Nietzsche does not tell us what this is, but it is becoming increasingly evident that it is the *self-overcoming* of *ressentiment*. This self-overcoming can be achieved by the gifted few; it is the affirmation and joy of life – *the redemption and purification of nature.*

Nietzsche stresses the parallels between the need for religious faith and the philosopher's need for metaphysical comfort. "Metaphysics is still needed by some, but so is that impetuous *demand for certainty* that today discharges itself in scientific-positivistic form among great masses – the demand that one *wants* by all means something to be firm . . . this is still the demand for foothold, support – in short, the *instinct of weakness* that, to be sure, does not create sundry religions, forms of metaphysics, and convictions but does – preserve them" (*GS* 347). Nietzsche's point is underscored by a philosopher who was influenced by him – Richard Rorty, who argues that, although modern philosophy no longer appeals to a transcendent God for ultimate grounding, it is still obsessed with the search for *rational* foundations. The "god terms" of modern philosophy are "rationality," "objectivity," and "reality." Rorty seeks to show – very much in the spirit of Nietzsche – that the attempt to discover permanent metaphysical and/or epistemological *foundations* or fixed "rational" *grounds* for our morality or politics is a doomed project. Like Nietzsche, Rorty (1989) calls for liberation from these futile and debilitating illusions. Like Nietzsche, he calls for abandoning the vocabularies in which vestiges of "God's shadows" are still present.

What about the other question: "When may we begin to *naturalize* humanity with a pure, newly discovered, newly redeemed nature?" This is closely related to the question about de-deification. From the beginning of Western philosophy, and most emphatically in Plato and Aristotle, there has been an attempt to specify the *essential* attributes of human beings that distinguish them from the rest of nature. For the Greeks it is *logos*. In Nietzsche's philosophical ambience – whether shaped by Kant or by Hegel – there is still the persistent drive to isolate "rationality" or "spirit" (*Geist*) as the essential attribute of human beings. For Kant and Hegel, human beings are natural creatures, but presumably *more* than natural. Nietzsche challenges this "prejudice"; or, rather, he raises *hard* questions about whether – and in what sense – human beings are *more* than just brute animals. His writings overflow with animal imagery when he speaks about different types of human beings. At times, he comes close to suggesting that all human behavior, including human rationality, can be explained by physio-psychological forces as they are manifested in history and culture. Insofar as there are still philosophical attempts to distinguish human beings from other animals and the rest of nature by appealing to some version of rationality, we have not yet *naturalized* humanity. Nietzsche mocks the philosophical attempt to *demarcate* what is distinctive about human beings by appealing to their "higher nature."

> To translate man back into nature; to become master over the many vain and overly enthusiastic interpretations and connotations that have so far been scrawled and painted over that eternal basic text of *homo natura*; to see to it that man henceforth stands before man as even today, hardened in the discipline of science, he stands before the *rest* of nature, with intrepid Oedipus eyes and sealed Odysseus ears, deaf to the siren songs of old metaphysical bird catchers who have been piping at him all too long, "you are more, you are higher, you are of a different origin!" – that maybe a strange and insane task, but it is a *task* – who would deny that? Why did we choose this insane task? Or, putting it differently: "why have knowledge at all?" (*BGE* 230)

Once again, we see the contemporary relevance of Nietzsche. One of the most controversial philosophical issues today is whether there is something distinctive about human beings that *demarcates* them from nonrational animals and the rest of nature. Many philosophers today (following Kant) are convinced that "human rationality," "the space of reasons," or "conceptual normativity" clearly demarcate human beings from the rest of nature. This is the "more" that separates human beings from other animals. Brandom, a strong proponent of such a view, makes this point emphatically when he claims that we humans are *sapient* and that nonrational animals are only *sentient*. His entire philosophical project can be viewed as developing a sharp *demarcation* between discursive rational creatures and the rest of nature – including nonhuman animals.[24] He seeks to delineate the "normative exceptionalism" that is characteristic of our rational discursive practices. Brandom and others who share his views about conceptual normativity are opposed by those who argue that we can give a naturalistic account of human rationality and normativity. There is no doubt where Nietzsche stands – clearly on the side of those who seek to naturalize rationality. Of course, his conception of nature is much richer and more complex than that of those who identify nature with what we learn *exclusively* from the empirical natural sciences. I suspect that if Nietzsche were alive today, he might still ask, "When will all these shadows of god no longer darken us?" (*GS* 109).

Throughout his oeuvre, Nietzsche advances a multifaceted critique of morality and religion – especially Christianity. His genealogical critique is shocking because he claims that Christianity, when unmasked, is not what it professes to be – a religion of universal love – but arises from *ressentiment* and self-hatred. Christianity and its morality are most dangerous because of their *life-denying* consequences – fostering the creation of weak, tame, herd animals. Nietzsche's critique of religion and morality becomes even more intense in his mature works.

> Every naturalism in morality – that is, every healthy morality – is dominated by an instinct of life; some commandment of life is fulfilled by a determinate canon of "shalt" and "shalt not"; some inhibition and hostile element on the path of life is thus removed. *Anti-natural* morality – that is, almost every morality which has so far been taught, revered, and preached – turns, conversely, *against* the instincts of life: it is *condemnation* of these instincts, now secret, now outspoken and impudent. When it says, "God looks at the heart," it says No to both the lowest and the highest desires of life, and posits God as the *enemy of life*. The saint in whom God delights is the ideal eunuch. Life has come to an end where the "kingdom of God" begins. (*TI* "Morality as Anti-Nature" 4)[25]

The above passage illustrates what I have called Nietzsche's "double reading." In many of his works, Nietzsche categorically condemns morality and the "moral world order." But in this passage, he contrasts "every *healthy* morality" dominated by "an instinct of life" with an "*anti-natural morality*," which turns "against the instincts of life." The intensity of his condemnation of existing European religions and morality opens the space for the possibility of a healthy *life-affirming morality* – a morality that Nietzsche identifies with *naturalism* in morality.

Nietzsche asks, when will we begin to naturalize humanity "with a pure, newly discovered, newly redeemed nature" (*GS* 109)? What does he mean by a "newly redeemed nature"? I want to offer an interpretation that helps to clarify what "naturalizing humanity" means. We have already indicated the negative task of this naturalizing: rooting out any vestige of "God's shadows," anything that is not immanent and worldly in accounting for human actions. Nietzsche takes the crisis of his time – the crisis of European culture – to be the powerful force that is turning human beings into tame, domesticated, herd animals. With the death of God – the God we have murdered – and the unraveling of Christianity, European nihilism spreads like a fungus where there is a loss of any significant meaning to life. Nietzsche loathed what he calls the "last man" – the contented, satisfied, unadventurous, happy philistine who is the product of such a culture. In his darker moments, Nietzsche thinks this will be the inevitable outcome of European civilization. He had no faith that democracy, socialism, or the demands for freedom and equality would save human beings from this spreading sickness – they are only its latest manifestations. Despite his graphic portrayal of this all-consuming nihilism, this is not where Nietzsche leaves us. In *The Gay Science*, the joyful celebration of life indicates the possibility of *transforming* life-denying values. Nietzsche disdains those who think of themselves as improvers of humankind; he mocks those who think we need to "overcome" our "evil" sinful passions. Nevertheless, he does think that there are a few, rare, lonely individuals who have the creativity, individuality, and strength to live their lives in a style that does not negate life but affirms it; they create themselves anew. These life-affirming individuals have a deep, tragic sense of human suffering. Unlike those weak individuals who invent false religious illusions to "justify" their suffering, Nietzsche's life-affirming individuals do not seek to escape suffering. They have the courage to embrace suffering and loneliness *honestly*, without any illusions, and simultaneously affirm the joy of living.[26] If such creative, artistic, life-affirming individuals arise in the future, then we will really begin to naturalize humanity with a "pure, newly discovered, newly redeemed nature." It is pure because all vestiges of "God's shadows" – all metaphysical illusions – have been removed from nature. It is newly discovered because only now, after more than two thousand years, nature is no longer contaminated by Christianity and moralism. It is *redeemed* by those few exceptional life-affirming individuals who have the strength and power to engage in the reevaluation of existing life-destroying values. I stress the "iffiness" of this, because it is never completely clear whether Nietzsche is expressing a hope for the future or only expressing a counterfactual view about what would purify and redeem nature.[27]

What does affirmation of life mean? At a minimum, it demands the reevaluation of the dominant, stubborn, life-negating values. It requires recognition that suffering is not an "evil"; suffering is *constitutive* of the affirmation of life. Affirmation of life involves a *total practical* change of how one lives one's life. To use the Wittgensteinian expression, it involves changing one's "form of life" so that one not only *thinks* differently but *feels* and *acts* differently. The affirmation of life is not a remote ideal – a *telos* that one strives to achieve. It is a *process* of *becoming*, a continuous process of self-creativity. In *Twilight of the Idols* (1888), Nietzsche writes, "I, too speak of a 'return to nature,' although it is really not a going back but an *ascent* – up into the high, free, even terrible nature and naturalness where great tasks are something one plays with, one *may* play with" (*TI* "Skirmishes of an Untimely Man" 48). We can approach this life-affirming becoming from the perspective of two of Nietzsche's most important ideas: eternal recurrence and the will to power. The ethical import of eternal recurrence is brought out in the thought experiment introduced in *GS* 341.

> What if some day or night a demon were to steal into your loneliest loneliness and say to you: "This life as you now live it and have lived it you will have to live once again and innumerable times again; and there will be nothing new in it, but every pain and every joy and every thought and every sign and everything unspeakably small or great in your life must return to you, all in the same succession and sequence – even this spider and this moonlight between the trees and even this moment and I myself. . . ." Would you not throw yourself down and gnash your teeth and curse the demon who spoke thus? Or have you once experienced a tremendous moment when you would have answered him: 'You are a god, and never have I heard anything more divine.' (*GS* 341)[28]

The exceptional individual who lives in a life-affirming manner will "*long for nothing more fervently* than for this ultimate eternal confirmation and seal" (*GS* 341). This life-affirming individual exuberantly and joyously manifests the will to power. His power is not domination but the *empowerment* that comes with the affirmation of life. Power is the overcoming of resistance – the resistance against everything that drags humans down from achieving nobility.[29] "We negate and have to negate because something in us *wants* to live and affirm itself" (*GS* 307). Nature is redeemed only when life-denying Christian morality is thoroughly negated – only when those exceptional individuals *purge* themselves of everything that is life-denying. They are the rare individuals that have the power and creative artistic strength to transform and reevaluate the decadent values of European nihilism; they are the ones who celebrate life joyously. They are the individuals who are capable of giving *style* to their character.

> To 'give style' to one's character – a great and rare art! It is practiced by those who survey all the strengths and weaknesses that their nature has to offer and then fit them into an artistic plan until each appears as art and reason and even weaknesses delight the eye. Here a great mass of second nature has been added: there a piece of first nature removed – both times through long practice and daily work at it. . . . In the end, when the work is complete, it becomes clear how it was the force of a single taste that ruled and shaped everything great and small. (*GS* 290)[30]

I want to step back and reflect on the different eyes with which Nietzsche sees nature and naturalism. Primarily, there is Nietzsche's experience of immanence, his complete commitment to a "this-worldly" approach to all issues. He relentlessly seeks to negate and destroy anything that claims to transcend this natural world. Nothing exists beyond the world of nature. He is a master in exposing and destroying the illusions and prejudices that blind us from focusing on the dark, instinctual, *contradictory*, *chaotic* drives that operate beneath (and beyond the reach of) our conscious illusions. He is a "master of suspicion." Nietzsche leaves no room for fixed order, permanence, or inherent rationality in nature. Throughout the history of Western philosophy, philosophers have appealed to some version of the appearance/reality distinction. There is the world that we immediately encounter, the world as it appears to us, but there is a reality beyond or behind this world that grounds it – the "true world."[31] Nietzsche challenges this appearance/reality distinction just as he challenges the classic distinction of becoming and being. Nietzsche not only develops a multi-faceted critique of religion but also seeks to root out "God's shadows." From Nietzsche's point of view, it is only a conceit of modernity that it has escaped dogmatism. A new form of dogmatism has arisen – one that appeals to metaphysical and epistemological foundations. Nietzsche raises hard, intractable questions about the philosophical obsession with "rational justification." Much more important are good *taste* and *instincts*. Although Nietzsche approaches nature primarily from the perspective of human nature, he harshly criticizes an anthropomorphism that projects superstitions onto the natural world. What most people take to be the natural world is thoroughly contaminated by religious and moral prejudices. That is why nature needs to be purified. Like Spinoza, Nietzsche denies free will and teleology. Nietzsche is also wary of the devious ways in which scientists smuggle their personal and philosophical prejudices into their scientific theories, although he has a healthy respect for what we learn from the sciences. Contrary to those who interpret Nietzsche as denying that there is *any* knowledge or truth, Nietzsche seeks to show what is involved in gaining *authentic* knowledge and truth – namely, honesty and courageously *struggling* with irreconcilable contradictions. This is the mark of "high culture": only the weak seek to reconcile these contradictions. Nietzsche denies that there is a view from nowhere; there is only perspectival knowledge. He denies that empirical science is our *only* approach to the natural world. Nature is rich, diverse, chaotic, and overflowing. Nietzsche calls for the de-deification of nature; nature needs to be purified of the religious, moralistic, and metaphysical prejudices that have contaminated it. In his darker moments, Nietzsche suggests that there is no escape from the spreading of life-denying nihilism, through which meaningless mediocrity dominates and pervades the world. Nature is *redeemed* only when (and if) those few rare gifted individuals purge themselves of the vestiges of life-denying values and live their lives in a joyous life-affirming manner – those who think, feel, and act in a creative manner, those who create themselves anew and incorporate tragic suffering into their form of life. Book IV of *The Gay Science* opens with Nietzsche's commitment to *amor fati*.[32]

> I want to learn more and more to see what is necessary in things as what is beautiful in them – thus I will be one of those who make things beautiful. *Amor fati*: let that be my love from now on! I do not want to wage war against ugliness. I do not want to accuse; I do not even want to accuse the accusers. Let *looking away* be my only negation! And, all in all and on the whole: some day I want only to be a Yes-sayer! (*GS* 276)

Nature is redeemed when this joyous self-affirmation of life is *embodied* in those "free spirits" who embrace tragic suffering. They are the ones whose *every* thought, feeling, and action is an expression of "Yes-saying" to life.[33] From one perspective, Nietzsche's suspicion cuts deeper than Marx's. Nietzsche would disdain Marx's appeal to socialized nature. He might well claim that Marx's transactional understanding of man and nature still does not grasp what is required for the redemption of a purified nature – what is required to be a free spirit and a "Yes-sayer."

7
Freud: Human Nature, Psychic Reality, and Cosmological Speculation

There is an intriguing legend about Freud's decision to become a medical student – a legend he initiated. When Freud was sixteen, he had an epiphany when he heard a recitation of Goethe's essay on nature: "[I]t was hearing Goethe's beautiful essay on Nature read aloud at a popular lecture by Professor Carl Brühl just before I left school that decided me to become a medical student" (Freud 1925: 8). There is a deep irony about this legend.[1] Goethe portrays "mother nature" as the romantic, living, breathing vital source of activity and energy – close in spirit to Schelling's description of nature in his *Naturphilosophie* and a strong departure from Kant's mechanical conception of nature in the *Critique of Pure Reason*. Peter Gay notes that the essay that so deeply affected Freud was "an emotional and exclamatory hymn celebrating an *eroticized Nature* as an embracing, almost smothering, ever-renewed mother" (Gay 2006: 24, emphasis added). When Freud actually became a medical researcher, this was not the idea of nature that inspired him. On the contrary, he vehemently repudiated a "romantic" understanding of nature. He was caught up in the growing positivist spirit that dominated so many late nineteenth-century German and Viennese natural scientists.[2] Nature consists exclusively of knowledge yielded by natural science. The mentors that inspired Freud were dedicated to the idea that all genuine knowledge is natural science; all phenomena, including biological and psychological phenomena, are to be explained by the same deterministic laws that explain physio-chemical phenomena. Freud, in effect, repressed the turbulent emotions that attracted him to Goethe's conception of a vital living nature.[3] Even at this early stage of his career, there were growing tensions between his positivist credo and the ideas welling up inside him that did not fit his "official" commitment to a tough-minded mechanistic and quantified conception of nature.

> In the long run, he [Freud] was not able to force all his thinking into the Positivists' mechanistic world picture. But as Ricoeur points out, Freud never disavowed the Positivists' "fundamental convictions" and "like all his Vienna and Berlin teachers, he continued to see in science the sole discipline of knowledge, the single rule of intellectual honesty, a world view that excludes all others, especially that of the old religion." (Whitebook 2017: 110)

There was another source of the emotional tension that Freud was experiencing. He began his medical career as an experimental researcher dedicated to careful microscopic observation. But he also started a practice as a clinician of nervous disorders – and it wasn't going well. In 1895, the twenty-nine-year-old Freud received a grant to study with the charismatic Jean-Martin Charcot in Paris. He went to Paris to further his study of nervous disorders. At Salpêtrière, the famous Paris hospital complex where Charcot lectured, Freud cultivated his interest in hysteria and neurotic disorders. Freud's initial interest in hysteria was stimulated by his work with his colleague, Josef Breuer.

> Charcot taught Freud that instead of dismissing neuroses as the mere dross of existence, one should treat them with the utmost respect because they could unlock important secrets of nature. . . . By the time Freud returned to Vienna, he had made the transition from neurophysiology to psychopathology. He was no longer primarily a research scientist but had become, despite his antipathy to medicine, a clinician. In neuroses – in "the sick soul" – Freud found the domain that would allow him to make the great discoveries concerning human nature he had been vainly pursuing elsewhere. (Whitebook 2017: 111)

Freud faced several serious problems. As a struggling clinician, he needed to discover the best techniques to cure, or at least alleviate, the symptoms of his patients. This was closely connected with the need to develop a better understanding of the root causes of hysteria. Freud also had to contend with the prejudice of many of his fellow Viennese scientists who dismissed questions concerning the psyche – especially the "sick soul" – as merely theological or metaphysical. Finally, Freud tried to fit the study of hysteria, and neuroses more generally, into the positivist world view that he embraced. He experimented with a variety of clinical techniques, including electrotherapy, hypnosis, and catharsis. Although he achieved modest successes with hypnosis and catharsis, he quickly became disenchanted with them as techniques for curing neuroses. Freud was convinced that the root causes of hysteria were somehow related to the unconscious mental life of his patients. He hypothesized that the key to understanding hysteria and neuroses involved patients' "repressed sexuality."[4] Freud struggled to fit these speculations into a genuinely scientific understanding of the dynamics of human nature.

The "Project for a Scientific Psychology" (1895) is a crucial document in Freud's development.[5] The "Project" sets out to analyze the psychic apparatus by using a principle borrowed from physics – the constancy principle. Freud sought to elaborate a *quantitative* treatment of psychic energy. The opening statement of the "Project" indicates how Freud sought to emulate the physics of his time.

> The intention [of this project] is to furnish a psychology that shall be a natural science; that is, to represent psychical processes as quantitatively determinate states of specifiable material particles, thus making those processes perspicuous and free from contradiction. Two principal ideas are involved: (1) What distinguishes activity from rest is to be regarded as [a quantity] Q, subject to the general laws of motion. (2) The neurones are to be taken as the material particles. (Freud 1895: 295)[6]

The material particles subject to the laws of motion are *neurons* in the brain. The "new" psychology is to be grounded in the anatomy of the brain. But there are already deep tensions in the "Project."

> Thus the 1895 "Project" belongs to a whole period of scientific thought. What is most interesting is the manner in which Freud, by extending this thought, transforms it to the breaking point. In this regard, the "Project" stands as the greatest effort Freud ever made to force a mass of psychical facts within the framework of quantitative theory. . . . As one enters more deeply into the "Project," one has the impression that the quantitative framework and the neuronic support recede into the background, until they are no more than a given and convenient language of reference which supplies the necessary constraint for the expression of great discoveries. (Ricoeur 1970: 73)

When Freud addresses the interplay of pleasure and unpleasure, cathexis, desire, inhibitions, and verbal images in the "Project," it becomes apparent that these phenomena exceed his mechanistic quantitative energy framework. Although committed to a framework of the quantitative constancy principle and to grounding his science in the neurons of the brain, Freud is describing psychic life in a manner that departs from his "official" mechanistic quantitative framework. He was on his way to describing psychic life that is *independent* of any reference to material neurons. Yet Freud never completely gave up on the appeal to a quantitative framework – the "economics" of psychic life. We detect the direct influence of the "Project" in the final chapter of *The Interpretation of Dreams* (1900).[7] Ricoeur argues that the distinctive characteristic of psychoanalysis is the integration of *energetic* (economic) discourse and *interpretative* discourse into a unified framework.[8]

During the 1890s, Freud was engaged in his lonely struggle to discover the structure and dynamics of psychic reality – a reality that, he believed, had never been *systematically* understood. This psychic reality provides the key to the understanding of human nature, which had become Freud's primary concern. The way to gain access to this psychic reality is through the study of psychological disturbances and illnesses – the "sick soul." Freud was aware that previous thinkers – "poets and philosophers" – had insights into the dynamics of unconscious psychic life. But he felt that *no one* prior to him had explored psychic life in a systematic manner. "'Through abnormality,' as Thomas Mann put it, Freud would 'succeed in penetrating most deeply into the darkness of human nature,' into the sickness caused by the strain of man's 'position between nature and spirit, between angel and brute'" (Whitebook 2017: 101). Freud was taking a radical turn in his exploration of human nature. Philosophers from the time of Plato and Aristotle had developed theories of the soul and theories of human nature. Nevertheless, no one before Freud had systematically argued that there is a deep unconscious psychic life that shapes and determines who we are and become – an unconscious psychic life that is never completely accessible to consciousness.[9]

Freud's primary project was to probe the depths of human nature and the role that the unconscious repressed material and unconscious drives (*Triebe*) play in determining who we become.[10] The task of the psychoanalyst is to enable patients to overcome strong resistances and to acknowledge their repressed desires, emotions, ideas, and conflicts. Throughout his career, Freud refined his understanding of psychic life and eventually expanded the scope of his speculations to deal with group psychology and the discontents of civilization. In the 1890s Freud had already developed the hypothesis that the source of the symptoms of his hysterical and neurotic patients involved their repressed sexual experiences; they were suffering from deep psychic resistances, defenses, inhibitions, and conflicts. He also discovered the important role of transference (and countertransference) between the patient and the analyst and its significance for psychoanalytic treatment. In *The Interpretation of Dreams*, he carefully analyzed dreamwork (*Traumwerk*) – the complicated formation of dreams that combines manifest and latent content. The source of the manifest content is some incident from recent waking daily life; the source of the latent content is a *repressed* incident from the patient's life.[11] Dreams are an expression of wish fulfillments – including those dreams which, on the surface, appear to contradict one's conscious wishes.[12] Contrary to those who dismissed dreams as meaningless, Freud argues that dreams have a *meaning*, and the task of the analyst is to discover their secret meaning.[13] In a beautiful passage from *The Interpretation of Dreams*, Freud states that dreams enable us to grasp a picture of the development of the human species:

> [D]reaming is on the whole an example of regression to the dreamer's earliest condition, a revival of his childhood, of the instinctual impulses which dominated it and of the methods of expression which were then available to him. Behind this childhood of the individual we are promised a picture of phylogenetic childhood – a picture of the development of the human race, of which the individual's development is in fact an abbreviated recapitulation influenced by the chance circumstances of life. We can guess how much to the point is Nietzsche's assertion that in dreams 'some primaeval relic of humanity is at work which we can now scarcely reach any longer by a direct path'; and we may expect that the analysis of dreams will lead into a knowledge of man's archaic heritage, of what is psychically innate in him. Dreams and neuroses seem to have preserved more mental antiquities than we could have imagined possible; so that psycho-analysis may claim a high place among the sciences which are concerned with the reconstruction of the earliest and most obscure periods of the beginnings of the human race. (Freud 1900: 548–9)

At the *deepest* level, the source of the latent content of a dream is the patient's infantile sexuality.[14] Like the pearl diver in Shakespeare's *Tempest*, the analyst has to overcome many obstacles to reach the depth of his patient's unconscious. He does not initially discover pearls but rather the dross that is buried in the unconscious. Yet, insofar as this dross is the basis for discovering the patient's repressions and resistances, they are the pearls for psychanalysis for overcoming the patient's resistances.

A dream, Freud claimed, is like a rebus consisting of many disparate elements, visual and verbal. In order to analyze and interpret a dream, the analyst needs to pay careful attention to the separate elements of the dream puzzle. Freud insists that the most trivial incidents of a dream are indispensable. He analyzed some of his own dreams, including the famous dream of Irma's injection.[15] The reason why dreams require *interpretation* is that in dreamwork there is both distortion and condensation. Initially, Freud moved from using hypnosis to the cathartic method developed by

Breuer, whereby the patient was encouraged to recall and emotionally release the unconscious conflict that was the source of her symptoms. But cathartic emotional release had its limitations. Frequently, the hysterical or neurotic symptoms would disappear temporarily, only to reappear again. As an alternative to catharsis, Freud developed the method of "free association" – a method that is not really "free" because the psychoanalyst can discover hidden connections and deeply repressed conflicts that elude the conscious awareness of the patient.[16]

Freud combined what he was discovering as a clinician with the theoretical framework he was developing to describe and explain his clinical observations.[17] We witness this in the two topographic models of the psyche. The first model proposed three areas of the human psyche: the conscious, the preconscious, and the unconscious, which Freud abbreviated as "Cs.," "Pcs.," and "Ucs." These are three "agencies," each following its own "rules." The major contrast, however, is between the conscious/preconscious and the unconscious. The preconscious consists of memories and knowledge that are not presently conscious but can be brought and made accessible to consciousness.

Before exploring in greater detail Freud's understanding of the unconscious, we need to elaborate Freud's battle with those philosophers who fail to recognize the role of the unconscious and think that human psychic life can be fully accounted for by the appeal to consciousness. Modern philosophy, beginning with Descartes, takes as its starting point the *primacy* of consciousness. Although thinkers such as Schopenhauer and Nietzsche suggested that there are unconscious drives that affect consciousness, Freud sought to justify the unconscious not only as a descriptive concept (an adjective) but also as a *substantive* concept or system having its own distinctive dynamics and "logic." In the 1912 paper "A Note on the Unconscious in Psychoanalysis" and in the first part of the 1915 paper "The Unconscious," Freud characterizes the unconscious in relation to consciousness. As Ricoeur notes,

> At the outset the quality of being unconscious is still understood in relation to consciousness: it is simply the attribute of what has disappeared but can reappear; the nonknown is on the side of the unconscious; the unconscious is something we assume and reconstruct from signs derived from consciousness, since it is from consciousness that memories disappear and in consciousness they reappear. (Ricoeur 1970: 118)

Freud, however, introduces a further distinction. There are instincts and representations that are so deep that they are *excluded* from consciousness.

From 1920 onwards Freud worked out another conception of personality – often given the concise title of 'the second topography'. According to the classical account, the principal reason for this was the ever-greater consideration demanded by the unconscious defences – a consideration which supposedly made it impossible to go on identifying the poles of defensive conflict with the systems we have been describing above – i.e. the repressed with the Unconscious and the ego with the Preconscious-Conscious.

In reality the motives for the revision in question cannot be reduced to this idea. . . . One of the chief discoveries that made it necessary was that of the role played by the various identifications in the formation of the personality and of the permanent structures which they leave within it (ideals, critical agencies, and self-images). In its schematic form, this second theory involves three 'agencies': the *id*, instinctual pole of the personality; the *ego*, which puts itself forward as representative of the whole person, and which, as such, is cathected by narcissistic libido; and the *superego* or agency of judgment and criticism, constituted by the internalisation of parental demands and prohibitions. (Laplanche and Pontalis 1988: 452)[20]

The id is the *primal source* of psychic energy, but it conflicts with the ego and the superego. In the second topography, it becomes clear that the repressing ego is, for the most part, *unconscious*. The id, however, is the "great reservoir" of libido and instinctual energy. Like the initial characterization of the unconscious, the id consists of "contradictory" instincts that are not coherently organized. Sometimes Freud describes the id as "chaos." Although he refers to the ego in his earliest writings, in the second topography he emphasizes the unconscious dimension of the ego. The ego takes on a variety of functions that include reality testing, the temporal ordering of mental processes, and rational thought. They also include "rationalization" and the defense against instinctual demands. The ego is a mediator that attempts to reconcile contradictory demands. It is menaced by *three* kinds of dangers – from the external world, from the libido of the id, and from the severity of the superego. The superego's relation to the ego may be compared to that of a judge or censor. Conscience and the formation of ideals are functions of the superego. The superego is the heir of the Oedipus complex insofar as it is constituted by the internalization of parental prohibitions. One part of the ego sets itself apart from another part and judges it critically. The second topography refines Freud's understanding of psychic reality and expands his understanding of human nature. Both topologies have *universal* significance; they are applicable to *all* human beings. They reveal the deep structure of who we are and who we become.[21]

Thus far, I have been elucidating Freud's distinctive understanding of human nature. To deepen my analysis, I want to introduce two further concepts: *chance* and *sublimation*. The importance of chance events in determining who we become is beautifully illustrated in Freud's essay on Leonardo Da Vinci.

> If one considers chance to be unworthy of determining our fate, it is simply a relapse into a pious view of the Universe which Leonardo himself was on the way to overcoming when he wrote that the sun does not move.... We naturally feel hurt that a just God and a kindly providence do not protect us better from such influences during the most defenceless period of our lives. At the same time we are all too ready to forget that in fact *everything to do with our life is chance*, from our origin out of the meeting of spermatozoon and ovum onwards – chance which nevertheless has a share in the law and necessity of nature, and which merely lacks any connections with our wishes and illusions. The apportioning of the determining factors of our life between 'necessities' of our constitution and the 'chances' of our childhood may still be uncertain in detail; but in general it is no longer possible to doubt the importance precisely of the first years of our childhood. We all still show too little respect for Nature which (in the obscure words of Leonardo which recall Hamlet's lines) 'is full of countless causes ['*ragoni*'] that never enter experience'.
>
> *Every one of us human beings corresponds to one of the countless experiments in which these* 'ragoni' *of nature force their way into experience.* (Freud 1910a: 137, emphasis added)[22]

What Freud calls "chance" is what many philosophers call "contingency." Normally we think of contingency as some external event that unexpectedly affects us. Freud, of course, acknowledges such chance events. But the chance that he speaks of here concerns our psychic life – especially the chance events of our early childhood – events over which we have no control. Nature is full of countless *ragoni* that play a significant role in who we become. We are, so to speak, thrown into a world that is not of our own making – a world that is the source of pain and suffering. If we pursue the logic of Freud's thinking, we must give up the illusion that we can have complete control over our unconscious lives. We never achieve this type of autonomy. This passage about chance calls to mind the famous passage in which Freud speaks of three blows that humanity has suffered as a result of the progress of science. The first was when Copernicus challenged the view that the earth is at the center of the universe – it is only a tiny speck in a vast universe. The second was Darwin's great discovery of evolution wherein human beings can no longer be considered as being at the center of the universe. The third great blow is due to psychoanalysis.

> But human megalomania will have suffered its third and most wounding blow from the psychological research of the present time which seeks to prove to the ego that it is not even master in its own house, but must content itself with scanty information of what is going on unconsciously in its mind. We psycho-analysts were not the first and not the only ones to utter this call to introspection; but it seems to be our fate to give it its most forcible expression and to support it with empirical material *which affects every individual*. (Freud 1916: 285, emphasis added).

This passage is frequently misinterpreted as an expression of Freud's profound pessimism about human nature. On the contrary, I think it expresses Freud's *realism* and his sustained critique of the false illusions about human nature that were once called "superstitions." In this respect, Freud closely follows Spinoza's critique of superstitions and illusions. Despite his critique of the naïve Enlightenment convictions about the "goodness" of human beings, Freud represents what might be called the radical tradition of the "dark Enlightenment."[23] Like Nietzsche, Freud is committed to ruthless honesty, where we do not gloss over what we discover about human nature – even the disturbing features of our unconscious lives. We should recall what Ricoeur said about Marx, Nietzsche, and Freud as practitioners of the hermeneutics of suspicion: "All three begin with suspicion concerning the illusions of consciousness, and then proceed to employ the stratagem of deciphering; all three, however, far from being detractors of 'consciousness' aim at extending it" (Ricoeur 1970: 34). These thinkers enlarge our consciousness by tearing away false illusions and enabling us to gain a depth of knowledge about our psychic lives. This cannot be overemphasized because it shows how firmly Freud was committed to the Enlightenment ideal of striving for genuine knowledge, including self-knowledge – even when this knowledge is extremely disturbing and painful.

There is another mistaken idea advanced by some of Freud's critics (and even by some of his defenders). Freud is accused of a kind of reductive thinking where all "higher" achievements of human beings are to be fully explained by the unconscious dynamics of our infantile sexuality. Freud refers to this criticism in the opening paragraph of his psychoanalytic study of Da Vinci.

> When psychiatric research, normally content to draw on frailer men for its material, approaches one who is among the greatest of the human race, it is not doing so for the reasons so frequently ascribed to it by laymen. 'To blacken the radiant and drag the sublime into the dust' is no part of its purpose, and there is no satisfaction for it in narrowing the gulf which

separates the perfection of the great from the inadequacy of the objects that are its usual concern. But it cannot help finding worthy of understanding everything that can be recognized in those illustrious models, and it believes there is no one so great as to be disgraced by being subject to the laws which govern both normal and pathological activity with equal cogency. (Freud 1910a: 63)[24]

We touch here upon one of the most important (and least developed) Freudian concepts – sublimation. Throughout his work, Freud frequently refers to sublimation. Sublimation is the process motivated by an individual's sexual instincts that develops aims independent of sexuality. The main types of activity described by Freud as sublimated are artistic creativity and intellectual endeavor.[25] The importance of the concept of sublimation is evident in the famous lectures that he gave at Clark University in 1909. In his fifth and final lecture, Freud introduces the concept of sublimation.

> Owing to their repressions, neurotics have sacrificed many sources of mental energy whose contributions would have been of great value in the formation of their character and in their activity in life. We know of a far more expedient process of development, called '*sublimation*,' in which the energy of the infantile wishful impulses is not cut off but remains ready for use – the unserviceable aim of the various impulses being replaced by one that is higher, and perhaps no longer sexual. It happens to be precisely the components of the *sexual* instinct that are specially marked by a capacity of this kind for sublimation, for exchanging their sexual aim for another one which is comparatively remote and socially valuable. It is probable that we owe our highest cultural successes to the contributions of energy made in this way to our mental functions. Premature repression makes the sublimation of the repressed instinct impossible; when repression is lifted, the path to sublimation becomes free once more. (Freud 1910: 53–4)

Freud's analysis of Da Vinci is also based on the concept of sublimation. "The core of his nature, and the secret of it, would appear to be that after his curiosity had been activated in infancy in the service of sexual interests he succeeded in sublimating the greater part of his libido into an urge for research" (Freud 1910a: 80–1). In *The Ego and the Id* (1923), Freud reiterates the significance of sublimation. He speaks of the ego's energy as "desexualized and sublimated." "If this displaceable energy is desexualized libido, it may be described as *sublimated* energy" (Freud 1923: 45).

The importance of sublimation cannot be underestimated in Freud's theory of human nature. But problems arise when we scrutinize sublimation more carefully. Freud never adequately *explains* the mechanism of sublimation. He *describes* but does not *explain* it. As Laplanche and Pontalis note, "Because Freud left the theory of sublimation in such a primitive state we have only the vaguest hints as to the dividing-lines between sublimation and processes akin to it (reaction-formation, aim-inhibition, idealisation, repression). Similarly, although Freud held the capacity to sublimate to be an essential factor in successful treatment, he never described its operation in concrete terms" (Laplanche and Pontalis 1988: 433).[26] Problems are compounded when we seek to understand how aggressive instincts are sublimated. Suppose we ask: How are we to explain why some outstanding geniuses like Da Vinci and Goethe are able to transform and sublimate their basic sexual drives, while the repressions and resistances of other human beings are so strong that they suffer from debilitating neurotic symptoms? Of course, we can give a *post hoc* account – that because the repression and resistances of neurotic patients are so intense, they are unable to sublimate their sexual energy. But this is *not* a scientific explanation of the phenomenon – only its redescription. Freud is a master of describing and distinguishing between neurotic patients who block any type of sublimation and artists like Da Vinci who succeed in creative sublimation. But if we are looking for a scientific account to explain why some individuals are able to sublimate their sexual energy in creative ways, and others find this impossible, we will not find it. This is a problem with many of Freud's "explanations" of psychic life: they do not explain why some chance events are so destructive, and others are so productive. Freud himself at times comes close to admitting that here we reach the limits of psychoanalysis. He might add that if we take seriously the hypothesis that chance events affect our unconscious lives, then it is foolish to try to give a *causal* account of what is the result of *ragoni* and chance. He never claims that we can give an *adequate* account of human creativity; we can specify only the psychic conditions that allow for the creativity of geniuses like Goethe and Da Vinci.

In the "Postscript" to his *Autobiographical Study* (1925), Freud writes: "My interest, after making a lifelong *detour* through the natural sciences, medicine and psychotherapy, returned to the cultural problems which had fascinated me long before, when I was a youth scarcely old enough for thinking" (Freud: 1925: 72). Freud is even more explicit about his turn to cultural issues and speculation in the "Postscript" to *The Question of Lay Analysis* (1926):

> After forty-one years of medical activity, my self-knowledge tells me that I have never really been a doctor in the proper sense. I became a doctor through being compelled to deviate from my original purpose; and the

triumph of my life lies in having, after a long and roundabout journey, found my way back to my earliest path. I have no knowledge of having had any craving in my early childhood to help suffering humanity ... In my youth I felt an overpowering need to understand something of the riddles of the world in which we live and perhaps even to contribute something to their solution. (Freud 1926: 253)

In his journey to discover the "riddles of the world," Freud's first endeavor was to understand the economics, dynamics, and structure of *individual* psychic life – especially the unconscious. From the 1890s until the 1920s, his primary focus was on the *individual*, although, of course, an individual can be understood only in her interactions with others – especially with parents and siblings. Beginning in the 1920s, with *Beyond the Pleasure Principle* (1920), *Group Psychology and the Analysis and the Ego* (1921), *The Ego and the Id* (1923), *The Future of an Illusion* (1927), and *Civilization and Its Discontents* (1930), Freud's thinking took a bolder speculative turn. To fully understand human nature, the study of *individual* psychic life was no longer sufficient. One needed to understand human beings in relation to society, culture, and civilization. Freud now introduces *Thanatos* and *Eros* as *cosmological forces of nature*.

Beyond the Pleasure Principle is a crucial text because in it Freud explicitly revises his theory of instincts and advances the hypothesis of a primitive death instinct – *Thanatos* – and the all-encompassing life instinct – *Eros*. This is one of Freud's most difficult texts – some have called it "scandalous." Many of Freud's closest psychoanalytic followers rejected Freud's claims about the death instinct, as well as the dualistic battle between *Thanatos* and *Eros*.[27] Rather than attempt to evaluate Freud's dubious arguments and his speculative appeals to alleged biological evidence to support his claims about the death instinct, I want to focus on three points: first, what led Freud to postulate a death instinct; second, how he understands the death instinct and its relation to *Eros*; and third, what the consequences of postulating the duality of *Thanatos* and *Eros* are for Freud's understanding of human nature.

Starting with the first point, Freud cites a number of phenomena that are the basis for postulating a death instinct. He was deeply disturbed by the war neuroses of many soldiers returning from the brutality and cruelty of World War I. He sought to explain the obsessive compulsion to repeat traumas that were so painful. He even drew upon what seemed to be the innocent "fort-da" game of his infant grandson. He was intrigued by the repetition of the "fort" stage of the child's game – the stage that signifies the painful experience of his mother's departure. The reason why these phenomena are so important for Freud is that they appeared to challenge what had been a cardinal principle of psychoanalysis – that all drives seek pleasurable satisfaction. Why did the repetition of painful experiences play such a significant role? Freud "speculated" (his word) that there must be something *beyond* the pleasure principle: "[W]e come now to a new and remarkable fact, namely that the compulsion to repeat also recalls from the past experiences which include no possibility of pleasure, and which can never, even long ago, have brought satisfaction even to instinctual impulses which have since been repressed" (Freud 1920: 20). There "must" be something more primitive than the pleasure principle: "there really does exist in the mind a compulsion to repeat which overrides the pleasure principle" (Freud: 1920: 22).

Moving on to the second point, Freud now makes one of his speculative leaps.

> At this point we cannot escape a suspicion that we may have come upon the track of a universal attribute of instincts and perhaps of organic life in general which has not hitherto been clearly recognized or at least not explicitly stressed. *It seems, then, that an instinct is an urge inherent in organic life to restore an earlier state of things* which the living entity has been obliged to abandon under the pressure of external disturbing forces, that is, it is a kind of organic elasticity, or, to put it another way, the expression of the inertia inherent in organic life. (Freud 1920: 36)[28]

Note that Freud here speaks of a universal attribute in *all* organic life (not just human life). All organic life (even simple cells) seek to return to what is an earlier state of things – what is inorganic. "If we are to take it as a truth that knows no exception that everything living dies for *internal* reasons – becomes inorganic once again – then we shall be compelled to say that '*the aim of all life is death*' and looking backwards, that '*inanimate things existed before living ones*'" (Freud 1920: 38). Freud is not making the trivial point that all living beings die, but rather that the *aim* of all life is death. There is an *active* tendency in all organic life to return to the inorganic – to die. It is almost as if Freud – contrary to Spinoza – is postulating a reverse *conatus* principle. Rather than striving to enhance power, all living beings aim to *diminish* their power and return to an inorganic state. Prior to *Beyond the Pleasure Principle*, Freud held that the pleasure principle is the principle that governs all instinctual behavior and that there are ego instincts that aim at self-preservation. Marcuse notes: "At the earliest stage of its development, Freud's theory is built around the antagonism between sex (libidinous) and ego (self-preservation) instincts; at the latest stage, it is centered on the conflict between the *life instincts* (*Eros*) and the *death instinct*" (Marcuse 1966: 22). Freud does *not* limit the scope of the death instinct to human beings; it is applied to all animate beings; it is a *biological* principle.

We are not yet done with the leaps that Freud makes. Suppose, for the sake of argument, we accept Freud's claim that there is a tendency in all organic beings to return to an inorganic state. This *by itself* does not tell us anything about aggression or outward destruction. We could, in principle, acknowledge that there is a death instinct without introducing aggressiveness and outward destruction. Yet it is clear that Freud does think of the death instinct – at least in human beings – as the instinct that accounts for aggressiveness and destruction. Freud introduces this connection of death and aggressiveness in a most hesitant manner.

> In the obscurity that reigns at present in the theory of instincts, it would be unwise to reject any idea that promises to throw light on it. We started out from the great opposition between life and death instincts. Now object-love itself presents us with a second example of a similar polarity – that between love (or affection) and hate (or aggressiveness). If only we could succeed in relating these two polarities to each other and in deriving one from the other! From the very first we recognized the presence of a sadistic component in the sexual instinct. As we know, it can make itself independent and can, in the form of a perversion, dominate an individual's entire sexual activity. . . . But how can the sadistic instinct, whose aim it is to injure the object, be derived from Eros, the preserver of life? Is it not plausible to suppose that this sadism is in fact a death instinct which, under the influence of the narcissistic libido, has been forced away from the ego and has consequently only emerged in relation to the object? . . . If such an assumption as this is permissible, then we have met the demand that we should produce an example of the death instinct – though, it is true, a displaced one. (Freud 1920: 53–4)

Note the sheer tentativeness of this passage and the sly use of questions that really turn out to be affirmations: "If only we could," "Is it not plausible," "If such an assumption as this is permissible." In short, despite these suggestions, Freud does not provide any direct *arguments* to support the thesis that the death instinct is a primary source of human destructiveness and aggressiveness.[29]

Finally, regarding the third point: although Freud has very little to say about the life instinct (*Eros*) in *Beyond the Pleasure Principle*, he affirms that *Thanatos* and *Eros* are two great opposing *forces of nature*.[30] *Eros* now encompasses everything that Freud has ascribed to sexuality, but it is also the principle of unification.[31] The death instinct strives toward death and destruction; the life instinct strives to form ever greater unities. These two instincts are present in *every* human being and are *fused* in different ways. They are frequently intertwined with each other.

Suppose we bracket the gaps in Freud's argument and accept his claim that there are two great opposing forces in nature: *Thanatos* and *Eros*. The death instinct is the *active* biological tendency of all organic life to return to a quiescent inorganic state. When directed *outward*, the death instinct is a primary source of aggressiveness and destruction. Furthermore, let us accept Freud's understanding of *Eros* as the name for the life instincts (including sexuality). The positive role that Freud assigns to *Eros* is like a return to Goethe's conception of eroticized nature that he found so inspiring when he was a teenager. Nature turns out to be the great drama of the battle of *Eros* and *Thanatos*. Freud adamantly held to his late theory of instincts to the end of his life, despite criticism of many of his followers. He consistently rejected the view that human beings are naturally good and are corrupted only by society. He consistently rejected the view that human beings can be completely domesticated and shaped by sociological and economic conditions. There is no way that we can *eliminate* human aggressiveness, even though it can be sublimated in productive ways. Although Freud's criticisms of communism and Marxism are crude, he believed that by abolishing private property, "we deprive the human love of aggression of one of its instruments. . . . Aggressiveness was not created by property" (Freud 1930: 113). From Freud's earliest reflections on the unconscious to his late theory of instincts, Freud argues that there is something deep in human nature – one's primary instincts – that cannot be eliminated. Recall Freud's early description of the unconscious as timeless and exempt from contradiction. This means that both aggressive and erotic instincts *simultaneously* exist together – and can be fused.[32] Whatever the vicissitudes of these instincts, they are rooted in the unconscious and the id. If we seek to repress the aggressive instincts (derivative of the death instinct), then we will be threatened by the "return of the repressed." Freud would not be surprised by the outbreaks of sheer aggressiveness at different stages of civilization (including in the contemporary world). Freud's late theory of instincts becomes a *critical standard* for evaluating civilization and its discontents.

We witness the dynamic of the battle of *Thanatos* and *Eros* in *Civilization and Its Discontents* (*Das Unbehagen in der Kultur*) (1930).[33] Based on Freud's firmly held theory of instincts, civilization "describes the whole sum of the achievements and the regulations which distinguish our lives from those of our animal ancestors and which serve two purposes – namely to protect men against nature and to adjust their mutual relations" (Freud 1930: 89). Freud focuses on the discontents of civilization, wherein human beings experience frustration because it is *impossible* to completely satisfy their instinctual drives. Early in the essay, Freud raises the question: What is the purpose of life? Frequently, when this question is raised, one presupposes that there is (or ought to be) an *objective* purpose to life. Freud shares Max Weber's thesis of the disenchantment of nature wherein there is no independent or objective meaning or purpose of life. Freud transforms the question into what is *actually* the behavioral aim of human life: What do human beings "demand of life and wish to achieve in it? The answer to this can hardly be in doubt. They strive after happiness; they want to become happy and to remain so. This endeavor has two sides, a positive and a negative aim. It aims, on the one hand, at an absence of pain and unpleasure, and, on the other, at the experiencing of strong feelings of pleasure" (Freud 1930: 76). Intense pleasure is only episodic and *cannot* be permanently realized. We are creatures threatened by suffering from three sources: our own body, from the external world, and from our relations with other human beings. Freud speaks of the achievements of civilization, including the increasing technological mastery of nature and the high development of artistic and intellectual culture. For all its positive achievements, civilization does not bring about happiness. Freud is scornful of those who think we can escape from civilization to a more primitive blissful state. There is no escape from civilization and from the suffering that we experience. "The programme of becoming happy, which the pleasure principle imposes on us . . . cannot be fulfilled; yet we must not – indeed, we cannot – give up our efforts to bring it nearer to fulfillment by some means or other" (Freud 1930: 83). The best we can achieve is some balance between protecting ourselves from suffering, pain, and unpleasure and occasional episodic bursts of intense pleasure – primarily due to the satisfaction of sexual desires. There is no golden rule that applies to every human being. Intense love comes into opposition with civilization, and civilization threatens love with substantial restrictions. Civilization prevents us from fully satisfying both our sexual *and* our aggressive instincts. Civilization has to use its utmost resources to limit the destructiveness of our aggressive instincts, but it also limits the fulfillment of intense sexual pleasure.

There is still one more twist in the discontents and malaise that we experience as a result of civilization. This is due to a sense of guilt. There are two origins for this: "one arising from fear of authority, and the other, later on, arising from fear of the super-ego" (Freud 1930: 127). Although there is a non-pathological sense of guilt that arises when we express remorse for something that we regret, there is also an "unconscious sense of guilt" that arises from the need for punishment – when authority is *internalized*. (This is a point that Nietzsche makes in the *Genealogy of Morals*.) "[A]ggressiveness is introjected, internalized; it is, in point of fact, sent back to where it came from – that is, it is directed towards his own ego" (Freud 1930: 123). Freud emphasizes the analogy between the development of the individual and the development of civilization. "It can be asserted that the community, too, evolves a super-ego under whose influence cultural development proceeds" (Freud 1930: 141). He claims that the sense of guilt is the most important problem in the development of civilization. "[T]he price we pay for our advance in civilization is a loss of happiness through the heightening of the sense of guilt" (Freud 1930: 134).

> And now, I think, the meaning of the evolution of civilization is no longer obscure to us. It must present the struggle between Eros and Death, between the instinct of life and the instinct of destruction, as it works itself out in the human species. This struggle is what all life essentially consists of, and the evolution of civilization may therefore be simply described as the struggle for life of the human species. And it is this battle of the giants that our nurse-maids try to appease with their lullaby about Heaven. (Freud 1930: 122)

Freud concludes *Civilization and Its Discontents* in an almost mock Olympian manner by declaring that he has "not the courage to rise up before my fellow-men as a prophet, and bow to their reproach that I can offer them no consolation: for at bottom that is what they are all demanding – the wildest revolutionaries no less passionately than the most virtuous believers" (Freud 1930: 145).[34]

Before drawing together the strands of Freud's distinctive understanding of nature, I want to underscore a subtext in *Civilization and Its Discontents*. One can easily draw the conclusion that the malaise of civilization is so intractable that nothing can be done about it. We are doomed to frustration and unhappiness. When Freud speaks of civilization and reality, he is referring to the *existing* civilization, with its restrictions and constraints. This is what Marcuse calls the "performance principle": "the prevailing historical form of the *reality principle*" (Marcuse 1966: 35). Although Freud refuses to be a prophet and affirms that no social, political, or economic arrangements in society will eliminate the conflicts generated by the erotic and aggressive instincts, he indicates that changes in society can alleviate *excessive* repression and better prepare us to face reality. Although we cannot remove all suffering, we can *ameliorate* suffering. For example, Freud acknowledges that during his lifetime, most extra-genital sexual satisfactions were forbidden as perversions. "The requirement, demonstrated in these prohibitions, that there shall be a single kind of sexual life for everyone, disregards the dissimilarities, whether innate or acquired, in the sexual constitution of human beings; it cuts off a fair number of them from sexual enjoyment, and so becomes the *source of serious injustice*" (Freud 1930: 104, emphasis added).

This remark takes on special significance in light of the greater tolerance for diverse sexual practices today – even though there is still great resistance to anything that deviates from the norm of heterosexual practices. Consequently, Freud allows for the possibility of *reforming* existing structures of society so that there will be less repression and suffering – even if we cannot completely eliminate them. In a fascinating footnote, he clearly indicates what is wrong with the education of young people. He also suggests how we may better prepare children for the future they will confront.[35] In short, Freud's subtext is that if we have a more accurate understanding of human nature and the sources of suffering and unhappiness, we can take steps to reform those practices that cause so much pain. This subtext of *Civilization and Its Discontents* tends to be ignored because of Freud's polemical stance. He strongly opposes the view that we can achieve happiness by eliminating the taboos, laws, and customs that impose restrictions on us. But once we realize that it is impossible to achieve complete and sustained happiness, there is plenty of room for *realistic* reform that takes account of the limitations of human nature. Freud never explores the type of social reform that is implicit in his understanding of human nature and civilization. Nevertheless, it should be clear that the more accurately we understand psychic reality and human nature – the more accurately we understand the sources of human suffering and pain – the more realistic we can be about ameliorating excessive psychic suffering and repression.[36] This is the aim of the psychoanalysis of individuals, and it can serve as a critical standard for alleviating the discontents of civilization.

I want to conclude by drawing together the various strands of Freud's conception of nature, especially human nature. At an early age, Freud was inspired by Goethe's conception of eroticized nature.[37] This initial attraction to a romantic conception of nature was suppressed when Freud became a medical researcher. He accepted a positivist conception of nature. Influenced by his mentors in Vienna, Freud sought to develop psychology as a rigorous quantitative natural science. In the 1895

"Project," he sought to ground his "new" psychology on the constancy principle and neurons in the brain. But, increasingly, he came to realize that the structure and dynamics of psychic life are independent of its somatic base. No understanding of human nature is adequate unless we systematically explore psychic life. Freud's treatment of pathological nervous disorders provided him with insights for comprehending the psychic life of *all* human beings. He insisted that dreams – even those that seem chaotic – have meaning. The task of the psychoanalyst – with the help of the analysand – is to discover the "secret meaning" of dreams. In *The Interpretation of Dreams*, Freud engaged in the remarkable task of analyzing his own dreams. He sought to show that, when properly analyzed, dreams are the expression of unconscious wish fulfillments. Freud became aware of the need to elaborate a theoretical structure to provide a framework for what he was discovering in his clinical work. In its first form – the first topography – Freud distinguished three systems or "agencies": the conscious, the preconscious, and the unconscious. He made his most radical claims about the unconscious – a timeless system that is the *primary* source of drives and the locus of what is repressed. From an early stage of his development, in his study of hysteria, Freud realized the importance of repressed infantile sexuality both for interpreting dreams and for understanding the source of neurotic symptoms in his patients. He also cultivated the psychoanalytic method of "free association" in order to gain insight into the repressed traumas of his patients. The second topography of the id, ego, and superego (*Es, Ich, Über-Ich*) provided a still deeper insight into psychic life and enabled Freud to explore the "unconscious sense of guilt" that resulted from the harshness of the superego. From the 1890s until the 1920s, he was primarily concerned with the *individual* psyche – although, of course, individuals are shaped by their interactions with other human beings, especially parents and siblings. Beginning in the 1920s, he gave full expression to his speculative impulse. He advanced his late theory of instincts in *Beyond the Pleasure Principle*, framing it as the battle between *Thanatos* and *Eros*. These were no longer thought of as drives restricted to the human psyche but as *biological* forces in *all* organisms. Freud went even further in his speculations. He followed the pre-Socratics in suggesting that *Thanatos* and *Eros* are *cosmological principles of all of Nature*.[38] In this more speculative mode, Freud claimed a deep affinity between his conception of love and Plato's Eros – especially as portrayed in the *Symposium* (Freud 1925a: 218). Once Freud advanced the hypothesis of the perpetual *intertwined* battle of *Thanatos* and *Eros*, he turned his attention to how these competing drives play out in civilization. Although human beings seek to maximize pleasure and minimize pain, they can never achieve complete happiness. It is impossible to completely satisfy or even completely sublimate the primary instincts.[39]

I have argued that it is a mistake to read *Civilization and Its Discontents* as advocating a pessimistic outlook. It is pessimistic *only* if we hold on to the illusion that we can achieve the type of happiness that avoids all suffering and pain. Freud's outlook is *realistic* – realistic in the sense of acknowledging our limitations and finitude. Human beings are neither angels nor devils. Heinz Kohut makes a similar point when he notes that "our capacity to acknowledge the finiteness of [our] existence" – our embeddedness in nature – "and to act in accordance with this painful discovery" represents a great "psychological achievement" that enhances human dignity (Kohut 1966: 264). Once we realize that we are motivated by *both* love and aggressiveness and that it is utopian to think that there is any social or civilized state that can avoid all conflict and frustration, then we can begin to think realistically about *reforms* that can alleviate human misery. Freud did not pursue this project, although he is deeply committed to the idea that a more honest understanding of human nature enables us to ameliorate some of the taboos and customs that are the source of so much suffering. Finally, I want to return to the thesis that, as a great destroyer of illusions, Freud stands in the tradition of the Enlightenment that is committed to relentless and honest self-knowledge – even when it reveals disturbing truths. Freud pursued a deeper understanding of psychic life and human nature. Human beings are subject to the larger cosmological forces of nature – the perpetual battle of *Thanatos* and *Eros*. They determine who we are and who we can become.

What Freud leaves us with is the demand for honest self-knowledge, even when this reveals the darkness of the human soul, the traumas, and suffering that cannot be avoided. In his *New Introductory Lectures*, Freud gives an eloquent statement of the aim of psychoanalytic therapy. "Its intention is, indeed, to strengthen the ego, to make it more independent of the super-ego, to widen its field of perception and enlarge its organization, so that it can appropriate fresh portions of the id. Where id was, there ego shall be. It is a work of culture – not unlike the draining of the Zuider Zee" (Freud 1933: 80).[40] In *Civilization and Its Discontents*, Freud draws the analogy between the individual and culture; he speaks of a cultural ego and superego. The above statement may also be taken as a guide to what *should* be the aim of civilization: to strengthen the ego and make it more independent of the cultural superego. This is not a "royal road" to illusory happiness but a realistic guide for living one's life. Freud stands in the best

Socratic tradition of the relentless pursuit of self-knowledge – no matter where it leads. Freud certainly would endorse the Socratic declaration in Book I of the *Republic*, "for the argument is not about just any question, but about the way one should live" (Plato 1991: 352d).

Coda

Marx, Nietzsche, and Freud are suspicious of the pretensions of philosophy as being an autonomous "rational" discipline that can provide us with objective knowledge of nature. More specifically, they are suspicious of the philosophical appeal to consciousness, which has been fundamental for modern philosophy since the time of Descartes. "Consciousness" is "false consciousness" because it conceals and mystifies the underlying nature and reality. Marx, Nietzsche, and Freud are great destroyers of illusions. They seek to tear away the masks, deceptions, and self-deceptions that distort the human-in-nature. They stand in Spinoza's tradition of "Radical Enlightenment." Spinoza challenged belief in the transcendent God of the Abrahamic religions; such a belief was nothing but a debilitating superstition. In the eighteenth century, there was a retreat from Spinoza's "Radical Enlightenment." Philosophers of the "moderate Enlightenment," like Kant, desperately sought to reconcile a strong conception of nature governed by strict deterministic universal laws with a *practical* faith in a transcendent God. But Marx, Nietzsche, and Freud would have none of this. To them, the attempt to reconcile knowledge and faith – to "deny knowledge in order to make room for faith" (Kant 1998: B xxx) – was nothing more than the search for an illusionary "metaphysical comfort." Nietzsche and Freud agree with Marx's proclamation: "The abolition of religion as people's *illusory* happiness is the demand for their *real* happiness. The demand to abandon illusions about their condition is a *demand to abandon a condition which requires illusions*. The criticism of religion is thus in *embryo* a *criticism of the vale of tears* whose *halo* is religion" (Marx 1997:

250). Marx, Nietzsche, and Freud are not just great destroyers of illusions. They destroy the pretensions and prejudices of philosophers in order to uncover a deeper, more profound understanding of the human-in-nature – one that leaves behind all vestiges of what Nietzsche calls "God's shadows" (Nietzsche 2001: 109).

Although Marx, Nietzsche, and Freud were sharp critics of "consciousness," they differ in the distinctive character of their critiques. Marx's approach is best illustrated in his interpretation of Hegel's *Phenomenology*. The *Phenomenology* begins its exploration with natural consciousness and then moves to self-consciousness, reason, and spirit. Marx argues that Hegel's starting point results in mystification and concealment. "The great thing in Hegel's *Phenomenology* and its final result . . . is simply that Hegel grasps the self-development of man as a process, objectification as loss of the object, as alienation and transcendence of this alienation; that he thus grasps the nature of *work* and comprehends objective man, authentic because actual, as the result of his *own work*" (Marx 1997: 321). Work – more specifically, labor – and the way it is *deformed* and alienated is Marx's starting point in his critique of consciousness. Nietzsche and Freud have different starting points. The appeal to consciousness obscures the role of the *unconscious* instincts (*Triebe*) in determining who we are and who we become. Nietzsche's approach to instincts is more intuitive and imaginative than Freud's, but no less insightful. Freud initially carries out his battle against the deep scientific prejudice that all mental events are conscious. In his first topography, where he distinguished three agencies, the category of the unconscious seemed the most dubious to his scientific colleagues. Freud took a radical turn. His discovery of unconscious drives (both sexual and aggressive) was key for the new discipline – psychoanalysis. The unconscious is not just an *adjective* for describing a deeper level of psychic activity; it is an independent *agency*. It is the source of *all* psychic energy and the locus of what is repressed. The unconscious is chaotic, timeless, and completely amoral. It knows no contradiction. Consequently, "contradictory" unconscious instincts exist *simultaneously*. They demand complete *intense* satisfaction and fulfillment. Nietzsche agrees with Freud that our basic instincts are contradictory and cannot be reconciled in a harmonious whole. Nietzsche and Freud warn us about the *introjection* of aggressive instincts – the turning of aggression against oneself. For Nietzsche, this is like a *poison* and results in *ressentiment*. For Freud, this internalization of aggressiveness results in the excessive harshness of the superego and increases the unconscious sense of guilt.

Although Marx does not appeal to unconscious instincts in his characterization of human nature, he can serve as a corrective to Nietzsche and Freud. Nietzsche and Freud are deeply skeptical of the very idea of a socialized human and of projects of social reform. Nevertheless, as Marcuse notes, Freud's reality principle is a historical *performance* principle. When Freud speaks of the reality principle, he means reality as it *currently* exists. He also speaks of repression that is excessive – what Marcuse calls "surplus repression" (Marcuse 1966: 35). Suffering, trauma, repression, and resistance can never be completely eliminated; they are *constitutive* of psychic life and, consequently, of human nature. The more we refine our understanding of the dynamics of psychic life, the better we will be able to take steps to alleviate excessive repression and suffering. Unfortunately, Freud never systematically explored a program of social reform that can change existing reality. One great difference between Nietzsche and Freud is that Nietzsche believes that gifted, exceptional individuals can become "Yes-sayers"; they can live affirmative lives. They can even celebrate the fulfillment of aggressive instincts when directed outward. Freud does not share Nietzsche's enthusiasm for life affirmation. The best that humans can achieve is an uneasy *compromise* between the demand for the intense satisfaction of instinctual drives and minimizing human misery by avoiding painful experiences. For Nietzsche, life-affirming individuals seek out pain and suffering in order to strengthen themselves. From Nietzsche's perspective, Freud's compromise is a cop-out, whereas, from Freud's perspective, Nietzsche's celebration of the joy of life is an unrealistic phantasy. Nietzsche's great fear is that civilization is turning human beings into domestic animals by taming life-affirming instincts and leading us to what he calls the "last man" – human beings without any powerful instincts and emotions (Nietzsche 2008: 9–10). With his sharp ironic wit, he might even accuse Freud of celebrating the "last man" with his "realistic" compromise between seeking pleasure and minimizing unpleasure, pain, and suffering.

Finally, I want to return to the thinker with whom I began – Spinoza. Marx, Nietzsche, and Freud are all thinkers shaped by Spinoza's philosophy of immanence. In different ways they seek to get rid of "God's shadows" – shadows that have and continue to distort the understanding of the human-in-nature. Although their respective conceptions of nature differ significantly from Spinoza's rationalistic conception, they are all naturalists in the spirit (if not the letter) of Spinoza. *They believe that everything in this world can be given a naturalistic explanation.* They are scornful of any appeal to conceptual normativity or morality that is "beyond" nature. Both Nietzsche and Freud seek to give positive *naturalistic* accounts of the origin of morality. Marx, from the beginning of his career, set out to challenge the is/ought dichotomy that has been taken as foundational for morality. The specter of Spinoza hovers over Marx's, Nietzsche's, and Freud's conceptions of the human-in-nature. It is not surprising that Spinoza has inspired recent interpretations of Marx, especially in France and Italy. This is evidenced in the appeal to transindividuality – a theme that can be traced back to Spinoza – that provides a fresh approach to understanding individuality and challenges the traditional dichotomy of the individual and the collective. This has led to new readings of Marx, Nietzsche, and Freud. Nietzsche recognizes his affinity with Spinoza. Recall the five points that Nietzsche mentions when he recognizes himself in Spinoza: "he denies the freedom of the will, teleology, the moral world order, the unegoistic, and evil" (Nietzsche 1976: 92). Finally, Freud's naturalistic account of psychic life, and especially his naturalistic account of the origins of human morality, is very much in the spirit of Spinoza. These affinities are compatible with Marx's, Nietzsche's, and Freud's *transactional* understanding of the human-in-nature. One of the great ironies of the history of thought is that Spinoza, whose rationalistic metaphysics was taken to be the paradigm of a discredited philosophical dogmatism, turns out to be the thinker who has stimulated fresh and thought-provoking interpretations of Marx, Nietzsche, and Freud.

Concluding Remarks

In my introduction, I indicated three interrelated purposes in writing this book – not least to correct the ignorance about how the past thinkers from Spinoza to Freud conceive of nature, why they conceive of nature in their distinctive ways, and the significance of the varied ways in which they conceive of nature and naturalism. There is actually a fourth purpose, but it is implicit in the other three. Nature is not a marginal or peripheral concept; it is central for each of the thinkers examined. I have now completed my intellectual journey and hope it is evident that the tradition that includes Spinoza, Hume, Kant, Hegel, Marx, Nietzsche, and Freud presents us with an extremely rich and varied portrait of the vicissitudes of nature – one that involves tensions and even contradictions among them, but also hidden affinities. There is no grand narrative or synthesis. Rather, we have an account of the different illuminating approaches to nature. In each case, I have also sought to show how these varied accounts of nature are related to the overall intellectual projects of these thinkers. I do not think that the views of any of the thinkers are passé. Each presents us with insights and challenges that must be confronted in thinking about humans and nature today. My hope is that this study will provide the basis for a creative dialogue that elucidates both the strengths and the weaknesses of these thinkers. I have made it clear that I reject the very idea of an ahistorical study of nature. Despite the claims by some of the examined thinkers that we can achieve a concept of nature standing for all time, my approach is thoroughly *historical*. Each of the thinkers I have examined roots their thought about nature in specific historical concerns, which I have sought to elucidate. The various conceptions of nature are rooted in the historical intellectual environment that sets the context for the issues that each thinker confronts.

I want to return to Marx's famous eleventh thesis on Feuerbach: "The philosophers have only *interpreted* the world in various ways; the point is, to *change* it" (Marx 1997: 402). No slogan is more appropriate today for confronting the current ecological crisis. Marx, of course, was not aware of the crisis we face today, but he was certainly aware that capitalism exploits human beings and nonhuman nature. During the past few decades, our practices have been destroying nature, and they are likely to destroy the human species unless we dramatically change human behavior. The serious issue we face today is whether there are sufficient efforts to meet the present crisis. Frankly, the evidence is discouraging. There is, of course, lots of talk about climate change and the destruction of the earth by fossil fuels. And there are gestures toward meeting these challenges. But the actions taken by the governments are weak and insufficient in light of the catastrophe that is already the extreme weather changes that seem to erupt every day.

Marx is also relevant for thinking though the current ecological crisis in more specific ways. This ecological crisis is not an isolated crisis that can be separated from the imperatives of capitalism. Thinkers like Nancy Fraser (and many others) have emphasized that the ecological crisis is deeply connected with the dynamics of contemporary capitalism and its background conditions. Building on the insights of Marx, Fraser (2021) is developing an enlarged view of Marxism in order to show how the current ecological crisis is constitutive of contemporary capitalism. In many parts of the world, problems are compounded by the authoritarian leaders who deny – despite the best scientific evidence – that climate change brought about by human actions is real. Even Marx's early talk of the "humanized nature," when properly understood, is relevant today. What Marx means by "humanized nature" is changing the human's relationship to nature so that we can change behavior in the way in which we systematically conceive and initiate practices to bring about a more rational approach to the "human-in-nature" whereby nature becomes sustainable and becomes a condition for human flourishing.

The second area of concern today in confronting nature – especially human nature – is human aggressiveness. Even if we reject Freud's postulation of a death instinct, we must recognize that human aggressiveness is innate to human nature. Today, human aggressiveness is ever more present throughout the world. It is manifested in hate crimes and violent attacks on people of color, homosexuals, and transgender persons. If Freud is right, human aggressiveness can never be eliminated; but it can be sublimated into creative cultural behavior. However, as Freud warns us, aggressiveness can never be completely and successfully sublimated. If instead we attempt to repress all human aggressiveness, we risk the forceful return of the repressed – a phenomenon that appears manifest today throughout the world.

A prolegomenon serves a double function: it serves as a warning of obstacles and limitations and as a guide to what we can know. To illustrate what I mean, I want to return to the theme of causality in nature that runs like a red thread through all the thinkers I have examined. It is explicitly discussed in Spinoza, Hume, and Kant, but Hegel, Marx, and Freud also have distinctive conceptions of causality. Dissenting from these philosophers, Nietzsche warns us that the appeal to causal determination may be a misleading representation of the chaos of existence. In my discussion, three important dimensions of causality have emerged: the *logical* (Spinoza), the *psychological* (Hume and Freud), and the *critical* (Kant). Although there are problematic issues in the way each of these thinkers deals with causality, they highlight the features of causality that must be faced today in developing an adequate conception of the relation of human beings to the rest of nature that meets the present ecological crisis. Many of the ways in which we speak of the transaction of humans and nature today are completely inadequate. I can illustrate this with reference to Kant, who tells us that every event is related to another event by a determinate rule. His major claim is that the principle of causality is a synthetic *a priori* judgment about the way in which natural events are related to each other. Kant presupposes that we have *criteria* for distinguishing one event from another event. "Everything **that happens** presupposes a previous state, upon which it follows without exception according to a rule" (*CPR* A 445/B 473). I call this "event causality." However, Kant's ontology of separate events that are connected in this manner is outdated. In the physical sciences, deterministic laws have been replaced by statistical laws based on probability. Furthermore, with the development of quantum mechanics, it no longer makes sense to speak of a *single* determinate event in the physical world. When we turn to new sciences such as neuroscience, cognitive science, and ecology, the meaning of causality and its role in explanation changes. Thus, it no longer makes sense to speak of a *univocal* concept of causality in the sciences – and certainly not of causality based on "event causality." In short, we need to face the full complexity of developing new ways of speaking of causality if we are to develop an adequate conception of the relations of humans to the rest of nature.

We can also illustrate the need to rethink the relations of humans to the rest of nature with the recent concern for sustainability. "Sustainability" became a quasi-technical term with the establishment of the Brundtland Commission by the United Nations in 1983. When four years later the Commission released a final report, it defined "sustainability" as development "that meets the needs of the present without compromising the future generations to meet their own needs" (World Commission 1987). The concept of sustainability has now spread to many different domains: there is sustainable farming, sustainable building, etc. The three "pillars" of sustainability are environment, economy, and society. However, when we turn to the details of what is meant by "sustainability," there are a number of complex problems. I would like to illustrate these problems by telling an anecdote. My family has a country house in the northern Adirondacks. One of the joys of country life – especially during the summer and fall months – is the farmer's market in Keene Valley, NY, where the local farmers bring their produce. Thanks to the market, we can enjoy locally grown meat, vegetables, and fruits, as well as locally produced cheese, yogurt, and home-baked bread. Several of the farms coming to the market employ the principle of sustainable farming. For example, Asgaard Farm & Dairy has movable chicken coops that allow for natural fertilization of the soil and grass used for the grazing of their beef cattle. The taste of the chicken meat from the Asgaard farm is delicious and far superior to anything one can buy in a supermarket. However, there is one serious problem: the cost of their chicken is normally three to four times the cost of the chicken available in supermarkets. Consequently, the Keene Valley farmer's market is primarily frequented by middle and upper-middle class families who have second homes in the area, while local residents and working-class families shop at the local supermarket where food is much less expensive.

I tell this anecdote because it illustrates the dilemma of sustainability. In its current state, the practice of sustainability exists primarily for the middle and upper-middle class, not for ordinary working people and the poor. We face the same dilemma when we speak of low-cost housing, which is almost never built on sustainable principles. To be blunt, sustainability today is a class phenomenon – not something that is universal. It may be a noble idea to envision global sustainability, but it glosses over the real social and economic problems we face today. Sustainability, as it exists now, is for the rich developed countries, not the countries mired in poverty.

Thus, if we are to develop a new conception of the relations of humans with the rest of nature, we must honestly face the dilemmas of sustainability as they actually exist.

Let me mention the third area where my work can serve as a prolegomenon: the "hard problem" of human motivation. Suppose we become clearer about what needs to be done to meet the urgent environmental crisis we face today. How are we to motivate people to make the decisions and sacrifices that need to be made now? This is not merely a theoretical problem but a practical one. This is especially problematic when we take into account that millions of people throughout the world do not believe that climate change is a real or serious problem. From the widespread resistance to the vaccines during the COVID-19 pandemic, we have learned that there is and will be resistance to doing anything about climate change. I certainly do not see any clear or easy solution to the problem of motivation. But unless we honestly confront it, we can be skeptical about stopping or even slowing down the destruction of our planet.

I do not want to conclude on a pessimistic note. There are different things that can be done to meet the growing environmental crisis. My basic plea is for honesty and serious realism – realism that requires rethinking the relation of humans and nature today. My hope is that my study may help in this process.

Notes

Preface

1 I was delighted to discover that one of my favorite philosophers of science and biology, Peter Godfrey-Smith, shares my enthusiasm for *Experience and Nature*. In 2014 he wrote a "belated" review of the book. He writes, "*Experience and Nature* is – despite its excesses, its endless repetition, its occasional incomprehensibility – the best book written in the pragmatic lineage so far" (Godfrey-Smith 2014: 290).
2 See my account of the rise and demise of American naturalism in Bernstein 2020.
3 My monograph, *Pragmatic Naturalism: John Dewey's Living Legacy*, is a critical discussion of contemporary liberal naturalism. I hope my monograph will be read in conjunction with *The Vicissitudes of Nature*.

Introduction

1 Contemporary thinkers like John McDowell, who have been deeply influenced by Kant, argue that we need a more open and liberal conception of nature – one that departs from Kant's "disenchanted" conception of nature, which is so fundamental for the first *Critique*. See McDowell 2008. For a critical discussion of McDowell's (and other) versions of liberal naturalism, see Bernstein 2020.

Chapter 1 Spinoza: Founder of Modern Naturalism

1   For the full text of the ban, see Yovel 1989: 3.
2   See Nadler 1999 and 2011, and S. James 2012 for a discussion of the reactions to Spinoza's *Theological-Political Treatise*.
3   For a detailed analysis of the *Theological-Political Treatise* that focuses on Spinoza's polemics, see S. James 2012. For a historical analysis of the significance and influence of the *TPT*, see Israel 2001. For explorations of the contemporary significance of the *TPT*, see Althusser 1976, Deleuze 1990, Negri 1991, and Balibar 1998.
4   I use capital letters when I refer to Spinoza's distinctive meaning of "Substance" and "Nature."
5   Yovel argues that what distinguishes Spinoza from his predecessors is a philosophy of immanence, which Spinoza developed with systematic sophistication:

> The philosophy of immanence is not a specific doctrine but a mode of philosophizing, a paradigmatic approach that knew several varieties in modern thought. If we were to characterize it in short (paying the price of a schematic simplification), we might say it claims three things:
>
> (1) The world (with its temporal projection into the past and future) is the comprehensive horizon of being, and the only context of meaningful questions concerning what there is. The image of a transcendent world, of the Beyond of being is a groundless (if not incoherent) metaphysical vision that should not overshadow the immanent world or be allowed to interfere in its affairs.
> (2) This world (through the humans in it) is also the sole possible source of valid norms – in morality, law, politics, even religion – and of any justified use of political authority and coercion intended to support that norm in practice.
> (3) To the extent that liberation, emancipation, spiritual exaltation – even "salvation" – is possible for humans, they must originate from this world and be realized by it.

   This passage is from the unpublished English translation of Yovel's Hebrew edition of the *Ethics*.
6   This sentence appears in a letter written to Albert Burgh, a former student who had converted to Catholicism (and urged Spinoza to convert). Rebecca Goldstein describes the rich context of this letter and what it reveals about Spinoza as a Jew and as a philosopher. See Goldstein 2006: 166–73. In her book, Goldstein, who was originally educated as an orthodox Jew, tells the charming story of how she came to discover Spinoza. She presents an imaginative reconstruction of his life and an elegant account of his philosophical vision.
7   In citing passages from the *Ethics*, I have followed the procedure of listing the part, followed by the definition, demonstration, axiom or proposition, fol-

lowed by the scholium and its number when there is more than one scholia. Thus, "IP33s1" refers to Part I, Proposition 33, scholium 1. When referring to Preface or Appendix, I list the part followed by "Preface" or "Appendix." Thus, "III Preface" refers to the Preface to Part III. The passages from the *Ethics* follow Edwin Curley's translation; see Spinoza 1985.

8   In the scholium to IP33 Spinoza explains what he means by "necessary," "impossible," and "contingent":

> A thing is called necessary either by reason of its essence or by reason of its cause. For a thing's existence follows necessarily either from its essence and definition or from a given efficient cause. And a thing is also called impossible from these same causes – viz. either because its essence, *or* definition, involves a contradiction, or because there is no external cause which has been determined to produce such a thing.
>
> But a thing is called contingent only because of a defect of our knowledge. For if we do not know that the thing's essence involves a contradiction, or if we do not know very well that its essence does not involve a contradiction, and nevertheless can affirm nothing certainly about its existence, because the order of causes is hidden from us, it can never seem to us either necessary or impossible. So we call it contingent or possible. (IP33s1)

9   Although Spinoza was deeply influenced by Descartes, he was also a radical critic of Descartes. He rejects Descartes' conception of God and his dualism of two types of substances – the mind and the body, where the mind is characterized by the attribute of thought and the body by the attribute of extension. He also rejects the Cartesian conception of free will (and of a God who possesses free will). Even though Spinoza uses Descartes' terms, "substance," "attribute," and "mode," he defines these terms in a way that is antithetical to Descartes' meaning. He mocks Descartes' appeal to the pineal gland in the brain to explain how the mind is connected to the body and how the mind and body interact: "Indeed, I cannot wonder enough that a Philosopher of his caliber – one who had firmly decided to deduce nothing except from principles known through themselves, and to affirm nothing which he did not perceive clearly and distinctly, one who had so often censured the Scholastics for wishing to explain obscure things by occult qualities – that such a Philosopher should assume a Hypothesis more occult than any occult quality" (V Preface).

10 Michael Della Rocca, one of the leading commentators on Spinoza, writes: "The purity of Spinoza's commitment to explanation can best be articulated in terms of his commitment to the Principle of Sufficient Reason (hereafter, the 'PSR') and to his naturalism. ... In Spinoza, unlike Leibniz, the PSR takes on an outsized importance – it's rationalism on steroids, but for the fact that, in Spinoza's eyes, this total commitment to the PSR is completely natural" (Della Rocca 2008: 4). Della Rocca argues that Spinoza's complete commitment to PSR is the key for understanding his philosophy. "Rethinking Spinoza in light of the Principle of Sufficient Reason promises

to be important not only for our understanding of Spinoza, but also for our understanding of the philosophical issues Spinoza deals with and that continue to trouble philosophers today" (Della Rocca 2008: p. ix).

11 For a moving description by Spinoza of his dedication to pursuing the highest human perfection and directing his efforts to understanding the highest good – viz. knowledge of what is eternal, a knowledge that is the source of true joy – see his *Treatise on the Emendation of the Intellect* in Spinoza 1985b.

12 Aaron Garrett notes:

> Commentators have placed different degrees of emphasis on the importance of the *mos geometricus* for understanding the *Ethics*. At one extreme, Harry Wolfson discounts it, remarking, "there is no logical connection between the substance of Spinoza's philosophy and the form in which it is written" [Wolfson 1934: 55]. At the other extreme, the most dominant French Spinoza scholar of the twentieth century, Martial Gueroult, places it at center stage, as does his great successor Alexandre Matheron and some of Spinoza's most important critics such as Hegel and critical commentators like Harold Joachim. (Garrett 2003: 17)

Garrett himself offers a distinctive interpretation of Spinoza's use of the *mos geometricus*. He claims that "the most important function of the *mos geometricus* is tied up with what Spinoza calls "emendation" in the *TEI* [*Treatise on the Emendation of the Intellect*], ridding oneself of inadequate ideas so that those adequate ideas that already make up our minds can better be expressed" (Garrett 2003: 17).

13 See also Henry Allison's discussion of the significance of the geometric method (Allison 1987: 38–41). Allison argues that it is the most adequate vehicle for presenting Spinoza's philosophy:

> Not only does it allow Spinoza to deduce, or at least attempt to deduce, all his conclusions from a single first principle – namely, the concept of God – and to illustrate the absolute necessity governing all things, but, for these very reasons, it presents his view of the universe in the form in which, according to his theory of knowledge, it can be adequately grasped by the intellect. Such a form is therefore, from Spinoza's point of view, necessary for the realization of his practical goal. (Allison 1987: 43)

14 The phrase *Deus sive Natura* shocked many of Spinoza's contemporaries – and still shocks many who believe in a God who creates nature as depicted in the beginning of Genesis. But it delights those who (mis-)read Spinoza as a *manqué* reductive naturalist or materialist. Hampshire makes an interesting suggestion about this phrase: "Perhaps *Deus sive Natura* is intended to be a proper name in a peculiar and technical sense of "proper name" which interests logicians; it is introduced as *necessarily* having *unique* reference: it is unlike other names in that there is only one thing to which it can be applied" (Hampshire 1951: 32, n. 1). By the end of the *Ethics*, we also realize that when "God," "Substance," and "Nature" are *adequately* defined,

they have *identical senses*. Note that in this revealing passage, Spinoza also uses the expression "reason, *or* cause." This also indicates an identity of cause and reason. This is the primary way in which Spinoza speaks of "cause." Later I will discuss some of the other ways in which he uses the term "cause."

15 Many of Spinoza's claims about God sound like traditional religious claims and seem to suggest that God is some sort of superperson who acts and establishes final ends. But a primary aim of the *Ethics* is to show that this way of thinking about God is misleading and, indeed, false. It is a fiction of the human imagination. A primary goal of the *Ethics* is to draw us away from a personalized conception of God and to lead us to a more rational, philosophical, and impersonal understanding of God as identical with Nature and Substance. This does not mean that talk about God is dispensable. Rather, it means that we have to think about God in a radically different way from the Abrahamic religions. Jonathan Bennett points out that the temptation to think of God as a superperson is compounded by the English translation of the *Ethics*:

> It is a nuisance that English has pronouns which are always used for people and not freely used for anything else. We use 'he' for God, thinking of God as a person; if we came to think of God as impersonal, we should switch to 'it'. No such choice faced Spinoza, because none of his half-dozen languages has personal pronouns. In Latin, for example, he had to use a masculine pronoun for God, to agree with the masculine noun *Deus*; but this masculinity is grammatical only, and implies nothing about the nature of the object. Whereas in English we must use 'he' in referring to a man and 'it' in referring to a pebble, in Latin a single pronoun serves for both, since *homo* and *calculus* are both masculine. As for 'his', 'hers', and 'its': there is a single Latin word for all of these, whatever the gender of the relevant noun. (Bennett 1984: 34)

16 Spinoza never explicitly defines what he mean by "expression" – a term that appears throughout the *Ethics*. For a discussion of the meaning of "expression" in the *Ethics*, see Deleuze 1990.

17 I have omitted the explanations that Spinoza provides to clarify the meaning of ID6 and ID8. Spinoza uses the term *natura* (nature) and its cognates in a variety of senses. He distinguishes three primary senses of "nature": (1) the universe or cosmos; (2) kind; and (3) essence. But some of Spinoza's uses of "nature" depart from these three senses. As I have indicated, when I capitalize "Nature," I am using the expression in the first sense – as the name of the entire cosmos or universe. When Spinoza uses the term "nature" in the titles of the second and third parts of the *Ethics*, he is using it in a way that is close to the more traditional sense of "essence": the distinctive and distinguishing character of the mind or the affects. Spinoza, however, departs from the traditional use of "essence" since he rejects the distinction between essential and accidental attributes of substance. See the entry for "Nature" in Curley's glossary, in Curley 1985: 647.

18 See Spinoza's discussion of two types of definition in his letter to Simon de Vries, February 1663, in Spinoza 1995: 91–4.
19 Hampshire makes a similar point in an even stronger way. Spinoza's definitions "are not offered as one of a set of possible and convenient definitions of Substance, Cause and God, but as the only possible or consistent set of definitions; to conceive the world except in terms of these notions, so defined, is demonstrably to be involved in contradiction or to be using words without attaching any clear meaning to them" (Hampshire 1951: 25–6). I do not want to deny that Spinoza's claims about his "real" definitions are open to criticism. Many of Spinoza's successors, including Hume, Kant, Hegel, and Peirce, have criticized Spinoza's definitions and their immediate availability to the unprejudiced mind.
20 Della Rocca provides a lucid account of Descartes' understanding of substance, attribute, and mode. He shows why Spinoza finds Descartes' account unsatisfactory and why Spinoza advocates substance monism. See Della Rocca 2008: 33–58.
21 Hampshire clarifies Spinoza's argument that the very idea of a plurality of substances is ultimately self-contradictory. See Hampshire 1951: 26–32.
22 For differing interpretations of the relation of modes to Substance, see Curley 1969, Della Rocca 2008, and Melamed 2013.
23 Hampshire brings out the subtlety of Spinoza's determinism and shows how it is compatible with Spinoza's distinctive understanding of human freedom. See Hampshire 1971, esp. p. 197. Scholars debate how to interpret Spinoza's necessitarianism. Don Garrett argues that Spinoza is committed to strict necessitarianism – "the doctrine that every actual state of affairs holds with strict metaphysical necessity" (D. Garrett 2018: 125). In contrast, Edwin Curley and Gregory Walski "agree that, for Spinoza, God exists as a matter of strict metaphysical necessity and that every finite mode follows with strict metaphysical necessity from God's nature when taken together with previous finite modes. They deny, however, that Spinoza regards finite modes themselves as existing with strict metaphysical necessity" (D. Garrett 2018: 125). Curley and Walski call their interpretation "moderate necessitarianism," which they contrast with Garrett's "strict necessitarianism." See Curley and Walski 1999. Both Garrett's original essay, "Spinoza's Necessitarianism," and his reply to his critics, "Postscript Necessitarianism Revisited," are in D. Garrett 2018.
24 Some commentators prefer to use the term "panentheism" to describe Spinoza's position, in order to stress that, for Spinoza, whatever is, is *in* God: "Whatever is, is in God, and nothing can be or be conceived without God" (IP13). Later I will consider the famous pantheism controversy that erupted in Germany at the end of the eighteenth century.
25 Spinoza scholars agree that the *Ethics* presents a thoroughgoing and principled attack on teleology in physics and theology. Bennett (1984) goes further and claims that Spinoza also rejects – or is committed to rejecting – teleological explanations of human actions. Bennett admits that Spinoza

frequently talks as if human actions can be understood teleologically, but he notes that Spinoza is being inconsistent in his claims. Martin Lin challenges Bennett's interpretation. He presents strong arguments to show that "[t]here is nothing in his [Spinoza's] metaphysics or philosophy of mind that forbids teleological explanations of human actions. In fact, there is good reason to think that his account of mental content commits him to them" (Lin 2006: 318).

26 Della Rocca characterizes Spinoza's naturalism as the "thesis that everything in the world plays by the same rules; there are no things that are somehow connected with each other but that are not governed by the same principles" (Della Rocca 2008: 5).

27 See Bernstein 2020.

28 Joseph Rouse (2015) never mentions Spinoza, but he takes up the challenge of giving a nonreductive naturalist account of human conceptual abilities.

29 Spinoza's conception of "idea" has been extensively debated. Daisie Radner provides one of the best explications of the meaning and role of ideas in Spinoza. She carefully distinguishes between the object of an idea and what an idea represents:

> The key to Spinoza's theory of the nature of representation is his distinction between the object of the idea and that which the idea represents. The term "the object of the idea" is not synonymous with the term "that which is represented by the idea," although in some cases the two terms have the same reference. The object and the thing represented stands in two different relations to the idea. . . . The relation between the idea and its object is explicated in terms of the distinction between objective and formal reality. The relation between the idea and what it represents is explicated in terms of the resemblance of the thing represented to the object of the idea. (Radner 1971: 346)

See also Brandom's discussion of the importance of the distinction between the object of an idea and what an idea represents in Brandom 2002: 34–40; 121–42.

30 Although Spinoza clearly rejects Cartesian *ontological dualism* that presupposes that the mind and the body are two different types of substances, there is a more neutral sense in which Spinoza's theory is dualistic. The causal order of ideas in the mind and the causal order of bodily events are conceptually independent – neither is reducible to the other. Both these orders describe and explain *one and the same reality*. This "dualism" is an application of the metaphysical principle that the two attributes – of thought and extension (and their modes) – are conceptually independent and are attributes (and their modes) of the one and only Substance. Because Spinoza claims that there is an infinity of attributes of God, and each is conceptually independent, it follows that there would be an infinite number of ways to describe and explain *one and the same reality* – God, Substance, or Nature – even though we, human beings, are limited to the knowledge of just two of these attributes – thought and extension.

31 There are some striking similarities between Spinoza's and Donald Davidson's identity theories. See Davidson 2001. Indeed, Davidson acknowledges his indebtedness to Spinoza in Davidson 1999. For a discussion of the similarities and differences between Spinoza and Davidson, see Della Rocca 1996 and 2008.
32 Although Spinoza wrote long before the development of the theory of evolution, his understanding of the continuity throughout Nature is analogous to Dewey's naturalistic evolutionary account of nature. Both reject all versions of ontological dualism. I explore Dewey's naturalism in Bernstein 2020.
33 There is a new English translation of the *Ethics* by Michael Silverthone and Matthew Kisner that is based on a new Latin edition. It takes account of a hand-copied manuscript of the *Ethics* discovered in the Vatican Library in 2010. See Spinoza 2018. Silverthorne and Kisner's translation departs from Curley's in speaking of "three kinds of cognition" rather than "three kinds of knowledge."
34 Sellars makes it clear that in speaking of "things imagined" he means things conceived, "for I am using 'image' in this sense as a metaphor for conception. ... The philosopher, then, is confronted by two conceptions, equally public, equally non-arbitrary, of man-in-the world and he cannot shirk the attempt to see how they fall together in one stereoscopic view" (Sellars 1963: 5).
35 Sellars acknowledges the similarity between his manifest/scientific distinction and Spinoza's distinction between the first two kinds of knowledge. But he goes on to say: "But if in Spinoza's account, the scientific image, as he interprets it, dominates the stereoscopic view (the manifest image appearing as a tracery of explainable error), the very fact that I use the analogy of stereoscopic vision implies that as I see it the manifest image is not overwhelmed in the synthesis" (Sellars 1963: 8–9). Sellars is mistaken about Spinoza. The first kind of knowledge, which is dependent on imagination, is a form of *knowledge*. It is not overwhelmed by the second form of knowledge, *ratio*. On the contrary, it is only from the perspective of *ratio* that we can explain the power and limitations of the first kind of knowledge. Spinoza seeks to give a *rational account* of why the first kind of knowledge misleads us. From a *functional* point of view, Sellars' understanding of a synoptic stereoscopic vision of man-in-the-world corresponds to Spinoza's third kind of knowledge where we grasp the relation between the first two forms of knowledge. From the perspective of Sellars' synoptic vision of man-in-the-world and Spinoza's third kind of knowledge, we come to have a deeper knowledge of ourselves and our place in nature. For Spinoza, the highest form of knowledge is one where we are able to understand how the first two kinds of knowledge are related to each other. Spinoza characterizes this third type of knowledge as *scientia intuitiva*. Sellars would reject such a characterization as a variant of the "myth of the given." Nevertheless, Spinoza's third kind of knowledge is close to what Sellars takes to be the aim of philosophy: "The aim of philosophy, abstractly formulated, is to understand how things in the broadest possible

36 For a helpful discussion of what Spinoza means by "formal essence," see D. Garrett 2009.
37 Bennett criticizes not only the doctrine of intuitive knowledge but also two other interlinked doctrines: Spinoza's claims about the mind's eternity and his claims about the intellectual love of God. Bennett concludes his critique of these three interlinked doctrines by declaring: "Those of us who love and admire Spinoza's philosophical work should in sad silence avert our eyes from the second half of Part 5" (Bennett 1984: 375).
38 For a full account of Yovel's interpretation of the third kind of knowledge, see "Knowledge as Alternative Salvation," Yovel 1989: ch. 6.
39 Curley discusses the problems of finding an English equivalent for *affectus*: "*Emotion* has the disadvantage of suggesting a passive state, whereas an *affectus* may well be active." Furthermore, "emotion" suggests "an exclusively psychological state (whereas an *affectus* is a state both of the mind and of the body)" (Curley 1985: 625). Finding English equivalents for Spinoza's Latin in his analysis of *affectus* is treacherous and can cause enormous confusion. *Laetitia* is sometimes translated as "pleasure," sometimes as "joy"; *tristitia* has been translated as "pain," "sorrow," or "sadness." I use Curley's translations because his English translation of the *Ethics* is commonly available. He translates *laetitia* as "joy" and *tristitia* as "sadness."
40 The Latin original follows Spinoza 1925. This passage is a striking example of how an excessive focus on the geometric method can distort the semantic richness of the *Ethics*. Throughout the *Ethics*, not just in his prefaces, scholia, and appendices, Spinoza uses irony, sarcasm, and even humor to ridicule his opponents. When Spinoza speaks of conceiving "of man in Nature as a dominion within a dominion" and says that man "disturbs" rather than follows the order of Nature, he is mocking the Cartesian doctrine that human beings have free will and absolute power over their actions. It is also hard to resist the speculation that the last two sentences in the above passage implicitly refer to the way in which Spinoza was cursed when he was excommunicated from Amsterdam's Jewish community.
41 This scholium also illustrates another important aspect of the *Ethics*. Spinoza does not simply develop logical demonstrations of his theses. He supports his claims by considering objections to them and answering these objections.
42 Spinoza draws his conclusions from what he takes to be logically necessary demonstrations (and not from empirical observations). But it is striking how much of his analysis of the bodily manifestation of affects has been borne out by recent neurobiological research. See, e.g., Damasio 2003. Allison writes: "Since . . . [Spinoza] assumes that mental and physical phenomena are subject to the same set of universal laws and are to be understood in terms of the same model of scientific explanation, Spinoza anticipated the method and world view of modern rational science to a much greater degree than Descartes" (Allison 1987: 125).

43 See also Bennett's discussion of causality in Bennett 1984: 111–24.
44 Spinoza considers the objection that experience shows that the mind does influence the body by a mysterious act of mental will. He squarely confronts this objection and shows that experience actually supports his account of the identity of the mental and bodily action. There is no such thing as a mental decision or volition that is distinct from a bodily appetite. On the contrary, "[a]ll these things, indeed, show clearly that both the decision of the Mind and the appetite and the determination of the Body by nature exist together – or rather are one and the same thing, which we call a decision when it is considered under, and explained through, the attribute of Thought, and which we call a determination when it is considered under the attribute of Extension and deduced from the laws of motion and rest" (IIIP2s).
45 For an illuminating reconstruction of Spinoza's *conatus* argument, see D. Garrett 2002. I also fully agree with Garrett's claim about Spinoza's naturalistic account of intentionality. "Any attempt to explain the origins of intentionality as emergent in nature is Spinozistic in spirit, if not in letter; Spinoza's proposal that substantiality is intrinsically related to self-preservation is one possible contribution to that project" (D. Garrett 2018: 380).
46 In a section of Part III entitled "Definitions of Affects," Spinoza explains that he does not recognize any "difference between human appetite and desire. For whether a man is conscious of his appetite or not, the appetite still remains one and the same."
47 One of the reasons why it is difficult to translate *affectus* into English is because it includes actions, passions, and desires.
48 See Yovel's interpretation of secular salvation in Yovel 1989: 167–71.
49 I use the expressions "ethics" and "moral philosophy" as rough synonyms. Spinoza's conception of ethics is much broader than contemporary understandings of moral philosophy and moral theory. It also encompasses what Hegel calls *Sittlichkeit* (ethical life).
50 I agree with Hampshire when he writes:

> To interpret Spinoza as expecting emancipation solely from an intellectual understanding of causes is not entirely correct. It is equally incorrect to represent him as defining freedom simply as knowledge of the causes that determine my emotions and actions. Reason is the expression of my primary desire of self-assertion as a thinking being, of the urge to extend my own activity and freedom as far as I can. I am to the highest degree free when I am engaged in an intellectual inquiry, and when the subject of this inquiry is the order of my thought, as an instance of something that may be understood *sub specie aeternitatis*, and not as it is affected by particular causes in the common order of nature. My happiness then consists, first, in immunity from hatred of particular things, and from the other negative and depressive passions, an immunity that an adequate understanding of causes necessarily brings; secondly, it consists in the positive enjoyment of my own freedom *as* freedom, as the active exercise of the power of thought. (Hampshire 1971: 197–8)

51 See Omri Boehm's discussion of nihilism in Boehm 2014. Boehm notes that Nietzsche considered Spinoza to be a kindred spirit and cites a famous passage from one of Nietzsche's letters.

> I have a *precursor*, and what a precursor! I hardly knew Spinoza: that I should have turned to him just *now*, was inspired by "instinct." Not only is his over-all tendency like mine – making knowledge the *most powerful* affect – but in the five main points of his doctrine I recognize myself; this most unusual and loneliest thinker is closest to me precisely in these matters: he denies the freedom of the will, teleology, the moral world order, the unegoistic, and evil. Even though the divergences are admittedly tremendous, they are due more to the difference in time, culture, and science. *In summa*: my lonesomeness, which, as on very high mountains, often made it hard for me to breathe and made my blood rush out, is now at least a twosomeness. Strange. (Nietzsche 1976: 92)

For a discussion of the similarities between Spinoza and Nietzsche, see Deleuze 1988.

52 For an excellent account of the ethical and political consequences of Spinoza's conception of human freedom and its contemporary relevance, see S. James 2012.

53 In an illuminating article, Daniel Garber examines a tension – an apparent dilemma – in Spinoza: "Our rational need for other people seems to conflict with other demands of complete rationality. If what we seek is perfect rationality, perfect freedom, then we would seem to be drawn into ourselves and our relation with God, and drawn away from other humans, while if reason draws us into society, then we would seem to be drawn away from exemplifying the model of a human nature better than our own" (Garber 2004: 184–5). Garber provides a brilliant solution to this dilemma – one that depends on the realization that perfect freedom is an idealization, something that can never be achieved in this world by human beings. Consequently, "we realize that our need for society is not temporary, not a provisional state until we attain the freedom to which we aspire, but a permanent and inevitable feature of human existence" (Garber 2004: 204).

54 Many commentators have noted the parallels between Freud and Spinoza, especially with regard to the need to achieve rational knowledge of the causes of our unconscious desires. See Hampshire 1971 and Yovel 1989. For a contentious article challenging the significance of what Spinoza and Freud presumably share in common, see de Deugd 2004.

55 Some thinkers claim that a moral theory acknowledging the existence of moral norms is, by definition, non-naturalistic. Such a claim begs the crucial issue. Spinoza as an ethical naturalist is not denying that there are ethical norms. Rather, he is claiming that we can account for such norms from within nature.

56 See the entry "Spinoza" in Bayle 1965: 288–338.

57 There are four versions of Spinoza's first name: Baruch (Hebrew), Benedictus (Latin), Bento (Portuguese), Benedict (English). They all mean "blessed."

58 For a discussion of Heine's enthusiasm for Spinoza and his influence on Heine's own "adventure of immanence," see Yovel 1989a: 52–65. In the twentieth century, Spinoza has inspired thinkers in a wide variety of fields. Arne Naess (2008) takes Spinoza as an inspiration for the "Deep Ecology Movement." Damasio (2003) explores how Spinoza's approach to joy, sorrow, and the feeling brain anticipates some of the most recent discoveries in neurobiology.
59 See Singer 1961.
60 See Althusser 1976, Deleuze 1988, and Balibar 1998.
61 Della Rocca lists the many ways in which Hume's philosophy is the antithesis of Spinoza's. See Della Rocca 2008: 281–2.
62 See my discussion of contemporary naturalism in Bernstein 2020.
63 See Brandom 1994: 4–7.

Chapter 2 Hume: The Experimental Method and the Science of Man

1 Hume published Books I and II of the *Treatise* together. Subsequently he published Book III.
2 Page references are to the revised second edition of the *Treatise* (Hume 1978).
3 Later we will see that Hume's claim that impressions of sensation "arise in the soul originally from unknown causes" is one of the sources of his skepticism.
4 Stroud notes that Hume's "'revolution' in philosophy takes for granted the theory of ideas, and concentrates on what must be added to it, what else must be true of human beings, in order to explain why they think, feel and act in ways they do" (Stroud 1977: 9). My own interpretation of Hume is close to and inspired by Stroud.
5 In his *Enquiry Concerning Human Understanding*, Hume declares:

> It seems to me, that the only objects of the abstract sciences or of demonstrations are quantity and number, and that all attempts to extend this more perfect species of knowledge beyond these bounds are mere sophistry and illusion. . . . All other enquiries of men regard only matter of fact and existence; and these are evidently incapable of demonstration. . . . When we run over libraries, persuaded of these principles, what havoc must we make? If we take in our hand any volume; of divinity or school metaphysics, for instance; let us ask, *Does it contain any abstract reasoning concerning quantity or number? No. Does it contain any experimental reasoning concerning matter of fact and existence?* No. Commit it then to the flames: for it can contain nothing but sophistry and illusion. (Hume 1975: 163–5)

6 See the section entitled "Of skepticism with regard to the senses" in Hume 1978 for Hume's complicated (and convoluted) account of how we come to

believe in the continued existence and independence of objects in the empirical world of matters of fact.

7   In 1905, Norman Kemp Smith wrote a two-part article in *Mind* entitled "The Naturalism of Hume" (Kemp Smith 1905 and 1905a). At the time, his interpretation of Hume was not influential. It was overshadowed by logical positivist interpretations of Hume. But in the past few decades, there has been an increasing appreciation of Kemp Smith's naturalistic interpretation of Hume. Hume, like Spinoza, never uses the expression "naturalism," although it is the term adopted by his commentators to identify Hume's orientation toward nature, including human nature. On Hume's naturalism, see Stroud 1977, Mounce 1999, and D. Garrett 2004 and 2015. One of the most controversial issues among Hume scholars has been the relation of Hume's naturalism to his skepticism. For a comprehensive discussion of Hume's skepticism, see Fogelin 1985, 1994, and 2009. D. Garrett (2004) carefully analyzes Fogelin's arguments and shows that Hume's naturalism is compatible with his "mitigated" skepticism. Showing that Hume's naturalism and skepticism are compatible is now becoming the dominant position among Hume scholars, although they disagree about *how* they are compatible.

8   Stroud argues that Hume's refinement of the British empiricist theory of ideas is his least original contribution to philosophy of human nature. The primary purpose of his version of the theory of ideas is to provide the foundations for a new original "science of man" (see Stroud 1977: 9). While it may be the least original contribution to his philosophy of human nature, nevertheless, Hume's *distinctive* version of the theory of ideas is foundational for him. Hume begins each book of the *Treatise* with an affirmation of the doctrine that all perceptions of the mind consist of impressions and ideas. Furthermore, when the consequences of this doctrine are developed, they lead to Hume's moderate or "mitigated" skepticism.

9   See the section "Of the reason of animals" in Hume 1978, where Hume suggests some of the ways in which "beasts" (nonhuman animals) are similar to, and yet different from, human animals. For Hume, nature encompasses inanimate nature, animate nature, and human nature. There are differences *within* nature, but no ontological breaks or gaps exist within nature.

10 When Hume uses the expression "experimental method of reasoning," he is not limiting it to the performance of actual experiments. Rather, it has a broad meaning – the observation of matters of fact based on experience.

11 Stroud notes:

> Despite the suggestions in the more programmatic parts of Hume's writings that the association of ideas, on the analogy of the principle of universal gravitation, can account for everything that goes on in the mind, when he actually gets down to the detailed business of explaining the origins of some of our most pervasive forms of thinking, feeling and acting, he does not force everything into a rigid associationist mould. (Stroud 1977: 37)

12 Hume speaks of "reasoning" from cause to effect and from effect to cause, but this use of "reasoning" does not mean that the appeal to reason is sufficient to *justify* these inferences.
13 The full title of the *Abstract* is *An Abstract of a Book lately published; Entituled, A Treatise of Human Nature, &c. Wherein The Chief Argument of that Book is farther Illustrated and Explained*. It was published anonymously in 1740. For a fascinating and illuminating account of the discovery that the anonymous *Abstract* was actually written by Hume himself, see J. M. Keynes and P. Straffa's introduction to Hume 1965. Since the publication of this book, further evidence confirms that Hume was the author of the *Abstract*.
14 The author of the *Abstract* (Hume) refers to the author of the *Treatise* (Hume) in the third person.
15 If one asks the question, of how we account for custom, Hume thinks we can go no further in our explanation. It is simply a matter of fact that this is how the mind operates. He clearly states this in his *Enquiry*.

> For wherever the repetition of any particular act or operation produces a propensity to renew the same act or operation, without being impelled by any reasoning or process of the understanding, we always say, that this propensity is the effect of *Custom*. By employing that word, we pretend not to have given the ultimate reason of such a propensity. We only point out a principle of human nature, which is universally acknowledged, and which is well known by its effects. Perhaps we can push our enquires no further, or pretend to give the cause of this cause; but must rest contented with it as the ultimate principle, which we can assign, of all our conclusions from experience. It is sufficient satisfaction that we can go so far, without repining at the narrowness of our faculties because they will carry us no farther. (Hume 1975: 43)

16 Passages such as this one lead some commentators to suggest that Book II of the *Treatise* should be read before Book I. As Hume proceeds in Book I, it becomes increasingly evident that we need to appeal to feelings, sentiments, and passions to fully understand what is fundamental for understanding cause and effect. But it is only in Book II that we have a full-scale discussion of feelings, sentiments, and passions.
17 Compare the way in which Hume characterizes belief in the *Enquiry*: "Whenever any object is presented to the memory or senses, it immediately, by the force of custom, carries the imagination to conceive that object, which is usually conjoined to it; and this conception is attended with a feeling or sentiment, different from the loose reveries of the fancy. In this consists the whole nature of belief" (Hume 1975: 48).
18 One may well ask what kind of impression is a "determination of the mind"? Normally, Hume thinks of impressions as discrete and separate units. Is a "determination" a discrete and separate unit – like a sensible impression of a red patch or an impression of reflection – like fear?
19 The question raised in the previous note is also applicable to "propensity." Is propensity a discrete and separate unit? Both "determination" and

"propensity" share the *grammar* of "power"; yet Hume rejects that there is an impression of power. For a subtle interpretation of Hume's claim that necessity exists in the mind, see Stroud 1977: 77–95.

20   Kant's claim that Hume awakened him from his "dogmatic slumber" makes perfect sense. In Kant's terminology, Hume demonstrated that causality is not an *analytic* principle justified by pure reason. Kant's transcendental philosophy seeks to show that, although not analytic, the necessary connection between cause and effect is a *synthetic a priori* principle – a principle that is established by an appeal to the understanding (*Verstand*). In his *Prolegomena*, Kant says:

> I freely admit that the remembrance of *David Hume* was the very thing that many years ago first interrupted my dogmatic slumber and gave a completely different direction to my researches in the field of speculative philosophy. I was very far from listening to him with respect to his conclusions, which arose solely because he did not completely set out his problem but only touched on a part of it, which, without the whole being taken into account, can provide no enlightenment. . . . So I tried first whether *Hume's* objection might not be presented in a general manner, and I soon found that the concept of the connection of cause and effect is far from being the only concept through which the understanding thinks connections of things *a priori*; rather, metaphysics consists wholly of such concepts. I sought to ascertain their number, and once I had successfully attained this in the way I wished, namely from a single principle, I proceeded to the deduction of these concepts, from which I henceforth became assured that they were not, as *Hume* had feared, derived from experience, but had arisen from the pure understanding. (*P* 4:260)

Kant accuses Hume of the failure to recognize that there are synthetic *a priori* principles. If Hume were to respond to Kant, he would challenge the very idea of synthetic *a priori* principles. The profound philosophical differences between Hume and Kant are indicated by their competing stances toward synthetic *a priori* principles. For Hume, there are *no* synthetic *a priori* principles. It is an empty class. For Kant, recognizing that there are synthetic *a priori* principles is the *key* to understanding the possibility of experience and scientific knowledge of the world.

21   Hume does not clearly specify the differences among "sentiments," "emotions," "passions," "feelings," and "impressions of reflection." At times, he suggests that they are different names for the same mental phenomenon. To use a philosophical term that Hume does not use, they all belong to the same *category* – a feature of the mind that must be sharply distinguished from the category of reason. Furthermore, what he says about the feeling that distinguishes belief from mere conception is applicable to all feelings: namely, that it is *impossible* by words to *describe* these feelings, sentiments, etc., and that everyone must be conscious of them in their own breast.

22   Hume's point that *only* another proposition (something that is true or false) can be in conflict with a proposition is analogous to the famous claim by

Donald Davidson that *only* a belief (something that is either true or false) can be in conflict or contradict another belief.

23 Commenting on the above passage, Stroud writes:

> In order to try to understand what Hume is getting at, let us say that the sorts of things that are true or false are 'propositions'. They are 'representative' entities in that they represent things to be a certain way, and they are true if and only if things are as the proposition represents them to be. Only propositions, so understood, are the proper 'objects of reason'. Hume appears to be saying that the only way something could be opposed to, or in conflict with, reason is by being opposed to, or in conflict with, one of the 'objects of reason'. But something can be in conflict or contradiction with a particular proposition only if it differs in truth-value from that proposition, and so whatever can be in conflict or contradiction with a proposition must be something that itself has a truth-value. And the only things that have truth-values, the only things that are either true or false, are 'representative' entities such as propositions.
>
> But a passion or emotion is what Hume calls an 'original existence, compleat in itself'; it is not a proposition at all. When I have a certain passion, then I am in a particular state; I undergo a certain 'modification of existence'. And Hume concludes that passions do not 'represent' things to be a certain way; they just exist, or are *felt*. (Stroud 1977: 159, emphasis added)

Reason belongs to the *cogitative* part of our nature; sentiments belong to the *sensitive* part. Hume makes his point dramatically when he writes:

> 'Tis not contrary to reason to prefer the destruction of the whole world to the scratching of my finger. 'Tis not contrary to reason for me to chuse my total ruin, to prevent the least uneasiness of an *Indian* or person wholly unknown to me. 'Tis as little contrary to reason to prefer even my own acknowled'd lesser good to my greater, and have a more ardent affection for the former than the latter. . . . In short, a passion must be accompany'd with some false judgment, in order to its being unreasonable; and even then 'tis not the passion, properly speaking, which is unreasonable, but the judgment. (Hume 1978: 416)

24 Hume knows that we do speak of actions and even passions as *unreasonable*, but he thinks that this is just a loose way of speaking and is quite compatible with his view. "He thinks an action is said to be 'unreasonable' only when it is 'accompany'd with' some judgment or proposition which is itself 'unreasonable' or 'contrary to reason'. If we do or feel something only because we believe that p, and it is in fact false that p, then our action or passion might be said to be unreasonable" (Stroud 1977: 159–60).

25 "[Hume's] main aim throughout is to establish that the uniformities, and therefore necessities, are present to the same degree in human affairs as in the operations of inanimate matter, since for him that is a necessary condition of there being a science of man" (Stroud 1977: 154).

26 Hume's work *Dialogues Concerning Natural Religion* was published posthumously, like Spinoza's *Ethics*. See Hume 2012. Nevertheless, during their lifetimes, both authors were condemned as infidels and atheists.

27 Although Hume speaks of perceptions as present "before the mind," this manner of speaking is misleading insofar as it suggests that the mind is *independent* of its perceptions – as if the mind is something before which perceptions appear. Hume, however, claims that the mind is nothing but its perceptions.

> For my part, when I enter most intimately into what I call *myself*, I always stumble on some particular perception or other, of heat or cold, light or shade, love or hatred, pain or pleasure. I never catch *myself* at any time without a perception, and never can observe anything but the perception. (Hume 1978: 252)

Consider also his metaphor of the mind as a kind of theater:

> The mind is a kind of theatre, where several perceptions successively make their appearance; pass, re-pass, glide away, and mingle in an infinite variety of postures and situations. . . . The comparison of the theatre must not mislead us. They are *the successive perceptions only*, that constitute the mind; nor have we the most distant notion of the place, where these scenes are represented, or of the materials, of which it is compos'd. (Hume 1978: 253, emphasis added)

The mind consists of successive perceptions with *no* theater or *place* in which they occur.

28 For the analysis of Hume's "mitigated" skepticism, see D. Garrett 2004.

29 Hume never adequately treats yet another deep problem. He presupposes that each and every perception is a *discrete* unit. This claim is fundamental for his understanding of perceptions and for his analysis of simple impressions and ideas. However, he never gives a satisfactory account of how we *individuate* these discrete impressions and ideas. What is the *criterion* for distinguishing one simple impression from another? Suppose I open my eyes and see a red patch, and then quickly blink. Now suppose I stare at the red patch for five minutes without blinking. Do both of these qualify as experiencing simple sensible impressions? Or does the five-minute stare consist of a plurality of impressions? William James, in his *Principles of Psychology* (1980), provides a sharp and, in my opinion, devastating critique of Hume's "atomistic" account of perceptions. He argues that Hume not only distorts experience but also substitutes an "intellectual abstraction" for the continuous *flow* of experience.

30 Hume acknowledges the tension between his philosophical reflections and what we naturally believe.

> The natural consequence of this reasoning shou'd be, that our perceptions have no more a continu'd than an independent existence; and indeed philosophers have so far run into this opinion, that they change their system, and distinguish . . . betwixt perceptions and objects, of which the former are suppos'd to be interrupted, and perishing, and different at every different return; the latter to be uninterrupted, and to observe a continu'd existence and identity. But however philosophical this new system may be esteem'd,

I assert that 'tis only a palliative remedy, and that it contains all the difficulties of the vulgar system, with some others, that are peculiar to itself. There are no principles either of the understanding or fancy, which lead us directly to embrace this opinion of the double existence of perceptions and objects, nor can we arrive at it by passing thro' the common hypothesis of the identity and continuance of our interrupted perceptions. Were we not first persuaded, that our perceptions are our only objects, and continue to exist even when they no longer make their appearance to the senses, we shou'd never be led to think, that our perceptions and objects are different, and that our objects alone preserve a continu'd existence. 'The latter hypothesis has no primary recommendation either to reason or the imagination, but acquires all its influence on the imagination from the former.' (Hume 1978: 211)

31 Hume is proud to consider himself an empiricist and to appeal to experience (rather than reason) to justify the claims about matters of fact. However, his conception of experience based on his doctrine of perceptions ineluctably leads to paradoxes and skeptical doubts. Kant's critique of Hume is that Hume fails to understand the *distinctive* character of experience.
32 For an exploration of some of the similarities and differences between Spinoza and Hume, see Popkin 1979.
33 Brandom is a powerful representative of this anti-naturalist attitude that stresses the non-naturalistic character of human reason. See Brandom 1994.

Chapter 3 Kant: Copernican Turn – Nature, Reason, and Freedom

1 Kant uses the term "reason" in a generic sense that includes all forms of discursive rationality. In his critical philosophy he distinguishes "understanding" (*Verstand*) – the source of the *categories* – from "reason" (*Vernunft*), the faculty that seeks to transcend possible experience – the source of what he calls *Ideas*.
2 When citing passages from the *Critique of Pure Reason* (*CPR*), I follow the standard practice of referring to the A and B editions. English translations are from the Cambridge edition of the *Critique* (Kant 1998).
3 The editors of the new Cambridge translation of the *Critique* use boldface type (rather than the contemporary convention of italics) to indicate Kant's original emphasis. For the rationale of their typographical decision, see their introduction to *CPR* (Kant 1998: 76). I follow the editors of the Cambridge translation of the *CPR* and *CJ* (Kant 2000) in using boldface type for Kant's original emphasis.
4 In citing passages from the *Cambridge Edition of the Works of Immanuel Kant*, I omit references to the editor's footnotes.

5   This second aspect of a metaphysics of nature presents a number of difficulties for Kant. Some passages of his *Metaphysical Foundations of Natural Science* read as if Kant is blurring the line between a pure science of nature and the physics of his time. This leads some commentators, like Stephan Körner, to suggest that the whole of the first *Critique* is an attempt to elucidate the presuppositions of Newtonian physics – the science of Kant's day. Consequently, Körner argues that, as physics progresses, we need to reconstruct the presuppositions of the new physics.

> Its [the *Critique*'s] doctrine of space and time as *a priori* particulars and forms of perception might need replacing by a new notion of space-time; and its three analogies by a different set. Whitehead's *Concept of Nature* and other works of his could be regarded . . . as attempts in this direction. Any philosophical physicist undertaking this task could learn a great deal not only from Kant's general approach, but also from the results of his examination of the science of his day. (Körner 1955: 87, cited in Strawson 1966: 120)

This historicizing of the *Critique* is certainly antithetical to Kant's intention of developing a transcendental philosophy that is universal and necessary. P. F. Strawson (among many others) rejects this "historicized" understanding of the *Critique*.

> If it [Körner's view of the *Critique*] were the only possible view, the *Critique* as a whole would be a less interesting work than we hoped. Accepting this view would amount to giving up the idea that we may find in the Principles further elaboration of the general conclusions of the Transcendental Deduction into more detailed statements of generally necessary conditions of the possibility of any experience of objective reality such as we can render intelligible to ourselves. Instead we should have to look at the Transcendental Deduction itself in a new light, knowing that in general we have to be content with historical metaphysics: accounts of the fundamental framework of ideas within which scientific thinking has been conducted at this or that period, or is conducted now. (Strawson 1966: 120)

Michael Friedman defends an opposing view. Against those interpreters of Kant, like Strawson, who seek "to downplay and even dismiss the philosophical relevance of Kant's engagement with contemporary science [of his time]," Friedman argues:

> Although this attempt to read Kant, as far as possible, in independence from the details of his scientific context is therefore understandable, I believe it is also profoundly mistaken. Kant's philosophical achievement consists precisely in the depth and acuity of his insight into the state of the mathematical exact sciences as he found them, and, although these sciences have since radically changed in ways that were entirely unforeseen (and unforeseeable) in the eighteenth century, this circumstance in no way diminishes Kant's achievement. (Friedman 1992: p. xii)

6   Sometimes Kant uses the term "metaphysical" in a more restricted sense, as when he distinguishes transcendental principles from metaphysical principles. For example, in the third *Critique*, he writes:

> A transcendental principle is one through which the universal *a priori* condition under which alone things can become objects of our cognition at all is represented. By contrast, a principle is called metaphysical if it represents the *a priori* condition under which alone objects whose concept must be given empirically can be further determined *a priori*. (*CJ* 5:181)

7   Friedman remarks that Kant leaves us in the dark concerning the precise nature of how empirical causal laws are grounded in the transcendental principles. See his attempt to elucidate this grounding in Friedman 1992a.

8   The full title of the *Prolegomena* is *Prolegomena to Any Future Metaphysics That Will Be Able to Come Forward as a Science*. It was published in 1783, two years after the first edition of the *CPR*. For an illuminating discussion of Kant's relation to Hume, see Gary Hatfield's introduction to the *Prolegomena* in Hatfield 2002.

9   Many commentators claim that Kant's primary targets were Leibniz and Wolff, but Omri Boehm (2014) argues that Kant set out to refute Spinoza's rationalism.

10 The adjectives "analytic" and "synthetic," when used to characterize *methods*, are not to be confused with their use in characterizing *judgments* or *propositions*.

11 Despite the almost universal agreement among Kant scholars that the Transcendental Deduction (especially as reformulated in the second edition) is the most crucial stage in Kant's overall argument, there is still fierce disagreement about (a) what precisely is the argument (or arguments) of the Deduction, and (b) what precisely it proves. For an illuminating discussion of the textual and philosophical problems of interpreting the Transcendental Deduction, see Henrich 1994.

12 In what I am calling Kant's "descent," he introduces the schematism and the threefold synthesis. In his account of the application of the categories to objects of the senses, Kant highlights the importance of the transcendental synthesis of the imagination.

> We therefore have a pure imagination, as a fundamental faculty of the human soul, that grounds all cognition *a priori*. By its means we bring into combination the manifold of intuition on the one side and the condition of the necessary unity of apperception on the other. Both extremes, namely sensibility and understanding, must necessarily be connected by means of this transcendental function of the imagination, since otherwise the former would to be sure yield appearances but no objects of an empirical cognition, hence there would be no experience. (*CPR* A 124)

Compare this with the following passage from the B edition:

> Now since all of our intuition is sensible, the imagination, on account of the subjective condition under which alone it can give a corresponding intuition

to the concepts of understanding, belongs to **sensibility**; but insofar as its synthesis is still an exercise of spontaneity, which is determining and not, like sense, merely determinable, and can thus determine the form of sense *a priori* in accordance with the unity of apperception, the imagination is to this extent a faculty for determining the sensibility *a priori*, and its synthesis of intuitions, **in accordance with the categories**, must be the transcendental synthesis of the **imagination**, which is an effect of the understanding on sensibility and its first application (and at the same time the ground of all others) to objects of the intuition that is possible for us. (*CPR* B 151–2)

Having emphasized the heterogeneous differences between understanding and sensibility – between concepts and intuitions – Kant argues that imagination enables a *mediation* between understanding and sensibility. This is essential for explaining how the pure concepts of the understanding apply to sensible (empirical) intuitions. Despite the brief remarks about the imagination in the first *Critique*, some interpreters (like Heidegger and Arendt) have stressed its importance for a proper understanding of Kant's critical philosophy. Arendt claims that "the role of imagination for our cognitive faculties is perhaps the greatest discovery Kant made in the *Critique of Pure Reason*" (Arendt 1992: 80).

13 Kant scholars debate the relation between the table of judgments of the Transcendental Logic and the pure concepts of the understanding. For a comprehensive analysis of Kant's theory of judgment, and how the table of judgments is related to the pure concepts of understanding, see Longuenesse 1998.

14 One of the most contentious debates in Kant interpretation concerns the relation between sensibility (the faculty of receptivity) and understanding (the faculty of spontaneity). There are those who maintain that the two faculties are absolutely separate and heterogeneous. And there are those, like McDowell, who maintain that "receptivity does not make an even notionally separable contribution to the co-operation" between receptivity and spontaneity (McDowell 1996: 9).

15 Kant and Hume scholars have debated whether Kant successfully answers Hume's doubts.

16 For an illuminating discussion of the thing in itself, which seeks to answer the objections of many of Kant's critics, see Allison 1983.

17 In the second edition of the *CPR* Kant added a section entitled "Refutation of idealism."

18 The idealism that Kant criticizes – "the claim that there are none other than thinking beings" – should not be confused with the transcendental idealism that he defends – the claim that, by virtue of our sensibility and understanding, we prescribe *a priori* universal principles to experience and nature. It is transcendental idealism that provides the justification for empirical realism.

19 One of the reasons for using the expression "prolegomena" in the title, *Prolegomena to Any Future Metaphysics That Will Be Able to Come Forward as a Science*, is to emphasize the need to supplement the *Prolegomena* with the metaphysical

foundations of natural science in order to *complete* the project of a critical metaphysics of nature.

20 For a discussion of the role of systematicity in Kant's conception of nature, see Guyer 2005.

21 One great difference between Kant and those logical positivists who also reject the very possibility of a transcendent metaphysics is that the positivists think that once we realize the illegitimacy of such a metaphysics, we can dismiss metaphysical questions. For Kant, on the contrary, we cannot simply dismiss these questions. They continue to haunt us – even when we realize that we cannot answer them. In this sense, Kant has a deeper grasp of our existential situation, where we desperately want answers to questions that we cannot satisfactorily answer. When Kant introduces the Transcendental Dialectic, he declares:

> The transcendental dialectic will therefore content itself with uncovering the illusion of transcendental arguments, while at the same time protecting us from being deceived by it; but it can never bring it about that transcendental illusion (like logical illusion) should even disappear and cease to be an illusion. For what we have to do with here is a natural and unavoidable illusion which itself rests on subjective principles and passes them off as objective. . . . Hence there is a natural and unavoidable dialectic of pure reason, not one in which a bungler might be entangled through lack of acquaintance, or one that some sophist has artfully invented in order to confuse rational people, but one that irremediably attaches to human reason, so that even after we have exposed the mirage, it will still not cease to lead our reason on with false hopes, continually propelling it into momentary aberrations that always need to be removed. (*CPR* A 298/B 354–5)

22 In the section of the *Critique* entitled "The Transcendental Doctrine of Method," Kant writes:

> When I hear that an uncommon mind has demonstrated away the freedom of the human will, the hope of a future life, and the existence of God, I am eager to read the book, for I expect that his talent will advance my insights. I am completely certain in advance that he will not have accomplished any of this, not because I believe myself already to be in possession of incontrovertible proofs of these important propositions, but rather because the transcendental critique, which has revealed to me the entire stock of our pure reason, has completely convinced me that just as pure reason is entirely inadequate for affirmative assertions in this field, even less will it know what to do in order to be able to assert something negative about these questions. For where would the supposed free-thinker derive his knowledge that, there is, e.g., no highest being? This proposition lies outside the field of possible experience, and therefore beyond the boundaries of all human insight. (*CPR* A 753/B 781)

23 In the *CPR*, the discussion of natural causality and the causality of freedom occurs in the context of the "system of cosmological ideas." Neither

the thesis nor the antithesis of the third antinomy mentions *human* freedom. Thesis: "Causality in accordance with laws of nature is not the only one from which all appearances of the world can be derived. It is also necessary to assume another causality through freedom in order to explain them" (*CPR* A 444/B 472). Antithesis: "There is no freedom, but everything in the world happens solely in accordance with laws of nature" (*CPR* A 445/B 473).

24 There is a potential terminological confusion between the expression "transcendent" and "transcendental." The primary use of "transcendental" designates the universal and necessary *a priori* conditions of possible experience. The primary use of "transcendent" is the purported "metaphysical realm" that is *beyond* experience. Normally, "transcendental" refers to the pure *a priori* conditions for the possibility of experience. However, when Kant speaks of the "transcendental idea of freedom," he is speaking of an idea that is *beyond* possible experience. In an important footnote, Kant states:

> For the understanding does not permit among **appearances** any condition that is itself empirically unconditioned. But if an **intelligible** condition, which therefore does not belong to the series of appearances as a member, may be thought for a conditioned (in appearance), without thereby interrupting in the least the series of empirical conditions, then such a condition could be admitted **as empirically unconditioned**, in such a way that no violation of the empirically continuous regress would occur anywhere. (*CPR* A 531/B 559)

25 For a comprehensive discussion of the pantheism controversy, see Beiser 1987: 42–91.

26 Several interpreters of Kant claim to elucidate how one and the same action is causally determined and yet free. I find their defenses unpersuasive. Allison, for example, says as a first response, "Kant neither has the need nor the right to assert dogmatically . . . that, given sufficient knowledge, we could infallibly predict human actions" (Allison 1983: 326). Such prediction is based on the presupposition of the principle of the uniformity of nature, and this principle is merely a regulative idea. However, the primary issue here is *not* about the uniformity of nature; it is about the claim that one and the same action is causally determined and yet is free. Allison then suggests that we take a closer look at the concept of practical freedom, especially the incentive – the reason for an action. We need to appreciate an essential aspect of Kant's theory of agency: viz. "the principle that an incentive can only determine an agent to act insofar as the agent incorporates that incentive into his rule of action" (Allison 1983: 327). But Kant is clear that practical freedom *presupposes* and is *grounded* in transcendental freedom. Although we can grasp the "abstract" or formal solution of the third antinomy, this does not help to explain how one and the same action is determined by natural causes and is also free. For other attempts to show how Kant seeks to explain how the transcendental idea of freedom is compatible with natural necessity, see Wood 1984, 1999, and Watkins 2005.

27 Earlier I suggested that the thing in itself is merely a negative concept – a concept indicating what things would be if they were not conditioned and represented by us. But interpreting the relation between appearance and thing in itself is more complicated. Paul Franks distinguishes three different interpretations of the relation of appearance to thing in itself.

> 1. *The Two Methods Interpretation*: On this view, Kant speaks of things in themselves nonreferentially and thus without any ontological commitment whatsoever. The point of the distinction between things in themselves and appearances is not to pick out some realm of entities beyond the reach of our knowledge. Instead, the point is to pick out a method for thinking of the very same objects that are accessible to our knowledge, a method for thinking of them as independent of the necessary conditions of our knowledge. . . .
> 2. *The Two Aspects Interpretation*: On this view, Kant speaks of things in themselves referentially, but he is referring to a nonphenomenal aspect of the very same objects that are accessible to our knowledge. . . .
> 3. *The Two Existents Interpretation*: On this view, Kant speaks of things in themselves referentially, and he is committed to the existence of entities distinct from sensible objects of our knowledge. (Franks 2005: 39)

For a review of competing interpretations of the relation of thing in itself and appearance and a defense of the two aspects interpretation, see Quarfood 2004, ch. 1.

28 The new Cambridge translation of *CJ* translates *bestimmend* as "determining" and *reflectirend* as "reflecting" – used as modifiers of *Urteilskraft* (the power of judgment). For justification of these translations, see "Note on the Translation" in Kant 2000: pp. xlvi–ix.

29 The phrase "There must still be a ground of the unity of the supersensible that grounds nature with that which the concept of freedom contains practically" (*CJ* 5:176) raises the tantalizing possibility that the *unity* of the supersensible grounds the *unity* of nature and freedom. But Kant does not explicitly explain how the "unity of the supersensible" grounds the unity of nature and freedom.

30 Concerning the possibility of freedom, Kant in the *CPR* denies not only that he has been trying to establish the *reality* of freedom, but also that he has been trying to establish the *possibility* of freedom. "[W]e have not even tried to prove the possibility of freedom; for this would not have succeeded either, because from mere concepts *a priori* we cannot cognize anything about the possibility of any real ground or any causality" (*CPR* A 558/B 586). His sole concern has been to show that "nature at least **does not conflict with** causality through freedom" (*CPR* A 558/B 586).

31 I have phrased this hypothetically, because one may want to accept much of what Kant says about the distinctive character of reason and yet reject Kant's understanding of nature. This is the strategy of McDowell, who defends a liberal naturalism that rejects the "disenchanted" concept of nature that

Kant endorses. "[W]e need to see ourselves as animals whose *natural being is permeated with rationality*, even though rationality is appropriately conceived in Kantian terms" (McDowell 1996: 85, emphasis added). For a fuller description of what McDowell means by "liberal naturalism," see McDowell 2008. For a critical discussion of his version of liberal naturalism, see Bernstein 2020.

32 In the passage that I cited earlier, from the introduction to the third *Critique* (*CJ* 5:196), Kant links the concept of purposiveness of nature with the role that the power of judgment plays in mediating the concepts of nature and freedom.

33 Kant typically uses the expression *organisierte Wesen* (organized beings) to refer to what we now call "organisms." An organism is *self-organized*.

34 Although Kant refers to "mechanism" in all three *Critiques*, he characterizes what he means by "mechanism" in different ways. For a discussion of the different meanings of "mechanism" and how "mechanism" is related to natural causality, see Quarfood 2004, Zuckert 2007, McLaughlin 2014, and Ginsborg 2015.

35 The concept of purposiveness plays a fundamental role in both parts of the *CJ*. Some Kantian scholars claim that the meaning of purposiveness in aesthetic judgment differs from its meaning in teleological judgment. For a discussion of competing interpretations, see Ginsborg 2015. Karen Ng explores how the discussion of purposiveness in the first *Critique* is related to purposiveness in the third *Critique* (see Ng 2020: 23–64).

36 See Ng (2020: 23–64) for a discussion of the issues concerning empirical concepts and nature that were left unresolved in the first *Critique*. Kant was vigorously challenged about his concept of nature, especially by his former student Herder. For a discussion of Herder's criticism of Kant, and Kant's scathing responses to Herder, see Zammito 1992, Lord 2011, and Zuckert 2014. Kant was scandalized when Jacobi and Herder claimed that his transcendental idealism was compatible with Spinozism.

37 Quarfood presents an account of the problem Kant confronted in the third *Critique*:

> In the *Critique of the Power of Judgment*, originally published in 1790, Kant turned his attention to teleological explanations in biology. The problem he confronted here was that there were features of organisms that appear to be intractable for the kind of explanations in terms of causal laws appropriate for ordinary physical objects (what Kant calls "mechanism"). Organisms are characterized by their capacities for reproduction, growth (which involves radical transformation of ingredients taken up from outside), and regeneration (for instance compensation for the loss of a part), capacities which in Kant's view are utterly different from anything else met with in nature (*CJ* 5:371–372). What leads us to view objects with such capacities in teleological terms is that the casual relations they exhibit can be seen "as law-governed only if we regard the cause's action as based on the idea of the effect, with this idea as the underlying condition under which the cause itself can produce that

effect" (*CJ* 5:367). It is thus the need for explanation in terms of law that, in the absence of mechanistic explanations, forces us to adopt a teleological view of organisms, in which a purpose (the "idea of the effect") is taken into consideration. Even though organisms like all objects of experience are subject to the causal principle, this alone does not take us very far in explaining their characteristics. (Quarfood 2004: 146)

38   This passage introduces Ginsborg's essay "Kant on Understanding Organisms as Natural Purposes" (Ginsborg 2015: 255–80). She explores two questions in this essay. The first is why we have to regard organisms as purposes. The second, "more fundamental question" is "what is it to regard an organism as a purpose, given that we must also regard it as a product of nature?" (Ginsborg 2015: 256).

39   Kant draws a sharp distinction between two types of objective purposiveness: external purposiveness and internal purposiveness. Ng gives a clear account of the differences between these two kinds of objective purposiveness:

> External purposiveness "is called either usefulness (for human beings) or benefit (for any other creature)," and we make judgements as to the relative purposiveness of objects whenever they are taken simply as means (*CJ* 5:367). We can see many examples of relative or external purposiveness in nature: sandy soil is beneficial for spruces, and hence, sand is relatively purposive when considered in connection with the existence and thriving of spruces; grass is beneficial, necessary in fact, for the existence of cattle, sheep, and horses; these animals in turn are beneficial for human civilization (*CJ* 5:367–9). It is clear that artifacts also fall under this general description of external purposiveness, insofar as they are created as "means that other causes employ purposively" (*CJ* 5:367). We build houses as a means for achieving the purpose of dwelling (or renting), and we make hammers as the means for achieving the purpose of hammering; in short, external purposiveness displays relations of utility. In order to articulate the meaning of internal purposiveness, a case in which "*everything is an end and reciprocally also a means*" (*CJ* 5:376), Kant turns to the concept of a natural purpose or end (*Naturzweck*), describing it as follows: "But in order to judge something that one cognizes as a product of nature as being at the same time an end, hence *natural end* [*Naturzweck*], something more [than the comparison with a product of art] is required if there is not simply to be a contraction here. I would say provisionally that a thing exists as a natural end *if it is cause and effect of itself*" (*CJ* 5:370–1). (Ng 2020: 51–2)

40   Kant claims that we can never *know or explain* organized beings (organisms) by an appeal to mechanistic principles:

> For it is quite certain that we can never adequately come to know the organized beings and their internal possibility in accordance with merely mechanical principles of nature, let alone explain them; and indeed this is so certain that we can boldly say that it would be absurd for humans even to make such an attempt or to hope that there may yet arise a Newton who could make

comprehensible even the generation [*Erzeugung*] of a blade of grass according to natural laws that no intention has ordered; rather we must absolutely deny this insight to human beings. (*CJ* 5:400)

41 The new Cambridge edition of the *CJ* translates *Zweck* as "end" rather than "purpose" and *Naturzweck* as "natural end." *Zweckmässigkeit* is translated as "purposiveness."
42 Zammito argues that the "discovery" of the new faculty of reflecting judgment in the third *Critique* transformed Kant's cognitive theory. See Zammito 1992: 151–77.
43 Kant explicitly says that the contrasting maxims (T and A) of the reflecting power of judgment "do not in fact contain any contradiction" (*CJ* 5:387). Consequently, the assertion of T and A is *not* really an antinomy. Yet, as frequently happens with Kant, the situation turns out to be more complicated. Some commentators argue that the assertion of T and A is a *genuine* antinomy – and this is the antinomy that Kant seeks to resolve. See Quarfood 2004 for a discussion of competing interpretations of the antinomy and a textual analysis of the entire Dialectic. See also Zuckert's interpretation of the antinomy of teleological judgment and the problems that it poses in Zuckert 2007: 146–69.
44 For a discussion of the meaning of mechanical inexplicability in Kant, see Ginsborg 2015. Ginsborg also provides a controversial interpretation of Kant's claim that organisms are purposes:

> If biological investigation is to be possible, we must regard the apparent regularities displayed by organisms as lawlike. Yet organisms are mechanically inexplicable, which is to say that we cannot regard the lawlikeness of these regularities as deriving from the fundamental lawlikeness displayed by the workings of inorganic matter. Our only alternative, therefore, is to regard the regularities manifested by the behavior as lawlike in the sense of conforming to *normative law*. (Ginsborg 2015: 278)

Ginsborg's normative interpretation relies heavily on the following passage from the first (unpublished) introduction to the third *Critique*:

> A teleological judgment compares the concept of a product of nature as it is with one of what it **ought to be** [*was es sein soll*]. Here the judging of its possibility is grounded in a concept (of the end) that precedes it *a priori*. There is no difficulty in representing the possibility of products of art in such a way. But to think of a product of nature that there is something that it **ought to be** and then to judge whether it really is so already presupposes a principle that could not be drawn from experience (which teaches only what things are). (*CJ* 20:240)

45 The precise meaning of purpose as a regulative principle for describing organisms is open to different interpretations. For a discussion of these and their consequences for different visions of Kant's philosophy of biology, see Huneman 2007.

46 Luca Illetterati argues that, taking into account the strict conditions for a science of nature that Kant specifies in his *MFN*, Kant denies the possibility of grounding a science of living beings.

> In the *CPJ*, Kant, rather than grounding the possibility of a science of living being, denies the very possibility of it. The acknowledgment of the impossibility of a "Newton of a blade of grass" (*CJ* V 400.16–20) and the acknowledgment of the impossibility of knowing the organizing principle of natural objects – which remains, according to Kant, an *"inscrutable principle"* (*CJ* V 424.29) – implies the impossibility of knowing the essential structure of living beings and consequently of a scientific biology. (Illetterati 2014: 96)

47 Quarfood recognizes that such a claim appears to contradict Kant's insistence on the regulative function of teleology. He suggests that when a distinction is made between a biological and a metaphilosophical perspective, it is possible to construe teleology as being *constitutive* in biology but *regulative* in philosophy. However promising this may be for resolving the tensions in Kant, there is *no* textual evidence in the third *Critique* to support this distinction between a *constitutive* biological perspective and a regulative *metaphilosophical* perspective. Kant *never* claims that in biology teleology is a *constitutive principle*. Quarfood also claims that "Aristotelian functions . . . are to be seen as valid at the *object level* of biological investigation. The denial of their objectivity only takes place at a further *meta level* reflection. For the biologist, organisms exhibit functions as a matter of course" (Quarfood 2004: 152). Commenting on this claim, Zammito writes: "I can find no passage in Kant that warrants ascribing to him this concession to biological practitioners" (Zammito 2006: 764).

Chapter 4 Hegel: Nature and *Geist*

1 "[R]eceptivity does not make an even notionally separable contribution to the co-operation" between receptivity and spontaneity (McDowell 1996: 9).
2 For an illuminating discussion of what Hegel appropriated from Fichte and Schelling, see Ng 2020. I want to acknowledge my debt to Karen Ng for her insights into the role of internal purposiveness and its relation to judgment in Hegel's philosophy. For a discussion of how Hegel departs from Schelling, especially Hegel's rejection of Schelling's appeal to "productive forces," see Stone 2013.
3 The interpretation of this initial triad – being, nothing, and becoming – is widely disputed. See, e.g., Houlgate 2006 and Pippin 2019.
4 See Ng 2020: ch. 3 for a discussion of the development of the speculative identity thesis from the *Differenzschrift* to the *Science of Logic*.
5 Whenever I refer to Hegel's concepts of Nature and Spirit (*Geist*), I capitalize the words.

6   Hegel uses the expression *Geist* in a more expansive and a more restrictive sense. In the *Phenomenology of Spirit*, *Geist* encompasses all the stages from Consciousness, Self-Consciousness, Reason, and Spirit (in its more restricted sense) – the stage that dialectically emerges from Reason. *Geist* has sometimes been translated as "mind" and more recently as "spirit," but neither English expression captures the richness of *Geist*. I follow the current practice of translating *Geist* as "spirit."
7   Hegel frequently speaks of Nature and Spirit in a global sense, but there are different stages, degrees, and (nonreducible) domains of both Nature and Spirit. Distinguishing different manifestations of Nature and Spirit is central for comprehending the continuity, identity, and nonidentity of Nature and Spirit.
8   See Pippin 1989, 2002; Brandom 1994.
9   McDowell, who is deeply influenced by a Hegelian interpretation of Kant, writes:

> We need to recapture the Aristotelian idea that a normal mature human being is a rational animal, but without losing the Kantian idea that rationality operates freely in its own sphere. The Kantian idea is reflected in the contrast between the organization of the space of reasons and the structure of the realm of natural law. Modern naturalism is forgetful of second nature; if we try to preserve the Kantian thought that reason is autonomous within the framework of that kind of naturalism, we disconnect our rationality from our animal being, which is what gives us our foothold in nature. The upshot is a temptation to drop the Kantian thought and naturalize our rationality in the manner of bald naturalism. . . . [*W*]*e need to see ourselves as animals whose natural being is permeated with rationality, even though rationality is appropriately conceived in Kantian terms*. (McDowell 1996: 85, emphasis added)

10 There is a vigorous debate about Hegel's naturalism. For references to those who favor a naturalistic interpretation of Hegel and those who oppose such an interpretation, see Ng 2020: 4, n. 2. Frequently, interpreters who argue that Hegel is an anti-naturalist assume (implicitly or explicitly) that the only viable version of naturalism is a reductive, physical, mechanical, materialistic version of it – what McDowell labels "bald naturalism." Indeed, one of the sources of confusion in debates about whether Hegel is a naturalist or an anti-naturalist is the widely different conceptions of naturalism held by those involved in these debates. For a helpful discussion of a cluster-based conception of different naturalistic strands, see Stone 2013. (There is an analogous confusion in the debates about metaphysical and nonmetaphysical interpretations of Hegel. All too frequently, opponents hold widely divergent conceptions of what constitutes metaphysics.)
11 See Lord 2011 for the complex story of Kant's encounters with Spinozism. See also Boehm 2014 for an argument that the *CPR* is intended as a critique of Spinoza.
12 Compare Schelling's explanation of *Natura naturans* and *Natura naturata* with Spinoza's explanation in *Ethics*, IP29s:

> [B]y *Natura naturans* we must understand what is in itself and is conceived through itself, *or* such attributes of substance as express an eternal and infinite essence, i.e. . . . God, insofar as he is considered as a free cause.
>
> But by *Natura naturata* I understand whatever follows from the necessity of God's nature, *or* from any of God's attributes, i.e., all the modes of God's attributes insofar as they are considered as things which are in God, and can neither be nor be conceived without God.

13 These passages from Schelling's *First Outline of a System of the Philosophy of Nature* (Schelling 2004) are cited in Ng 2020: 72.

14 Ng argues that internal purposiveness is integral not only to the way in which Hegel conceives of nature but both integral and constitutive of Hegel's conception of the Concept (*Begriff*).

> The idea of internal purposiveness is the Kantian ancestor and model for Hegel's concept of the Concept, and Hegel repeatedly attests to its importance, claiming that "reason is *purposive activity*," and more emphatically, that internal purposiveness is "Kant's great service to philosophy". . . . Although the details of Kant's own account are, to be sure, much disputed, what is indisputable is Hegel's unequivocal endorsement of Kant's conception of internal purposiveness and his insistence that it plays a positive, constitutive role with respect to the activities of reason and thought. (Ng 2020: 6)

15 For a detailed reconstruction of Hegel's arguments that "internal purposiveness" is not merely a regulative principle of nature but a constitutive principle of nature and self-consciousness, see Ng 2020: ch 3.

16 This raises the complex issue of whether Hegel is committed to some version of hylozoism or hylomorphism. Willem deVries has no hesitancy in speaking of Hegel's view of nature as similar to Aristotle's hylomorphism, because he wants to stress that, although there are differences between what is inorganic and organic, there is no sharp *ontological* break between them.

> Hegel's philosophies of nature and spirit are very much Aristotelian, and it is profitable to think of Hegel's view of nature as similar to Aristotle's hylomorphism; the objects of a lower stage offer the material for the further mediation, the new structures and forms of the higher stages. Even more important, Hegel also adopts a teleological worldview like that we find in Aristotle. That the lower stages of nature are material for the higher stages, are the potentiality of the higher stages, entails that their own actuality is achieved in the higher stage. Nature points toward and exists for the sake of spirit, not because nature is someone's means for realizing an intention to create spirit, but *because spirit is the force dwelling within the differentiation of nature. It is the nature of nature, its Concept, to provide the necessary conditions for the realization of spirit and to be itself an essential part of that realization.* (deVries 1988: 45, emphasis added)

Ng takes a more cautious approach to the issue of hylozoism:

> Far from committing himself to hylozoism, Hegel is in fact, throughout his career, highly critical of employing notions of force and living force as explana-

tory paradigms. Further, Hegel does *not* view nature as one big giant organism; rather, in a modernized Aristotelian vein and consistent with a contemporary division of labor, Hegel distinguishes carefully between physical/mechanical processes, chemical processes, and biological/organic processes, demonstrating a subtle understanding of their connections and disconnections, their identity and their differences. (Ng 2020: 63)

17 Pinkard presents a lucid account of the continuity and differences between nonhuman animals and humans in Pinkard 2012: ch. 1. Pinkard characterizes Hegel's Aristotelianism as a "disenchanted Aristotelian naturalism." By "disenchanted," a term he adopts from Max Weber, Pinkard means a naturalism that does not include any reference to supernatural *entities*. I think Ng's expression "modernized Aristotelian" is more felicitous for describing Hegel's appropriation of Aristotle. For a comprehensive discussion of the relation between Aristotle and Hegel, see Ferrarin 2001. See also Williams 2007 for a discussion of how Hegel is influenced by, and departs from, Aristotle.

18 Kantian Hegelians typically stress the distinctiveness, the *sui generis* quality of conceptual normativity. They contrast this conceptual normativity with the rest of nature. Naturalistic (or pragmatic) Hegelians stress the *continuity* and *unity* of nature and Geist. They reject the claim that conceptual normativity can be sharply demarcated from the rest of nature. Later I will consider how these different and opposing stances on the status of discursive conceptual normativity have shaped and continue to shape philosophical debates in the twentieth and twenty-first centuries.

19 As mentioned earlier, one of the sources of confusion in debates about Hegel's naturalism or anti-naturalism results from the different conceptions of what constitutes naturalism. An illustration of this is the dispute between Beiser and Garner. Beiser claims that German idealists, including Hegel, are naturalists. See Beiser 2002 and 2005. Of course, Hegel and the German idealists reject the type of mechanical naturalism defended by Baron d'Holbach, Diderot, and de la Mettrie. Commenting on the disagreement between Beiser and Garner, Stone notes, "Beiser maintains, the idealists regard nature as a self-organizing whole, and in this they accept the naturalist thesis that "everything in nature happens according to laws . . . of necessity", and they also accept that nature is pervaded by mechanism. They merely reject "a naturalism that claims everything is explicable *only* according to mechanical laws . . . a radical or narrow mechanism" (Beiser 2005: 69)" (Stone 2013: 61). Ironically, "Gardner identifies the same position as anti-naturalist. Gardner explains that while the idealists saw themselves as pursuing a naturalist project – taking naturalism in a broad and non-mechanistic sense (as Beiser also does) – their position was "historically revealed to be not 'genuinely naturalistic' after all", but to be supernaturalistic by later standards (Gardner 2007: 46)" (Stone 2013: 62). The dispute between Beiser and Gardner has parallels with current disputes about whether what McDowell labels "bald naturalism" is the only form of "genuine" naturalism or whether a liberal naturalism is viable. McDowell's understanding of liberal naturalism can

be traced back to Hegel's (and Aristotle's) nonreductive "broad naturalism." "Broad naturalism" is Stone's term for characterizing Hegel's naturalism.

20 John Findlay, is his Foreword to the English translation of the *Philosophy of Nature*, eloquently expresses this naturalistic theme in Hegel: "There is, for Hegel, nothing ideal or spiritual that does not have its roots in Nature, and which is not nourished and brought to full fruition by Nature" (Findlay 1970: p. xiii).

21 Hegel is drawing upon Aristotle's conception of second nature. Both Dewey and McDowell are post-Hegelian thinkers who draw upon an Aristotelian/Hegelian conception of second nature to develop a richer form of naturalism. For a discussion of Dewey's and McDowell's conception of liberal naturalism, see Bernstein 2020.

22 Lucas Corti, in his unpublished paper "Hegel's Account of Biological Normativity: The 'Is' and 'Ought' of the Animal Organism," develops a detailed analysis of Hegel's conception of *biological normativity*. Ginsborg (2015) argues that biological normativity is already present in Kant's understanding of the internal purposiveness of organisms. Her thesis supports Hegel's *positive* interpretation of Kant's concept of internal purposiveness. This does not diminish the crucial difference between Kant and Hegel. For Kant, ascribing normativity to biological creatures is only a *regulative* way of *judging* organisms. For Hegel, it is a *constitutive* feature of organisms and indeed a constitutive feature of Nature.

23 This provides another perspective for seeing how Kantian Hegelians present a distorted picture of Hegel. They focus on the normativity characteristic of *discursive language* and tend to think that this normativity is *sui generis*. Consequently, they fail to do justice to the Hegelian insight that there are *degrees* of normativity.

24 Actuality (*Wirklichkeit*) is one of the most ubiquitous and important concepts in Hegel's system. Hegel sharply distinguishes actuality and existence. Actuality is Hegel's appropriation of the Aristotelian concept of *energeia*. Actuality denotes both the activity of internal purposiveness and its product. When something becomes actual, it achieves its true ideal form. Actuality is fundamental for understanding Nature, Spirit and Logic. See Ng 2020: ch. 4 for a detailed analysis of the meaning of actuality. See also Rocío Zambrana's (2015) account of actuality. Rahel Jaeggi nicely illustrates the distinctive Hegelian meaning of actuality:

> For Hegel, an entity can be real or possess reality without being actual or exhibiting actuality. Thus, a human child is a real human being but, insofar as it has yet to develop the full potential implicit in the concept of a human being, and hence does not yet correspond to its concept, it lacks actuality. . . . "*Verwirklichung*" refers to the process of development through which an entity actualizes the potential implicit in its concept in this Hegelian sense. (Jaeggi 2018: p. xix).

It is important to stress that there are *degrees* or stages of actualization.

25 During his lifetime, Hegel published only four books: the *Phenomenology of Spirit* (1807); the *Science of Logic*, in 3 vols (1812–16); the *Encyclopaedia of the Philosophical Sciences*, originally published in 1816 but revised in 1827 and 1830; and *Elements of the Philosophy of Right*, published in 1820. The *Phenomenology* has received the greatest attention – especially in Anglo-American and French Hegel scholarship. Recently, Hegel scholars have turned their attention to the *Science of Logic* for its importance in comprehending Hegel's philosophical system – a text that was central for the interpretation of Hegel by the nineteenth-century British idealists. Hegel divides his *Encyclopaedia* into three parts: *Logic, Philosophy of Nature*, and *Philosophy of Spirit*. Hegel published the *Encyclopaedia* as a guide for students who attended his lectures. After Hegel's death, his editors published the *Encyclopaedia* and supplemented it with his lecture notes and student notes (*Zusätze*). No attempt has been made to publish an English translation of the entire *Encyclopaedia* as a *single* text. Sections of the *Encyclopaedia* have been translated and published as separate books. See Hegel 1970, 1971, and 1991. The *Philosophy of Subjective Spirit* is only the *first* part of the *Philosophy of Spirit*. Consequently, it is a fragment of a fragment. The history of both the German editions and English translations of the *Philosophy of Subjective Spirit* (and related materials) is extremely tangled. See deVries 1988 and Williams 2007 for discussions of this complex publication record. Michael Petry has published a bilingual translation of the *Philosophy of Subjective Spirit* (with additional material). See Hegel 1978. For a recent analysis of the *Philosophy of Subjective Spirit*, see deVries 1988. For an early discussion of the *Philosophy of Spirit*, see Dewey's 1897 lecture on Hegel in Dewey 2010.

26 The *Encyclopaedia* section, "The Phenomenology of Spirit," is not to be confused with the more ambitious 1807 work the *Phenomenology of Spirit*.

27 Soul (Anthropology); Consciousness (The Phenomenology of Spirit), and Spirit (Psychology) are the three main divisions of Subjective Spirit.

28 There are significant parallels between Hegel's analysis of habit and the analysis of habit in James' *Principles of Psychology* (1890). The concept of habit is also fundamental for Peirce and Dewey. All three philosophers understood habit as providing a transition to rationality – or to what Dewey (1983) calls "intelligence."

29 This quotation is from the *Zusatz* to §410 of the 1830 edition of the *Encyclopaedia*. The *Zusätze* are additions taken from student notes of Hegel's lectures. Some Hegel purists think that one should never rely on these *Zusätze*. Findlay, in his foreword to *Hegel's Philosophy of Nature*, makes this judicious remark about the *Zusätze*:

> It must, however, be remembered that Hegel's *Encyclopaedia* was a condensed, arid compendium, put out as a foundation for detailed comment and explanation in lectures. Without such material as is provided by the editorial *Zusätze* it would be largely uninterpretable, a monumental inscription in Linear B. Many scholars have written as if those who first published the *Zusätze* deserved blame, whereas they deserve boundless gratitude. (Findlay 1970: p. vii)

I have cited passages from the *Zusätze* only when they are consistent with passages from Hegel's main text.

30 As Pinkard notes,

> Hegel accuses Kant of staying only at the level of the "understanding" and of not therefore adequately grasping the "speculative" nature of this enterprise. The Kantian philosophy, as Hegel often says, stays at the level of "consciousness," by which he means that it takes the opposition of subject and object as fundamental, as the "final dichotomy," together with its attendant and one-sided notion that it is the object that functions normatively as the "truth-maker" for our judgments about it. This attitude, which Hegel also identifies as the standpoint of "representational" thought (of *Vorstellung*), is on Hegel's account not so much false as it is one-sided: the subject/object split is not a metaphysical division already present at hand in the world but is itself normatively established as a moment in the space of the reasons. (Pinkard 2005: 24)

31 See Testa 2013 for an insightful discussion of how Hegel's analysis of soul and body relates to his naturalism.
32 This passage, quoted in Testa 2013: 29, is from the remark (*Anmerkung*) to §410 of the 1827 edition of the *Encyclopaedia*.
33 For a discussion of the relation between Dewey's and Hegel's conception of habit, see Levine 2015 and Testa 2017.
34 Recently, there has been a revival of recognition of the philosophical importance of habit for illuminating issues in a variety of disciplines, including neuroscience, cognitive science, social psychology, and social theory. This builds on the central role of habit – especially critical habits – in the classical pragmatic thinkers. Dewey's conception of habit is clearly indebted to Hegel. For a collection of essays concerning the contemporary relevance of habit, see Caruana and Testa 2021.
35 One of the standard and persistent criticisms of Hegel is that he so stresses universality, sameness, and identity that he neglects difference and nonidentity. According to this caricature, all difference is sublated (*aufgehoben*), and consequently all difference is eliminated. This caricature is not only misleading and false; it fails to recognize that Hegel may justifiably be called the *philosopher of difference*. This is beautifully illustrated in the 1807 *Phenomenology*. In the movement from Consciousness to Self-Consciousness, Reason, and Spirit, we continually discover that just when we think we have achieved a "successful" sublation, *difference* and *negativity* break out, and this motivates the movement of the dialectic. Hegel characterizes the *Phenomenology* as a "highway of despair." *Difference is not obliterated; it is integral to the process of sublation* (*Aufhebung*).
36 This passage, cited in Hegel 2007: 11, is from the *Zusatz* to §381of the 1830 edition of *Encyclopaedia*. It is passages like this that seem to support the interpretation that Spirit leaves Nature behind, and that Hegel ultimately assigns logical and metaphysical priority to Spirit. Such an interpretation is *one-sided*. It does not do justice to the important way in which Spirit does *not* leave

Nature behind but incorporates the *truth* of Nature. Robert Williams brings out the subtlety and complexity of Hegel's conception of the relation of Nature and Spirit. Commenting on this passage, he writes:

> The priority of nature over spirit is suspended by spirit itself in its self-development. While Hegel expresses this suspension too negatively when he says that nature 'has disappeared' in spirit, a closer reading reveals that it is only nature's immediacy and absolute priority that are suspended. Nature does not simply disappear, but continues on a higher level in spirit.
>
> Nature continues to be the indispensable other of spirit. . . . Spirit begins in 'slumbering' subjection to nature; it must negate the immediacy of nature, and come to itself in and through a suspension of the externality and priority of nature. Spirit 'is absolute negativity, because in nature the concept has its complete but external objectivity, has suspended this its externalization, and in this suspension has become identical with itself. Spirit is this identity only as it returns to itself out of nature [*Encyclopaedia* 1830, §381].' Hegel's retrieval of Aristotle is not a simple repetition. Although spirit emerges from nature, it does not emerge in a natural way, or by natural causality. Spirit is self-grounding and self-liberating. (Williams 2007: 11–12)

37 For a discussion of the abusive criticism of the *Philosophy of Nature*, see Houlgate 1998 and Rand 2007. For a balanced interpretation that clarifies Hegel's project and notes some of its deficiencies, see Pinkard 2005.

38 DeVries explicates what he means by empirical sensitivity concerning the *Philosophy of Subjective Spirit*, but his insights are just as relevant to the *Philosophy of Nature*. See deVries 1988: chs. 2 and 3. Sebastian Rand (2007) advances the most thorough critique of the claim that Hegel's *Philosophy of Nature* is an *a priori* science (in the Kantian sense of *a priori*). He argues that taking the *Philosophy of Nature* to be a pure *a priori* science is the major obstacle to appreciating how it contributes to Hegel's narrative of the emergence and actualization of freedom.

39 Stone describes the relation of the philosophy of nature and empirical science as follows: "[F]or Hegel there is continuity between philosophy and science: philosophy of nature draws out, extends and realises the dimension of ordering thought that is already operative in empirical science" (Stone 2013: 66).

40 Peirce distinguishes three basic categories: Firstness, Secondness, and Thirdness. He criticizes Hegel for neglecting Secondness, the category of struggle, resistance, sheer otherness, and brute existence. Consequently, Peirce claims that Hegel lacks "a healthy sense of reality." "The capital error of Hegel which permeates his whole system in every part of it is that he almost altogether ignores the Outward Clash" (Peirce 1992: 233). Peirce's criticism of Hegel has affinities with that of a long line of critics that includes Schelling, Kierkegaard, Feuerbach, Levinas, and Derrida. Presumably, Hegel is so logocentric, so rationalistic, so obsessed with universality, and with the Concept (*Begriff*) that he neglects, or refutes singularity, individuality, and the sheer otherness of the other. Robert Stern (2007) carefully considers Peirce's

interpretation and criticisms of Hegel. He argues that what Peirce calls "Secondness" plays an essential role in Hegel's philosophy. Peirce claims: "Not only does Thirdness suppose and involve the ideas of Secondness and Firstness, but never will it be possible to find any Secondness or Firstness in the phenomenon that is not accompanied by Thirdness. If the Hegelians confined themselves to that position they would find a hearty friend in my doctrine" (Peirce 1998: 177). Thirdness corresponds to what Hegel calls "conceptuality." Stern shows that Hegel is indeed a "hearty friend," because this is Hegel's position when we translate it into the Peircian categories of Secondness and Thirdness. When Hegel affirms the *otherness* and *opposition* between Spirit and Nature, he acknowledges the dyadic Secondness that stands between Spirit and Nature. Another way of making this point is to focus on Peirce's understanding of *Aufheben*. Peirce, like many critics of Hegel, assumes that when something is *aufgehoben*, it is "refuted" and obliterated. But this neglects Hegel's fundamental thesis that *aufgehoben* means not merely refuted but also *preserved and raised up*. Spirit does not eliminate the otherness of Nature; it *preserves*, yet also transforms, it.

41 The philosophical thesis that we never encounter anything but our own mental ideas is sometimes called "metaphysical idealism." William Maker (1998) argues that this is not Hegel's view, and that Hegel is a powerful critic of metaphysical idealism.

42 See Pippin's perceptive remarks about logic as the "realm of shadows" and the way in which Hegel's "*Realphilosophie* . . . [returns] us to the embodied form of these making-intelligibility-possible forms, *Natur* and *Geist*" (Pippin 2019: 28–9).

43 I skip over the stage of chemism. Although Hegel stresses this stage as the "differentiated object," he admits that it is frequently "lumped together with mechanism." "But mechanism and chemism are also very definitely distinct from one another; specifically, this is because in the mode of mechanism the object is, initially, only indifferent relation to itself, whereas the chemical object proves to be strictly related to what is other" (Hegel 1991a: 277–8). For a clarification of this obscure claim, and how the category of chemism is related to Hegel's understanding of the chemistry of his time, see Burbidge 1996.

44 Let us recall that when Hegel praises Kant's distinction between external and internal purposiveness, he indicates that it opens the way to Life and the Idea. The logical concept of Life is implicit in the idea of internal purposiveness and becomes fully explicit in the culmination of the *Logic* – the Absolute Idea. Ng's book (2020) seeks to clarify the meaning of the *logical* concept of Life in Hegel's system and its importance for Hegel's concept of the Concept. For a discussion of the significance of Life in Hegel's system, see Khurana 2013 and 2017.

45 "Pure Spirit" is not to be confused or identified with Absolute Spirit. Absolute Spirit is not pure or abstract; it is concrete, i.e., fully determinate. The movement in the *Philosophy of Spirit* is from *Seele*, the most primitive form of Spirit,

to Subjective, Objective, and finally, to Absolute Spirit – the full actualization of Nature.
46 Ironically, so-called "left Sellarsians" tend to be critical of the naturalistic strands in Sellars' thinking. Sellars himself was neither a "left" nor a "right" Sellarsian. He sought to show how conceptual normativity and a naturalistic scientific account of the world can be joined together in a stereoscopic philosophic vision of humans in the world. See my discussion of Sellars in Bernstein 2020.
47 See Pippin 1989 and 2002.
48 Richard Rorty characterizes Dewey's philosophy as "a kind of naturalization of Hegel – Hegel without the split between nature and spirit" (Rorty 2006: 34). Dewey might respond that this naturalization is already implicit in Hegel.
49 For a detailed discussion of Dewey's living legacy in contemporary philosophy, see Bernstein 2020.

Chapter 5 Marx: The Transaction of Nature and Social Man

1 After declaring the futility "of all [his] previous endeavors," he writes:

> Meanwhile I had acquired the habit of making excerpts from all the books I was reading, from Lessing's *Laocoön*, Solger's *Erwin*, Winckelmann's *History of Art*, Luden's *German History*. While doing this, I scribbled down some reflections. At the same time I translated Tacitus' *Germania*, Ovid's *Tristium libri*. With the aid of grammar books I began the private study of English and Italian, but as yet not achieved anything. I read Klein's book on criminal law and his *Annals*, and a lot of the most recent literature, though the latter only incidentally. (Marx 1997: 45–6)

2 See Marx 1997: 151–202.
3 This is one of Marx's earliest references to how theory becomes a material force when it is "gripped by the masses."
4 The entire sixth thesis is:

> Feuerbach resolves the religious essence into the human essence. But the human essence is no abstraction inherent in each single individual. In its reality it is the ensemble of the social relations.
>
> Feuerbach, who does not enter upon a criticism of this real essence, is consequently compelled:
>
> 1) To abstract from the historical process and to fix the religious sentiment as something by itself and to presuppose an abstract – isolated – human individual.
> 2) Essence, therefore, can be comprehended only as 'genus', as an internal,

dumb generality which naturally unites the many individuals. (Marx 2000: 172).

There have been competing interpretations of this sixth thesis by commentators, including Althusser and Ernst Bloch (see Althusser 2005: 219–47 and Bloch 1986: 249–86). For a comprehensive, detailed, incisive, philological, semantic, and philosophical interpretation of this thesis, see "Afterword: Philosophical Anthropology or Ontology of Relations? Exploring the Sixth Thesis on Feuerbach" in Balibar 2017.

5   To move smoothly between Marx's own voice and my discussion of his claims, I am keeping masculine gender for "laborer", "worker," "producer," and similar nouns rather than using gender-neutral pronouns that are more appropriate in such instances.

6   Norman Geras (2016) distinguishes two ways of thinking about human nature. The first is when we think of human as a constant and fixed universal entity that does not change with the variability of history. The second is when human nature is variable and takes on different forms in different historical circumstances. Marx clearly rejects the first conception. When he speaks of "species-being," he is using it in a non-Feuerbachian sense. The term "species-being" designates a changing ensemble of social relationships that are degraded and deformed in the historical system of private property and wage labor, but which can be transformed by revolutionary practice. For a nuanced interpretation of Marx's "dialectical naturalism" that also rejects a fixed or static conception of *Gattungswesen* (species-being), see Khurana 2022.

7   This is why Marx says that even raising the wages of the laborer does not alter his objective alienation. It "would therefore be nothing but a *better slave-salary* and would not achieve either for the worker or for labor human significance and dignity" (Marx 1997: 298).

8   I use the word "transaction" rather than "interaction" because the latter suggests *two* elements of interacting. But the relation between man's natural being and the rest of nature is *not* one of two elements interacting. It is a single dynamic process. The point I want to emphasize is similar to Balibar's conception of "transindividuality" – a concept he attributes to Marx and traces back to Spinoza. See Balibar 2020, especially the section "Philosophies of the Transindividal: Spinoza, Marx, Freud." See also Read 2016 for a discussion of transindividuality in Marx.

9   When Marx criticizes Hegel in the *Paris Manuscripts*, he declares:

> The *human quality* of nature, of nature produced through history, and of man's products appears in their being *products* of abstract spirit and hence phases of *mind, thought-entities*. The *Phenomenology* is thus concealed and mystifying criticism, unclear to itself, but inasmuch as it firmly grasps the *alienation* of man – even though man appears only as mind – *all* the elements of criticism are implicit in it, already *prepared* and *elaborated* in a manner far surpassing the Hegelian standpoint. (Marx 1997: 320–1)

10 In the *Paris Manuscripts* Marx frequently refers to the relationship of man and woman to illustrate both the degradation of human beings in a system of private property and what the humanizing of nature means. In the context of criticizing "crude communism," where only a community of labor has been "universalized" and is the consummation of envy and leveling down, he writes:

> The immediate, natural, necessary relationship of human being to human being is the *relationship* of *man* to *woman*. In this *natural* species-relationship man's relationship to nature is immediately his relationship to man, as his relationship to man is immediately his relationship to nature, to his own *natural* condition. In this relationship the extent to which the human essence has become nature for man or nature has become the human essence of man is *sensuously manifested*, reduced to a perceptible *fact*. From this relationship one can thus judge the entire level of mankind's development. From the character of this relationship follows the extent to which *man* has become and comprehended himself as *generic being*, as *man*; the relationship of man to woman is the *most natural* relationship of human being to human being. It thus indicates the extent to which man's *natural* behavior has become *human* or the extent to which his *human* essence has become a *natural* essence for him, the extent to which his *human nature* has become *nature* to him. In this relationship is also apparent the extent to which man's *need* has become *human*, or the extent to which his *human* essence has become a *natural* essence for him, to the extent to which his *human nature* has become *nature* to him. In this relationship is also apparent the extent to which man's *need* has become *human*, thus the extent to which the *other* human being, as human being, has become a need for him, the extent to which he in his most individual existence is at the same time a social being. (Marx 1997: 303)

11 Several commentators have criticized Marx, claiming that he thinks of nature as primarily a resource to be exploited. But this completely neglects Marx's insight about the transactional understanding of society and nature. Indeed, a number of thinkers have recently suggested that Marx's historical transactional understanding of man, society, and nature can be employed to deal with the current ecological crisis that has taken place under capitalism. See Moore 2015 and Fraser 2021.

12 In this context, Kolakowski is using "humanized" in a *generic* sense, wherein nature is shaped by man's social activity. This use needs to be distinguished from the sense used by Marx when he speaks of nature becoming humanized by man's free spontaneous activity.

13 Yovel makes a similar point when he writes: "Through human labor and material (and mental) production, man and nature constitute a dialectical unity, in which everything else inheres. It is their separation that becomes an abstraction – a false reflection of reality that is, however, inevitable under the economic alienation in which we live and thus must affect and prejudice our minds, beliefs, and culture" (Yovel 1989: 79).

14 For a comprehensive critique of Althusser's interpretation of the "two Marxs," see Jaffe 2014 and Geras 2016.

15 See Marx 2000: 379–423.
16 See also Schmidt's statement about the notebooks that comprise *Grundrisse*:

> From the point of view of his intellectual development, they represent the connecting link between the Paris Manuscripts and the fully-formed materialist economics of the mature Marx. The *Grundrisse*, despite their partially fragmentary character, contain without a doubt Marx's most philosophically significant statements. . . . A study of this work can contribute in particular to the demolition of the legend, which still presses heavily on discussions of Marx, that only the thought of the 'young Marx' is of philosophical interest, and that the later, factually economic, problematic buried all the original impulse of real humanism. (Schmidt 1971: 213–14, n. 43)

17 One of the most explicit statements of the significance of the distinction between objectification (*Vergegenständlichung*) and alienation (*Entfremdung*) appears in the *Grundrisse*:

> Stress is placed not on the state of objectification but on the state of alienation, estrangement, and abandonment, on the fact that the enormous objectified power which social labour has opposed to itself as one of its elements belongs not to the worker but to the conditions of production that are personified in capital. So long as the creation of this material form of activity, objectified in contrast to immediate labour power, occurs on the basis of capital and wage-labour, and so long as this process of objectification in fact seems to be a process of alienation as far as the worker is concerned, or to be the appropriation of alien labour from the capitalist's point of view, so long will this distortion and this inversion really exist and not merely occur in the imagination of both workers and capitalists. But this process of inversion is obviously merely a historical necessity, a necessity for the development of productive forces from a definite historical starting-point, or basis, but in no way an absolute necessity of production; it is, rather, ephemeral. The result and the immanent aim of the process is to destroy and transform this basis itself, as well as this form of the process. Bourgeois economists are so bogged down in their traditional ideas of the historical development of society in a single stage that the necessity of the objectification of the social forces of labour seems to them inseparable from the necessity of its alienation in relation to living labour. But as living labour loses its immediate, individual character, whether subjective or entirely external, as individual activity becomes directly general or social, the objective elements of production lose this form of alienation. They are then produced as property, as the organic social body in which individuals are reproduced as individuals, but as social individuals. (Marx 2000: 419–20)

18 See Marx 2000: 452–546.

Chapter 6 Nietzsche: Nature and the Affirmation of Life

1. I quoted this passage earlier in the chapter on Spinoza (see n. 51), but it takes on an enriched meaning here in my discussion of Nietzsche.
2. All passages from *The Gay Science* are from Nietzsche 2001, abbreviated *GS* and followed by section number.
3. All passages from *Beyond Good and Evil* are from Nietzsche 2000, abbreviated *BGE* and followed by section number.
4. Although both Spinoza and Nietzsche are sharply critical of the Abrahamic religions, they recognize (like Marx) that these traditional religions serve the function of giving meaning to human suffering for the "multitude."
5. Walter Kaufmann was one of the first American commentators to expose the origin and baselessness of these distortions. See Kaufmann 1974 [1950]. See also Yovel 1986.
6. I agree with the hermeneutical principle proposed by Richard Schacht:

    > The interpretation of Nietzsche is a notoriously tricky business. He says things in various places that are hard to square with virtually every interpretation of his thought that attributes definite positions of one sort or another of him. In trying to decide what to make of them and how much weight to give to them and in considering what lines of interpretation to favor and disfavor, I believe that considerable weight should be given to pervasive concerns and convictions of his that are evident in a broad range of his writings, even if he sometimes says things (in print or in his notebooks) that are at apparent or actual variance with them. One is well advised to read him comprehensively before jumping to conclusions with respect to the import and upshot of any such passage, proceeding with care in considering what to make of any particular passage in his writings, published as well as not. (Schacht 2012: 192)

7. All passages from *On the Genealogy of Morals* are from Nietzsche 2000a, abbreviated *GM* and followed by essay number and section number.
8. Bernard Williams makes a perceptive observation about the use of the word "claim." "'[C]laim', for Nietzsche, is . . . rarely the right word. It is not only too weak for some things he says and too strong for others; we can usefully remember, too, (or perhaps pretend) that even when he sounds insistently or shrilly expository, he is not necessarily telling us something, but *urging us to ask something*" (Williams 2006: 303, emphasis added).
9. For an illuminating discussion of the complexities of Nietzsche's understanding of nihilism, see Schacht 1983 and 1995, and Janaway 2007.
10. Compare this passage with *BGE* 200, in which Nietzsche contrasts those "weaker human beings" who desire that the war of internal oppositions should come to a harmonious end of tranquilized "happiness," and those "enigmatic men" who wage war against themselves.
11. In *GS*, Nietzsche describes consciousness as follows:

    > My idea is clearly that consciousness actually belongs not to man's existence as an individual but rather to the community-and herd-aspects of his nature;

that accordingly, it is finely developed only in relation to its usefulness to community or herd; and that consequently each of us, even with the best will in the world to *understand* ourselves as individually as possible, 'to know ourselves', will always bring to consciousness precisely that in ourselves which is 'non-individual', that which is 'average'; that due to the nature of consciousness – to the 'genius of the species' governing it – our thoughts themselves are continually as it were *outvoted* and translated back into the herd perspective. (*GS* 354)

12 For a discussion of some of the contemporary varieties of naturalism, see Bernstein 2020.
13 See Schacht 1983 and 2012.
14 Williams makes a similar point: "The word 'Wissenschaft', unlike the English word 'science' in its modern use, does not mean simply the natural and biological sciences – they are, more specifically, 'Naturwissenschaft'. It means any organized study or body of knowledge, including history, philology, criticism and generally what we call 'the humanities'" (Williams 2006: 314).
15 Brian Leiter (2013) provides a number of references indicating Nietzsche's knowledge of the sciences of his day.
16 Nietzsche makes many negative comments about science. For example, in *GS* 373, entitled "'Science' as prejudice," Nietzsche attacks "the pedantic Englishman Herbert Spencer." In this context, he writes:

> So, too, it is with the faith with which so many materialistic natural scientists rest content: the faith in a world that is supposed to have its equivalent and measure in human thought, in human valuations – a 'world of truth' that can be grasped entirely with the help of our four-cornered little human reason – What? Do we really want to demote existence in this way to an exercise in arithmetic and an indoor diversion for mathematicians? Above all, one shouldn't want to strip it of its *ambiguous* character: that, gentleman, is what *good* taste demands – above all, the taste of reverence for everything that lies beyond your horizon! That the only rightful interpretation of the world should be one to which *you* have a right; one by which one can do research and go on scientifically in *your* sense of the term (you really mean *mechanistically*?) – one that permits counting, calculating, weighing, seeing, grasping, and nothing else – that is a crudity and naiveté, assuming it is not a mental illness, an idiocy. Would it not be quite probable, conversely, that precisely the most superficial and external aspect of existence – what is most apparent; its skin and its sensualization – would be grasped first and might even be the only thing that lets itself be grasped? Thus, a 'scientific' interpretation of the world, as you understand it, might still be one of the *stupidest* of all possible interpretations of the world, i.e. one of those most lacking in significance.

17 Leiter claims that Nietzsche *had* to be a *Speculative* M-Naturalist "given the primitive state of psychology in the nineteenth century. A Speculative M-Naturalist simply does *not* claim that the explanatory mechanisms essential to his theory of why humans think and act are supported by existing scientific *results*" (Leiter 2013: 581). Presumably, as empirical psychology

develops, Nietzsche's hypotheses will be confirmed or disconfirmed by actual scientific results and empirical evidence.

18 Leiter's idea of the "Humean Nietzsche" is based on Barry Stroud's characterization of Hume's naturalism. Stroud writes:

> [Hume] wants to do for the human realm what he thinks natural philosophy, especially in the person of Newton, had done for the rest of nature.
>
> Newtonian theory provides a completely general explanation of why things in the world of nature happen as they do. It explains various and complicated physical happenings in terms of relatively few extremely general, perhaps universal, principles. Similarly, Hume wants a completely general theory of human nature in order to explain why human beings act, think, perceive and feel in all the ways they do. . . . [T]he key to understanding Hume's philosophy is to see him as putting forward a general theory of human nature in just the way that, say, Freud or Marx did. They all seek a general kind of explanation of the various ways in which men think, act, feel and live. . . . The aim of all three is completely general – they try to provide a basis for explaining *everything* in human affairs. And the theories they advance are all, roughly, deterministic. (Stroud 1977: 3–4)

19 See Acampora 2006, Janaway 2007, and Schacht 2012.

20 Leiter disparagingly calls Janaway's characterization "Laundry List Naturalism." He deems it a damning criticism when he asks, "Why are *these* a set of views a philosophical naturalist *ought* to hold?" (Leiter 2013: 577). Leiter's "question" is revealing, because it shows that he is imposing his *own* conception of what a philosophical naturalist ought to hold. He does not ask, "What does Nietzsche understand by nature and naturalism?" Schacht points out that Janaway is not dealing with the question of what a philosophical naturalist *ought* to hold, but rather, is describing how Nietzsche understands naturalism. "Janaway rightly observes and emphasizes that Nietzsche's methods are often 'discontinuous with those of empirical scientific inquiry' rather than based or modeled on it, and that 'explanatory facts about me, even if located somehow in my psychophysiology, are essentially shaped by *culture*'" (Schacht 2012: 191 [see Janaway 2007: 47]). Given the widespread disagreement about what a philosophical naturalist *ought* to hold, Leiter never justifies *his* conception of philosophical naturalism.

21 Developing an adequate *philosophical* conception of nature is once again in the foreground in contemporary philosophy. In contrast to a concept of nature and naturalism based on the modern natural sciences, the "rule of law" and the "disenchanted" concept of nature, McDowell proposes a liberal naturalism that takes account of the "second nature" of human beings. See McDowell 1996 and 2008 There are many contemporary versions of liberal philosophical naturalism that reject the thesis that the natural sciences *alone* provide an adequate account of nature. A philosophical naturalism need not be based *exclusively* on explanations (even speculative ones) "modeled" on the empirical sciences. For a critical discussion of liberal naturalism, see Bernstein 2020.

22 For a subtle analysis of what Nietzsche means by psychology, and why it is "the Queen of the sciences," see Pippin 2010: ch. 1.
23 The German original follows Nietzsche 2013: 122. It is typical of Nietzsche's biting irony that he uses the word "redeemed" (*erlösen*) to characterize a purified nature that, in a Christian context, is associated with Christ.
24 See Brandom 1994: 4–7.
25 All passages from *Twilight of the Idols* are from Nietzsche 1976a, abbreviated *TI* and followed by section title and number.
26 A dominant concern of *GS* is "honesty" (*Redlichkeit*) and the primacy of an "intellectual conscience," which Nietzsche sharply distinguishes from "moral conscience" (*GS* 319, 344).
27 Nietzsche does assert that there have been historical life-affirming creative individuals. For example, consider his depiction of Goethe:

> Goethe – not a German event, but a European one: a magnificent attempt to overcome the eighteenth century by a return to nature, by an *ascent* to the naturalness of the Renaissance – a kind of self-overcoming on the part of that century.... he did not retire from life but put himself into the midst of it; he was not fainthearted but took as much as possible upon himself, over himself, into himself. What he wanted was *totality*; he fought the mutual extraneousness of reason, senses, feeling, and will (preached with the most abhorrent scholasticism by *Kant*, the antipode of Goethe); he disciplined himself to wholeness, he *created* himself. (*TI* "Skirmishes or an Untimely Man" 49)

28 Compare this passage with *GS* 304: "Basically I abhor every morality that says: 'Do not do this! Renounce! Overcome yourself!' But I am well disposed towards those moralities that impel me to do something again and again from morning till evening, and to dream of it at night, and to think of nothing else than doing this *well*, as well as *I* alone can!"
29 In the *Antichrist* Nietzsche declares:

> What is good? Everything that heightens the feeling of power in man, the will to power, power itself.
> What is bad? Everything that is born of weakness.
> What is happiness? The feeling that power is *growing*, that resistance is overcome. (Nietzsche 1976: 570)

For an analysis of power as the overcoming of resistance, see Reginster 2006.
30 This passage about shaping oneself seems to be in tension with the ideal of self-affirmation in the doctrine of eternal recurrence. See Janaway's discussion of the various ways in which this tension can be addressed (Janaway 2007: 263–5). Alexander Nehamas, who has developed a distinctive and influential interpretation of Nietzsche highlighting the value of artistic self-creation, elucidates the "giving style" of the passage as follows:

> The value of everything depends on its contribution to a whole of which it can be seen as a part.... But what is it to affirm the whole of which all these fea-

tures and events have been made parts? The answer is provided by the thought of the eternal recurrence. . . . the thought that if one were to live over again, one would want the very life one has already had, exactly the same down to its tiniest detail, and nothing else. (Nehamas 1998: 142).

See also Nehamas 1985 for his full account of Nietzsche.
31 In "How the 'True World' Finally Became a Fable" Nietzsche declares: "The true world – we have abolished. What world has remained? The apparent one perhaps? But no! *With the true world we have also abolished the apparent one*" (*TI* "How the 'True World' Finally Became a Fable" 6)
32 For a discussion of the significance of *amor fati*, see Yovel 1986.
33 Compare this with Spinoza's claim in the *Ethics*: "*A free man thinks of nothing less than of death, and his wisdom is a meditation on life, not on death*" (IVP67).

Chapter 7 Freud: Human Nature, Psychic Reality, and Cosmological Speculation

1 Freud's claims about himself are never quite as straightforward as they initially appear. Kurt Eissler (1978) challenges this legend. Furthermore, the essay on nature that Freud mentions was not written by Goethe. See Peter Gay's discussion of Freud's "mythmaking" in initiating this legend in Gay 2006: 24–6; see also Whitebook 2017: 75–7.
2 I use the expression "positivist spirit" in a broad sense to refer to the commitment that it is natural science and natural science *alone* that yields *genuine* knowledge of the world. Peter Gay describes the positivist spirit of Brücke, one of Freud's mentors.

> Brücke's philosophy of science was no less formative for Freud than his professionalism. He was a positivist by temperament and by conviction. Positivism was not an organized school of thought so such as a pervasive attitude toward man, nature, and styles of inquiry. Its votaries hoped to import the program of the natural sciences, their findings and methods, into the investigation of all human thought and action, both private and public. (Gay 2006: 34)

Gay also notes that Freud reiterated this positivist credo on many occasions.

> To Freud, Brücke and his brilliant associates were the chosen heirs of philosophy. Freud's forceful disclaimer that psychoanalysis has no world view of its own, and could never generate one, was his way of paying tribute to his positivist teachers years later: psychoanalysis, he summed up the case in 1932, "is a piece of science and can adhere to the scientific world view." In short, psychoanalysis is, like all the sciences, devoted to the pursuit of truth and to the unmasking of illusions. It might have been Brücke speaking. (Gay 2006: 35)

3   We will see the return of nature as a living vital force in Freud's speculations about *Eros* as a cosmological force.
4   See Freud's account of his experience with hypnosis and catharsis as well as his eventual discovery of psychoanalytic "free association" in Freud 1925.
5   Freud subsequently abandoned the "Project"; it was not published during his lifetime.
6   In a letter to Wilhelm Fliess, dated May 25, 1895, Freud writes: "I am plagued with two ambitions: to see how the theory of mental functioning takes shape if quantitative considerations, a sort of economics of nerve-force, are introduced into it; and secondly, to extract from psychopathology what may be of benefit to normal psychology" (Freud 1954: 119–20).
7   See Freud 1900. Freud's writings are like a palimpsest. Although Freud constantly engages in self-criticism and rejects or modifies earlier ideas, his earlier views (like his commitment to a quantitative understanding of psychic life) frequently appear just below the surface of his more developed views. For example, although Freud abandoned the 1895 "Project," the opening of *Beyond the Pleasure Principle* is almost a verbatim translation of the constancy principle – the increase and decrease of the "quantity of excitation" between pleasure and unpleasure (see Freud 1920).
8   A paradigmatic example of Freud's combination of an economic and an interpretative perspective is his analysis of the famous "fort-da" game of a young infant (his grandson). In *Beyond the Pleasure Principle* Freud carefully observes the repetitive pattern of an infant playing with a wooden reel attached to a string – a game of disappearance and return. He then offers an *interpretation* of this sequence of events that is related to the disappearance and reappearance of the child's mother. "It was related to the child's great cultural achievement – the instinctual renunciation (that is, the renunciation of instinctual satisfaction) which he had made in allowing his mother to go away without protesting. He compensated himself for this, as it were, by himself staging the disappearance and return of objects within his reach" (Freud 1920: 15). Freud then relates this repetitive pattern of behavior to the interplay of unpleasure due to the disappearance of the mother and the pleasure experienced upon her return. Freud uses this example to show that "even under the dominance of the pleasure principle, there are ways and means enough of making what is itself unpleasurable into a subject to be recollected and worked over in the mind" (Freud 1920: 17). It is Freud's observation and interpretation of this child's game that initiates his discussion of what is *beyond* the pleasure principle.
9   One of the strangest and most controversial periods of Freud's life entails his complex emotional and intellectual relation with Wilhelm Fliess – a time that has been labeled Freud's "creative illness" or "madness." The letters between Freud and Fliess were almost destroyed (Freud wanted them to be destroyed), but through the intervention of his good friend and dedicated follower Marie Bonaparte and his daughter Anna, they were saved, but carefully guarded. Long after Freud's death, Anna published an edited German edition in 1950.

The English translation was published in 1954 with the title *The Origins of Psycho-Analysis*. It was only in 1985 that Jeffrey Masson retranslated the correspondence and published an *unedited* version. The title, *The Origins of Psycho-Analysis*, is appropriate and revealing. In addition to what we discover about Freud's most intimate life, his turbulent passions, and his homosexual infatuation with Fliess, the letters are a gold mine for following the process of Freud's understanding of psychic life – a process that culminated in Freud's self-analysis in the *Interpretation of Dreams*. These letters belie the image of Freud as the rational objective positivist scientist. They reveal how Freud's "madness played an essential constitutive role as the medium through which Freud discovered psychoanalysis" (Whitebook 2017: 171). Freud was on his journey of discovering psychoanalysis – the *new science of human nature*. For a detailed analysis of Freud's personal relationship with the eccentric Fliess, as well as what Freud's letters reveal about the origins of psychoanalysis, see ch. 6, "Dear Magician," of Whitebook 2017.

10   In the Standard Edition, *Trieb* is translated as "instinct," even though Freud distinguishes *Trieb* and *Instinkt*. A *Trieb* is more plastic and indeterminate than the fixed instincts of nonhuman animals.

> An *Instinkt*, for Freud, is a rigid, innate, behavioral pattern, characteristic of animal behavior: e.g., the innate ability and pressure of a bird to build a nest. It is the essence of an *Instinkt* that it could not have a vicissitude: the pattern of behavior that it fuels and directs is preformed and fixed. A *Trieb*, by contrast, has a certain plasticity: its aim and direction is to some extent shaped by experience. (Lear 1991: 123–4)

Lear describes a drive as follows: "The drive *considered psychologically* is a mental stimulus . . . The drive *considered physiologically* is a purely physiological process. Here we may not be dealing with two different things, but with two different ways in which the same thing is considered" (Lear 1991: 122–3). Although Freud consistently distinguishes what is psychological from what is physiological, he seeks to show that what is psychical is grounded in biology. He describes a drive as a *frontier* concept – the psychic representative of biological stimuli.

11   Freud writes,

> The numerous [free – RJB] associations produced by the dreamer led to the discovery of a thought-structure which could no longer be described as absurd or confused, which ranked as a completely valid psychical product, and of which the *manifest* dream was no more than a distorted, abbreviated and misunderstood translation, and for the most part a translation into visual images. These *latent dream-thoughts* contained the meaning of the dream, while its manifest content was simply a make-believe, a façade, which could serve as a starting-point for the associations but not for the interpretation. (Freud 1925: 43–4)

12   Freud defends his thesis about dreams as wish fulfillments against a variety of objections in Freud 1933.

13 Freud is not merely interested in explaining dreamwork and defending his thesis that dreams are meaningful wish fulfillments. He suggests that the analysis of dreams provides the basis for understanding human nature and an insight into the psychic beginnings of the human race.

14 Freud explains,

> In my search for the pathogenic situations in which the repressions of sexuality had set in and in which symptoms, as substitutes for what was repressed, had had their origin, I was carried further and further back into the patient's life, and ended by reaching the first years of his childhood. What poets and students of human nature had always asserted turned out to be true: the impressions of that early period of life, though they were for the most part buried in amnesia, left ineradicable traces upon the individual's growth and in particular laid down the disposition of any nervous disorder that was to follow. But since these experiences of childhood were always concerned with sexual excitations and the reaction against them, I found myself faced with the fact of *infantile sexuality* – once again a novelty and a contradiction of one of the strongest human prejudices. (Freud 1925: 33)

Freud, denies, however, that *all* dreams have sexual content.

15 For an illuminating discussion of this dream, see Whitebook 2017: 198–204.

16 In his *Autobiographical Study*, Freud makes the following comment about "free association":

> It may seem surprising that this method of free association, carried out subject to the observation of the *fundamental rule of psychoanalysis* [the rule that patients should say whatever comes into their heads, even if they think it to be irrelevant, nonsensical, embarrassing or distressing – RJB], should have achieved what was expected of it, namely the bringing into consciousness of the repressed material which was held back by resistances. We must, however, bear in mind that free association is not really free. The patient remains under the influence of the analytic situation even though he is not directing his mental activities on to a particular subject. We shall be justified in assuming that nothing will occur to him that has not some reference to that situation. (Freud 1925: 40–1)

17 When Freud was exploring the memories of his patients, they reproduced childhood scenes of being sexually seduced by a grown-up. Initially he believed these stories, but later came to realize that they were not always truthful reports. Freud reports that his error shook his confidence.

> When, however, I was at last obliged to recognize that these scenes of seduction had never taken place, and that they were only phantasies which my patients had made up or which I myself had perhaps forced on them, I was for some time completely at a loss. . . . When I had pulled myself together, I was able to draw the right conclusions from my discovery: namely, that the neurotic symptoms were not related directly to actual events but to wishful phantasies, and that as far as the neurosis was concerned *psychical reality was of more importance than material reality*. (Freud 1925: 34, emphasis added)

Although Freud came to realize that many of the "memories" of seduction were "phantasies," he did *not* deny that some of his patients had been actually sexually seduced.
18 For a helpful discussion of the unconscious and some of its problematic aspects, see MacIntyre 2004.
19 Freud's *own* intellectual development bears a rough analogy to his moving description of Rome in *Civilization and Its Discontents*, where all the layers of the past are preserved. The Rome example is introduced as an analogy to psychic life, where "nothing that once has come into existence will have passed away and all the earlier phases of development continue to exist alongside the latest one" (Freud 1930: 70).
20 There has been a controversy concerning the English translation of *Ich* and *Es* as "ego" and "id" by James Strachey in the English Standard Edition. *Ich* and *Es* are ordinary German words that would normally be translated as "I" and "it." Translating *Ich* as "ego" and *Es* as "id" makes Freud sound as if he is introducing a more technical, rigid distinction than is suggested by the German words *Ich* and *Es*. Strachey translates *Über-Ich* as "super-ego."
21 Freud typically announces his views in a forceful, and sometimes dogmatic, manner, but he is acutely aware of the fallibility of science, including psychoanalysis. In the final lecture of *The New Introductory Lectures on Psycho-Analysis*, where he defends a scientific worldview against its religious critics, Freud states, "The path of science is indeed slow, hesitating, and laborious" (Freud 1933: 174).

> We put forward conjectures, we construct hypotheses, which we withdraw if they are not confirmed, we need much patience and readiness for any eventuality, we renounce early convictions so as not to be led by them into overlooking unexpected factors, and in the end our whole expenditure of effort is rewarded, the scattered findings fit themselves together, we get an insight into a whole section of mental events, we have completed our task and now we are free for the next one. (Freud 1933: 174)

22 Commenting on this passage, Rorty writes,

> It is hard nowadays to recapture how startling it must have been when Freud first began to describe conscience as an ego ideal set up by those who are "not willing to forgo the narcissistic perfection of . . . childhood." If Freud had made only the large, abstract, quasi-philosophical claim that the voice of conscience is the internalized voice of parents and society, he would not have startled. . . . What is new in Freud is the *details* he gives us about the sort of thing which goes into the formation of conscience, his explanations of why certain very concrete situations and persons excite unbearable guilt, intense anxiety, or smoldering rage. (Rorty 1989: 31)

23 Consider Yovel's description of the "dark Enlightenment":

> From Machiavelli and Hobbes, to Darwin and Marx, and up to Nietzsche, Freud, and Heidegger – and passing through Spinoza . . . – this process of

> dark enlightenment proved a sharp awakening from religious and metaphysical illusions, incurring pain and conflict in its wake. For it challenged accepted self-images and enshrined cultural identities, and thereby endangered a whole range of vested psychological interests. But for those very reasons, it was also a *movement of emancipation*, serving to inspire a richer and more lucid self-knowledge in man, even at the price of unflattering consequences which often shock and dismay. This was the true "Oedipal drive" – not of Freud's Oedipus but of the original protagonist of Sophocles' tragedy, of whom Freud himself is an avid follower. (Yovel 1992: 136, emphasis added)

24 Later in this essay Freud writes, "Leonardo himself, with his love of truth and his thirst for knowledge, would not have discouraged an attempt to take the trivial peculiarities and riddles in his nature as a starting-point, for discovering what determined his mental and intellectual development. We do homage to him by learning from him" (Freud 1910a: 130–1).

25 Although Freud introduces the concept of sublimation in connection with the sexual instincts, he also speaks of the sublimation of the aggressive instincts. Both sexual instincts and aggressive instincts can be sublimated.

26 For a comprehensive overview of the psychoanalytic literature on sublimation, see Loewald 1988. But even Loewald admits that his study is a "fragment" and that there are many unresolved problems with sublimation that need to be explored.

27 Even Freud's most sympathetic interpreters have difficulty with this text. Whitebook thinks that "its argument contains gaps big enough to drive a proverbial truck through and deploys highly questionable empirical evidence in a cavalier manner to suit its purposes" (Whitebook 2017: 361). Gay writes that what is so unsettling is "Freud's yielding to flights of the imagination as uninhibited as any he had ever undertaken in print. The reassuring intimacy with clinical experience that marks most of Freud's papers, even at their most theoretical, seems faint here, almost absent" (Gay 2006: 398). Lear is even more extreme: "Freud admitted that the ground for postulating the death drive did not arise from within psychoanalytic observation and thinking, but from biology. . . .That is, Freud knew that there wasn't a shred of psychoanalytic evidence for the death drive" (Lear 1991: 13). To compound the problems, toward the end of his discussion, Freud raises the rhetorical question: "It may be asked whether and how far I am myself convinced of the truth of the hypotheses that have been set out in these pages. My answer would be that I am not convinced myself and that I do not seek to persuade other people to believe in them. Or more precisely, that I do not know how far I believe in them" (Freud 1920: 59). Despite this admission, and despite all the criticisms that Freud received, he steadfastly held to the hypothesis of a death instinct to the end of his life.

28 The death instinct is motivated by the Nirvana principle – a principle given currency by Schopenhauer and drawn from Buddhism. It is the tendency "to reduce, to keep constant or to remove internal tension due to stimuli" and is "one of our strongest reasons for believing in the existence of death

instincts" (Freud 1920: 55–6). In *The Ego and the Id*, Freud speaks of the "dangerous death instincts."

> The dangerous death instincts are dealt with in the individual in various ways: in part they are rendered harmless by being fused with erotic components, in part they are diverted towards the external world in the form of aggression, while to a large extent they undoubtedly continue their internal work unhindered. How is it then in melancholia the super-ego can become a kind of gathering-place for the death instincts?
>
> From the point of view of instinctual control, of morality, it may be said of the id that it is totally non-moral, of the ego that it strives to be moral, and of the super-ego that it can be super-moral and then become as cruel as only the id can be. It is remarkable that the more a man checks his aggressiveness towards the exterior the more severe – that is aggressive – he becomes in his ego ideal. (Freud 1923: 54)

29 It is typical of Freud to introduce some of his most controversial ideas in a "tentative" manner and then assume them as established facts. In *Civilization and Its Discontents*, after reviewing his initial discovery of the death instinct, he writes:

> To begin with it was only tentatively that I put forward the views I have developed here [in *Beyond the Pleasure Principle*], but in the course of time they have gained such a hold upon me that I can no longer think in any other way. To my mind, they are far more serviceable from a theoretical standpoint than any other possible one; they provide that simplification, without either ignoring or doing violence to the facts, for which we strive in scientific work. I know that in sadism and masochism we have always seen before us manifestations of the destructive instinct (directed outwards and inwards), strongly alloyed with eroticism; but I can no longer understand how we can have overlooked the ubiquity of non-erotic aggressivity and destructiveness and can have failed to give it its due place in our interpretation of life. (Freud 1930: 119–20)

Freud recognized the important role of aggressiveness long before the introduction of the death instinct. Laplanche and Pontalis declare:

> Freud as a rule keeps the expression 'aggressive instinct' (*Aggressionstrieb*) for that portion of the death instinct which is directed outwards, with the help, in particular, of the muscular apparatus. It should be remembered that for Freud this aggressive instinct (in the same way perhaps as the tendency towards self-destruction) cannot be conceived of at all without envisaging its fusion with sexuality. . . . The facts invoked by Freud in *Beyond the Pleasure Principle* . . . to justify his introduction of the idea of the death instinct are phenomena which give expression to the repetition compulsion – *and this has no special affinity with aggressive behaviour*. (Laplanche and Pontalis 1988: 19, emphasis added)

30 Freud, who was a great admirer of Plato, claims that his understanding of sexuality is close to Plato's Eros – especially "the all-inclusive and all-preserving Eros of Plato's *Symposium*" (Freud 1925a: 218).

31 Freud clarifies his terminology in a footnote to *Beyond the Pleasure Principle*.

> We came to know what the 'sexual instincts' were from their relation to the sexes and to the reproductive function. We retained this name after we had been obliged by the findings of psycho-analysis to connect them less closely with reproduction. With the hypothesis of narcissistic libido and the extension of the concept of libido to the individual cells, the sexual instinct was transformed for us into Eros, which seeks to force together and hold together the portions of living substance. What are commonly called the sexual instincts are looked upon by us as the part of Eros which is directed towards objects. Our speculations have suggested that Eros operates from the beginning of life and appears as a 'life instinct' in opposition to the 'death instinct' which was brought into being by the coming to life of inorganic substance. (Freud 1920: 60–1, n. 1)

Freud can be eloquent, even romantic, in his description of the love between a pair of lovers.

> When a love-relationship is at its height there is no room left for any interest in the environment; a pair of lovers are sufficient to themselves, and do not even need the child they have in common to make them happy. In no other case does Eros so clearly betray the core of his being, his purpose in making one out of more than one; but when he has achieved this in the proverbial way through the love of two human beings, he refuses to go further. (Freud 1930: 108)

32 *Eros* and *Thanatos*

> seldom – perhaps never – appear in isolation from each other, but are alloyed with each other in varying and very different proportions and so become unrecognizable to our judgement. In sadism, long since known to us as a component instinct of sexuality, we should have before us a particularly strong alloy of this kind between trends of love and the destructive instinct; while its counterpart, masochism, would be a union between destructiveness directed inwards and sexuality – a union which makes what is otherwise an imperceptible trend into a conspicuous and tangible one. (Freud 1930: 119)

33 Acknowledging Freud's explicit scorn of the distinction between "civilization" and "culture," the Standard Edition translates *Kultur* as "civilization" rather than "culture" (Freud 1927: 4, 6). A more accurate translation of *Unbehagen* is "unease" or "malaise." As the editors point out in their introduction, Freud suggested the title "Man's Discomfort in Civilization" in a letter to his translator, Joan Riviere; but it was she herself who came up with the title "Civilization and Its Discontents" (Freud 1930: 59–60).

34 Freud leaves us with an open "fateful question" for the future of the human species. Will human beings succeed in mastering the human instinct of aggression and self-destruction?

> Men have gained control over the forces of nature to such an extent that with their help they would have no difficulty in exterminating one another to the

last man. They know this, and hence comes a large part of current unrest, their unhappiness and their mood of anxiety. And now it is to be expected that the other of the two 'Heavenly Powers' . . . eternal Eros, will make an effort to assert himself in the struggle with his equally immortal adversary. But who can foresee with what success and with what result? (Freud 1930: 145)

Strachey points out that "this final sentence was added in 1931 – when the menace of Hitler was already beginning to be apparent" (Freud 1930: 145, n.1).

35 The footnote reads:

> That the education of young people at the present day conceals from them the part which sexuality will play in their lives is not the only reproach which we are obliged to make against it. Its other sin is that it does not prepare them for the aggressiveness of which they are destined to become the objects. In sending the young out into life with such a false psychological orientation, education is behaving as though one were to equip people starting on a Polar expedition with summer clothing and maps of the Italian Lakes. In this it becomes evident that a certain misuse is being made of ethical demands. The strictness of these demands would not do so much harm if education were to say: 'This is how men ought to be, in order to be happy and to make others happy, but you have to reckon on their not being like that.' Instead of this the young are made to believe that everyone else fulfils those ethical demands – that is, that everyone else is virtuous. It is on this that the demand is based that the young, too, shall become virtuous. (Freud 1930: 134, n. 1)

In making this criticism, Freud is clearly suggesting that there is a better way to educate the young: one based on a more realistic account of human nature.

36 This is at the heart of Marcuse's concept of "surplus repression" (Marcuse 1966: 224). Marcuse recognizes that it is impossible to eliminate all psychological repression, but the surplus repression can be eliminated. The difficulty with Marcuse's thesis is that he imagines a state of society wherein our deepest instincts are gratified, where "reason and instinct could unite" (Marcuse 1966: 235). But given Freud's understanding of the immortal battle of *Thanatos* and *Eros*, this is impossible.

37 In an address he gave in 1930 when he received the Goethe Prize, he said: "Goethe always rated Eros high, never tried to belittle its power, followed its primitive and even wanton expressions with no less attentiveness than its highly sublimated ones and has, as it seems to me, expounded its essential unity throughout all its manifestations no less decisively than Plato did in the remote past" (Freud 1930a: 210). For further discussion of Freud, see Bernstein 1998 and 2002.

38 In his text *On Nature*, Empedocles posits Love and Strife as the two cosmic forces of creation and destruction (Curd 2011: 83–8).

39 We need to keep in mind that the satisfaction of *both* erotic and aggressive instincts is pleasurable – yields happiness.
40 The passage is from the conclusion of the thirty-first lecture. This lecture presents one of Freud's clearest statements of the relations among the id, ego, and superego.

References

Acampora, C. D. (2006) Naturalism and Nietzsche's Moral Psychology. In Ansell-Pearson (ed.) 2006, pp. 314–33.
Allison, H. E. (1983) *Kant's Transcendental Idealism*. Yale University Press, New Haven.
Allison, H. E. (1987) *Benedict de Spinoza: An Introduction*, rev. ed. Yale University Press, New Haven.
Althusser, L. (1976) Elements of Self-Criticism. In L. Althusser, *Essays in Self-Criticism*, trans. G. Lock, NLB, London, pp. 101–61.
Althusser, L. (2005) *For Marx*, trans. B. Brewster. Verso, New York.
Anderson, R. L. (2017) Friedrich Nietzsche. In *The Stanford Encyclopedia of Philosophy*, ed. E. N. Zalta. https://plato.stanford.edu/entries/nietzsche/.
Ansell-Pearson, K. (ed.) (2006) *A Companion to Nietzsche*. Wiley-Blackwell, Malden.
Arendt, H. (1992) *Lectures on Kant's Political Philosophy*, ed. R. Beiner. University of Chicago Press, Chicago.
Avineri, S. (2019) *Karl Marx: Philosophy and Revolution*. Yale University Press, New Haven.
Baier, A. C. (1991) *A Progress of Sentiments: Reflections on Hume's* Treatise. Harvard University Press, Cambridge, Mass.
Balibar, E. (1998) *Spinoza and Politics*, trans. P. Snowdon. Verso, New York.
Balibar, E. (2017) *The Philosophy of Marx*, trans. C. Turner, updated new ed. Verso, New York.
Balibar, E. (2020) *Spinoza, the Transindividual*, trans. M. G. E. Kelly. Edinburgh University Press, Edinburgh.
Bayle, P. (1965) *Historical and Critical Dictionary: Selections*, trans. R. H. Popkin. Bobbs-Merrill Company, Indianapolis.
Beiser, F. C. (1987) *The Fate of Reason: German Philosophy from Kant to Fichte*. Harvard University Press, Cambridge, Mass.

Beiser, F. C. (2002) *German Idealism: The Struggle against Subjectivism 1781–1801*. Harvard University Press, Cambridge, Mass.
Beiser, F. C. (2005) *Hegel*. Routledge, New York.
Bennett, J. (1984) *A Study of Spinoza's Ethics*. Hackett Publishing Company, Indianapolis.
Berlin, I. (1948) *Karl Marx: His Life and Environment*. Oxford University Press, London.
Bernstein, R. J. (1998) *Freud and the Legacy of Moses*. Cambridge University Press, Cambridge.
Bernstein, R. J. (2002) *Radical Evil: A Philosophical Interrogation*. Polity, Cambridge.
Bernstein, R. J. (2020) *Pragmatic Naturalism: John Dewey's Living Legacy*. Kindle Direct Publishing.
Biro, J., and Koistinen, O. (eds) (2002) *Spinoza: Metaphysical Themes*. Oxford University Press, New York.
Bloch, E. (1986) *The Principle of Hope*, trans. N. Plaice, S. Plaice, and P. Knight, vol. 1. MIT Press, Cambridge, Mass.
Boehm, O. (2014) *Kant's Critique of Spinoza*. Oxford University Press, New York.
Brandom, R. B. (1994) *Making It Explicit: Reasoning, Representing, and Discursive Commitment*. Harvard University Press, Cambridge, Mass.
Brandom, R. B. (2002) *Tales of the Mighty Dead: Historical Essays in the Metaphysics of Intentionality*. Harvard University Press, Cambridge, Mass.
Burbidge, J. W. (1996) *Real Process: How Logic and Chemistry Combine in Hegel's Philosophy of Nature*. Toronto University Press, Toronto.
Caruana, F., and Testa, I. (eds) (2021) *Habits: Pragmatist Approaches from Cognitive Science, Neuroscience, and Social Theory*. Cambridge University Press, Cambridge.
Clark, M., and Dudrick, D. (2006) The Naturalisms of *Beyond Good and Evil*. In Ansell-Pearson (ed.) 2006, pp. 148–67.
Collingwood, R. G. (1945) *The Idea of Nature*. Clarendon Press, Oxford.
Curd, P. (ed.) (2011) Empedocles of Acragas. In *A Presocratics Reader: Selected Fragments and Testimonia*, trans. R. D. McKirahan and P. Curd, 2nd ed., Hackett Publishing, Indianapolis, pp. 73–100.
Curley, E. (1969) *Spinoza's Metaphysics: An Essay in Interpretation*. Harvard University Press, Cambridge, Mass.
Curley, E. (ed.) (1985) *The Collected Works of Spinoza*, trans. E. Curley, vol. 1. Princeton University Press, Princeton.
Curley, E., and Walski, G. (1999) Spinoza's Necessitarianism Reconsidered. In Gennaro and Huenemann (eds) 1999, pp. 241–62.
Damasio, A. (2003) *Looking for Spinoza: Joy, Sorrow, and the Feeling Brain*. Harcourt, New York.
Davidson, D. (1999) Spinoza's Causal Theory of the Affects. In Yovel (ed.) 1999, pp. 95–111.
Davidson, D. (2001) Mental Events. In D. Davidson, *Essays on Actions and Events*, 2nd ed., Clarendon Press, Oxford, pp. 207–27.
De Caro, M., and Macarthur, D. (eds) (2004) *Naturalism in Question*. Harvard University Press, Cambridge, Mass.

de Deugd, C. (2004) Spinoza and Freud: An Old Myth Revisited. In Yovel and Segal (eds) 2004, pp. 227–52.
Deleuze, G. (1988) *Spinoza: Practical Philosophy*, trans. R. Hurley. City Lights Books, San Francisco.
Deleuze, G. (1990) *Expressionism in Philosophy: Spinoza*, trans. M. Joughin. Zone Books, New York.
Della Rocca, M. (1996) *Representation and the Mind-Body in Spinoza*. Oxford University Press, New York.
Della Rocca, M. (2008) *Spinoza*. Routledge, New York.
deVries, W. A. (1988) *Hegel's Theory of Mental Activity: An Introduction to Theoretical Spirit*. Cornell University Press, Ithaca.
Dewey, J. (1981) *The Later Works of John Dewey, 1925–1953*, ed. J. A. Boydston, vol. 1: *1925: Experience and Nature*. Southern Illinois University Press, Carbondale.
Dewey, J. (1983) *The Middle Works of John Dewey, 1888–1924*, ed. J. A. Boydston, vol. 14: *1922: Human Nature and Conduct: An Introduction to Social Psychology*. Southern Illinois University Press, Carbondale.
Dewey, J. (2010) Hegel's Philosophy of Spirit: 1897, University of Chicago. In *John Dewey's Philosophy of Spirit, with the 1897 Lecture on Hegel*, ed. J. R. Shook and J. A. Good, Fordham University Press, New York, pp. 93–176.
Eissler, K. R. (1978) Creativity and Adolescence: The Effect of Trauma in Freud's Adolescence. *The Psychoanalytic Study of the Child*, 33, pp. 466–517.
Ferrarin, A. (2001) *Hegel and Aristotle*. Cambridge University Press, Cambridge.
Findlay, J. N. (1970) Foreword. In Hegel 1970, pp. v–xxv.
Fogelin, R. (1985) *Hume's Skepticism in the* Treatise of Human Nature. Routledge & Kegan Paul, London.
Fogelin, R. (1994) *Pyrrhonian Reflections on Knowledge and Justification*. Oxford University Press, Oxford.
Fogelin, R. (2009) *Hume's Skeptical Crisis: A Textual Study*. Oxford University Press, Oxford.
Franks, P. W. (2005) *All or Nothing: Systematicity, Transcendental Arguments, and Skepticism in German Idealism*. Harvard University Press, Cambridge, Mass.
Fraser, N. (2021) Climates of Capital: For a Trans-Environmental Eco-Socialism. *New Left Review*, 127, pp. 94–127.
Freud, S. (1895) *Project for a Scientific Psychology*. In Strachey (ed.) 1953, vol. 1, pp. 281–391.
Freud, S. (1900) *The Interpretation of Dreams (Second Part)*. In Strachey (ed.) 1953, vol. 5, pp. 339–627.
Freud, S. (1910) *Five Lectures on Psycho-Analysis*. In Strachey (ed.) 1957, vol. 11, pp. 1–56.
Freud, S. (1910a) *Leonardo Da Vinci and a Memory of His Childhood*. In Strachey (ed.) 1957, vol. 11, pp. 57–138.
Freud, S. (1915) "The Unconscious." In Strachey (ed.) 1957, vol. 14, pp. 159–215.
Freud, S. (1916) *Introductory Lectures on Psycho-Analysis* (Part III). In Strachey (ed.) 1963, vol. 16.

Freud, S. (1920) *Beyond the Pleasure Principle*. In Strachey (ed.) 1955, vol. 18, pp. 1–64.
Freud, S. (1921) *Group Psychology and the Analysis and the Ego*. In Strachey (ed.) 1955, vol. 18, pp. 65–143.
Freud, S. (1923) *The Ego and the Id*. In Strachey (ed.) 1961, vol. 19, pp. 1–66.
Freud, S. (1925) *An Autobiographical Study*. In Strachey (ed.) 1959, vol. 20, pp. 1–74.
Freud, S. (1925a) *The Resistances to Psycho-Analysis*. In Strachey (ed.) 1961, vol. 19, pp. 211–24.
Freud, S. (1926) *The Question of Lay Analysis*. In Strachey (ed.) 1959, vol. 20, pp. 177–258.
Freud, S. (1927) *The Future of an Illusion*. In Strachey (ed.) 1961, vol. 21, pp. 3–58.
Freud, S. (1930) *Civilization and Its Discontents*. In Strachey (ed.) 1961, vol. 21, pp. 57–146.
Freud, S. (1930a) *The Goethe Prize*. In Strachey (ed.) 1961, vol. 21, pp. 205–14.
Freud, S. (1933) *New Introductory Lectures on Psycho-Analysis*. In Strachey (ed.) 1964, vol. 22, pp. 1–182.
Freud, S. (1954) *The Origins of Psycho-Analysis: Letters to Wilhelm Fliess, Drafts and Notes: 1887–1902*, trans. E. Mosbacher and J. Strachey. Basic Books, New York.
Friedman, M. (1992) *Kant and the Exact Sciences*. Harvard University Press, Cambridge, Mass.
Friedman, M. (1992a) Causal Laws and the Foundations of Natural Science. In Guyer (ed.) 1992, pp. 161–99.
Garber, D. (2004) Dr. Fischelson's Dilemma: Spinoza on Freedom and Sociability. In Yovel and Segal (eds) 2004, pp. 183–207.
Gardner, S. (2007) The Limits of Naturalism and the Metaphysics of German Idealism. In Hammer (ed.) 2007, pp. 19–49.
Garrett, A. V. (2003) *Meaning in Spinoza's Method*. Cambridge University Press, Cambridge.
Garrett, D. (2002) Spinoza's *Conatus* Argument. In Biro and Koistinen (eds) 2002, pp. 127–58.
Garrett, D. (2004) 'A Small Tincture of Pyrrhonism': Skepticism and Naturalism in Hume's Science of Man. In Sinnott-Armstrong (ed.) 2004, pp. 68–98.
Garrett, D. (2009) Spinoza on the Essence of the Human Body and the Part of the Mind That is Eternal. In Koistinen (ed.) 2009, pp. 284–302.
Garrett, D. (2015) *Hume*. Routledge, New York.
Garrett, D. (2018) *Nature and Necessity in Spinoza's Philosophy*. Oxford University Press, New York.
Gay, P. (2006) *Freud: A Life for Our Time*. W. W. Norton, New York.
Gemes, K., and Richardson, J. (eds) (2013) *The Oxford Handbook of Nietzsche*. Oxford University Press, Oxford.
Gennaro, R. J., and Huenemann, C. (eds) (1999) *New Essays on the Rationalists*. Oxford University Press, New York.
Geras, N. (2016) *Marx and Human Nature: Refutation of a Legend*. Verso, New York.
Ginsborg, H. (2015) *The Normativity of Nature: Essays on Kant's* Critique of Judgement. Oxford University Press, Oxford.

Godfrey-Smith, P. (2014) John Dewey's *Experience and Nature*. *Topoi*, 33/1, pp. 285–91.
Goldstein, R. (2006) *Betraying Spinoza: The Renegade Jew Who Gave Us Modernity*. Schocken Books, New York.
Goy, I., and Watkins, E. (eds) (2014) *Kant's Theory of Biology*. Walter de Gruyter, Berlin.
Gutting, G. (ed.) (2005) *Continental Philosophy of Science*. Blackwell Publishing, Malden.
Guyer, P. (2005) *Kant's System of Nature and Freedom: Selected Essays*. Oxford University Press, New York.
Guyer, P. (ed.) (1992) *The Cambridge Companion to Kant*. Cambridge University Press, Cambridge.
Hammer, E. (ed.) (2007) *German Idealism: Contemporary Perspectives*. Routledge, New York.
Hampshire, S. (1951) *Spinoza*. Faber & Faber, London.
Hampshire, S. (1971) Spinoza and the Idea of Freedom. In S. Hampshire, *Freedom of Mind and Other Essays*, Princeton University Press, Princeton, pp. 183–209.
Hatfield, G. (2002) Translator's Introduction. In Kant 2002, pp. 31–47.
Hegel, G. W. F. (1969) *Hegel's Science of Logic*, trans. A. V. Miller, ed. H. D. Lewis. Humanity Books, Amherst.
Hegel, G. W. F. (1970) *Hegel's* Philosophy of Nature*: Being Part Two of the* Encyclopaedia of the Philosophical Sciences *(1830)*, trans. A. V. Miller. Clarendon Press, Oxford.
Hegel, G. W. F. (1970a) *Hegel's Philosophy of Nature*, ed. and trans. M. J. Petry, 3 vols. George Allen and Unwin, London.
Hegel, G. W. F. (1971) *Hegel's* Philosophy of Mind*: Being Part Three of the* Encyclopaedia of the Philosophical Sciences *(1830), together with the* Zusätze *in Boumann's Text (1845)*, trans. W. Wallace and A. V. Miller. Clarendon Press, Oxford.
Hegel, G. W. F. (1977) *The Difference Between Fichte's and Schelling's System of Philosophy*, trans. H. S. Harris and W. Cerf. SUNY Press, Albany.
Hegel, G. W. F. (1978) *Hegels Philosophie des subjektiven Geistes / Hegel's Philosophy of Subjective Spirit*, ed. and trans. M. J. Petry, 3 vols. D. Reidel Publishing Company, Dordrecht.
Hegel, G. W. F. (1991) *Elements of the Philosophy of Right*, ed. A. W. Wood, trans. H. B. Nisbet. Cambridge University Press, Cambridge.
Hegel, G. W. F. (1991a) *The Encyclopaedia Logic*, with the Zusätze: Part I of the *Encyclopaedia of Philosophical Sciences* with the Zusätze, trans. T. F. Geraets, W. A. Suchting, and H. S. Harris. Hackett Publishing Company, Indianapolis.
Hegel, G. W. F. (2007) *Lectures on the Philosophy of Spirit, 1827–8*, trans. R. R. Williams. Oxford University Press, New York.
Hegel, G.W.F. (2007a) *Philosophy of Mind*, trans. W. Wallace and A. V. Miller, revised with introduction and commentary by M. Inwood. Clarendon Press, Oxford.
Henrich, D. (1994) *The Unity of Reason: Essays on Kant's Philosophy*, ed. R. Velkley, trans. J. Edwards *et al.* Harvard University Press, Cambridge, Mass.
Houlgate, S. (1998) Introduction. In Houlgate (ed.) 1998, pp. xi–xxvii.

Houlgate, S. (2006) *The Opening of Hegel's Logic: From Being to Infinity.* Purdue University Press, West Lafayette.

Houlgate, S. (ed.) (1998) *Hegel and the Philosophy of Nature.* SUNY Press, Albany.

Hume, D. (1965) *An Abstract of* A Treatise of Human Nature 1740: *A Pamphlet hitherto unknown by David Hume,* reprinted with an introduction by J. M. Keynes and P. Sraffa. Archon Books, Hamden.

Hume, D. (1975) *Enquiries Concerning Human Understanding and Concerning the Principles of Morals,* ed. L. A. Selby-Bigge and P. H. Nidditch, 3rd ed. Clarendon Press, Oxford.

Hume, D. (1978) *A Treatise of Human Nature,* ed. L. A. Selby-Bigge and P. H. Nidditch, 2nd rev. ed. Oxford University Press, Oxford.

Hume, D. (1993) *An Abstract of* A Treatise of Human Nature. In D. Hume, *An Enquiry Concerning Human Understanding,* ed. E. Steinberg, 2nd ed. Hackett Publishing Company, Indianapolis, pp. 125–38.

Hume, D. (2012) *Dialogues Concerning Natural Religion,* ed. D. Coleman. Cambridge University Press, Cambridge.

Huneman, P. (2007) Introduction: Kant and Biology? A Quick Survey. In Huneman (ed.) 2007a, pp. 1–36.

Huneman, P. (ed.) (2007a) *Understanding Purpose: Kant and the Philosophy of Biology.* University of Rochester Press, Rochester.

Illetterati, L. (2014) Teleological Judgment: Between Technique and Nature. In Goy and Watkins (eds) 2014, pp. 81–98.

Israel, J. I. (2001) *Radical Enlightenment: Philosophy and the Making of Modernity, 1650–1750.* Oxford University Press, New York.

Jaeggi, R. (2018) *Critique of Forms of Life,* trans. C. Cronin. Harvard University Press, Cambridge, Mass.

Jaffe, A. (2014) Alienation from "Species-Being": An Investigation of Marx's Philosophical Anthropology. Ph.D. dissertation, New School for Social Research, New York.

James, S. (2012) *Spinoza on Philosophy, Religion, and Politics:* The Theologico-Political Treatise. Oxford University Press, New York.

James, W. (1890) *Principles of Psychology,* 2 vols. Holt, New York.

Janaway, C. (2007) *Beyond Selflessness: Reading Nietzsche's* Genealogy. Oxford University Press, New York.

Kant, I. (*CPR* [1998]) *Critique of Pure Reason,* ed. and trans. P. Guyer and A. W. Wood. Cambridge University Press, Cambridge.

Kant, I. (*CJ* [2000]) *Critique of the Power of Judgment,* ed. P. Guyer, trans. P. Guyer and E. Matthews. Cambridge University Press, Cambridge.

Kant, I. (*P* [2002]) *Prolegomena to Any Future Metaphysics That Will Be Able to Come Forward as Science.* In Kant 2002, pp. 29–169.

Kant, I. (*MFN* [2002]) *Metaphysical Foundations of Natural Science.* In Kant 2002, pp. 171–270.

Kant, I. (2002) *Theoretical Philosophy after 1781,* eds. H. Allison and P. Heath, trans. G. Hatfield, M. Friedman, H. Allison, and P. Heath. Cambridge University Press, Cambridge.

Kaufmann, W. (1974 [1950]) *Nietzsche: Philosopher, Psychologist, Antichrist*, 4th ed. Princeton University Press, Princeton.
Kaufmann, W. (ed.) (2000) *Basic Writings of Nietzsche*. The Modern Library, New York.
Kemp Smith, N. (1905) The Naturalism of Hume (I). *Mind*, 14/54, pp. 149–73.
Kemp Smith, N. (1905a) The Naturalism of Hume (II). *Mind*, 14/55, pp. 335–47.
Khurana, T. (2013) Life and Autonomy: Forms of Self-Determination in Kant and Hegel. In Khurana (ed.) 2013, pp. 155–193.
Khurana, T. (2017) *Das Leben der Freiheit: Form und Wiklichkeit der Autonomie*. Suhrkamp, Berlin.
Khurana, T. (2022) Genus-Being: On Marx's Dialectical Naturalism. In *Nature and Naturalism in Classical German Philosophy*, ed. L. Corti, J.-G. Schülein. Routledge, London.
Khurana, T. (ed.) (2013) *The Freedom of Life: Hegelian Perspectives*. August Verlag, Berlin.
Kohut, H. (1966) Forms and Transformations of Narcissism. *Journal of the American Psychoanalytic Association*, 14/2, pp. 243–72.
Koistinen, O. (ed.) (2009) *The Cambridge Companion to Spinoza's* Ethics. Cambridge University Press, New York.
Kolakowski, L. (1968) *Toward a Marxist Humanism: Essays on the Left Today*, trans. J. Zielonko Peel. Grove Press, New York.
Körner, S. (1955) *Kant*. Penguin Books, Baltimore.
Laplanche, J., and Pontalis, J.-B. (1988) *The Language of Psychoanalysis*, trans. D. Nicholson-Smith. Karnac Books, London.
Lear, J. (1991) *Love and Its Place in Nature: A Philosophical Interpretation of Freudian Psychoanalysis*. Noonday Press, New York.
Leiter, B. (2004) The Hermeneutics of Suspicion: Recovering Marx, Nietzsche, and Freud. In Leiter (ed.) 2004, pp. 74–105.
Leiter, B. (2013) Nietzsche's Naturalism Reconsidered. In Gemes and Richardson (eds) 2013, pp. 576–98.
Leiter, B. (2015 [2002]) *Nietzsche on Morality*, 2nd ed. Routledge, New York.
Leiter, B. (ed.) (2004) *The Future for Philosophy*. Clarendon Press, Oxford.
Levine, S. (2015) Hegel, Dewey, and Habits. *British Journal of the History of Philosophy*, 23/4, pp. 632–56.
Lin, M. (2006) Teleology and Human Action in Spinoza. *The Philosophical Review*, 115/3, pp. 317–54.
Loewald, H. (1988) *Sublimation: Inquiries into Theoretical Psychoanalysis*. Yale University Press, New Haven.
Longuenesse, B. (1998) *Kant and the Capacity to Judge: Sensibility and Discursivity in the Transcendental Analytic of the* Critique of Pure Reason, trans. C. T. Wolfe. Princeton University Press, Princeton.
Lord, B. (2011) *Kant and Spinozism: Transcendental Idealism and Immanence from Jacobi to Deleuze*. Palgrave Macmillan, New York.
Lukács, G. (1971) *History and Class Consciousness: Studies in Marxist Dialectics*, trans. R. Livingstone. MIT Press, Cambridge, Mass.

MacIntyre, A. (2004) *The Unconscious: A Conceptual Analysis*, rev. ed. Routledge, New York.
Maker, W. (1998) The Very Idea of the Idea of Nature, or Why Hegel Is Not an Idealist. In Houlgate (ed.) 1998, pp. 1–27.
Marcuse, H. (1966) *Eros and Civilization: A Philosophical Inquiry into Freud*. Beacon Press, Boston.
Marx, K. (1997) *Writings of the Young Marx on Philosophy and Society*, ed. and trans. L. D. Easton and K. H. Guddat. Hackett Publishing Company, Indianapolis.
Marx, K. (2000) *Karl Marx: Selected Writings*, ed. D. McLellan. Oxford University Press, New York.
Masson, J. M. (ed.) (1985) *The Complete Letters of Sigmund Freud to Wilhelm Fliess, 1887–1904*, trans. J. M. Masson. Harvard University Press, Cambridge, Mass.
McDowell, J. (1996) *Mind and World: With a New Introduction*. Harvard University Press, Cambridge, Mass.
McDowell, J. (2008) Naturalism in the Philosophy of Mind. In De Caro and Macarthur (eds) 2004, pp. 91–105.
McLaughlin, P. (2014) Mechanical Explanation in the "Critique of the Teleological Power of Judgment." In Goy and Watkins (eds) 2014, pp. 149–66.
Melamed, Y. Y. (2013) *Spinoza's Metaphysics: Substance and Thought*. Oxford University Press, New York.
Moore, J. W. (2015) *Capitalism in the Web of Life: Ecology and the Accumulation of Capital*. Verso, New York.
Mounce, H. (1999) *Hume's Naturalism*. Routledge, London.
Nadler, S. (1999) *Spinoza: A Life*. Cambridge University Press, Cambridge.
Nadler, S. (2011) *A Book Forged in Hell: Spinoza's Scandalous Treatise and the Birth of the Secular Age*. Princeton University Press, Princeton.
Naess, A. (2008) Spinoza and the Deep Ecology Movement. In *The Ecology of Wisdom: Writings by Arne Naess*, ed. A. Drengson and B. Devall, Counterpoint, Berkeley, pp. 230–51.
Negri, A. (1991) *The Savage Anomaly: The Power of Spinoza's Metaphysics and Politics*, trans. M. Hardt. University of Minnesota Press, Minneapolis.
Nehamas, A. (1985) *Nietzsche: Life as Literature*. Harvard University Press, Cambridge, Mass.
Nehamas, A. (1998) *The Art of Living: Socratic Reflections from Plato to Foucault*. University of California Press, Berkeley.
Ng, K. (2020) *Hegel's Concept of Life: Self-Consciousness, Freedom, Logic*. Oxford University Press, New York.
Nietzsche, F. (1976) *The Portable Nietzsche*, trans. and ed. W. Kaufmann. Penguin Books, New York.
Nietzsche, F. (*TI* [1976a]) *Twilight of the Idols or, How One Philosophizes with a Hammer*. In Nietzsche 1976, pp. 463–563.
Nietzsche, F. (1976b) *The Antichrist*. In Nietzsche 1976, pp. 565–56.
Nietzsche, F. (*BGE* [2000]) *Beyond Good and Evil: Prelude to a Philosophy of the Future*. In Kaufmann (ed.) 2000, pp. 179–435.

Nietzsche, F. (*GM* [2000a]) *On the Genealogy of Morals*. In Kaufmann (ed.) 2000, pp. 437–599.
Nietzsche, F. (*GS* [2001]) *The Gay Science: With a Prelude in German Rhymes and an Appendix of Songs*, ed. B. Williams, trans. J. Nauckhoff. Cambridge University Press, Cambridge.
Nietzsche, F. (2008) *Thus Spoke Zarathustra: A Book for All and None*, trans. A. Del Caro, ed. A. Del Caro and R. B. Pippin. Cambridge University Press, Cambridge.
Nietzsche, F. (2013) *Philosophische Werke in sechs Bänden*, ed. C.-A. Scheier, vol. 5: *Die fröhliche Wissenschaft, Wir Furchtlosen (Neue Ausgabe 1887)*. Felix Meiner Verlag, Hamburg.
Peirce, C. S. (1992) *The Essential Peirce: Selected Philosophical Writings*, vol. 1: *1867–1893*, ed. N. Houser and C. Kloesel. Indiana University, Bloomington.
Peirce, C. S. (1998) *The Essential Peirce: Selected Philosophical Writings*, vol. 2: *1893–1913*, ed. the Peirce Edition Project. Indiana University, Bloomington.
Petry, M. J. (1970) Introduction. In Hegel (1970a), vol. 1, pp. 11–177.
Pinkard, T. (2005) Speculative *Naturphilosophie* and the Development of the Empirical Sciences: Hegel's Perspective. In Gutting (ed.) 2005, pp. 19–34.
Pinkard, T. (2012) *Hegel's Naturalism: Mind, Nature, and the Final Ends of Life*. Oxford University Press, New York.
Pippin, R. B. (1989) *Hegel's Idealism: The Satisfactions of Self-Consciousness*. Cambridge University Press, Cambridge.
Pippin, R. B. (2002) Leaving Nature Behind: Or Two Cheers for "Subjectivism." In Smith (ed.) 2002, pp. 58–75.
Pippin, R. B. (2010) *Nietzsche, Psychology, and First Philosophy*. University of Chicago Press, Chicago.
Pippin, R. B. (2019) *Hegel's Realm of Shadows: Logic as Metaphysics in* The Science of Logic. University of Chicago Press, Chicago.
Plato, (1991) *The Republic of Plato*, trans. A. Bloom, 2nd ed. Basic Books, New York.
Popkin, R. H. (1979) Hume and Spinoza. *Hume Studies*, 5/2, pp. 65–93.
Putnam, H. (1999) Hilary Putnam: The Vision and Arguments of a Famous Harvard Philosopher. In Pyle (ed.) 1999, pp. 44–54.
Pyle, A. (ed.) (1999) *Key Philosophers in Conversation: The* Cogito *Interviews*. Routledge, New York.
Quarfood, M. (2004) *Transcendental Idealism and the Organism*. Almqvist & Wiskell International, Stockholm.
Radner, D. (1971) Spinoza's Theory of Ideas. *The Philosophical Review*, 80/3, pp. 338–59.
Rand, S. (2007) The Importance and Relevance of Hegel's *Philosophy of Nature*. *The Review of Metaphysics*, 61/2, pp. 379–400.
Read, J. (2016) *The Politics of Transindividuality*. Haymarket Books, Chicago.
Reginster, B. (2006) *The Affirmation of Life: Nietzsche on Overcoming Nihilism*. Harvard University Press, Cambridge, Mass.
Ricoeur, P. (1970) *Freud and Philosophy: An Essay on Interpretation*, trans. D. Savage. Yale University Press, New Haven.

Rorty, R. (1989) *Contingency, Irony, and Solidarity*. Cambridge University Press, Cambridge.
Rorty, R. (2006) *Take Care of Freedom and Truth Will Take Care of Itself: Interviews with Richard Rorty*, ed. E. Mendieta. Stanford University Press, Stanford.
Rouse, J. (2015) *Articulating the World: Conceptual Understanding and the Scientific Image*. University of Chicago Press, Chicago.
Schacht, R. (1983) *Nietzsche*. Routledge, London.
Schacht, R. (1995) Beyond Nihilism: Nietzsche on Philosophy, Interpretation, and Truth. In R. Schacht, *Making Sense of Nietzsche: Reflections Timely and Untimely*. University of Illinois Press, Chicago, pp. 62–80.
Schacht, R. (2012) Nietzsche's Naturalism. *Journal of Nietzsche Studies*, 43/2, pp. 185–212.
Schelling, F. W. J. (2004) *First Outline of a System of the Philosophy of Nature*, trans. K. R. Peterson. SUNY Press, Albany.
Schmidt, A. (1971) *The Concept of Nature in Marx*, trans. B. Fowkes. NLB, London.
Sellars, W. (1963) Philosophy and the Scientific Image of Man. In W. Sellars, *Science, Perception and Reality*, Ridgeview Publishing Company, Atascadero, pp. 1–40.
Sellars, W. (1997) *Empiricism and the Philosophy of Mind*. Harvard University Press, Cambridge, Mass.
Singer, I. B. (1961) The Spinoza of Market Street, trans. M. Glicklich and C. Hemley. In I. B. Singer, *The Spinoza of Market Street*, Farrar, Straus & Cudahy, New York, pp. 3–24.
Sinnott-Armstrong, W. (ed.) (2004) *Pyrrhonian Skepticism*. Oxford University Press, Oxford.
Smith, N., and O'Keefe, P. (1980) Geography, Marx and the Concept of Nature, *Antipode*, 12/2, pp. 30–9.
Smith, N. H. (ed.) (2002) *Reading McDowell: On* Mind and World. Routledge, New York.
Spinoza, B. (1925) *Ethica*. In *Spinoza Opera*, ed. C. Gebhardt, vol. 2. Carl Winters Universitätsbuchhandlung, Heidelberg, pp. 41–308.
Spinoza, B. (1985) *Ethics*. In Curley (ed.) 1985, pp. 399–617.
Spinoza, B. (1985a) *Letters: August 1661–August 1663*. In Curley (ed.) 1985, pp. 157–218.
Spinoza, B. (1985b) *Treatise on the Emendation of the Intellect*. In Curley (ed.) 1985, pp. 3–45.
Spinoza, B. (1995) *The Letters*, trans. S. Shirley. Hackett Publishing Company, Indianapolis.
Spinoza, B. (2018) *Ethics Proved in Geometrical Order*, ed. M. J. Kisner, trans. M. Silverthorne and M. J. Kisner. Cambridge University Press, Cambridge.
Stern, D. S. (ed.) (2013) *Essays on Hegel's* Philosophy of Subjective Spirit. SUNY Press, Albany.
Stern, R. (2007) Peirce, Hegel, and the Category of Secondness. *Inquiry*, 50/2, pp. 123–55.

Stone, A. (2013) Hegel, Naturalism and the Philosophy of Nature. *Hegel Bulletin*, 34/1, pp. 59–78.
Strachey, J. (ed.) (1953–1974) *The Standard Edition of the Complete Psychological Works of Sigmund Freud*, trans. J. Strachey *et al.* The Hogarth Press, London.
Strawson, P. F. (1966) *The Bounds of Sense: An Essay on Kant's* Critique of Pure Reason. Methuen, London.
Stroud, B. (1977) *Hume*. Routledge & Kegan Paul, London.
Stroud, B. (2004) The Charm of Naturalism. In De Caro and Macarthur (eds) 2004, pp. 21–35.
Testa, I. (2013) Hegel's Naturalism or Soul and Body in the *Encyclopedia*. In Stern (ed.) 2013, pp. 19–35.
Testa, I. (2017) Dewey, Second Nature, Social Criticism, and the Hegelian Heritage. *European Journal of Pragmatism and American Philosophy*, IX/1. https://doi.org/10.4000/ejpap.990
Watkins, E. (2005) *Kant and the Metaphysics of Causality*. Cambridge University Press, Cambridge.
Whitebook, J. (2017) *Freud: An Intellectual Biography*. Cambridge University Press, Cambridge.
Williams, B. (2006) *The Sense of the Past: Essays in the History of Philosophy*, Princeton University Press, Princeton.
Williams, R. R. (2007) Translator's Introduction. In Hegel 2007, pp. 1–56.
Wolfson, H. (1934) *The Philosophy of Spinoza: Unfolding the Latent Process of His Reasoning*, vol. 1. Harvard University Press, Cambridge, Mass.
Wood, A. W. (1984) Kant's Compatibilism. In Wood (ed.) 1984, pp. 73–101.
Wood, A. W. (1999) *Kant's Ethical Thought*. Cambridge University Press, Cambridge.
Wood, A. W. (ed.) (1984) *Self and Nature in Kant's Philosophy*. Cornell University Press, Ithaca.
World Commission on Environment and Development (1987) *Our Common Future*. https://sustainabledevelopment.un.org/content/documents/5987our-common-future.pdf
Yovel, Y. (1986) Nietzsche and Spinoza: *amor fati* and *amor dei*. In *Nietzsche as Affirmative Thinker: Papers Presented at the Fifth Jerusalem Philosophical Encounter, April 1983*, ed. Y. Yovel, Martinus Nijhoff, Dordrecht, pp. 183–203.
Yovel, Y. (1989) *Spinoza and Other Heretics*, vol. 1: *The Marrano of Reason*. Princeton University Press, Princeton.
Yovel, Y. (1989a) *Spinoza and Other Heretics*, vol. 2: *The Adventures of Immanence*. Princeton University Press, Princeton.
Yovel, Y. (2018) *Kant's Philosophical Revolution: A Short Guide to the* Critique of Pure Reason. Princeton University Press, Princeton.
Yovel, Y. (ed.) (1999) *Desire and Affect: Spinoza as Psychologist*. Little Room Press, New York.
Yovel, Y., and Segal, G. (eds) (2004) *Spinoza on Reason and the "Free Man."* Little Room Press, New York.
Zambrana, R. (2015) *Hegel's Theory of Intelligibility*. University of Chicago Press, Chicago.

Zammito, J. H. (1992) *The Genesis of Kant's* Critique of Judgment. University of Chicago Press, Chicago.

Zammito, J. H. (2006) Teleology Then and Now: The Question of Kant's Relevance for Contemporary Controversies over Function in Biology. *Studies in History and Philosophy of Biological and Biomedical Sciences*, 37/4, pp. 748–70.

Zuckert, R. (2007) *Kant on Beauty and Biology: An Interpretation of the* Critique of Judgment. Cambridge University Press, Cambridge.

Zuckert, R. (2014) Organisms and Metaphysics: Kant's First Herder Review. In Goy and Watkins (eds) (2014), pp. 61–77.

Index of Names

Acampora, Christa Davis 165
Allison, Henry 22, 23, 24, 39–40, 212n 13, 217n 42, 231n 26
Althusser, Louis 7, 47, 148
Anderson, Lanier 159
Arendt, Hannah 229n 12
Aristotle 23, 25, 111, 113, 117, 120, 126, 171, 238n 16, 239n 17, 240n 21
Avineri, Shlomo 146–7

Baier, Annette 62
Balibar, Etienne 47, 246n 8
Bayle, Pierre 44
Beiser, Frederick 45–6, 239n 19
Bennett, Jonathan 34, 213n 15, 214n 25, 217n 37
Berlin, Isaiah 135
Boehm, Omri 45, 219n 51, 228n 9
Borges, Jorge Luis 46
Brandom, Robert 5, 6, 48, 116, 128, 171–2, 215n 29, 226n 33
Breuer, Josef 178, 182
Brücke, Ernst Wilhelm von 253n 2
Burgh, Albert 210n 6

Charcot, Jean-Martin 178
Clark, Maudemarie 165

Collingwood, Robin George 123
Copernicus, Nicolaus 75, 186
Corti, Lucas 240n 22
Curley, Edwin 214n 23, 217n 39

Damasio, Antonio 220n 58
Darwin, Charles 186
Davidson, Donald 216n 31, 224n 22
Deleuze, Gilles 47
Della Rocca, Michael 27, 47, 211n 10, 214n 20, 215n 26
Descartes, René viii–ix, 3, 23, 24, 25, 31, 35, 40, 49, 55, 109, 131, 182, 211n 9
deVries, Willem 115, 120, 122, 238n 16, 243n 38
Dewey, John vii–viii, 6–7, 11, 119–20, 123, 128, 240n 21, 241n 28, 242n 34, 245nn 48–9
Diderot, Denis 44
Dudrick, David 165

Eissler, Kurt 253n 1
Eliot, George 46
Empedocles 261n 38
Euclid 3, 17–18, 70

Feuerbach, Ludwig 137–8, 205, 245n 4
Fichte, Johann Gottlieb 6, 45, 94, 105, 108, 112–13
Findlay, John 240n 20, 241n 29
Fliess, Wilhelm 254n 9
Fogelin, Robert J. 221n 7
Franks, Paul 232n 27
Fraser, Nancy 205
Freud, Sigmund viii, 3, 7, 8–10, 131, 132, 161, 162, 177–99, 200, 201, 202–3, 206, 219n 54, 253–62nn 1–40
Friedman, Michael 78, 227n 5, 228n 7

Garber, Daniel 46, 47, 219n 53
Gardner, Sebastian 239n 19
Garrett, Aaron 212n 12
Garrett, Don 214n 23, 218n 45, 221n 7
Gay, Peter 177, 253n 2, 258n 27
Geras, Norman 246n 6
Ginsborg, Hannah 98–9, 103, 234n 38, 235n 44, 240n 22
Godfrey-Smith, Peter 209n 1
Goethe, Johann Wolfgang von 45, 46, 177, 189, 193, 196, 252n 27, 261n 37
Goldstein, Rebecca 210n 6
Gueroult, Martial 212n 12
Guyer, Paul 85

Hampshire, Stuart 17–18, 23, 25–6, 33, 34–5, 38–9, 212n 14, 214nn 19,21,23, 218n 50
Hatfield, Gary 80
Hegel, Georg Wilhelm Friedrich viii, 3, 6, 7, 11, 19, 28, 29, 45, 47, 51, 94, 105, 107–28, 131, 134–5, 137, 138, 143, 155, 156, 171, 201, 206, 236–45nn 1–49, 246n 9
Heidegger, Martin 229n 12
Heine, Heinrich 46, 220n 58
Herder, Johann Gottfried 45, 111, 233n 36

Houlgate, Stephen 121
Hume, David viii, 3–4, 6, 7, 10, 29, 47, 50–71, 72, 78–9, 80, 84, 106, 109, 125, 131, 132, 138, 206, 220–6nn 1–33, 251n 18
Hutcheson, Francis 55

Illetterati, Luca 236n 46
Israel, Jonathan 2, 16, 45

Jacobi, Friedrich Heinrich 45, 111, 233n 36
Jaeggi, Rahel 240n 24
James, William 225n 29, 241n 28
Janaway, Christopher 165–6, 251n 20
Joachim, Harold 212n 12

Kant, Immanuel viii, 3, 4–6, 7, 10, 11, 12, 29, 45, 47, 48, 71, 72–106, 107, 108, 109, 110, 111, 112, 113–14, 124, 125, 126, 128, 131, 138, 171, 177, 200, 206, 223n 20, 226–36nn 1–47, 240n 22
Kaufmann, Walter 249n 5
Kemp Smith, Norman 54, 221n 7
Kierkegaard, Søren 45
Kisner, Matthew 216n 33
Kohut, Heinz 198
Kolakowski, Leszek 145–6, 247n 12
Körner, Stephan 227n 5

Laplanche, J. 185, 188–9, 259n 29
Lear, Jonathan 255n 10, 258n 27
Leibniz, Gottfried Wilhelm 44, 45, 79, 109, 228n 9
Leiter, Brian 163–5, 166, 167, 250nn 15,17, 251nn 18,20
Leonardo Da Vinci 186, 187, 188, 189, 258n 24
Lessing, Gotthold 45, 46
Levine, Steven 115, 116
Lin, Martin 215n 25
Locke, John 4, 109
Loewald, Hans 258n 26

Lord, Beth 111–12
Lukács, Georg 147

McDowell, John 5, 107, 209n 1, 229n 14, 232n 31, 236n 1, 237nn 9–10, 239n 19, 240n 21, 251n 21
McLellan, David 150
Maker, William 244n 41
Malamud, Bernard 46
Malebranche, Nicolas 31
Mann, Thomas 180
Marcuse, Herbert 183–4, 191–2, 195, 202, 261n 36
Marx, Karl viii, 3, 7, 10, 131, 132, 133–56, 161, 168, 176, 187, 200, 201, 202, 203, 205, 206, 245–8nn 1–18
Matheron, Alexandre 212n 12
Mendelsohn, Moses 45

Naess, Arne 220n 58
Negri, Antonio 47
Nehamas, Alexander 252n 30
Newton, Isaac 3, 4, 54, 55, 66, 73, 124
Ng, Karen 109–10, 114, 233nn 35–6, 234n 39, 236n 2, 238nn 14,16, 244n 44
Nietzsche, Friedrich viii, 3, 7, 8, 10, 43, 45, 131, 132, 157–76, 182, 187, 195, 200, 201, 202–3, 206, 219n 51, 249–53nn 1–33

Overbeck, Franz 157

Peirce, Charles Sanders 122, 241n 28, 243n 40
Petry, Michael 121–2
Pinkard, Terry 111, 114–15, 116–17, 122, 124, 239n 17, 242n 30
Pippin, Robert 6, 244n 42
Plato 171, 197, 199, 259n 30
Pontalis, Jean-Bertrand 185, 188–9, 259n 29
Putnam, Hilary 48

Quarfood, M. 99–100, 101, 104, 233n 37, 235n 43, 236n 47
Quine, Willard Van Orman viii, 163

Radner, Daisie 31, 215n 29
Rand, Sebastian 243n 38
Reinhold, Karl Leonhard 45
Ricardo, David 139
Ricoeur, Paul 7, 131–2, 155, 178, 180, 182, 187
Rorty, Richard 170, 245n 48, 257n 22
Rouse, Joseph 49, 66, 162, 215n 28
Ruge, Arnold 136

Schacht, Richard 162–3, 165, 166, 249n 6
Schelling, Friedrich Wilhelm Joseph ix, 6, 45, 94, 105, 108, 111, 112, 177, 236n 2
Schmidt, Alfred 147, 248n 16
Schopenhauer, Arthur 182, 258n 28
Sellars, Wilfrid viii, 32–3, 128, 167, 216nn 34–5, 245n 46
Silverthorne, Michael 216n 33
Singer, Isaac Bashevis 46
Smith, Adam 139
Smith, John E. vii
Spencer, Herbert 250n 16
Spinoza, Baruch viii, ix, 2–3, 6, 7, 10, 11, 15–49, 50, 51, 66, 69, 70, 71, 72, 79, 106, 111–12, 131, 138, 157, 158, 168, 187, 200, 202, 203, 206, 210–20nn 1–63, 238n 12, 249n 4, 253n 33
Stern, Robert 243n 40
Stone, Alison 237n 10, 239n 19, 243n 39
Strachey, James 257n 20, 261n 34
Strawson, Peter Frederick 227n 5
Stroud, Barry 1, 54, 55, 59, 65, 69, 220n 4, 221nn 8,11, 224nn 23,25, 251n 18

Testa, Italo 115, 117, 118

Voltaire 44

Walski, Gregory 214n 23
Westphalen, Jenny von 133–4
Westphalen, Ludwig von 133
Whitebook, Joel 178, 180, 255n 9, 258n 27
Williams, Bernard 249n 8, 250n 14
Williams, Robert 243n 36
Wizenmann, Thomas 45

Wolff, Christian 79, 228n 9
Wolfson, Harry 212n 12
Wood, Allen 85

Yovel, Yirmiyahu 2, 17, 19, 24, 34, 38, 44, 75–6, 158, 210n 5, 217n 38, 247n 13, 257n 23

Zammito, John H. 235n 42, 236n 47
Zuckert, Rachel 235n 43

General Index

a priori judgments and principles
 66, 77, 78, 80, 81, 83, 104,
 108
 synthetic 4, 76, 79, 80, 81, 86, 89,
  206, 223n 20
acosmism 28
actualization of nature 6, 116, 127,
 240n 24
affects 18, 34, 35–6, 40–1, 43,
 217n 42, 218n 47
 active 41
 derivative 41
 passive 41, 42
 primary 40–1
 see also passions
agency 114, 116, 231n 26
aggressiveness 193, 194, 195, 198,
 205–6, 258n 25, 259n 29,
 260n 34, 262n 39
 directed outward 202
 internalization of 201
 sublimation of 206
alienation 137, 248n 17
 alienated labor 7, 138–41, 142, 143,
  144, 147, 148, 149, 151, 152,
  156, 201, 246n 7
 from nature 155

analytic philosophical method 80,
 228n 10
anthropomorphism 2, 16, 28, 30, 175
appearance / thing in itself distinction
 6, 92, 94–5, 97, 105, 108, 175
architectonic design 95, 100
Autobiographical Study (Freud) 189,
 255n 11, 256nn 14,16

being and nothing 109, 127
Beyond Good and Evil (Nietzsche) 158,
 162
Beyond the Pleasure Principle (Freud) 9,
 190–1, 192, 197, 254nn 7–8,
 260n 31
Bible 16
biological normativity 240n 22
blessedness 42
bondage 41, 43
Brundtland Commission 207

capitalism 7, 139, 141, 142, 145, 148,
 149, 152, 155
 alienating character of 154
 contemporary 205
 dynamics and contradictions of
  154, 155, 156

capitalism (*cont.*)
  exploitative 7, 145, 149, 151, 205
  nature and 150–1
  political economy of 149
  revolutionary transformation of 152
  see also alienation
Cartesian dualism 31, 72, 211n 9, 215n 30
catharsis 182
causality
  causa sui 22, 26, 38, 51, 71, 158
  causal determinism 165
  causal laws 77, 89, 228n 7, 233n 37
  causal necessity 65, 66, 70, 71, 72, 76
  causal principle 4, 56, 73, 76, 79, 89
  cause and effect 56, 57, 58, 60, 79, 89, 100, 125
  critical account of *see* Kant and *below*
  event causality 206
  external causation 37, 38, 40, 41, 43, 46, 47, 211n 8
  Freud and 178, 179, 186, 189, 196, 206
  horizontal and vertical causality 38
  Hume and 3, 4, 10, 50, 56, 63, 65–6, 69, 71, 72, 79, 125, 206, 223n 20
    negative conception of causality 4
    nonrational account of causality 56, 218n 45
  Kant and 5, 10, 73–4, 89, 90–4, 98, 100, 105, 125, 206
  logical account of *see* Spinoza and *below*
  mechanistic account of 5, 98
  necessary connection and 4, 17, 60–3, 65, 66, 69, 71, 72, 79, 89, 223n 20
  Nietzsche and 164, 206
  psychological account of *see* Freud and; Hume and *above*
  rationalist conception of 79, 93–4

  Spinoza and 10, 29, 37–40, 71, 72, 206
  through freedom 5, 73, 74, 88, 90, 91, 93, 105, 106, 230n 23
chance 186
chemism 124, 125, 126, 244n 43
Christianity 168, 172, 173
  see also God
Civilization and Its Discontents (Freud) 9, 190, 193–5, 196, 198, 257n 19, 259n 29, 260n 33
climate change 11, 145, 205, 208
conatus 40
concepts
  Hegel's Doctrine of the Concept 113, 125, 126, 135, 143, 238nn 14,16, 243n 40, 244n 44
  Kant on 4, 83, 86, 105
conceptual normativity 5–6, 172, 239n 18, 245n 46
conscience 159, 185, 252n 26, 257n 22
  bad conscience 169, 170
consciousness
  false 131, 132, 200
  Freud and 132, 182–5, 200, 201
    the conscious, the preconscious, and the unconscious 7, 8, 9, 118, 120, 131–2, 146, 147, 161, 181, 187, 190, 193, 197, 200, 201
  Hegel and 155, 201
  illusions of 132
  Marx and 132, 155, 200, 201, 202
  Nietzsche and 132, 200, 201, 249n 11
  primacy of 182
  self-consciousness 111, 114, 118, 143, 147, 155, 201, 238n 15
constancy principle 8, 179, 197, 254n 7
contiguity 56, 57, 62
Copernican Revolution, Kantian 4–5, 73, 74, 75, 88, 104, 106, 108
counter-transference 9, 180
COVID-19 pandemic ix, 208

Critique of Hegel's Philosophy of the State (Marx) 134
Critique of the Power of Judgment (Kant) 5, 95–6, 97, 98, 99, 100–1, 102, 103–4, 105, 106, 108, 113, 114, 228n 6, 232nn 28–9, 233n 37, 234nn 39–40, 235n 44
Critique of Practical Reason (Kant) 88, 97
Critique of Pure Reason (Kant) 4, 5, 45, 71, 73, 74–7, 78, 80–3, 85, 86–9, 90, 91, 92, 94, 95, 97, 98, 100, 104–5, 106, 108, 111, 112, 114, 125, 128, 177, 206, 227n 5, 230nn 21–3, 231nn 24,26, 232n 30
   Transcendental Aesthetic 81, 82–3
   Transcendental Analytic 77, 89, 112
   Transcendental Deduction 81, 227n 5, 228n 11
   Transcendental Logic 78, 81, 83, 229n 13
custom 58, 59, 62, 69, 71, 222nn 15,17

Das Kapital (Marx) 7, 138, 148, 149–50, 153, 154, 156
de-deification of nature 167, 168, 170, 176
death instinct (*Thanatos*) 9, 190, 191, 192–3, 195, 197, 198, 258nn 27–8, 260n 31
Deep Ecology Movement 220n 58
desire 40, 41, 43, 44
determinism
   causal determinism 165
   Kant and 89, 94, 106
   Nietzsche and 164
   Spinoza and 27, 214n 23
Deus sive Natura 20, 34, 212n 14
Difference Between Fichte's and Schelling's System of Philosophy (Hegel) 109, 112
disenchantment of nature 194, 209n 1, 232n 31, 239n 17, 251n 21

dogmatism 102, 175
dreamwork 8–9, 180–2, 183, 197, 255nn 11–12, 256nn 13–15

ecological crisis 11–12, 205, 247n 11
The Ego and the Id (Freud) 188, 190, 259n 28
Elements (Euclid) 18
Elements of the Philosophy of Right (Hegel) 123
empirical subjectivity 112
empiricism 3, 4, 47, 51, 53, 66, 79, 112, 221n 8, 226n 31
Encyclopaedia Logic (Hegel) 124, 125
Enlightenment 16, 111, 198
   "dark Enlightenment" 187, 257n 23
   "moderate Enlightenment" 16, 48, 200
   "Radical Enlightenment" 2, 16, 200
Enquiry Concerning Human Understanding (Hume) 54, 56, 65, 220n 5, 222nn 15,17
eroticized nature 177, 193, 196
eternal recurrence 161, 174, 252n 30
Ethics (Spinoza) 2, 3, 18–45, 50, 51, 66, 70, 71, 158, 217n 40
ethics, naturalistic 34, 42, 43, 44, 218n 49
event causality 206
   see also causality
exchange value 150
Experience and Nature (Dewey) vii
exploitation of nature 7, 145, 153, 156, 247n 11
   see also ecological crisis

false consciousness 131, 132, 200
   see also consciousness
fetishism of commodities 153–4
First Outline of a System of the Philosophy of Nature (Schelling) 112
"first philosophy" 66, 163
   see also metaphysics
Firstness, Secondness, Thirdness 122, 243n 40

food production 142–3
Foundations of the Metaphysics of Morals (Kant) 97
"free association" 8–9, 182, 197, 256n 16
free will 2, 26, 42, 43, 175, 217n 40
  Cartesian conception of 211n 9
freedom 41–2, 43, 46, 47, 118, 154, 155, 156, 219m 53, 231n 23, 232nn 29–30
  causality through 5, 73, 74, 88, 90, 91, 93, 105, 106, 230n 23
  degrees of 43
  Kant on 5, 73, 88, 89, 90–4, 96–7, 104, 105, 232nn 29–30
  moral freedom 92, 96
  and natural necessity 70, 94, 95, 106
  and nature 6, 94, 96, 105, 107, 108, 110
  practical freedom 92, 93, 94, 96, 97, 104, 231nn 26, 91
  as self-determination 154, 156
  transcendental freedom 91, 92, 93, 96–7, 104, 105
The Future of an Illusion (Freud) 190

The Gay Science (Nietzsche) 158–9, 162, 167–9, 170, 173, 176, 249n 11, 250n 16, 252n 28
Genealogy of Morals (Nietzsche) 159, 160–1, 169, 195
geometric method 3, 17–18, 19, 66, 70, 212nn 12–13
The German Ideology (Marx) 136, 142, 154
God
  anthropomorphic conceptions of 28, 30
  death of God 173
  Deus sive Natura 20, 34, 212n 14
  essence of 25, 27
  "God's shadows" 8, 157, 158, 162, 167, 168, 170, 172, 173, 175, 201, 202
  identification with Nature and Substance 2, 16, 17, 20–1, 22, 23, 24, 26, 28, 168, 213n 15
  immanence of 23, 24, 38
  intelligent designer concept 97
  transcendent God 2, 16, 23, 30, 48, 51, 88, 158, 168, 170, 200
good/evil distinction 161
good life 42
good philosophers, characteristics of 48
Group Psychology and the Analysis and the Ego (Freud) 190
Grundrisse (Marx) 7, 149, 150, 151, 152, 154, 156, 248n 16
guilt 194–5, 197, 201

habit 59, 62, 117–18, 119, 120, 241n 28, 242n 34
human-in-nature 7, 10, 155, 156, 201, 203, 205
  see also man-in-nature
human nature 9, 31, 34–5, 42, 50, 70, 246n 6, 247n 10, 251n 18
humanism, Marxist 148
humanization of nature 144, 149, 205, 247nn 10,12
hylozoism 238n 16
hysteria and neuroses 8, 178–9, 180, 182, 183, 184, 189, 197

id, ego, and superego 9, 184, 185, 195, 197, 198, 201, 257n 20, 259n 28, 262n 40
  see also the conscious, the preconscious, and the unconscious
identity theory of mind and body 31
illusions 10, 87, 104, 173, 187, 200–1
imagination 32, 33, 43, 68; 70, 216, 216n 35, 228n 12
immanence
  of God 23, 24, 38
  Hume and 51, 70, 72
  Nietzsche and 157–8, 166, 168, 175

Spinoza and 2, 3, 10, 23, 24, 30, 42, 44, 48, 70, 72, 157, 158, 168, 202, 210n 5
impressions and ideas
 Hume and 3, 4, 51–3, 56–7, 59, 60, 61–2, 64, 66–9, 106, 221n 8, 222n 18, 225n 29
 intentional content of 66, 67, 69
 original and secondary 64
 of reflection 52–3, 61, 63, 64
 of sensation 52, 53, 64
 simple and complex 52
inference 56, 57–8, 59, 62, 65
instincts 8, 161, 162
 Freud and 9, 181, 182, 185, 188, 190, 191–4, 195, 197, 201, 202, 255n 10
 Nietzsche and 169, 172, 175, 201, 202
 see also death instinct (*Thanatos*); life instinct (*Eros*); primary drives
intentionality 30, 48, 218n 45
The Interpretation of Dreams (Freud) 8, 180–1, 197, 255n 9
intuitions
 empirical 82, 83, 86, 88, 105, 229n 12
 pure 82, 83, 84
is/ought dichotomy 134, 143, 203

joy 40
 of life/living 170, 173, 202
 Nietzsche and 169, 174
 Spinoza and 40, 41, 43, 70, 212n 11, 217n 39, 220n 58
judgment
 determining judgment 5, 99, 100, 104
 reflecting judgment 5, 96, 99, 100, 102, 104, 105, 235nn 42–3
 teleological judgment 100–1, 102, 103, 104, 235n 44

Kantian dichotomies 6, 107–8, 109, 110, 111, 124

Kantian Hegelians 6, 110, 115, 128, 239n 18
knowledge
 disinterested 160
 imagination 32, 33, 43, 68, 70, 216, 216n 35, 228n 12
 intuitive 34, 70, 217n 37
 Kant and 87–8
 Nietzsche and 160, 161
 perspectival 159, 176
 rational 70
 self-knowledge 187, 198, 199, 258n 23
 Spinoza and 32–4, 70

labor
 alienated 7, 138–41, 142, 143, 144, 147, 148, 149, 151, 152, 156, 201, 246n 7
 wage labor 7, 142, 151, 155, 246n 7
"last man" 8, 10, 173, 202
laws of nature 2, 4, 24, 26, 27, 29, 30, 34, 41, 48, 72, 73, 84, 89, 92, 93, 143
liberal naturalism 30, 209n 1, 233n 31, 239n 19, 251n 21
liberal pragmatic naturalism viii
 see also nature and naturalism: pragmatic naturalism
life-affirmation 8, 10, 43, 173, 174–5, 176, 202, 252n 27
life instinct (*Eros*) 9, 190, 192, 193, 195, 197, 198, 260n 31
logical positivism 221n 7, 230n 21

man-in-the-world 32–3, 216nn 34–5
Marranos 1, 15, 17
mathematics 4, 18, 22, 33, 75, 80, 81, 83–4
mechanical materialism 137
mechanism 125–6, 233n 34, 244n 43
mechanistic conception of nature 38, 98, 102, 103, 111, 124–5, 234n 40, 239n 19

Meditations (Descartes) 24
Metaphysical Foundations of Natural Science (Kant) 77, 89, 98, 227n 5
metaphysical idealism 244n 41
metaphysics
　critical metaphysics 77–8, 230n 19
　Descartes and 24
　Hume and 66, 71, 72
　Kant and 71, 74–5, 77–8, 79, 80, 81, 86, 88, 89, 97, 98, 106
　of nature 77–8, 168, 227n 5, 230n 19
　Spinoza and 3, 21, 26, 32, 34, 37, 42, 44, 47, 72, 106
　transcendent metaphysics 86, 87, 88, 166, 230n 21
mind–body dualism *see* Cartesian dualism
miracles 66
monism 44, 70, 214n 20
moral philosophy 34, 35, 54, 62, 218n 49
morality 43, 64, 65, 203
　Christian 168, 172, 174
　Freud and 202, 203, 259n 28
　Hume and 64, 65
　Kant and 73, 104, 108
　Marx and 202, 203
　naturalistic account of 2, 3
　Nietzsche and 164, 167, 168, 172, 202, 252n 28
　　life-affirming 172
　Rorty and 170
　Spinoza and 2, 3
　theological conception of 42, 43
　see also ethics, naturalistic

Natura naturans 27, 28
Natura naturata 27, 28
natural sciences 2, 3, 4, 54, 75–7, 83, 84, 121, 122, 143, 163, 177
　a priori 75, 76, 77, 122
　empirical 72, 75, 76–7, 88–9
naturalizing humanity 148, 167, 170, 171, 172–3

nature and naturalism
　ahistorical approach to 11, 204
　Dewey and vii, viii, 6, 11
　enduring philosophical concern 1–2
　eroticized nature 177, 193, 196
　exploitation of nature 7, 145, 153, 156, 247n 11
　　see also ecological crisis
　Fichte and 112–13
　Freud and viii, 177–97
　Hegel and 107–28, 237n 10, 239n 19
　hermeneutics of suspicion 7–10, 131–99
　human-in-nature 7, 10, 155, 156, 201, 203, 205
　　see also man-in-nature
　humanization of nature 144, 149, 205, 247nn 10,12
　Hume and 50–71, 72, 251n 18
　identification of nature with God and Substance 2, 16, 17, 20–1, 22, 23, 24, 26, 28, 168, 213n 15
　Kant and 6, 11, 71, 72–106, 107–8, 112
　laws of nature 2, 4, 24, 26, 27, 29, 30, 34, 41, 48, 72, 73, 84, 89, 92, 93, 143
　liberal naturalism 30, 209n 1, 233n 31, 239n 19, 251n 21
　Marx and viii, 7, 138, 139–46, 150
　mechanistic conception of nature 38, 98, 102, 103, 111, 124–5, 234n 40, 239n 19
　Methodological Naturalism (M-Naturalism) 163–4, 165, 250n 17
　nature and Spirit (Geist) 6, 110, 111, 115, 116, 117, 120–1, 123, 124, 126–8, 239n 18, 242n 36
　nature–culture distinction 11
　Newtonian conception of 4
　Nietzsche and viii, 8, 161–8, 175, 251n 20

Nonhuman nature 29, 66, 132, 144, 145, 147, 155, 205
otherness of nature 116, 123, 124, 244n 40
philosophical conceptions of 2–7, 15–128, 251n 21
pragmatic naturalism 11, 128
reductive forms of naturalism 30, 49, 237n 10
revival of interest in viii, 11
Schelling and ix, 112, 115
social conditioning of nature 147
Speculative M-Naturalism 164, 165, 250n 17
Spinoza and viii, 2–3, 11, 15–49, 66, 69, 72, 111, 168
Naturphilosophie 108, 111, 112, 122
necessary connection 4, 17, 60, 61, 62, 63, 65, 66, 69, 71, 72, 79, 89, 223n 20
necessitarianism 27, 214n 23
New Introductory Lectures on Psycho-Analysis (Freud) 198, 257n 21
nexus effectivus 99
nexus finalis 99, 102
nihilism 8, 43, 45, 160, 161, 173, 174, 176, 219n 51
Nirvana principle 258n 28
nominal and real definitions 22
nonhuman animals 31–2, 108, 114, 116, 117, 140, 146, 147, 172, 239n 17, 255n 10
normative exceptionalism 172
normativity 49, 116–17, 240nn 22–3
  biological 240n 22
  conceptual 5–6, 172, 239n 18, 245n 46
A Note on the Unconscious in Psychoanalysis (Freud) 182
noumena 6, 85, 90, 105, 107, 110

objectification of labor 139, 151, 248n 17
  see also alienated labor; wage labor

objectivity 85, 122, 147, 159, 160, 161, 170, 236n 47, 243n 36
On Nature (Empedocles) 261n 38
organisms, understanding 98, 99–100, 101, 102, 103–4, 105, 106, 108, 234nn 38,40
original sin 43
The Origins of Psychoanalysis (Freud) 255n 9
Outlines of the Philosophy of Right (Hegel) 134

pantheism controversy 3, 28, 45–6, 92, 111, 214n 24
Paris Manuscripts (Marx) 136, 138, 148, 149, 150, 151, 153, 154, 155–6, 246n 9, 247n 10
passions 35, 41, 43, 46, 64, 65, 70, 224n 23
perceptions 225nn 27,29, 226n 30
  Hume and 3, 4, 66, 225nn 27,29, 226nn 30,31
  intentional content 67
  see also affects; impressions and ideas
"performance principle" 195, 202
Phenomenology of Spirit (Hegel) 109, 137, 201, 237n 6, 241n 25, 244n 45
Philosophy of Nature (Hegel) 121–2, 124, 126–7
Philosophy of Spirit (Hegel) 117, 119, 127, 241n 25
pleasure principle 183–4, 191, 194, 198, 254n 8
political economy 139, 140, 149, 155
positivism 178, 253n 2
  logical positivism 221n 7, 230n 21
Pragmatic Naturalism: John Dewey's Living Legacy (Bernstein) viii, 209n 3
praxis 132, 136, 137, 143, 149, 152, 155
  revolutionary *praxis* 136, 152, 155
primary drives 8, 10, 183, 198
  see also aggressiveness; sexuality
principle of sufficient reason 2, 18, 22, 29, 47, 50, 69, 211n 10

private property 139, 141, 142, 143, 144, 148, 155, 193
productive subjectivity 112
"Project for a Scientific Psychology" (Freud) 8, 179
Prolegomena to Any Future Metaphysics (Kant) 78–9, 80, 81, 84, 85, 90, 92, 93–4, 119n 19, 228n 8
propensity 61, 63, 222nn 15,19
psychic life 179–80, 183, 184, 186, 189, 190, 197, 198, 202, 203, 255n 9, 257n 19
psychic reality 8, 9, 180, 185, 196
psychoanalysis 8–9, 180–8, 187–90, 196, 197, 198, 201
purpose and purposiveness
  external purposiveness 104, 113, 234n 39, 244n 44
  Hegel and 113–14, 126
  internal purposiveness 104, 108, 113–14, 115, 117, 119, 120, 124, 126, 234n 39, 238nn 14–15, 240nn 22,24, 244n 44
  Kant and 5, 86–7, 95–6, 97–8, 99, 101, 102–3, 104, 105–6, 108, 113, 126, 233nn 32,35, 234n 39, 240n 22

The Question of Lay Analysis (Freud) 189–90

rationalism
  a priori reason 50, 55
  demonstrative or intuitive reason 50, 58, 70
  discursive rationality 6, 171–2
  Hume and 50–1, 58, 64–5, 69, 70
  Kant and 6, 72–3, 77, 79, 80, 81, 82, 86, 87, 105
  see also *Critique of Pure Reason*
  Leibniz and 168
  naturalizing rationality 172
  principle of sufficient reason 2, 18, 22, 29, 47, 50, 69, 211n 10
  rational knowledge 70

Spinoza and 2, 17, 18, 29, 30, 37, 48–9, 69, 168
reality principle 183, 184, 195, 202
receptivity 6, 82, 83, 107, 229n 14, 236n 1
religion
  Marxist critique of 135, 136, 200
  see also Christianity; God
Republic (Plato) 199
ressentiment 8, 161, 170, 172, 201
Romanticism, philosophical 111, 177

sadness 40, 70, 217n 39
Science of Logic (Hegel) 108–9, 113, 123, 135
  Absolute Idea 113, 135, 244n 44
scientific Marxism 148
second nature 116, 118, 119, 175, 237n 9, 240n 21, 251n 21
  see also habit
self-affirmation 176, 252n 30
self-consciousness 111, 114, 118, 143, 147, 155, 201, 238n 15
  see also consciousness
self-determination 152, 154, 156
self-esteem 43
self-knowledge 187, 198, 199, 258n 23
  see also knowledge
self-realization 152, 153
sensibility 6, 82, 83, 85, 86, 105, 229nn 12,14
sentiments 3, 39, 55, 62–6, 69, 71, 222n 16, 223n 21, 224n 23
sexuality 8, 179, 187, 188, 189, 192, 194, 196, 197, 256nn 14,17, 258n 25, 259n 30, 260nn 31–2, 261n 35
skepticism 53, 54, 66, 68, 69, 71, 84, 132, 165, 221n 7
social reform 196, 202
soul 9, 51, 52, 53, 63, 66, 166, 169, 178, 180, 198, 220n 3, 228n 12
  Hegel and 116, 117–18, 119, 120, 121, 241n 27, 242n 31

species-being 138, 141, 143, 144, 148, 149, 151, 156, 246n 6
speculative identity 6, 109, 110, 113, 119
Spirit (*Geist*) 110, 118–19
  Absolute Spirit 127, 244n 45
  actualization of 116, 120, 121, 124
  Hegel and 6, 110, 111, 115, 116, 117, 120–1, 123, 124, 126–7, 128, 201, 237nn 6–7, 239n 18, 242n 36
    spiritual phenomena 125–6
  Nature and 6, 110, 111, 115, 116, 117, 120–1, 123, 124, 126–8, 239n 18, 242n 36
  Pure Spirit 128, 244n 45
  self-determination of 124
  self-diremption and self-division 120
spontaneity 6, 91, 107, 112
subject–object dichotomy 119, 242n 30
subjective idealism 85
sublimation 186, 188–9, 206, 258nn 25–6
substance 23–6
  Aristotelian conception of 24
  Cartesian substances 24–5
  identification of God with 2, 17, 20–1, 22, 23, 24, 26
  modes of 21, 25, 26, 27, 34, 35, 38, 39, 40, 214nn 20,21,23, 221n 9, 237n 12
  ontological and conceptual independence 23, 24
  plurality of 24
  Spinoza's concept of 23–5, 47
  thought and extension, attributes of 25, 26, 31, 32, 42, 71, 215n 30
substance monism 214n 20
suffering 8, 9, 174, 194
  amelioration of 10, 196, 198, 202
supernatural, the 66, 162
superstitions 2, 16, 28, 30, 32, 175, 187, 200
"surplus repression" 202, 261n 36

sustainability
  class phenomenon 207
  dilemma of 207–8
Symposium (Plato) 197, 259n 30
synthetic philosophical method 80–1, 228n 10

teleology 103, 104, 125, 126, 175, 214n 25, 236n 47
  teleological judgment 100–1, 102, 103, 104, 235n 44
theism 16
  see also God
Theological-Political Treatise (Spinoza) 16, 19, 210n 3
Theses on Feuerbach (Marx) 136, 137–8, 141, 151, 154, 205
thing in itself 6, 84, 85, 92, 94, 95, 97, 105, 108, 232n 27
"this-worldliness" 2, 10, 17, 51, 72, 166, 175
  see also immanence
thought and extension, attributes of 25, 26, 31, 32, 42, 71, 215n 30
transactional relationship with nature 7, 10, 132, 142, 144, 146, 147, 153, 154, 155, 156, 203, 247n 11
transcendental freedom 91, 92, 93, 96–7, 104, 105
  see also freedom
transcendental idealism 82–3, 85, 92, 97, 99, 105, 108, 111, 114, 229n 18, 233n 36
transference 9, 180
transindividuality 203, 246n 8
Treatise of Human Nature (Hume) 3, 50, 51–6, 60–4, 67, 68, 69, 221n 8, 222n 16
  Abstract 56–60, 222n 13
Twilight of the Idols (Nietzsche) 174

the unconscious *see* the conscious, the preconscious, and the unconscious

"The Unconscious" (Freud) 182
understanding, faculty of 83, 84, 87, 90, 105, 108, 229n 12
universal subjectivity 85
use value 150

wage labor 7, 142, 151, 155, 246n 7
will to power 158, 165, 174
Wissenschaften 162–3, 250n 14

Young Hegelians 135, 136